Shakespeare in the North

Shakespeare in the North

Place, Politics and Performance in England and Scotland

Edited by Adam Hansen

EDINBURGH
University Press

Edinburgh University Press is one of the leading university presses in the UK. We publish academic books and journals in our selected subject areas across the humanities and social sciences, combining cutting-edge scholarship with high editorial and production values to produce academic works of lasting importance. For more information visit our website: edinburghuniversitypress.com

© editorial matter and organisation Adam Hansen, 2021, 2023
© the chapters their several authors, 2021, 2023

Edinburgh University Press Ltd
The Tun – Holyrood Road, 12(2f) Jackson's Entry, Edinburgh EH8 8PJ

First published in hardback by Edinburgh University Press 2021

Typeset in 11/13 Bembo by
IDSUK (DataConnection) Ltd

A CIP record for this book is available from the British Library

ISBN 978 1 4744 3592 5 (hardback)
ISBN 978 1 4744 3593 2 (paperback)
ISBN 978 1 4744 3594 9 (webready PDF)
ISBN 978 1 4744 3595 6 (epub)

The right of Adam Hansen to be identified as the editor of this work has been asserted in accordance with the Copyright, Designs and Patents Act 1988, and the Copyright and Related Rights Regulations 2003 (SI No. 2498).

Contents

Acknowledgements   vii
Notes on Contributors   viii

Introduction   1
   Adam Hansen

I: Shakespeare and the Early Modern North

1. Shakespeare's Northern Blood: Transfusing *Gorboduc* into *Macbeth* and *Cymbeline*   41
   Paul Frazer

2. 'Here are strangers near at hand': Anglo-Scottish Border Crossings Pre- and Post-Union   60
   Steven Veerapen

3. Shakespeare, King James and the Northern Yorkists   79
   Richard Stacey

4. North by Northwest: Shakespeare's Shifting Frontier   103
   Lisa Hopkins

II: Performing Shakespeare in the North

5. The People's Shakespeare: Place, Politics and Performance in a Northern Amateur Theatre   125
   Adam Hansen

6. Only Northerners Need Apply? Northern Broadsides and 'No-nonsense' Shakespeare   151
   Caroline Heaton

7. Shakespeare and Blackpool: The RSC's *A Midsummer Night's Dream* (2016): A Play for the Nation? 168
   Janice Wardle

8. William the Conqueror: The Only Shakescene in a Country 187
   Richard Wilson

III: Appropriating Shakespeare in the North

9. 'What is Shakespeare to Manchester'? Shakespearean Engagement in the North at the Turn of the Twentieth Century 219
   Monika Smialkowska

10. A Road by Any Other Name: Heaton History Group, a North East Suburb and Shakespeare 244
    Chris Jackson

11. Lancastrian Shakespeares: *Hamlet* and *King Lear* in North West England (2005–2014) 258
    Liz Oakley-Brown

12. Shakespeare's Cheek: *Macbeth*, *Dunsinane* and the Jacobean Condition 276
    James Loxley

Postscript: News from the North 298
   Willy Maley

Index 315

Acknowledgements

Many thanks to the editorial team at, and reviewers commissioned by, Edinburgh University Press, all of whom did an amazing job of getting this finished. The contributors also deserve great credit for their hard work and patience – I have learned so much from working with you, and am sure others will too. I'd like to thank David Walker, Mel Waters, David Stewart, Joe Street, Andy Feeney, Graham Hall and Monika Smialkowska for their companionship and insight, and Paul Frazer for his, as well as for reminding me of the 'Irish Question'. Thanking current colleagues emphasises how most of my understanding of Shakespeare was made in the North. This began a long time ago, and I'm sincerely grateful to those who helped shape that understanding: Anna Osborne and Michael Wagner, for their friendship; Tony Greenwood, for the letter, and much else besides; Mr Moorhouse, for *The Winter's Tale*, and not knowing all the answers; Mr Cann, for *Hamlet*; and Mrs Todd, for *Macbeth* (my first time studying and 'teaching' Shakespeare). Everyone involved with Shakespeare Club, at the Lit and Phil and 'on the road', warrants profound gratitude, especially Kay Easson, Ann Logan, Bruce Babington, Allan Bage, Tom Harrison, Bee Ward, and Hilary and Kelsey Thornton. Finally, huge and heartfelt thanks to The Crossings Community Group and Band, for helping me think, act, and play beyond borders; Helen and Gary Bate, for Spurn Head; Fay Garratt, Kirsty McNamara and Ted Carden, for the cover; Mila and Lars for taking me to see plays in Bradford and Manchester, for the two-volume Clark and Wright *Complete Works*, and for their love; Megan Holman, for everything she did; and dearest Angela, Joe, Leon, and Katie, simply for everything.

Notes on Contributors

Paul Frazer is Senior Lecturer in Early Modern Literature at Northumbria University, Newcastle upon Tyne. His research focuses on Elizabethan and early Jacobean drama, and he has published essays and articles on a range of works by William Shakespeare, Christopher Marlowe, Thomas Dekker and John Webster. Paul co-edited the Bloomsbury critical companion to *The White Devil* (2016), and is co-editing a new edition of *Gorboduc, or The Tragedy of Ferrex and Porrex* for Manchester Revels.

Adam Hansen is Senior Lecturer in English at Northumbria University. In addition to publishing numerous articles and chapters on early modern culture in its own time and after, he is the author of *Shakespeare and Popular Music* (2010), and co-editor of *Litpop: Writing and Popular Music* (2014), *Shakespearean Echoes* (2015), and *The White Devil: A Critical Reader* (2016). From 2014–19, he convened the free, monthly, public reading group Shakespeare Club at Newcastle's Lit and Phil, and at other locations in the North. His next book will be about Marlowe.

Caroline Heaton is Senior Lecturer (Research, Evaluation and Student Engagement) at Sheffield Hallam University, where she has held posts in course administration, widening participation policy and research, student engagement, and student experience research and evaluation. Between 2014 and 2016, Caroline undertook a Masters by Research in English, for which she reviewed a season of productions at the Royal Shakespeare Company in Stratford-upon-Avon. As a seasoned theatre-goer, Caroline has published many of these reviews in journals such as *Shakespeare* and *Early Modern Literary Studies*.

Lisa Hopkins is Professor of English at Sheffield Hallam University and co-edits *Shakespeare* (the journal of the British Shakespeare Association),

Marlowe Studies, Arden Early Modern Drama Guides and Arden Studies in Early Modern Drama. She writes mainly on Shakespeare, Marlowe and Ford, but has also published on Jane Austen, Bram Stoker, crime fiction, and literature on screen. She is currently working on two books, *Burial Plots in British Detective Fiction* and *Early Modern Drama and the Edge of Christendom*. Her most recent publication is *Greeks and Trojans on the Early Modern English Stage* (2020). *A Companion to the Cavendishes: Literature, Patronage, Material Culture*, which she has co-edited with Tom Rutter, is forthcoming from Arc Humanities Press.

Chris Jackson helped found a local history society based in Newcastle upon Tyne, Heaton History Group, in 2013, and has been its secretary ever since. She researches and writes about Heaton's history for the group's website: <www.heatonhistorygroup.org>

James Loxley is Professor of Early Modern Literature at the University of Edinburgh. Among his book publications are *Ben Jonson's Walk to Scotland: An Annotated Edition of the 'Foot Voyage'*, co-edited with Anna Groundwater and Julie Sanders (2015), *Shakespeare, Jonson and the Claims of the Performative*, co-authored with Mark Robson (2013), *Performativity* (2007) and *Ben Jonson* (2001). He has led a number of major research and public engagement projects, including an exhibition on Shakespeare and Scotland at the National Library of Scotland and a digital literary map of Edinburgh, Litlong (<https://litlong.org>).

Willy Maley is Professor of Renaissance Studies at the University of Glasgow. He is the author of *A Spenser Chronology* (1994), *Salvaging Spenser: Colonialism, Culture and Identity* (1997), and *Nation, State and Empire in English Renaissance Literature: Shakespeare to Milton* (2003). Among his edited volumes are studies of early modern Irish and British identities, including, with Brendan Bradshaw and Andrew Hadfield, *Representing Ireland: Literature and the Origins of Conflict, 1534–1660* (1993); and with David J. Baker, *British Identities and English Renaissance Literature* (2002). He has also edited several collections on Shakespeare and national identity, including, with Andrew Murphy, *Shakespeare and Scotland* (2004); with Philip Schwyzer, *Shakespeare and Wales: From the Marches to the Assembly* (Ashgate, 2010); with Margaret Tudeau-Clayton, *This England, That Shakespeare: New Angles on Englishness and the Bard* (2010); and with Rory Loughnane, *Celtic Shakespeare: The Bard and the Borderers* (2013). He is currently working on a monograph provisionally entitled *Mapping Milton: Geography and Empire in Seventeenth-Century Literature*.

Liz Oakley-Brown teaches and researches pre-modern literature and culture at Lancaster University, UK. Her chapter in this volume is aligned with her interests in the translation and adaptation of sixteenth- and seventeenth-century writing.

Monika Smialkowska is Senior Lecturer in Early Modern Literature at Northumbria University. Her current research interest lies in post-renaissance adaptations and appropriations of early modern authors and genres. She has published book chapters and journal articles on the topic, focusing chiefly on the ways in which the Shakespeare Tercentenary of 1916 was celebrated across the world, and on the ways the North East of England participated in the 2012 World Shakespeare Festival. She edited a special issue of Shakespeare on the topic of 'Shakespeare and the Great War' (2014). She is working on a monograph about the 1916 Shakespeare Tercentenary, and co-editing, with Edmund King, a collection of essays entitled *Memorialising Shakespeare: Commemoration and Collective Identity, 1916–2016* (forthcoming from Palgrave).

Richard Stacey is University Teacher 1500–1700 at the University of Glasgow. He has published on Shakespeare, and is currently working on a book titled *Literary Responses to the House of York, 1550–1615*.

Steven Veerapen is a Teaching Associate at the University of Strathclyde, having completed his PhD and Masters in Renaissance Studies there. His recent publications include the monograph *Slander and Sedition in Elizabethan Law, Speech, and Writing*, two popular histories (*Blood Feud: Mary Queen of Scots and the Earl of Moray* and *Elizabeth and Essex: Power, Passion, and Politics*), and he is currently working on a biographical study of James VI and I's consort: 'Anne of Denmark, Queen in Two Kingdoms'. His published articles include 'European unions: the Spanish wife and the Scottish widow in Shakespeare and Fletcher's Henry VIII and Ford's Perkin Warbeck' in *Early Modern Literary Studies* and 'Slanderisation and censure-ship: when good texts went bad in early modern England' in the *Journal of the Northern Renaissance*. Steven has written for *The Historian* and also published several series of novels set in the Stuart and Elizabethan eras. His research interests include early modern transmission of libellous material and Anglo-Scottish relations.

Janice Wardle is an independent scholar, recently retired from her position as Principal Lecturer at the University of Central Lancashire, where she taught courses in Renaissance Literature, Shakespeare, and Literature and Film. Her current research examines the adaptation of Shakespeare and Austen, and the representation of the lives of these authors in contemporary fiction, theatre and film. She has published essays in *Adaptation*, *Borrowers and Lenders: The Journal of Shakespeare and Appropriation*, and *The Journal of Adaptation in Film and Performance*. She has also contributed to the edited collection *After Austen: Reinventions, Rewritings, Revisitings* (2018).

Richard Wilson is Professor Emeritus in Shakespeare Studies at Kingston University, and author of *Worldly Shakespeare: The Theatre of Our Good Will* (2016); *Free Will: Art and Power on Shakespeare's Stage* (2013); *Shakespeare in French Theory: King of Shadows* (2007); *Secret Shakespeare: Essays on Theatre, Religion and Resistance* (2004); and *Will Power: Studies in Shakespearean Authority* (1993). He has edited many books on Renaissance culture, including *Shakespeare and Continental Philosophy* (2014); *Shakespeare's Book* (2008); *Theatre and Religion* (2003); *Region, Religion and Patronage* (2003); *Christopher Marlowe* (1999); and *New Historicism and Renaissance Drama* (1992). His forthcoming book is entitled *Modern Friends: Shakespeare's Fascist Followers*. Since 1999 he has been a Trustee of Shakespeare North, and is Academic Advisor on its project to rebuild the Elizabethan playhouse at Prescot (Knowsley) near Liverpool.

Introduction

Adam Hansen

When going North, wogs begin at Barnet.[1]

'Rights'

In Autumn 1985, the year after he had accepted the role of Poet Laureate, Ted Hughes published a remarkable but overlooked poem called 'Rights', in a regional journal, *Arts Yorkshire*.[2] 'Rights' describes an experience at the place shown on the front of this book: Bridestones, a gust-sculpted, sheep-strewn hulk of millstone grit on the Yorkshire-Lancashire border. Rooted in moorland, these rocks bloom high above the northern English Pennine towns and villages of Blackshaw Head, Burnley, Hebden Bridge, Todmorden, Mytholmroyd, Heptonstall, and Luddenden Foot. They occupy a landscape like the fictional 'Luddenstall' in J. B. Priestley's *The Good Companions* (1929), about which the novel's Inigo Jolliphant observes: 'It's ridiculous to say this place is in England – quite another country really'.[3] Priestley's Jolliphant was indeed in good company: according to a BBC publication from the same year, it 'may be truly said of the North of England that it is a nation within a nation'.[4] As this introduction's epigraph suggests, such ideas have had a persistent and at times cruder currency.

Musing not on this, but on the name of the rocks, and overcome (to the point of self-parody) by the earthy sensuality of the scene, Hughes' poem's speaker imagines all those who may have coupled there, but then gets back to the job in hand: reading Shakespeare's *Coriolanus* in peace and quiet. Apparently lost in reveries inspired by the play and the place, the speaker is all the more surprised when men with guns from the Halifax hunt bowl up to ask what they're doing there, on private land (only a bit less politely). The speaker responds that the place is public, not private, and since they are the public, they will stay. The stand-off descends into strong language and mutual incomprehension, with neither side claiming victory. The speaker then reflects that some things have changed – during the conversation, or since Shakespeare wrote *Coriolanus*? – and some things have not. As the hunt troops off over the peaty tussocks, the speaker remains, as the poem's last words have it, reading *Coriolanus*.[5]

Before we examine the definitions and terminology that could make sense of Shakespeare and the North, what, then, might we make of *this* rendering of Shakespeare *in* the North, and how might it illuminate what *Shakespeare in the North* is trying to do? Hughes published 'Rights' during the long gestation of his treatise, *Shakespeare and the Goddess of Complete Being* (1992). There, Hughes discusses how tragic conflict homes in on *Coriolanus*' Rome.[6] Yet 'Rights' suggests conflict occurs in one of the places Hughes called home, too. For the speaker could be a figuring of Hughes, remembering a moment from the years spent visiting his parents' house, The Beacon, the next hill or so over, just up the Calder Valley where he spent his early childhood. Or it could be Hughes reflecting on visiting his aunt Hilda Farrar early in 1985 to celebrate the Laureateship with family.[7] As he put it in a letter around that period: 'My wife and I come to the Hebden Bridge area at least four times a year'.[8]

For Hughes, in *Goddess* and elsewhere, Shakespeare can sometimes be a 'reconciliatory' force, connecting disparate and opposed traditions of poetry and politics.[9] As Hughes himself put it, writing at a time of multiple and extreme splits in the English 'national' psyche, between Catholic and Protestant, Stuart and Puritan, powerful and powerless, rich and poor, city and country, metropolis and regions, Shakespeare catalysed language to bond his audience – high and low – together.[10] Reading Shakespeare's bonding words afresh might fix a nation again in crisis.

However, in its scene of reading past divisions, 'Rights' does not admit reconciliation or resolution in the present. Conflicts and crises about power, place and property here are irresolvable and ongoing, and not restricted to a barney at some rocks on a moor. *Coriolanus*, in particular, evokes a range of conflicted responses for Hughes, because Shakespeare and Englishness do too, as Neil Corcoran explains:

> Inscribed in Hughes's very conception of Shakespeare ... is an element of self-contradiction which is the inevitable product of attachment to varieties of Englishness which cannot be comprehended under an ideal of national unity ... Hughes's Shakespeare is fractured at his very core.[11]

Since *Coriolanus* was written at a time of revolt in England's Midlands, and vividly depicts conflicts between plebeians and patricians, there are few more appropriate Shakespeare plays for inspiring someone to face down those who want to police a place for a bit of private slaughter. Yet, in *Goddess*, Hughes attributes the conflict in the play in part to the ignoble, treacherous and bestial body of Rome's people.[12] Though the play certainly licenses this interpretation (as it also suggests others), this is Hughes as 'authoritarian'.[13] Expressions of 'class rancour' are 'rare' in his work, and became rarer when he 'nailed his flag to the mast of the establishment' by becoming Laureate.[14] Neither was he averse to saying dehumanising things about those he would himself term the proletariat.[15] Nonetheless, this poem also shows how Hughes could 'strongly and even militantly' evoke 'cultural resistance to a 'courtly' ruling class'.[16] Given his background, he was, in fact, acutely conscious of class conflicts in England.[17] 'Rights' intimates that reading a play like *Coriolanus* was part of that resistance, and had been for some time. In a 1957 letter, Hughes commented on A. Alvarez's review of his first poetry collection, *The Hawk in the Rain*, noting that Alvarez seemed to think he had stolen from Shakespeare, specifically by echoing a word from *Coriolanus*: 'dispropertied' (2.1.218).[18] This word is used by the Tribunes Brutus and Sicinus to describe how Martius would deprive the people of 'freedoms', degrading them as 'camels in their war'. As its title and content suggest, 'Rights' revisits the play's contested terrain to set up arguments about property and freedom: who belongs here, and whom does here belong to? Moreover, in this contested terrain, who has the 'Rights' to Shakespeare, an entity Hughes described elsewhere as an artefact or property of a museum, fiercely defended by umpteen curators?[19] One thing seems clear: if Hughes belongs at Bridestones, on that northern English moor, so does Shakespeare. But if Hughes does not belong there, maybe Shakespeare doesn't either. And because this unresolved local dispute is mapped onto a broader landscape of national discourse and identity, manifested in and through Shakespeare, the resonance of 'Rights' is profound. To recollect Priestley's sense of the North being 'another country', as Hughes' Shakespeare is 'fractured', so too is Hughes' England. Of course, Hughes vs. the Halifax hunt *is* a local dispute, hardly some pitting of the North against what Hughes identified as a distinctly southern English mentality.[20] But 'Rights' undoubtedly rings with conflicts of various kinds: within the North; between the North and the South; within Hughes' thinking; and within Shakespeare as Hughes conceived him, and the 'nation' that Shakespeare, the North, and Hughes make up.

For, in contiguity with the 1984–5 miners' strike, 'Rights' appeared at a moment of conflict within and between the regions and communities constituting England and the archipelago of which it is a part. Even the Laureate-to-be, living off the fat of the land as country gent 'down South', offering platitudes about politics being some organic process, could not ignore the causes of this critical event. This is clear from a letter Hughes wrote in 1982 to Jack Brown, a fellow poet and Labour county councillor in Barnsley in the Yorkshire coalfields, lamenting the symptoms of Conservative party and southern English dominance, as Thatcherite neoliberal monetarist policies began to bite deep.[21] In other letters, Hughes attributed the destruction of northern England's coal industry to specific socio-cultural conflicts between those who employ and govern, and those employed (or unemployed) and ruled.[22] Of course, these conflicts do not map simply onto a North-South divide. But with the demise of Communism, Hughes referred to the northern English working classes as inhabiting reservations, like North American First Peoples.[23] In a post-industrial, post-Cold War world, they are now a 'musty superfluity' (1.1.213), as *Coriolanus* would put it.

Echoing Priestley's observation about 'Luddenstall' not being 'in England', 'Rights' brings these concerns into focus. As David Gervais has noted, 'the logic of Hughes' preoccupation with England is to lead to the dismantling of the notion of "Englishness" altogether'.[24] This was not something Hughes saw reason to celebrate – in one letter he lamented the impending fragmentation of the United Kingdom as comparable to Yugoslavia's violent demise.[25] However, even when in the admiring service of the nominal ruler of that kingdom (and other places besides), or on some hieratic, atavistic trip, Hughes would not evade the perplexed realities of where he wrote and what inspired him to write. Indeed, Hughes' previous period of serving the nation in the post-war years had conditioned him to realise what he articulates in 'Rights', if not elsewhere: Shakespeare exposes the fissures in those seemingly solid substances making up the friable fabric of a *dis*united kingdom.

During his national service in the early 1950s, Hughes was stationed at R.A.F. Patrington, in Yorkshire's East Riding.[26] Reading Shakespeare in his spare time, Hughes had occasion to reflect on his proximity to a northern English location – or the absence of it – that features significantly and repeatedly in the history plays:

RAVENSPURGH (otherwise RAVENSPURN, or RAVENSER). It was close to Spurn Head at the mouth of the Humber, near Kilnsea, but it was swept away by the encroachment of the ocean in the 16th cent. Here Bolingbroke arrived on July 4th, 1399, ostensibly to claim his father's estates.[27]

Also known as Ravenserodd, between the early 1200s and the later 1300s, and before it was 'washed away', this place had once held a Royal Charter as a bustling port at the end of a peninsula reaching into the North Sea.[28] Perhaps the fact that it stopped existing before Shakespeare's lifetime explains why – unlike Holmedon, Pomfret, or Gaultree – the northern location of Ravenspurgh does not figure in a recent list of significant Shakespearean 'Places . . . BRITAIN (OUTSIDE LONDON)'.[29] But as Edward Sugden's brief note reminds us, this many-named place that no longer exists is where, in *Richard II*, Henry Bolingbroke first returns from exile 'to touch our northern shore' (2.1.289), a moment and a place so important that the name 'Ravenspurgh' is repeated again in the next scene, and three times in 30 or so lines in 2.3. Then, when, in *The First Part of Henry the Fourth*, King Henry remembers arriving at Ravenspurgh, he experiences a painful difference between past and present, and between people's expectations and *realpolitik*, as now as monarch he has to fight a civil war against his one-time fellow rebels: 'even as I was then is Percy [Hotspur] now' (3.2.96). Comparably, Ravenspurgh is invoked by Hotspur with regret as a place 'where I first bowed my knee / Unto this king of smiles, this Bullingbrook' (1.3.251–2), a man who, 'while his blood was poor', sought his family's aid, 'Upon the naked shore of Ravenspurgh' (4.3.82–3). With Shakespeare's earlier rendering of later history in *The Third Part of King Henry VI*, King Edward remembers 'being thus arrived / From Ravenspurgh haven before the gates of York' (4.7.7–8). Ravenspurgh shifts in memory, sequence, and status; it is and is not there, geographically and temporally. Clearly Shakespeare was thinking for a long time about this place on the edge of northern England that was in his time no longer part of England, obsessively connecting this unstable location to his depiction of England's unstable monarchy, and doing so in history plays where lots of other bits of England's possessions get 'lost' too (*Henry V*, Epilogue.12). As Tony Harrison puts it, in a poem about England's North East: 'the sea works bits of England loose'.[30] So does Hughes' Shakespeare-infused 'Rights'. And so, this collection contends, does thinking about Shakespeare in the North. To echo Tom Nairn's famous question about the 'break-up' of Britain: the North may be a 'nation within a nation', but 'what does "national" *mean* in this context?'[31] With the 2015 Scottish referendum (and the (im)possibility of another), the 2016 Brexit vote, the results of the 2019 UK election, and as *Shakespeare in the North* testifies, such questions are unavoidable. Notable contributions here from James Loxley, Willy Maley, Liz Oakley-Brown and Richard Wilson suggest that current socio-political and cultural conditions explain why our context necessitates thinking about Shakespeare and the North, separately and together, in academia, and in the wider world.[32]

'Deep England', 'Deep North'

As if in dialogue with Nairn, the cultural theorist Stuart Hall reflected that 'what the nation means is an ongoing project, under constant reconstruction'.[33] This includes the nations constituting a particular North Atlantic archipelago:

> Historically speaking, Great Britain, and still more the United Kingdom, are comparatively recent and synthetic constructs that have often been contested and in flux in the past, just as they continue to be contested and in flux now.[34]

'Englishness', as a manifestation of part of these 'constructs', 'has had to be made and re-made in and through history'.[35] The early modern period was one of those moments in history when just such remaking occurred: 'Englishness was a contested resource as much for writers engaging with readers as for leaders mustering armies ... 'England' was a shifting entity'.[36] It remains so. Alex Niven rightly argues that 'the quest for an authentic national culture is ... a form of compensation for the elusiveness of the English nation state'.[37] Shakespeare has been implicated in that quest, being seen to compensate for England's elusive shiftiness with visions of holism and stability. But by thinking beyond the English North, and by querying such visions and perspectives, *Shakespeare in the North* seeks to make this rendering of Shakespeare, and of England, much harder. For as Nairn has suggested, it is now 'England's turn' – and, we might add, the 'turn' of its regions and borders too – to discover a 'renewed identity that can acknowledge the Bard of Avon' without being 'in thrall to the time-bound legacy' of jingoistic, imperialistic renderings.[38]

This requires us seeing that part of the way the North has been constructed has depended on ideas of what Englishness is, and the extent to which the North consolidates or contests these ideas. Because 'exclusivity has been central to the formation of Englishness', *Shakespeare in the North* stresses how such contestation occurs and why it is needful.[39] For example, constructions of 'Deep England' have had significant implications for constructions of the English North as 'England's other'.[40] Indeed, when 'Deep England' was made, so was a 'Deep North'.[41] At the turn of the twentieth century, Dave Russell suggests, 'dominant classes threatened by currents of modernism, urbanism and political radicalism' tried to develop 'a distinctive and defensive type of Englishness' drawing on 'a rich repertoire of cultural practices that celebrated the pre-industrial past . . . in which the south of England often stood proxy for the nation as a whole'.[42] Shakespeare was part of that repertoire: Graham Holderness notes how Walter Jerrold's 1912 book *Shakespeare-land* 'disengages from the real Edwardian Stratford to represent . . . an untroubled English pastoral . . . "the heart of England"'.[43] And Shakespeare is still part of that ideological performance: 'Shakespeare was born in the region that the Tourist Board now calls the Heart of England. From here he pumps out the lifeblood of the realm.'[44]

The divisive, debilitating effects of the 'Deep England' mythos on national identity, and on Shakespeare, have been and still are profound. 'Deep England' resided not only 'somewhere south in the fields', but also 'in the economic and ideological power of metropolitan cultural industries'.[45] These southern English economic and cultural industries included and still include the *Shakespeare* industry and the 'Shakespeare metropolitan academy'.[46] Inversely, these economic and cultural industries excluded and still exclude the North as a site of meaningful engagement with or constructions of Shakespeare, suggesting that Shakespeare and the North are fundamentally incompatible:

> Arthur Lloyd James, a member of the committee set up to determine pronunciation at the BBC, argued in 1939, 'You must not blame the BBC for killing dialect . . . the Lancashire comedian has killed the Lancashire dialect, and made Lancashire for ever afterwards impossible for the production of Shakespeare.'[47]

More recently, in 2011, the Royal Shakespeare Company (RSC) announced it would not be visiting Newcastle upon Tyne from Stratford-upon-Avon (as it had done every year since 1977), blaming cuts in funding due to the austerity policies of the Conservative-Liberal coalition government.[48] When the Company did come back to the city, in autumn 2013, Newcastle's buses bore the advertising legend: 'Shakespeare returns to Newcastle'.[49] This return was, of course, welcomed by the city and the Company. But if you were an educator, theatre-goer, theatre practitioner, or student working at any level with Shakespeare in the city, you might have opined: yes, the RSC had been away, but had Shakespeare? As Janice Wardle's chapter here on the RSC in Blackpool also asks: is there Shakespeare in the North without them? Such questions are a necessary response to the persistence of the 'Deep England' mythos, and how it implicates and circumscribes Shakespeare. In the service of that mythos, Shakespeare emerges as English (after a fashion), but never northern.

Just as Hughes' reader has no 'Rights' in claiming him (and yet still does), so other northern English writers explore the contradictions of collocating northernness and Shakespeare. In Harrison's 'Them & [uz]', for example, Shakespeare represents an exclusive form of cultural capital forcing anyone who wants to share in or possess it to change their language, demeanour and outlook. You have to alter who you are to do Shakespeare, and doing Shakespeare alters you. Harrison's speaker recollects being given the role of the Porter in *Macbeth* because his accent means he is one of those who speaks comic prose, not the poetry of kings.[50] In Harrison's view at this juncture, Leeds and literature (especially Shakespeare) are incompatible. Inhabiting one world means rejecting another. In 'A Good Read', the precocious, pretentious speaker consoles themselves after receiving another of their father's withering looks with the knowledge that he would never get excited by Shakespeare's *King Lear*.[51] Accordingly, Harrison suggests that Shakespeare represents something beyond or greater than bounded, specifically northern, lives and experiences. In 'Aqua Mortis', Harrison reflects on an aging father in Leeds, far from a son across the Atlantic who can be contacted only via technology better than Puck's powers. The poem concludes with that son echoing Prospero's book-burning resignation, in regret, and in italics emphasising distance (from source, father, or sentiment).[52] Even when reflecting on later life, and later in his career, Harrison conveys a sense that when you are in the North, Shakespeare occurs elsewhere, and still signifies geographical and social dislocation. In 'Fig on the Tyne', the speaker, rooted in North East England, imagines their dedicatee returning from Tokyo after playing Goneril.[53]

Of course, the irony inherent to articulating all this discontinuity is that Harrison, from and of the North, is writing poetry *using* and informed by Shakespeare, just as he writes poems inspired by those with no time to read poetry.[54] In a section of Harrison's play *Poetry or Bust*, a police constable makes a dire pun to tell the Airedale Bard, John Nicholson (1790–1843), that he is *barred* from selling books of his poems at Covent Garden Opera House in London: nodding at a bust of Shakespeare, the officer suggests *he* summoned the guard.[55] Shakespeare is monumentalised as an authority with the power to prohibit northern expression. And yet when Harrison's play was first staged at Yorkshire's Salts Mill in 1993, Nicholson was performed by the Northern Broadsides' Barrie Rutter, an actor and company acclaimed for their Shakespearean productions. As Caroline Heaton's chapter on the Broadsides in this collection reveals, when it comes to Shakespeare and the North, distinction and exclusion operate precisely because connection and inter-orientation can be imagined and at times realised.

Shakespeare in the North explores exactly these contradictions between Shakespeare and the North as (constructed as) mutually exclusive and mutually constitutive, because so many instances of Shakespeare in the North reveal them. For example, in his compendious and impressionistic account of *The North (and almost everything in it)*, Paul Morley records a factoid for '1588': 'William Shakespeare roams as far as Newcastle and Carlisle, possibly as a member of the Queen's Players'.[56] Unsurprisingly, given the way his characteristic prose style mingles the fantastical and the mundane, Morley offers no source or substantiation for this, or a gloss as to why this detail matters. Yet to record or fantasise about it suggests it *does* matter. Why? Because it seems implausible, or plausible, or desirable?

Morley also reminds us that where the BBC feared to tread, ITV did not. *Coronation Street*, the world's longest-running soap, celebrated and marketed because of the way it presents a quintessential northern English scene, had potentially Shakespearean roots:

> The working title of the show was Florizel Street, named after a character in Robert Louis Stevenson's detective short stories *The Suicide Club*, who was perhaps named after a character in Shakespeare's *Twelfth Night*, *The Winter's Tale* [sic] but a tea lady named Agnes remarked that Florizel sounded like a brand of disinfectant.[57]

Other sources corroborate Morley's claims about the Street's first name (if not always the detail about Agnes).[58] Equally, contributions from Monika Smialkowska and Chris Jackson in this collection emphasise that whatever the provenance of a fictional northern street, when it comes to *real* ones, Shakespeare has been built into the urban fabric across the English North, from Bootle in Merseyside, to Mancunian libraries, to Heaton in Tyneside.[59] But the error and happenstance in how Morley relates the story remain telling: it doesn't matter which Shakespeare play the name derived from, because the connection is tantalising enough, as too is the rejection. Apparently, Shakespeare is and is not part of the North's 'everything', which speaks volumes about the North, and about Shakespeare.

As Liberal as the North: Definitions, Challenges, Opportunities

Still, as we survey the 'North', what or where exactly do we mean? Emilia says, in *Othello*, 'I will speak as liberal as the north' (5.2.250), but she is not really talking about the North as a region (in Italy, Cyprus, England or otherwise). She means the north wind, and, with that simile, she implies that she will speak with freedom of expression and conscience, counteracting her silencing by Iago. Her liberated, gutsy speech has immediate effects: she condemns Iago, and schools Othello. However, pre-empting Gratiano's words in the close of the play ('All that's spoke is marred', 5.2.401), that liberated speech also has ambiguous, marring consequences: Iago kills her, and Othello kills himself. Her liberal expression is brutally repressed, her words strong but insubstantial, gesturing to a freedom that she cannot attain. Her words are just, in fact, words, and we all know what that play thinks about them: 'But words are words' says Brabantio (1.3.234).

Yet while Emilia may not be talking about *the* North, her compromised, ambiguous words help us begin to think about the challenges and opportunities of defining it, including norths *beyond* England (an idea Lisa Hopkins develops in her chapter in this collection). The North, whether immaterial wind or solid location, has long been associated with the kind of (potentially transgressive) liberality and liberty at which Emilia hints. Shakespeare offers other instances: when Joan La Pucelle practises her witchcraft, in *The First Part of Henry VI*, she calls on 'the lordly monarch of the north' (5.3.6), meaning either Lucifer or Zimimar (invoked by witches as 'king of the north', according to Reginald Scot in 1584).[60] Yet long before Shakespeare, Aristotle had described comparable assumptions about the incoherent freedom of the North:

> The nations that live in cold regions and those of Europe are full of spirit, but somewhat lacking in skill and intellect; for this reason, while remaining relatively free, they lack political cohesion and the ability to rule over their neighbours.[61]

These ideas inform Peter Davidson's remark that 'non-conformists go north (as they do in the British Isles)'.[62] There are strong historical reasons for recognising the North's capacity for generating alternative views of what freedom might look like: 'the North's experience of industrial and demographic change has made the region, or significant parts of it, a forcing ground of radical working-class political culture'.[63] As my own chapter in this collection indicates, such northern political cultures can prove significant for staging Shakespeare.

Perhaps, too, Emilia's airy, strong, empty, powerful, liberal, circumscribed words only alert us to the perception that the 'North' is flexible and indefinable, 'a shifting idea, always relative, always going away from us . . . Everyone carries their own idea of north within them'.[64] Harrison hints at something similar by prefacing the poem 'Facing North' with an epigraph from Louis MacNeice: 'The North begins inside'.[65] A recent exhibition in Newcastle upon Tyne's Baltic Art Gallery raised questions about this, but offered no answers, even as it touched upon the ideas of liberality Emilia voices:

> *From Blaydon to Shields, from Hull to Dundee,*
> *the passengers ask us: where can the north be?*
> *We appear to be in it, or are we at sea?*
> *Is it rivers and mines, is it you or just me? . . .*
> How do you know you're in the North? . . .
> Is this home, are we free?[66]

These kinds of refrains about multiple, subjective Norths climax in Morley's baggy rhapsodies: 'in the end the north is made up of lots of norths . . . norths within the north'.[67] There is some merit in such refrains, because, as with any region or community, heterogeneity is a cultural, geographical and social reality in whatever definition of 'North' we might settle upon. But even if we accept that 'there may be places . . . thought of as honorary norths', for the purposes of this collection we are simply defining North as 'the north (northern England or Scotland)'.[68] Though this definition may appear to exclude Ireland's North (which is, admittedly, ironic given the Northern Irish MacNeice's role here and elsewhere in representing diverse Norths), and may seem prosaic in contrast to those other more poetic refrains, it is meant as a usefully freeing, not to say liberal, designation for the region(s) in question.[69]

When we enquire whether the North is airy nothingness or solid reality, we begin to both problematise and clarify a working definition of it. To do more, we need to reflect critically on the state of play in understandings of early modern – and Shakespearean – northernness, and contemporary discourses about current northern regional identities and the 'North–South divide'. But why, indeed, think regionally at all? Edward Royle has rightly and eloquently expressed the problems and disadvantages of thinking regionally, not least because regions' identities are 'unstable, fluctuating and ambiguous': as we have seen and will see, the North is no exception.[70] Nonetheless, much is to be gained by thinking regionally, especially when we do so in relation to the discourse of 'critical regionalism'. For Klaus Lösch and Heike Paul, critical regionalism asks, in the first instance, 'How to define a region?' in a globalised age, when culture has been 'quite radically deterritorialized': 'What, then, is the relationship of region and culture? On a local-global continuum, is the region closer to the local or the global?' In response to these questions, critical regionalism 'tries to elucidate the hidden connections between the local/regional and the global which are mostly glossed over in self-conscious constructions of regional identities'. To do this, critical regionalism attends to the 'constitutive dialectic of the local and the global', especially when this dialectic involves 'questions of power and authority'. Lösch and Paul conclude: 'regions have to be conceptualized not as autonomous entities but as part of intricate global structures implying interdependencies of all kinds'.[71] These are liberating provocations for thinking about Shakespeare in the North – where the region is understood *not just* in terms of England, and where 'Shakespeare' embodies a long historical palimpsest, and a globally consumed, mediated and appropriated cultural authority, an icon finding a place in particular locales, connected with their own histories. And by thinking historically, and locally, we can certainly see why region mattered in Shakespeare's time: 'Even in an age of emerging nationhood, English men and women were still profoundly influenced by – and even drew their primary identity from – the parish, the town, and the county'.[72] So profound was this influence, suggests John M. Adrian, that 'the local' could serve as a 'site of active opposition to the national', in specific places: 'this applies more to regions like the Marches or the North than particular counties or towns'.[73] Thinking *regionally*, and of a region like the North, rather than simply *nationally*, is to think like an early modern, as much as someone in the 2000s:

> the majority of people . . . were never simply and invariably possessed by an overwhelming sense of their own distinctive identity as Englishmen, as Scotsmen, as Welshmen, or even as Irishmen. As in the rest of Europe, intense local and regional loyalties were always there to complicate and compromise.[74]

This regionality shaped Shakespeare, who 'grew up in the provinces, and received his education . . . from the provinces'.[75] Even if he didn't go

North, the North, in all its diverse significance, came to him: 'Four out of five consecutive Stratford schoolmasters were Lancashire men'.[76] In an 1999 interview with BBC 2's 'Newsnight', Stephen Greenblatt reflected on the 'Lancastrian Shakespeare' conference held at Hoghton Tower and the University of Lancaster (which explored the implications of Shakespeare's time in the North), to aver how though 'for so long we had talked of Shakespearean England as a monolith', we would now need to no longer.[77] However, that monolith is still all too often inscribed in commentary on what Shakespeare means now. In other words, even when work on Shakespeare does bring his relationship to contemporary discourses of Englishness to the fore, it all too often assumes that modern England is coherent, rather than a messy mass of conflicted communities and identities, as we have realised early modern England was itself. The local and regional are mistakenly subsumed by assumptions about the national, and about Shakespeare. As Alison Findlay and Richard Dutton suggest, such assumptions have afflicted understandings of Shakespeare:

> Even when Shakespeare was working at the centre of commercial and governmental power, he may have been artistically, emotionally and spiritually connected to a provincial alternative which deconstructed the monolithic and absolutist rhetoric of Elizabethan government.[78]

Of course, while we might accept the value of thinking regionally, maybe the North is not a region that can easily be thought into definitive and tangible existence. John Le Patourel emphasises that throughout history, 'the North of England has always been a vague notion without rigid territorial limits and encompassing considerable internal diversity'.[79] This is especially true in the 1500s where 'many if not most parts of the Tudor North were indistinguishable in their economy, wealth, social structure, and doubtless religious practices from southern lowland England'.[80] Even if regions and communities in the North *were* distinct from those in 'southern lowland England', those regions and communities were not sufficiently coherent to constitute a comprehensible 'north': 'the society of the borders was immensely different from that of the vale of York or south Lancashire'.[81] Arguably, what look like geographical and social distinctions might need to be framed differently: 'some of the contemporary discontents were not a conflict of north and south so much as centre versus peripheries: ... the feudal, Catholic, violent and backward characteristics of the Tudor north were characteristics of all provincial England'.[82] Cross-country aristocratic and material connections also meant that the

North was integrated into national not simply regional networks. The Duchy of Lancaster, for example, was not just a northern entity but also 'a living, working presence for Londoners', since it possessed 'vast holdings' in the capital.[83] In theological terms, too, the North was far from wholly Catholic in Shakespeare's period, nor was Catholicism confined to the North; accordingly, if Shakespeare *was* in the North because of a network of Catholic recusant and kinship connections, it was also because of the region's connections with the Midlands, the South, and the continent.[84]

It is for these reasons that in Shakespeare's plays what makes up the North is not always distinct, and what distinction there is must apparently be overcome. In *Richard II*, Henry's power depends on his ability to unite England's regions, as Scroop counsels Richard:

> Your uncle York is joined with Bullingbrook,
> And all your northern castles yielded up,
> And all your southern gentlemen in arms
> Upon his faction. (*Richard II*, 3.2.195–8)

For his part, Richard only sees the North in negative terms: 'I towards the north, / Where shivering cold and sickness pines the clime' (5.1.76–7). This means he fails to appreciate how potent – and necessary – integrating North and South might be. Later in the tetralogy, we learn why even defining the North distinctly is difficult. When Mortimer, Glendower and Hotspur divide England and Wales in 3.1. of *1 Henry IV*, Hotspur gets 'The remnant northward lying off from Trent' (3.1.78). The North, here, has no firmer designation or identity than that. And even this designation gets less firm as the scene progresses. Hotspur's ambition and his identity as 'this northern youth' (3.2.146) means he plans to alter the course of the river to claim more land as part of his 'remnant northward', liberally enlarging his domain and himself. Regional distinctions are, it seems, fluid.

Despite this emphasis on inexorable integration or fluidity, however, Shakespeare also contributes to discourses that make North and South distinct. This is how Henry IV describes the arrival at his court of a 'true industrious friend', after a journey from what we now call Humbleton in Northumberland, where Hotspur's triumph has preserved the northern boundaries of the new king's England against the Scots:

> Sir Walter Blunt, new lighted from his horse,
> Stained with the variation of each soil
> Betwixt that Holmedon and this seat of ours (*1 Henry IV*, 1.1.62–5)

Of course, this victory and this passage could be seen to manifest the coherence and integrity of an English geographical, national and political identity in the face of a foreign threat. But in a disunited kingdom, the very land 'Betwixt' the English North and the metropolitan, political core, centred on the king's authority, is itself composed of heterogeneous and plural identities. Hotspur's subsequent rebellion reveals that any coherence is at best momentary, because the 'variation' between 'each soil' of regions and territories *within* England is potentially as significant as any differences between England and Scotland.

In intimating this, Shakespeare would draw on what Andrew Hadfield has described as the 'long history and distinguished history' of the idea of the 'north' as distinct.[85] These perceived distinctions took many forms. To some, they were linguistic: George Puttenham noted that the language used in northern England was 'not so courtly nor so currant as our southerne English'.[86] Linguistic differences aligned with material variations: 'in the later middle ages and sixteenth century ... the prosperity gap between the north and south-east was widening'.[87] Differences *were* also theological. To a preacher in 1625, the North was one of the 'dark places of the kingdom'.[88] Prior to the Reformation, the northern regions' distance from 'the main Lollard centres of Oxford and London', their 'lower levels of literacy', and 'the immense power and influence of the northern monasteries', reduced potential heterodoxy. Because of this, *during* the Reformation, however, 'Catholicism at all social levels remained far stronger in the North than in the South'.[89] And Catholicism played a large part in events like the 1569 Northern Rebellion: 'concealed altarstones and holy-water vats were resurrected from the dunghills and gardens where they had been buried and became the focus for resistance to the Elizabethan settlement'.[90] Some historians have taken this resistance to what became the state religion further, to emphasise, again, the North's liberalism: 'the hall-mark of the north was not Catholicism but lack of enthusiasm for any religion'.[91]

Admittedly, when exploring the roots of a phenomenon like the 1569 Rebellion, K. J. Kesselring accepts that 'recent historical research has undermined theories of northern exceptionalism' when it comes to contemporaneous revolts against the Elizabethan state.[92] Indeed, Kesselring shows how the rebellion had international and national dimensions beyond regional concerns. Nonetheless, Kesselring also shows how 'insensitivity to local sentiment' regarding religious matters, along with 'widespread sympathy in the north for Mary [Queen of Scots]' helped foment rebellion, and underscored its cross-border complexities.[93] Kesselring notes how Thomas Norton, co-author of the north-fixated play *Gorboduc*, reflected on the rebellion, to observe that 'when the rebels shouted "*God save the Queen* . . . they have plainly showed it is not our Queen, Queen Elizabeth, that they mean"'.[94] To some, the Rebellion exemplified the fact that border dwellers were 'savage and more eager than others for upheaval'.[95] Norton's anxieties fed into the drama he and others produced, as Paul Frazer's chapter in this collection shows.

Of course, the Rebellion was *also* a reaction to the Tudor state's centralising, nation-building efforts, and failed in the face of these accordingly. As Helen M. Jewell notes, 'the Tudor period saw the end of the north-south divide as a major political concern'.[96] Yet Jewell also notes that subsequent centuries emphasised what the early modern period had inaugurated: 'there was already, before the industrial revolution, a distinction between north and south, and between northerners and southerners'.[97] Jewell's careful, long-view equivocation is echoed in other perspectives on the 'north-south divide'. While some scholars have argued that 'imagery used of the north actually changed very little between the medieval period and the nineteenth century', others have contended that the nineteenth-century's nation-building, manifested in politics and infrastructure, mitigated divides and distinctions.[98] However, as Stuart Rawnsley suggests, 'Far from negating regional economies and cultures, the "Industrial Revolution" actually intensified them', by exacerbating the already socially and geographically unequal distribution of resources and wealth.[99]

Obviously, as recent events suggest, we need to be careful and critical about perpetuating a 'space-myth' of the North as 'the Land of the Working Class . . . a symbol of the common unity of the British "folk"' set against 'London, the centre of authority and finance, and . . . the pastoral South of the gentry'.[100] But having surveyed the diverse historical perspectives on the North's definition and distinction (or otherwise), it seems politic nevertheless to concur with Alan R. H. Baker and Mark Billinge's view that '[t]he North-South divide – like all such regionalisation – has to be seen as a cultural construction . . . which could nonetheless be the basis for real thought and action'.[101] In turn, the 'modern liberal doctrine' emphasising the 'plurality of "norths"' warrants challenging because it risks overlooking the (English) North's very real and ongoing sociocultural difference from the (English) South.[102] Thus when contemporary parliamentarians confess that 'The exact extent of the north . . . is not prescribed by the government' they admit defeat when faced with defining terms, but they also seek to diffuse – or perhaps defuse? – the potential inherent in it.[103] Understandably, then, Niven cautions against dissolving northernness because doing so denudes the political power inherent to a community until recently read and felt as solidarity, in the North, and *elsewhere*: we might be able to counteract 'the structural inequalities of British society' by reimagining a socio-political 'system' of 'strong, energetic, regional provinces facing outwards to Europe and the rest of the world'.[104]

What the 2019 UK election result says about such solidarity and aspirations remains to be seen. But there can be no question that 'structural inequalities', differences and separations persist today. Much is at stake – including but beyond what we do with Shakespeare – when we realise this. As we combat 'geographical inequalities in work and welfare' by drawing on the 'legitimacy of more localised autonomy', that autonomy might itself 'draw upon the histories and cultural identities of localities and regions'.[105] Thinking about Shakespeare can seem a long way from thinking about 'structural' or 'geographical' inequalities. But this need not be the case if we appreciate more fully Shakespeare's inherence to 'the histories and cultural identities of localities and regions'. To ensure we do not do this at some abstract, theoretical level, we might think about the interactions of the terms in this collection's subtitle – place, politics and performance – focusing for a moment, to do so, on *The Winter's Tale*.

In Shakespeare's rewrite of Othello's tragic jealousy, does Emilia's liberal 'north' take on new forms? Maybe, if we consider that the Bohemian scenes in the play loosely accommodate 'the country remains of Catholic syncretism'.[106] To original audiences of *The Winter's Tale*, 'fair Bohemia' (4.1.21) might, indeed, have been code for an actual Catholic land: 'In 1577 [Edmund] Campion wrote from Prague to Robert Arden, a Jesuit operating near Stratford who is thought to have been related to Mary Arden, to encourage recruits to sail for "the pleasant and blessed shore of Bohemia".'[107] If you were minded to, then, you could link the English North West and far-off Bohemia in Shakespeare's time, realising how a regional province faced outward, to recollect Niven's terms.

For different but related reasons you can in ours too. Lucy Bailey's 2013 production of *The Winter's Tale* for the RSC juxtaposed a Sicily of aristocratic (un)ease with a Bohemia populated by northern English industrial workers on a hard-earned Wakes Week holiday in a seaside resort looking very much like Blackpool. Part of the production's brilliance involved the ways it set the play in the 1860s, just at the moment when Deep England (and by implication the 'Deep North') was in the process of construction. This was not just an historical, costume-drama setting, though. Perdita's lament that 'To me the difference forges dread' (4.4.20) refers to the dangers of the class distinction dividing her and Florizel; but her present tense reminds us that production took place in the year when Britain was named as 'the most unequal country in the West'.[108] Bailey suggested that with this play Shakespeare 'gives us a new dawn', even if the production's moment could not: 'It's a radical thought, even today, that Perdita, with a labourer's accent, should become queen'.[109] Yet Perdita didn't just have a 'labourer's' accent; she had a north-western English accent: when discussing 'bastards', her first 'a' was short and flat (/bæstədz/), while the nobles' Received Pronunciation drew out a long first 'a' (/bɑːstədz/). Class division intensifies as a conflict between English regions. Moreover, the potential of a lost Catholic world became a (similarly lost?) coherent, oppositional working-class identity, local and distinct, but connected to a wider world beyond Deep England, and beyond an institution of the metropolitan Shakespeare academy like the RSC.[110] In this regard, signifying Bohemia as industrial-era Blackpool made a lot of sense:

> The Illuminations were borrowed from the Kaiser's birthday celebrations, and the tower is borrowed from the Eiffel Tower; . . . The trams are very Middle European. You can imagine that it's the coast of Bohemia, if you're looking for the coast of Bohemia.[111]

We don't need to subscribe completely to Davidson's notion that 'the revenant narrative is essentially of the north . . . a product of occluded weather and broodings upon the fate of the dead', to observe the historical survivals ghosting through a production like this.[112] The networked North that existed whether Shakespeare went there or not, a North complicating the definitions and testing the limits of Englishness, is still with us. And so when it comes to Shakespeare's Catholicism and his time in the North, contributors to this collection are more or less bothered about establishing or pronouncing on 'where geographically and ideologically, Shakespeare was coming from in the 1580s'.[113] The 'howls of anguish' about the idea of a Catholic northern Shakespeare challenging the notion of 'the Anglocentric Bard of Protestant Power' arose because of the 'Catholic' tag, yes, but *also* in response to the northern designation, and how that makes Anglocentrism difficult because it contests the very idea that there is a solid, singular, essential 'Anglo', or, indeed 'Britain'.[114]

Bridges and/not Borders

Even as this introduction has thus far focused on Shakespeare in relation to the English North, the contributors and I have tried – if not succeeded – to avoid the trap of 'debate about real regional differences based on solid economic, political and historical factors' becoming 'subsumed . . . into fashionable analyses of "Englishness"'.[115] Indeed, by trying to ensure that the North in focus is never solely English, Scottish, or indeed Irish, we can understand it in such a way as to further query what is 'British'. To put this another way, identifying what might be perceived as distinctive about northern English communities and identities should not prevent us from seeing that distinctiveness replicated in other places, so that what seems distinctive is actually something shared.

Since, as Willy Maley and Rory Loughnane have confirmed, 'Celtic' is a contested term in itself but especially when related to Shakespeare, then, we might add, so is 'North', especially because of how 'Celtic' and 'northern' communities and identities interact with each other conceptually and materially.[116] These interactions have profound historical bases. 'Critical regionalism' is useful once again because it reminds us that a region might, in fact, be made up of the borders *between* regions, since borders themselves are 'entities that exhibit distinctly regional and transnational features'.[117] This is an important component in defining the North, because it helps us establish a sense of the North as something that *crosses* borders: not just 'the north as "northern England or Scotland"', as in Davidson's formulation, but *also* 'northern England *and* Scotland' (and Ireland), as in ours. To stress this may seem a modern preoccupation:

> The only way to counteract the geographical inequalities of the London-dominated capitalist state is by building up the English regions . . . But alongside the regionalist cause, we should also explore ways of connecting the English regions and the non-English nations, so that the boundary lines of our imagined national communities are transcended rather than reinforced.[118]

This progressive, provocative position (like the one taken by this collection) is not some desperate defence of the 'Union'. As such, it is not the same as saying, as the UK's Prime Minister recently did for reasons of political expediency, that 'there is no such thing as a border between England and Scotland'; clearly there is.[119] But, again, if we think like an early modern, we see how cross-border confluence was both unavoidable and problematic: influential work by Lisa Hopkins, and chapters in *Shakespeare in the North* by Steven Veerapen and Richard Stacey, make this evident.[120] When James I acceded, he tried to 'impose a new order' on the border between England and Scotland but few there were 'cooperative': '"Scotland will be Scotland, borders will be borders", rejoiced some Northumbrians as the king's plans for union died'.[121] Yet the Anglo-Scots border was, in reality, subject to 'pervasive interpenetration' in Shakespeare's day.[122] There were 'openings as well as boundaries'.[123] Scotland's relations with England *could* help establish new forms of cross-border nationhood: 'since the Scottish reformation of 1560, a new discourse of "British" amity based on shared religious identity and a shared enemy emerged'.[124] But the early modern borders – 'a region apart' – were also a place where existing conceptions of national identity might come unstuck.[125] This evinces the reality so influentially articulated by John Kerrigan: that the communities and cultures of the British 'linked and divided archipelago' were 'interactive entities' comprised of 'different ethnic and religious groups' with 'braided histories'.[126] Since in parts of northern England Scots were 'outnumbering the English', border inhabitants did not always possess 'a due sense of the primacy of national loyalties' and indulged at times in 'cross-border confederacy'; people were '"Scottish when they will, and English at their pleasure"'.[127] This meant that early modern Scotland and England were 'intimately related . . . domains'.[128] It also meant that border folk, as northerners, were seen as 'uncivilized, unruly, and not fully English'.[129]

Shakespeare was and is 'deeply implicated' in these 'archipelagic issues'.[130] His plays exhibit this conflicted inter-orientation of plural Norths. Many scholars have shown how those making up Shakespeare's England, especially in the history plays, are themselves made by their connected opposition to those in non-English locations, such as Scotland, Ireland and Wales: 'when King Henry speaks in praise of Hotspur [in *1 Henry IV* 3.2], he describes his martial virtues primarily in terms of the Scotsman [Douglas] he has conquered and made loyal'.[131] Staging this interdependence made sense, since from 1603 'Shakespeare . . . served the Scottish king', who sponsored his theatre company.[132] Yet Willy Maley's 'Postscript' in this collection crucially emphasises how northern England, Scotland and Ireland presented challenges to the Tudor and Stuart state, *especially* when these inter-orientations were apparent, in Shakespeare and in his society. It is no surprise that those currently discussing mores and identities in the 'debatable land' where 'the national border disappears like a track through a mire' should reach for their Shakespeare to make sense of them: 'A Scottish Romeo did not have to brave the wrath of his family to court an English Juliet, nor did the Juliets have to travel very far'.[133] Moreover, given the prominence of the bordered Irish 'North' in present political discussions, the northern cross-border interactions as evinced by Shakespeare are historical, but also ongoing. David Smith identified 'a 'Celtic fringe' of the very north of England, Cornwall, Wales, Scotland and Northern Ireland', united by distance from political business at Westminster, and shared socio-economic travails.[134] More recently, Niven has argued that 'radically' reconfiguring 'the centre-margins dynamic of the archipelago' involves '*breaking apart England itself and repositioning its fringes in close alliance with Welsh, Scottish and Irish nation-regions*'.[135] What might be described as (critical) regionalism is an entirely reasonable and predictable response to resurgent nationalism. This has been true in the past, and in various places: 'It was ultimately the acceptance of the French nation as mono-lithic (i.e. mono-national, mono-linguistic) which gave rise to the idea of the region as an "intermediate place".'[136] Yet with the rise of *English* nationalism in recent years, such a critical response is ever more vital.

For nationalists, including racists, of course, the nation is never safe, strong, or pure enough. Threats menace the nation's sanctity, whether from within or without. This requires the nation to police vigilantly its borders and sustain its discriminations, in '*a historical system of complementary exclusions and dominations*'.[137] But this desire to keep the nation secure means always creating new discriminations, and never stopping at the border. Policing borders evinces how permeable nations can be, and restlessness and anxiety inform exploitation and expansionism, material or military, laying claim to bits of one nation to keep another secure. Likewise, imperialism and (neo)colonialism make the 'nation' (or aspects of it) modular and portable beyond geographic limits. Law, education, modes of governance, commerce, technology and finance are mobilised and weaponised. So too are figurings of ethnicity – Englishness, for example, has itself at times represented a 'translatable identity' – and culture, including, in the case of the nations comprising the North Atlantic archipelago, the 'global Shakespeare cult'.[138] However, all this means that racism and nationalism display (and often simultaneously obscure or repress) an economic and psychological dependence on what or who lies beyond the border – and on the border itself – to make the national community what it is: 'It may be that all borderlands hum with the frequencies of the unconscious; after all, borders are where the fabric is thin'.[139] There is, as a result, a tragic dialectic at work here: the more obvious it becomes that a border is an arbitrary, contingent construct, the more violently it is enforced; the more a border is crossed, the more vigorously it is policed; and the more defined a border, the more likely – if far less easily – it will be crossed. Writing about another kind of border, but in resonant terms, Michel Foucault observed: 'limit and transgression depend on each other for whatever density of being they possess: a limit could not exist if it were absolutely uncrossable'.¹⁴⁰ In an age of renewed global mobilities, and reflecting on the forms and effects of borders past, Kapka Kassabova has, to an extent, updated Foucault's concerns:

> Once near a border, it is impossible not to be involved, not to want to exorcise or transgress something. Just by being there, the border is an invitation. Come on, it whispers, step across this line. If you dare.¹⁴¹

After all this, and mindful of the violence and tragedy all too often surrounding contemporary borders, can we conceive a modern North haunted by the early modern North, continuing to exist beyond and across borders? History's unstable borders might therefore present a 'laboratory of the future'.¹⁴² This may help us in querying the integrity of identities and formations those borders define, including nations themselves. We should accept the historic and contemporary evidence that 'Northern identities do not . . . develop or exist in splendid isolation', but link within and beyond the North.¹⁴³ As we do, we can also conceive of the productive, progressive exchanges that result when we bridge borders, and when we remember '*nobody* is fully English . . . every empirical Englishman contains something "non-English"'.¹⁴⁴

Shakespeare in the (Postcolonial?) North

We have shifted focus from northern England, to borders, to Scotland, and the world. This helps us appreciate how the flexible, inclusive North is often seen as another country. This also means we can appreciate the value of a postcolonial approach to thinking about *Shakespeare in the North*. In recent years, much excellent critical work has been done looking at Shakespeare's global significance, especially in relation to what has been happening in the world since so many countries and communities began to achieve independence from colonial and imperial powers. Such work is vital because it shows how the tools of domination – including language, especially *Shakespeare's* language – can be turned against those who dominate by those who were once dominated. In Sandra Young's words, in 2019's *Shakespeare in the Global South*, 'travelling across the globe, traditional Shakespeare has been dismantled and reimagined' by 'writers, activists and politicians'.¹⁴⁵

Shakespeare in the North is both informed by and yet keen to think beyond these kinds of potent analyses. For example, it would be a mistake to discount how brilliantly Young identifies how certain productions of Shakespeare focused on 'the struggle of the migrant' realise solidarities between globally diverse but historically contingent 'displaced and disempowered' communities in the 'heterogeneous urban spaces of the North'.[146] Likewise, we would concur with Young's view that we must identify 'pockets of vulnerability and disempowerment or what one might call "southerliness" in the North that result from diasporic mobilities' in the 'urban spaces of the global north'.[147] But perhaps it would also be a mistake to identify the causes of 'vulnerability and disempowerment' in the North – whether 'global' or local – as resulting from a single factor: there are many reasons why such 'pockets' of inequality (and often very large ones, at that) exist. Indeed, as we have seen, there are plural, heterogeneous Norths (again, global or otherwise). And while Young writes of the 'multiply diverse, unequal urban spaces of the North' she focuses on only two: Los Angeles and London.[148] London has no exclusive claim to accommodating diasporic, migrant identities (and we risk occluding vibrant histories of hybridity elsewhere, especially in the North, if we think so).[149] Moreover, while London is in the global North, it is also true that for those in the north of the country of which London is the capital, London is *not* the North.

Young also rightly critiques 'the predictable region-by-region framework' focusing on 'colourful local translocations' of Shakespeare in formulations such as 'Indian Shakespeare' or 'Shakespeare in Africa', because 'Shakespeare remains the dominant figure – the noun – and the region under focus is positioned as a colourful variant, qualifying the primary'.[150] Arguably, from its title alone, *Shakespeare in the North* succumbs to this tendency. But when the region in question is *within* a hegemonic domain, such as a post-imperial power like the United Kingdom, the imbalances Young describes start to take on a different form. What if the qualification of Shakespeare comes from inside what Young designates as a 'primary' location? What if Shakespeare is never settled or 'dominant', not least in the North, and in the archipelago of which the North is a part? What if the supposed 'centre' is itself fractured and diverse, and *de*centering happens there too? Young writes of moving beyond 'familiar dichotomies' of colonial and postcolonial thinking, but if we truly want to do so, we need to think in terms not only of the Global South she so acutely articulates, but also in terms of Shakespeare in the North.[151] It is undoubtedly right – ethically, politically, and in terms of any interest we might have in Shakespeare and ourselves – that we consider his work in relation to the 'various social groups who live in the penumbra of Western colonial cultures'.[152] Yet it would appear that in some accounts of postcolonial, globalised Shakespeare, engaging as they are, the 'local' is always already somewhere different to precisely the kind of homogeneous constructs of Western, national, 'British', 'Scottish' or 'English' geo-political identities and cultural practices that *Shakespeare in the North* aims to contest.

So, like Young, Craig Dionne and Parmita Kapadia legitimately observe that 'Shakespeare is rewritten, reinscribed, and translated to fit within the local traditions, values and languages of various communities and cultures around the world'.[153] Yet the collection that their comments preface does not feature any contributions focused on the 'various communities and cultures' in what Willy Maley – who provides *this* collection's 'Postscript' – has elsewhere termed the 'ubiquitous 'North', that is, anywhere North of Stratford'.[154] Maybe there is no need to: who cares about hearing more stories from already historically privileged and over-exposed people and places? However, many of the stories told in *Shakespeare in the North* have *not* been heard before, in part because the South's 'domination' of the North is 'discursive power: the authority to tell stories about this region'.[155] As we have seen throughout this introduction, one of the stories told about the North involves Shakespeare's presence in or absence from it, and the region's right to tell stories about itself using Shakespeare. Why bother, then, to describe things from 'the perspectives of the hegemonic cultures of the North'?[156] Because if local Shakespeares query the idea of a globally universal Shakespeare, then a northern Shakespeare exposes the myths of a national culture, and the reality of what we saw as perceived by both Hughes and Harrison as '*a dreadful schism in the British nation*'.[157]

Let's be clear: we cannot and would not downplay how enabling postcolonial scholarship has been for the thinking gathered in this collection; nor is it credible to blithely equate the specifics of what people and places enduring colonialism suffered with how some parts of the British archipelago were forcibly integrated. Whether or not the North was subject to what has been described as 'internal colonialism' might, indeed, be hard to say: Michael Hechter differentiated between how England's North and the 'Celtic fringe' (including Scotland) experienced 'the establishment of one national culture' (though this discrimination depends upon seeing distinctions between the two as solid).[158] We also need to be clear that, as Jyotsna G. Singh has argued, there are no 'guarantees of a progressive outcome' from seeing Shakespeare in relation to '"native" and minority cultures in a variety of locations', or, indeed, regions.[159] But by querying and diversifying the narratives of Shakespeare as laureate of a supposedly coherent 'nation', we make nativist Shakespeares harder to maintain, precisely because the places to which he is being made 'native' are shown to be contingent and far from coherent. We know that 'adaptation', of Shakespeare or otherwise, 'is a useful antidote against the worst excesses of nationalism', near or far.[160] Indeed, as Dionne and Kapadia put it: 'Countering England through Shakespeare, through its prized national poet, by making Shakespeare "native" to other peoples and cultures feels at first counterintuitive.'[161]

It might feel *especially* counterintuitive to do so by looking at Shakespeare in England's or Britain's regions, to not only contradict but also deconstruct the idea of 'nation'. But that, in fact, is what this collection seeks to do. It must be possible to 'plot how Shakespeare's texts, iconicity, and cultural capital' can 'reflect the uneasy relationship between the hegemonic and the subaltern, the West and the rest', by *also* emphasising the heterogeneity of 'the West' – including the regions and communities of the British archipelago – in the same way we should do with 'the rest'.[162] At a time when (too) many powerful people use Shakespeare 'as the ultimate tool to reform and unify a population into a cohesive identity', this would on the contrary be to 'unscript the desire for cohesion' when it comes to Shakespeare, and the nations he has been made to serve, in provocative and energising ways.[163]

Dionne and Kapadia celebrate the reality that 'Shakespeare's plays can no longer signify an exclusively British or even Western identity; instead they function as a site of contest reflecting manifold cultures'.[164] The point of *this* collection is that the 'cultures' *within* archipelagic Britain are themselves 'manifold', differentiated by 'uneven relations of power' and 'race, region, religion, class, subculture etc.', and we do those cultures, and Shakespeare, a disservice if we forget this.[165] So, while Dionne and Kapadia affirm that 'Local Shakespeares suggest powerful strategies of intervention', this collection concurs, but *intervenes* in different localities to do so. Through this, we come closer to Sonia Massai's take on how we need to refine and augment our understanding of globalised Shakespeare. To complement our sense of Shakespeare's role 'in the shaping of national cultures and dramatic traditions' we should conduct 'new investigations into a much wider variety of localities, including specific local, regional, national and supra-national "positions"'.[166]

Thinking of Shakespeare and the North – and using postcolonial models to do so – can also help us bring the processes, realities, opportunities and costs of 'glocalization' into focus, and empower us to deal with them.[167] As Young affirms, 'Global Shakespeare *is* local Shakespeares'.[168] In other words, and as an approach like critical regionalism would suggest, we can put the interchanges between different global localities to work, and we can use texts and figures like Shakespeare to do so:

> By drawing together the voices of a given region and allowing comparison with another space's structurally significant life situation, aesthetic artefacts help outsiders to interpret the terms of their exteriority, create ideological bridges, and set into play the resonances constituting mutual awareness ... The existence of a dialogue with other regions outside our own may thus provide a foothold for our collective entrance into the future.[169]

Postcolonial Shakespeares have taught us that there is no single, monolithic, ever-enduring Shakespeare to whom all must subject themselves, just as there is no single, monolithic ever-enduring form of control by which all are forever subjected. At the same time, following the shift to a post-imperial but still globalised new world socio-economic order, archipelagic nations and communities have had to find new roles and identities in relation to their past, each other, and the world. Part of doing so has involved thinking about the role of 'aesthetic artefacts' like those derived from Shakespeare, in and when appropriated by the various, conflicted, diasporic, devolving and devolved communities of the British Isles.[170] We must accept that there is 'more to Shakespeare's work' than serving 'conservative anglocentrism', 'global capitalism' or 'nationalist political agendas' (in the global South or North).[171] When we act on this acceptance we rejuvenate and revolutionise the 'provincial alternative' that scholars have realised was itself open to Shakespeare.[172]

In the 1930s, Ralph Vaughan Williams asked: 'Was anyone ever more local, or even parochial, than Shakespeare?'[173] Now, we might agree, but ask, local to *where* or *whom*? By doing just this, *Shakespeare in the North* tries to extend the cultural (and enhance the political) franchise for – and within – our communities, whatever their latitude. As recent academic and community work in and about Shakespeare in locations across the North East of England has shown, he can be an effective vehicle for people to come together in new ways to understand their locality, and themselves as social and political agents.[174] Belying its title, then, this book is not simply about Shakespeare (whatever forms 'he' takes), or the North (wherever it is). But it *is* wholly about what culture can do for others and to us, and what we can do with it, however conflicted and diverse 'we' are. Indeed, it is our diversity and our conflicts that make us, and the culture we make happen. Even as we become used to critical orthodoxies regarding Global Shakespeares, Scottish Shakespeares, Irish Shakespeares, and Welsh Shakespeares, perhaps at times we also need to think beyond the borders that such designations reinforce. And even if people are willing and able to speak of (or critique, or conflate) British and English Shakespeares, we are less used to hearing about them as anything other than a southern (or more often metropolitan) Shakespeare. Isn't it time, therefore, for *Shakespeare in the North*?

Shakespeare in the North

Growing out of a 2016 conference organised by the editor at Northumbria University and the Library of Newcastle's Literary and Philosophical Society, *Shakespeare and the North* curates the voices of emerging and established authors from within and beyond academia and Shakespeare studies. Together, chapters look backwards and forwards, offering a survey of historical change, with contributions on Shakespeare and northernness in the early modern period, as well as on later appropriations of his work in and beyond the North (this is, in part and deliberately, evident in the variations in tone, and different Shakespearean editions and formats for citing the plays used by different contributors). Subsequently, the contributions do what this introduction has tried to do: that is, reflect on links and differences between past and present, different cultural forms and literary genres, England and Scotland (and beyond), the local and the global. The collection is divided into three sections: 'Shakespeare and the Early Modern North', 'Performing Shakespeare in the North', and 'Appropriating Shakespeare in the North'. The first explores shifting relations between early modern northern places and power in Shakespearean drama, and the contexts informing and informed by that drama when it was initially conceived or performed. Paul Frazer considers Shakespeare's recycling of Thomas Sackville and Thomas Norton's *Gorboduc*, a play whose response to a period of political strife would speak to Shakespeare's sense of similar conditions decades later. Steven Veerapen discusses the staging of cross-border relationships in plays such as Shakespeare's *Henry V* and *Macbeth*, Ben Jonson's *Eastward Ho*, and Robert Greene's *The Scottish History of James the Fourth*. Richard Stacey develops the focus on cross-border matters to explore the Yorkist iconography and ideology underpinning James VI and I's complex claim to the throne of England, particularly in plays debating political authority such as *Macbeth* and *King Lear*. Ending the first section, Lisa Hopkins connects Shakespeare to Anthony Brewer's *The Lovesick King* and Richard Brome's *The Queen's Exchange* to show two related things: first, that the North stands in a charged relationship with the West, and second that where England's own North begins and ends is partially conditioned by the other countries which lie to the north of it.

After this coverage of early modern Shakespearean norths, the collection's next section considers significant instances of Shakespeare's staging and remaking in the North subsequently. Chapters in this section therefore emphasise the ways in which 'performing' Shakespeare in various ways on and beyond northern stages has constructed and queried both Shakespeare and the North. This involves looking at particular theatrical institutions or companies, and particular productions, all of which have much to say about the complexities and conflicts of performing Shakespeare in particular places. Drawing on extensive archival material, Adam Hansen evaluates the work of the People's Theatre, Newcastle upon Tyne, founded in 1911 by local members of the British Socialist Party, to ask: what might such a theatre make of Shakespeare? Looking at another period, and another company, Caroline Heaton shows how, following its formation in 1992, the Northern Broadsides has been a regular source of energetic productions of works by Shakespeare. The question of northern Shakespeares now is also addressed by Janice Wardle who explores a specific production of *A Midsummer Night's Dream* by the Royal Shakespeare Company at the Blackpool Grand Theatre in April 2016. This staging reveals not an antithetical comic opposition of Shakespeare and the North, but an ethically driven conversation designed to revive the performance of the play *and* northern communities.

Richard Wilson critically examines another recent instance of potential revival: in 2016, the Conservative then-Chancellor George Osborne's announcement of £11 million towards building a 'Globe of the North' in Liverpool. Wilson's chapter introduces the themes of the collection's final section, concerning the uses to which Shakespeare has been put in the North historically, and currently, beyond performances on stage, focusing on his appropriations in northern civic society, his incorporation within the fabric of northern cityscapes, and his figurings in diverse media today. Scrutinising previously neglected archives, Monika Smialkowska evinces how and why, in the early 1900s, Shakespeare was used in England's North West (in particular, Greater Manchester) to help build a sense of identity in local communities distinct from (though not necessarily oppositional to) nationhood and empire. Moving from England's North West to North East, Chris Jackson's chapter explores what happens when Shakespeare, northern locations and local history meet, focusing on a recent community research project on the origin of Shakespearean street names in Heaton,

Newcastle upon Tyne. We recross the Pennines in Liz Oakley-Brown's discussion of the 2005 film *Frozen* (dir. Juliet McKoen) and Jenn Ashworth's short story 'Doted' (2014). As Lancastrian visions of *Hamlet* and *King Lear* respectively, we see how these pre-modern plays of elite sensibilities help articulate the identity politics of contemporary culture. James Loxley then takes us once more across the Anglo-Scots border, and once more into the matter of nationhood, past and present, contending that Shakespeare's place in Scottish literary culture is a complicated business. Through a reading of David Greig's 2010 play *Dunsinane*, Loxley suggests that the kind of Jacobean moment which shaped Shakespeare is now visible again in the constitutional and cultural politics of early twenty-first-century Britain. Finally, Willy Maley's 'Postscript' surveys the preceding arguments' shared concerns and discontinuities. He reflects on what has changed in our understandings of 'Shakespeare in the North' since his own hugely influential contributions to debates about Shakespeare's relations to Englishness, Scottishness, and Britishness, and in response to the socio-political faultlines revealed by who and where we are now.

Notes

1. Title of a 1964 debate at the Oxford University Union, cited in Dave Russell, *Looking North: Northern England and the National Imagination* (Manchester and New York: Manchester University Press, 2004), 15. Barnet is one of London's northernmost boroughs. The abusive term 'wog' was – and sadly *is* – used by bigots to describe people from black and minority ethnic communities; this phrase is a reworking of the no-less bigoted, ill-informed, but sadly influential idiom that 'wogs begin at Calais'.
2. Hughes' most recent biographer, Jonathan Bate, does not mention the poem, in an otherwise inclusive study of the works; see *Ted Hughes: The Unauthorised Life* (London: William Collins, 2015).
3. J. B. Priestley, *The Good Companions* (Bradford: Great Northern Books, 2018), 443.
4. Cited in Russell, *Looking North*, 137.
5. Ted Hughes, 'Rights', first published in *Arts Yorkshire* (Oct/Nov 1985); republished in Paul Keegan (ed.), *Collected Poems* (London: Faber and Faber, 2003), 700–1.
6. Ted Hughes, *Shakespeare and the Goddess of Complete Being* (London: Faber and Faber, 1992), 293–4.
7. See Hughes, letter to Hilda Farrar (? February 1985), in Christopher Reid (ed.), *Letters of Ted Hughes* (Faber and Faber: London, 2007), 496–7.
8. Ted Hughes, letter to A. H. Greenwood, Headmaster of Colden J & I School (11 February 1985). Uncollected.

9. Neil Corcoran, 'A nation of selves: Ted Hughes's Shakespeare', in Willy Maley and Margaret Tudeau-Clayton (eds), *This England, That Shakespeare: New Angles on Englishness and the Bard* (Farnham: Ashgate, 2010), 185–200, 198.
10. See Ted Hughes, *A Choice of Shakespeare's Verse* (London and Boston: Faber and Faber, 1991), 174.
11. Corcoran, 'A nation', 198.
12. See Hughes, *Goddess*, 293–4.
13. John Lucas, *Modern English Poetry: From Hardy to Hughes* (London: Batsford, 1986), 194.
14. Neil Roberts, 'Class, war and the Laureateship', in Terry Gifford (ed.), *The Cambridge Companion to Ted Hughes* (Cambridge: Cambridge University Press, 2011), 150–61, 150–2.
15. See Hughes, letter to Daniel Weissbort, *Letters*, 115–16.
16. Roberts, 'Class', 160.
17. See Hughes, letter to Lucas Myers (19 June 1959), *Letters*, 146–7.
18. See Hughes, letter to Daniel Huws (October 1957), *Letters*, 111–12. All references in this introduction to *Coriolanus*, and any other Shakespearean plays thereafter cited parenthetically, are to William Shakespeare, *The Complete Works*, ed. Jonathan Bate and Eric Rasmussen (Basingstoke: Macmillan, 2008).
19. See Hughes, letter to the Editor of *The Observer* newspaper (17 January 1972), *Letters* 327.
20. See Hughes, letter to Gerald and Joan Hughes (19 June 1963), *Letters*, 220–1. Equally, for all his environmentalist credentials, Hughes was not himself above shooting and fishing, even acting as a grouse beater in the 1980s; see Hughes, letter to Jack Brown (3 February 1998), *Letters*, 704–5.
21. See Hughes, letter to Jack Brown (10 November 1982), *Letters*, 462–3.
22. See Hughes, letter to Joanny Moulin (6 April 1995); cited in Terry Gifford, 'Hughes' social ecology', in Gifford, *Cambridge Companion*, 81–93, 84.
23. On Hughes' use of 'superfluous' in these terms, see his letter to Lucas Myers (9 October 1989), *Letters*, 565–6.
24. David Gervais, 'Ted Hughes: An England beneath England', *English: Journal of the English Association*, 42: 172 (Spring 1993), 45–73, 70–1.
25. See Hughes, letter to Nick Gammage (15 December 1992), *Letters*, 617–21.
26. See Hughes, letter to Edna Wholey (1950), *Letters*, 9–10.
27. Edward H. Sugden, *A Topographical Dictionary to the Works of Shakespeare and his Fellow Dramatists* (Manchester: Manchester University Press, 1925), 427
28. R. A. Donkin, 'Changes in the Early Middle Ages', in H. C. Darby (ed.), *A New Historical Geography of England Before 1600* (Cambridge: Cambridge University Press, 1976), 75–135, 127. See also Pete Crowther, 'Ravenser and Ravenser Odd: The Early History of Spurn Head'. Available at: <https://www.wilgilsland.co.uk/page30.html> (last accessed 12 July 2019).
29. David Crystal and Ben Crystal, *Shakespeare's Words: A Glossary and Language Companion* (London: Penguin, 2002), 632.

30. Tony Harrison, 'Ghosts: Some Words Before Breakfast', *Selected Poems* (Harmondsworth: Penguin, 2013), 73.
31. Tom Nairn, *The Break-up of Britain: Crisis and Neo-Nationalism* (NLB, 1977; second edition, London: Verso, 1981), 368.
32. The popular appetite for discussions of 'Northernness' in the 2010s was evident in the success of Melvyn Bragg's BBC Radio 4 series *The Matter of the North* (2016), which followed Rory Stewart's 2014 BBC 2 television series, *Border Country: The Story of Britain's Lost Middleland* (2014). Simultaneously, the Shakespeare North project, based at Knowsley (http://www.shakespearenorth.org/) has attracted significant government funding and international media attention, and academics such as Richard Wilson – one of our contributors here – are heavily involved in this attempt to create a 'Globe of the North'. Comparable activities looking at English Shakespeares beyond London and Stratford-upon-Avon, and bridging academic and non-academic worlds, include the *Shakespeare in the North* exhibition curated by the current author, held at Newcastle's Literary and Philosophical Society (April 2016), and Nottingham University and the British Library's *Provincial Shakespeare Performance* venture.
33. Stuart Hall, 'Whose heritage?', in Jo Littler and Roshi Naidoo (eds), *The Politics of Heritage: The Legacies of 'Race'* (London: Routledge, 2005), 21–31, 25.
34. Linda Colley, *Acts of Union and Disunion: What has held the UK together – and what is dividing it?* (London: Profile Books, 2014), 4.
35. Robert Colls and Philip Dodd, 'Preface', in Colls and Dodd (eds), *Englishness: Politics and Culture 1880–1920* (Beckenham: Croom Helm, 1986), n.p.
36. John Kerrigan, *Archipelagic English: Literature, History and Politics 1603–1707* (Oxford: Oxford University Press, 2008), 12.
37. Alex Niven, '"Englishness" was never enough to build a nation on', *The Guardian* (20 November 2019). Available at: <https://www.theguardian.com/commentisfree/2019/nov/20/englishness-union-radical-vision-nationalisms> (last accessed 21 November 2019).
38. Tom Nairn, 'Postscript to Britain: England's turn?', in Mark Perryman (ed.), *Imagined Nation: England After Britain* (London: Lawrence and Wishart, 2008), 240–2.
39. Peter J. Taylor, 'Which Britain? Which England? Which North?', in David Morley and Kevin Roberts (eds), *British Cultural Studies: Geography, Nationality, and Identity* (Oxford: Oxford University Press, 2001), 127–44, 134–5; see also Taylor, 'The meaning of the North: England's "foreign country" within?', *Political Geography*, 12: 2 (March 1993), 136–55.
40. Taylor, 'Which Britain?', 134–5.
41. Stuart Rawnsley, 'Constructing "the North": space and a sense of place', in Neville Kirk (ed.), *Northern Identities: Historical Interpretations of 'The North' and 'Northernness'* (Aldershot: Ashgate, 2000), 3–22, 16.

42. Russell, *Looking North*, 7. See also Alun Howkins, 'The discovery of rural England', in Colls and Dodd (eds), *Englishness*, 62–88; Angus Calder, *The Myth of the Blitz* (1991; London: Pimlico, 2008), 180–208; and Paul Fussell, *The Great War and Modern Memory* (Oxford and New York: Oxford University Press, 1977), 231–69.
43. Holderness, 'Shakespeare-land', in Maley and Tudeau-Clayton (eds), *This England*, 201–19, 201.
44. Jonathan Bate, *The Genius of Shakespeare* (London and Basingstoke: Macmillan, 1997), 195–6.
45. Simon Featherstone, *Englishness: Twentieth-century Popular Culture and the Forming of English Identity* (Edinburgh: Edinburgh University Press, 2009), 101.
46. Martin Orkin, *Local Shakespeares: Proximation and Power* (London and New York: Routledge, 2005), 2.
47. Paul Morley, *The North (and almost everything in it)* (London: Bloomsbury, 2014), 117.
48. See 'Newcastle loses out to RSC budget cuts' <http://www.bbc.co.uk/news/uk-england-tyne-12281448> (25 January 2011); and Ian Youngs, 'RSC Returns to Newcastle after Cuts' <http://www.bbc.co.uk/news/entertainment-arts-21382076> (8 February 2013). Both last accessed 8 October 2013.
49. See Adam Hansen and Monika Smialkowska, 'Shakespeare in the North: regionalism, culture and power', in Paul Prescott and Erin Sullivan (eds), *Shakespeare on the Global Stage: Performance and Festivity in the Olympic Year* (London: Arden, 2015), 101–32.
50. Tony Harrison, 'Them & [uz]', *Selected Poems*, 102. On Harrison and Shakespeare, see Neil Rhodes, *Shakespeare and the Origins of English* (Oxford: Oxford University Press, 2007), 49–50.
51. Harrison, 'A Good Read', *Selected Poems*, 121.
52. Harrison, 'Aqua Mortis', *Selected Poems*, 117.
53. Harrison, 'Fig on the Tyne', *Selected Poems*, 268.
54. Harrison, 'A Good Read', *Selected Poems*, 121.
55. Harrison, 'From poetry or bust', in Carol Rutter (ed.), *Permanently Bard: Selected Poetry* (Bloodaxe: Newcastle Upon Tyne, 1995), 111–13, 111.
56. Morley, *North*, 497.
57. Ibid. 43.
58. See Russell, *Looking North* (199), who cites a memo by Tony Warren, the programme's creator, itself cited in D. Little, *The Coronation Street Story* (London: Boxtree, 1995).
59. On Bootle's Shakespearean streets, see <https://historic-liverpool.co.uk/bootle> (last accessed 12 November 2019).
60. See Scot, in Brinsley Nicholson (ed.), *The Discoverie of Witchcraft* (1584; London: Elliot Stock, 1886), 327.

61. Aristotle, *Politics*, 7.7., trans. T. A. Sinclair (Penguin: Harmondsworth, 1962), 410; cited in Peter Davidson, *The Idea of North* (London: Reaktion Books, 2017), 27.
62. Davidson, *Idea of North*, 208.
63. Russell, *Looking North*, 23.
64. Davidson, *Idea of North*, 10.
65. Harrison, 'Facing North', *Selected Poems*, 170. In 'Epilogue for W. H. Auden', from which Harrison derives his epigraph, MacNeice is himself citing Auden, in Auden and MacNeice's *Letters from Iceland* (London: Faber and Faber, 1937), 259.
66. Sean O'Brien and W. N. Herbert, 'In These Waters' (2018), poem for *Idea of North* Exhibition, Baltic Art Gallery, Gateshead (11 May – 30 September 2018). Italics in original.
67. Morley, *North*, 20.
68. Davidson, *Idea of North*, 22, 92.
69. The best coverage of Shakespeare's place in *this* North remains the essays collected in Mark Thornton Burnett and Ramona Wray (eds), *Shakespeare and Ireland: History, Politics, Culture* (Houndmills: Macmillan, 1997).
70. Edward Royle, 'Introduction: regions and identities', in Royle (ed.), *Issues of Regional Identity* (Manchester and New York: Manchester University Press, 1998), 1–13, 2.
71. Klaus Lösch and Heike Paul, 'Critical Regionalism: an introduction', in Klaus Lösch, Heike Paul and Meike Zwingenberger (eds), *Critical Regionalism* (Heidelberg: Universitäts Verlag Winter, 2016), 1–9, 3–4. See also Wendy Katz and Timothy Mahoney (eds), *Regionalism and the Humanities* (Lincoln: Nebraska University Press, 2008).
72. John M. Adrian, *Local Negotiations of English Nationhood, 1570–1680* (Basingstoke: Palgrave, 2011), 3.
73. Ibid. 34.
74. Linda Colley, 'Britishness and otherness: an argument', *Journal of British Studies*, 31: 4 (October 1992), 309–29, 314.
75. Peter Greenfield, 'Regional performance in Shakespeare's time', in Richard Dutton, Alison Findlay and Richard Wilson (eds), *Region, Religion and Patronage: Lancastrian Shakespeare* (Manchester: Manchester University Press, 2003), 243–51, 243.
76. E. A. J. Honigmann, *Shakespeare: The 'Lost Years'* (Manchester: Manchester University Press, 1985), 131.
77. Cited in Richard Wilson, 'Introduction: a torturing hour – Shakespeare and the martyrs', in Richard Dutton, Alison Findlay and Richard Wilson (eds), *Theatre and Religion: Lancastrian Shakespeare* (Manchester: Manchester University Press, 2003), 1–39, 31.
78. Alison Findlay and Richard Dutton, 'Introduction', in Dutton, Findlay and Wilson (eds), *Region, Religion and Patronage*, 1–31, 2.

79. John Le Patourel, "Is Northern History a Subject?", *Northern History* 12 (1976), 1–15, 12.
80. R. W. Hoyle, *The Pilgrimage of Grace and the Politics of the 1530s* (Oxford: Oxford University Press, 2001), 29.
81. Helen M. Jewell, *The North-South Divide: The Origins of Northern Consciousness in England* (Manchester and New York: Manchester University Press, 1994), 63.
82. Ibid. 64.
83. Richard Dutton, 'Shakespeare and Lancaster', in Dutton, Findlay and Wilson (eds), *Region, Religion and Patronage*, 143–68.
84. See Eamon Duffy, 'Bare ruined choirs: remembering Catholicism in Shakespeare's England', in Dutton, Findlay and Wilson (eds), *Theatre and Religion*, 40–57; and Mary A. Blackstone, 'Lancashire, Shakespeare and the construction of cultural neighbourhoods in sixteenth-century England', in Dutton, Findlay and Wilson (eds), *Region, Religion and Patronage*, 186–204.
85. Andrew Hadfield, 'The idea of the North', *The Journal of the Northern Renaissance*, 1 (2009), 1–14, 2–3.
86. Cited in M. Wakelin, *English Dialects: An Introduction* (London: 1972), 37.
87. Jewell, *North-South*, 104.
88. John Preston, Sermon before the House of Commons (1625), cited in J. E. C. Hill, 'Puritans and 'the Dark Corners of the Land', *Transactions of the Royal Historical Society*, 13 (1963), 77–102, 92.
89. Bruce M. S. Campbell, 'North-South dichotomies, 1066–1550', in Alan R. H. Baker and Mark Billinge (eds), *Geographies of England: The North-South Divide, Material and Imagined* (Cambridge: Cambridge University Press, 2004), 145–74, 146.
90. Duffy, 'Bare ruined choirs', 46.
91. S. M. Keeling, 'Reformation in the Anglo-Scottish Border Counties', *Northern History*, XV (1979), 41.
92. K. J. Kesselring, *The Northern Rebellion of 1569: Faith, Politics and Protest in Elizabethan England* (Basingstoke and New York: Palgrave Macmillan, 2010), 181.
93. Ibid. 21, 30.
94. Ibid. 159.
95. Jewell, *North-South*, 58.
96. Ibid. 5.
97. Ibid. 4.
98. Russell, *Looking North*, 35.
99. Rawnsley, 'Constructing', 3.
100. Rob Shields, *Places on the Margin: Alternative Geographies of Modernity* (London: Routledge, 1992), 211, 245.
101. Alan R. H. Baker and Mark Billinge, 'Cultural constructions of England's geography and history', in Baker and Billinge (eds), *Geographies of England*, 175–83, 181.
102. Alex Niven, *Folk Opposition* (Zero Books: Arlesford, 2012), 49.

103. James Wharton, Conservative MP (2015), cited in Helen Pidd, 'Where is the north of England? Don't ask the government', *The Guardian* (7 July 2015). Available at: <http://www.theguardian.com/uk-news/the-northerner/2015/jul/07/where-is-the-north-of-england-the-government-isnt-sure> (last accessed 24 October 2019).
104. Niven, *Folk Opposition*, 49.
105. Alan R. H. Baker and Mark Billinge, 'Material and imagined geographies of England', in Baker and Billinge (eds), *Geographies of England*, 1–14, 4.
106. Julia Reinhard Lupton, *Afterlives of the Saints: Hagiography, Typology, and Renaissance Literature* (Stanford: Stanford University Press, 1996), 197.
107. Wilson, 'Introduction: a torturing hour', 27.
108. Dan Hutton, 'Lucy Bailey: On folk culture, social division and directing The Winter's Tale', *Exeunt* (15 February 2013). Available at: <http://exeuntmagazine.com/features/lucy-bailey> (last accessed 13 December 2019).
109. Lucy Bailey, cited in *The Winter's Tale*, Programme, Royal Shakespeare Company (2013), n.p.
110. See also John Langton, 'The continuity of regional culture: Lancashire Catholicism from the late sixteenth to the early nineteenth century', in Edward Royle (ed.), *Issues of Regional Identity* (Manchester: Manchester University Press, 1998), 82–101.
111. Patrick Keiller, *Robinson in Space* (London: Reaktion Books, 1999), 231.
112. Davidson, *Idea of North*, 56.
113. Wilson, 'Introduction: a torturing hour', 15.
114. Honigmann, *Shakespeare*, 126; Wilson, 'Introduction: a torturing hour', 31.
115. Niven, *Folk Opposition*, 44.
116. Willy Maley and Rory Loughnane, 'Introduction: Celtic connections and archipelagic angles', in Maley and Loughnane (eds), *Celtic Shakespeare: The Bard and the Borderers* (Oxford and New York: Ashgate, 2013), 1–22, 3.
117. Claudia Sadowski-Smith, 'Critical regionalism and US borders', in Lösch, Paul and Zwingenberger (eds), *Critical Regionalism*, 39–56, 50.
118. Niven, '"Englishness"'.
119. Boris Johnson, cited in Torcuil Crichton, 'Boris Johnson and Nicola Sturgeon clash', *Daily Record* (1 July 2020). Available at: <https://www.dailyrecord.co.uk/news/politics/boris-johnson-nicola-sturgeon-clash-22283990> (last accessed 17 July 2020).
120. See Hopkins, *Shakespeare on the Edge: Border-Crossing in the Tragedies and the Henriad* (Aldershot: Ashgate, 2005).
121. David J. Baker, '"Stands Scotland where it did?" Shakespeare on the march', in Willy Maley and Andrew Murphy (eds), *Shakespeare and Scotland* (Manchester: Manchester University Press, 2004), 20–36, 22.
122. Baker, '"Scotland"', 28.
123. Willy Maley and Andrew Murphy, 'Introduction: then with Scotland first begin', in Maley and Murphy (eds), *Shakespeare and Scotland*, 1–19, 11.

124. Kesselring, *Rebellion*, 115; see also Jane E. Dawson, 'Anglo-Scottish Protestant culture and integration in sixteenth-century Britain', in Steven G. Ellis and Sarah Barber (eds), *Conquest and Union: Fashioning a British State, 1485–1725* (London: Routledge, 1995), 87–114.
125. Kesselring, *Rebellion*, 91.
126. Kerrigan, *Archipelagic English*, vii, 1, 2.
127. Kesselring, *Rebellion*, 91–2.
128. Baker, '"Scotland"', 23.
129. Steven G. Ellis, *Tudor Frontiers and Noble Power: The Making of the British State* (Oxford: Clarendon Press, 2005), 260.
130. Kerrigan, *Archipelagic English*, 18.
131. Vimada C. Pasupathi, 'The quality of mercenaries: contextualizing Shakespeare's Scots in *1 Henry IV* and *Henry V*', in Maley and Loughnane (eds), *Celtic Shakespeare*, 35–59, 50. See also Christopher Ivic's chapter 'Shakespeare's Elizabethan England/Jacobean Britain', in the same collection, 103–18.
132. Maley and Murphy, 'Introduction', in Maley and Murphy (eds), *Shakespeare and Scotland*, 2.
133. Graham Robb, *The Debatable Land: The Lost World Between Scotland and England* (London: Picador, 2019), 131.
134. Smith, *North and South*, 4.
135. Alex Niven, *New Model Island: How to Build a Radical Culture Beyond the Idea of England* (London: Repeater, 2019), 126. Italics in original.
136. Francesca Zantedeschi, 'Petrarch 1874: pan-national celebrations and Provençal regionalism', in Joep Leerssen and Ann Rigney (eds), *Commemorating Writers in Nineteenth-Century Europe: Nation-Building and Centenary Fever* (Basingstoke: Palgrave, 2014), 134–51, 148.
137. Etienne Balibar, 'Racism and nationalism', in Balibar and Immanuel Wallerstein, *Race, Nation, Class: Ambiguous identities* (London and New York: Verso, 1991), 37–67, 49. Italics in original.
138. Robert J. C. Young, *The Idea of English Ethnicity* (Oxford: Blackwell, 2008), 1, 228.
139. Kapka Kassabova, *Border: A Journey to the Edge of Europe* (London: Granta, 2018), xv.
140. Michel Foucault, 'A preface to transgression' (1963), in Donald F. Bouchard (ed.), *Language, Counter-Memory, Practice: Selected Essays and Interviews by Michel Foucault* (New York: Cornell University Press, 1977), 29–52, 34.
141. Kassabova, *Border*, xv.
142. Charles Bowden (ed.), *Juárez: The Laboratory of Our Future* (New York: Aperture, 1998); cited in Silvia Spitta, 'The in*Sur*gent imagination of Tijuana: transculturation, ironic disciplines, and transborder studies', in Lösch, Paul and Zwingenberger (eds), *Critical Regionalism*, 57–78, 70.
143. Kirk, 'Introduction', in *Northern* Identities, ix–xiv, xii.

144. Slavoj Žižek, *For They Know Not What They Do: Enjoyment as a Political Factor* (London: Verso, 2002), 110. As Ralph Waldo Emerson observed: 'Everything English is a fusion of distant and antagonistic elements. The language is mixed; the names of men are of different nations – three languages, three or four nations'; see Emerson, *English Traits and Representative Men* (London: Oxford University Press, 1923), 29. We might now reflect that some of these 'elements' may be closer (if no more or less antagonistic) too.
145. Sandra Young, *Shakespeare in the Global South: Stories of Oceans Crossed in Contemporary Adaptation* (London: Bloomsbury, 2019), 1.
146. Ibid. 103–25.
147. Ibid. 2–3.
148. Ibid. 105.
149. See Featherstone, *Englishness*, 180.
150. Young, *Shakespeare in the Global South*, 3.
151. Ibid. That said, this collection will not include discussion of Shakespeare in the wider 'global north', for several reasons. Such a designation denotes a vast and diffuse area, not only geographically: encapsulating what happens to Shakespeare in North America, Scandinavia and Siberia would be beyond the means of a single edited collection without significant danger of homogenisation, and would risk reproducing the kinds of already excellent work captured by activities such as the Canadian Appropriations of Shakespeare project (<http://www.canadianshakespeares.ca>).
152. Craig Dionne and Parmita Kapadia, 'Introduction: native Shakespeares: indigenous appropriations on a global stage', in Dionne and Kapadia (eds), *Native Shakespeares: Indigenous Appropriations on a Global Stage* (Ashgate: Aldershot, 2008), 1–15, 3.
153. Dionne and Kapadia, 'Introduction', 3.
154. Willy Maley, '"This sceptred isle": Shakespeare and the British problem', in John J. Joughin (ed.), *Shakespeare and National Culture* (Manchester: Manchester University Press, 1997), 83–108, 94–5.
155. Ewa Mazierska, 'Introduction: imagining the north of England', in Mazierska (ed.), *Heading North: The North of England in Film and Television* (Basingstoke: Palgrave, 2017), 1–35, 3.
156. Young, *Global South*, 107.
157. Tony Harrison, 'Classics Society', *Selected Poems* (Harmondsworth: Penguin, 2013), 100.
158. Michael Hechter, *Internal Colonialism: The Celtic Fringe in British National Development, 1536–1966* (London and Henley: Routledge and Kegan Paul, 1975), 5.
159. Jyotsna G. Singh, 'Afterword: the location of Shakespeare', in Dionne and Kapadia, *Native Shakespeares*, 233–9, 238.
160. Maley and Murphy, 'Introduction', in Maley and Murphy (eds), *Shakespeare and Scotland*, 13.

161. Dionne and Kapadia, 'Introduction', in Dionne and Kapadia (eds), *Native Shakespeares*, 1.
162. Ibid. 6.
163. Ayanna Thompson, *Passing Strange: Shakespeare, Race and Contemporary America* (Oxford: Oxford University Press, 2011), 15. See also Linda Colley, 'Shakespeare and the limits of national culture', Hayes Robinson Lecture Series, No. 2 (1999) <www.rhul.ac.uk/history/documents/pdf/events/hrcolley.pdf> (last accessed 17 July 2019).
164. Dionne and Kapadia, 'Introduction', in Dionne and Kapadia (eds), *Native Shakespeares*, 6.
165. Joughin, 'Introduction', in Joughin, *Shakespeare and National Culture*, 1–15, 6.
166. Sonia Massai, 'Defining local Shakespeare', in Massai (ed.), *World-wide Shakespeares: Local Appropriations in Film and Performance* (London and New York: Routledge, 2005), 3–11, 10.
167. See Roland Robertson, 'Glocalization: time-space and homogeneity-heterogeneity', in Mike Featherstone et al. (eds), *Global Modernities* (London: Sage, 1995), 23–44.
168. Young, *Global South*, 14.
169. Cheryl Temple Herr, *Critical Regionalism and Cultural Studies: From Ireland to the American Midwest* (Gainesville: University Press of Florida, 1996), 2, 9.
170. In addition to the works already discussed and cited in this introduction, one might also note Andrew Murphy and John Foster (eds), *Studies in Ethnicity and Nationalism (Special Issue): William Shakespeare, Ethnicity and Nationalism*, 16: 2 (October 2016); Willy Maley and Philip Schwyzer (eds), *Shakespeare and Wales: From the Marches to the Assembly* (Oxford and New York: Ashgate, 2010).
171. Maley and Murphy, 'Introduction', in Maley and Murphy (eds), *Shakespeare and Scotland*, 10.
172. Findlay and Dutton, 'Introduction', in Dutton, Findlay and Wilson (eds), *Region, Religion and Patronage*, 2.
173. Ralph Vaughan Williams, 'Should music be national?', from *National Music and Other Essays* (Oxford: Oxford University Press, 1934), 3–22. Available at: <http://spinnet.humanities.uva.nl/images/2013-10/vaughanwilliams1934.pdf> (last accessed 11 December 2019).
174. See Adam Hansen and Tony Prince, 'Shakespeare reading groups: education without the "Academy"?', *Transformations: The Journal of Inclusive Scholarship and Pedagogy*, 29: 1 (2019), 4–29; the report into the activities of Shakespeare Club, based at Newcastle upon Tyne's Literary and Philosophical Society from 2014–18 <https://gallery.mailchimp.com/feb16b1e537d94ce26e9fdba8/files/b2232efb-3a85-4322-84e6-8a93e94ac38a/Newsletter_Winter_email_19.01.pdf> (last accessed 13 December 2019); and the related blog for Shakespeare Club 'on the road' in Tyneside and Northumberland during 2019 <https://shakespeareclub918514705.wordpress.com/2019/09/27/the-bard-beyond-shakespeare-club-on-the-road> (last accessed 13 December 2019).

I

Shakespeare and the Early Modern North

1

Shakespeare's Northern Blood: Transfusing *Gorboduc* into *Macbeth* and *Cymbeline*

Paul Frazer

The accession of the Scottish king, James (Stuart) VI, to the English throne on 24 March 1603 prompted intense interest in the relationship between Britain's North and South, and the histories therein. James was the first monarch to try to unite the territories of Scotland with England and Wales, and he was afforded the opportunity to do so because his bloodline descended from Henry (Tudor) VII. With the help of a little Tudor mythology, James was also able to trace his origins to the Trojan founder of Britain (Brutus the grandson of Aeneas). England's new king may well have come from the North, but his mythic blood transcended regional geopolitics – drawing authority from Britain's most ancient legacy. For proponents of the Brutus myth, the legitimacy of James' blood was unassailable; but there were, of course, many sceptics. And as we might expect, geo-political posturing of this kind prompted substantial commentary and imaginative critique – not least on the popular stage, an important space for participatory political discussion.[1] In the years that followed James' accession, William Shakespeare wrote several plays that were intended to deconstruct the histories and legacies that James (and his regime) were laying claim to, and imitating and echoing earlier plays was an important part of his creative process. Yet in critical readings of Shakespeare's Jacobean writings, his use of the early Elizabethan tragedy *Gorboduc, or the Tragedy of Ferrex and Porrex* (first performed December 1561) has been neglected. Understanding more about how important this play was to Shakespeare can, however, tell us much about the relationship between political drama and the North in this period.

Thomas Norton and Thomas Sackville's *Gorboduc* is a remarkable text for many reasons, and we should be unsurprised to find that it exerted substantial influence over Shakespeare's dramatic writings. The first English play of its kind, Norton and Sackville's Senecan tragedy was written by two rising stars of the Inns of Court. Norton became an essential fixture in Elizabeth's parliaments, and a key propagandist voice against Elizabeth's enemies; and Sackville (first cousin of Elizabeth's mother, Anne Boleyn) would be elevated as first Baron Buckhurst in 1567 and would later succeed William Cecil as Lord Treasurer. *Gorboduc*'s first performance at the Inns' Christmas festivities was followed quickly by a royal performance before Elizabeth I at Whitehall Palace in January 1562. The play spoke directly to the queen, touching sensitive political pressure points; and several scholars have debated the centrality of its discussions of the succession dilemma.[2] Featuring less prominently among scholarly readings, however, is the play's interest in northern politics – most specifically, in the Stuart bloodline.

Gorboduc captured Shakespeare's imagination at a time of heightened interest in Britishness – in the embryonic years of the Union of England, Wales and Scotland, and in the period in which the histories of Britain were being forged and disseminated in print. Written in the months that followed the return to Scotland of Mary Stuart (Queen of Scots) on 19 August 1561, and first printed on 22 September 1565, two months after her marriage to Lord Henry Darnley (around the time that she became pregnant with her only child: the future King James VI and I), *Gorboduc*'s copious blood imagery glances repeatedly to the competing Catholic claim to the English throne that Mary personified throughout the 1560s until her execution in 1587. Drawn from a blend of classical, biblical and medieval chronicle sources, Norton and Sackville's tragedy invokes northern vocabularies and histories of northern identity and invasion, and it does so to force interpretive political adjacencies with Mary and her husband. In other words, it shapes the narrative and language of a mythic king (of North and South) to address the regional politics of its 1561 composition. This chapter argues that *Gorboduc*'s blood flows through the lines of several of the plays that Shakespeare wrote in the first decade of James' reign. Focusing on *Macbeth* and *Cymbeline*, I explore political critiques of England's Scottish king – most especially, James' gestation and the bloody circumstances that surrounded his parents and childhood (in the 1560s). *Macbeth* foregrounds a chilling blood-soaked child motif, inviting latent parallels with the Stuart dynasty and with James' physical inadequacies. Moreover, through the figure of Medea, *Macbeth* uses *Gorboduc*'s sustained interest in the unnatural maternity of Mary Stuart through the words and actions of Lady Macbeth. The narrative of *Cymbeline*'s heroine, Innogen, invokes similarly barbed imagery in a warped pastiche of Britain's mythic origins. In its construction of Innogen's persecutor Cloten, *Cymbeline* borrows the name from *Gorboduc*, and in doing so invokes another distant chronicle history of Welsh invasion and annexation of the North. This chapter concludes by reflecting upon the general antipathy that the British project seems to have provoked in English subjects (like Shakespeare) in the infancy of its realisation.

Gorboduc's Bloody North

Gorboduc has a relatively simple plotline: the eponymous king unwisely divides his kingdom into North and South, respectively between his two sons, Porrex and Ferrex. The realm is divided at the Humber estuary and river (in Yorkshire). Prompted by the deceitful advice and warnings of his advisor (the 'parasite' Tinder), northern Porrex (the younger) rebels against his brother and kills him; seeking vengeance, the Queen Mother Videna slays Porrex. Civil war ensues, in which king and queen are killed by the rebellious mob. (Here ends the Trojan bloodline of the first Briton, Brutus.) The remaining nobles crush the rebellion, and the play ends on a knife-edge as the traitorous Duke of Albany prepares to invade from his northern power base (Scotland).

Because the Gorboduc story was about the disastrous reign of a British king (and the end of the Brutus bloodline), it was a useful model for thinking about contemporary concerns. In 1561-2, the Elizabethan regime was in its infancy – still finding its way back to reform after the Catholic hiatus of Mary I. Numerically, the nation was substantially more Catholic than Protestant in the 1560s and, as the period wore on, the concentration of Catholics remained strongest in the English North.[3] The return of Mary Queen of Scots in 1561 gave northern resistance a political figurehead of substance. Mary was endorsed by Rome, and her claim to the throne was strong – stronger, Catholics argued, than that of the Tudor bastard Elizabeth I. Recently widowed and thereby removed from the French throne (at a time of war between England and France), Mary arrived at Leigh on 16 August – four months before the first performances of *Gorboduc*. Mary Stuart's blood was one of the prominent political concerns for English subjects because of the strength of her claim to their throne.

It is unsurprising then that Norton and Sackville's play was preoccupied by imagery of blood and birth – Elizabeth was dragging her heels over the succession, and her Catholic rival was on the market for a new husband. If Mary reproduced (and Elizabeth did not), the English crown would almost certainly restore Catholicism to the realm. Into this context, the first printed edition of *Gorboduc* emerged on 22 September 1565[4] (an important date that I will return to). The printed play was only 1794 lines in length – some 700 lines leaner than *Macbeth*. Nevertheless, *Gorboduc* uses the words 'blood' and 'bloody' (a combined total of) 48 times. Comparing this to Shakespeare's writing, the play which uses the word most often is the much longer *Henry V*: 46 instances in 3227 lines. (*Macbeth* uses it 41 times in 2477 lines.) In *Gorboduc*, the word blood is used on almost every page, with unusual concentration.

This seems in part to do with the sources that Norton and Sackville used to construct their version of the Gorboduc story. The most significant is the root source of the Brutus myth, Geoffrey of Monmouth's *Historia Regum Britannia*. Here Geoffrey traces the Trojan bloodline through to its cessation:

> After the death of Cunedagius, his son Rivallo succeeded him, a peaceful, prosperous young man who ruled the kingdom frugally. In this time it rained blood for three days and men died from the flies which swarmed. Rivallo's son Gurgustius succeeded him. Sisillius came after Gurgustius, then Jago the nephew of Gurgustius, then Kimarcus the son of Sisillius and after him Gorboduc.[5]

According to Andrew Hadfield, 'Geoffrey casts Brutus as a second Aeneas, his story as an epic to rival those of the ancient world, with the triumph of the Britons and their empire coming after periods of uncertainty, doubt and defeat'.[6] Indeed, the blood-rain motif above was recycled from the *Iliad*, from the passage in which Zeus intervenes to rain blood upon the Achaeans ('from air's upper region did bloody vapours rain, / For sad ostent much noble life should ere their times be slain') – a divine portent of the slaughter that the assembled Greeks will initially suffer (XI.47–8).[7] In Plutarch's account of the reign of Romulus, moreover, blood fell from the sky (alongside other plagues) as divine punishment on the city of Laurentum for harbouring the murderers of the Sabine king and joint ruler of Rome, Titus Tatius.[8] Within both Homer and Plutarch, blood-rain symbolises a forewarning of divine judgement and punishment in the context of a collaborative political regime. Geoffrey uses the motif in his account of King Gorboduc to herald the end of the Brutus bloodline, and the subsequent descent of Britain into generations of civil conflict.[9] Norton and Sackville's 1561-2 account of Gorboduc's reign was motivated by a desire to recall and think about this corruption of the British Trojan lineage.

Their version of the story also imposes an overt geo-political interest in northernness. Jaecheol Kim has read the play's 1570 reissue in relation to the 1569 Northern Rebellion, but critics have generally neglected the play's interest in the Scottish circumstances of the 1560s.[10] For as well as hinging upon two bloody invasions from the North (by Porrex, and then Fergus the Duke of Albany), *Gorboduc* also exudes a more subtle linguistic fascination with northern words and phrases – often in archaic terminologies, which may go some way to explaining the play's difficulty for modern readers. (With tongue in cheek, Peter C. Herman once claimed that 'finding *Gorboduc* interesting signals the onset of professional Alzheimer's'![11]) Queen Videna's speech at the beginning of 4.1 provides a useful starting point. This is the scene that follows Nuntius's report: that 'with bloody hand' (3.1.944) Porrex's northern forces have invaded his older brother's southern stronghold; and it immediately follows the dumbshow which summons three Furies 'clad in black garments sprinkled with blood and flames . . . each driving before them a king and queen which, moved by the Furies, unnaturally had slain their own children' (4.0.3–8). Videna uses the word 'mought/est' here four times (at lines 977, 1013, 1018 and 1026 of the Tydeman edition, though Tydeman modernises the latter two instances to 'might' and 'mightest'). A variant spelling of 'may/might', mought had, according to the *OED*, 'a continued existence in English regional use and in Scots until the 19th Century' (*v*.1.d. etym). Old English variations of mought are commonly recorded as Northumbrian in origin: traced to the Linsdisfarne Gospels and Durham Ritual Liturgical Texts. In the same speech (and multiple times elsewhere in the play), we have the verb 'reave' (and elsewhere 'bereave' and 'reft') – meaning to commit robbery, to plunder, pillage, to make raids. According to Lisa Hopkins, 'the word "reave" and its cognates recur [in *Gorboduc*] with extraordinary insistence . . . originally of German origin, the idea of reaving (now usually spelled "reiving") had become distinctively associated with the perennial unrest on the Scottish Border' – and specifically evoked northern border crossing and associated criminality.[12] Similarly, the play's use of 'lotting' (PHILANDER: 'As for dividing of this Realm in twain / And lotting out the same in equal parts' (1,1,149–50)) defines both the actions of 'dividing land into sections' (*OED*, *n*.1b) and also 'contributing a proportionate or allotted amount to municipal taxes and charges'. The latter practice was commonly known as 'scotting and lotting' (*n*.1a) in the Tudor period. The 1565 edition of the play also used words like 'perched' and 'yeld' which the *OED* traces to northern English and/or Scottish dialects ('perched' *v*.1 'etym'; 'yeld' *adj*. and *n*.). Furthermore, the northern King Porrex uses 'regrate' (4.2.1097) – a word traceable to Gavin Douglas' 1513 Scots translation of the *Aeneid*. None of these northern words are spoken before Gorboduc divides his kingdom; they seep into the language of the play as its narrative edges closer to civil war, and Albany announces his intention to invade.

In the penultimate scene of the play, the characters map Britain into four geo-political corners: represented by the dukes of Cornwall, Llogres (England), Camberland (Wales) and Albany (Scotland). This gathering of forces (to put down the rebellion) is not, however, a celebrated union – it fractures the northern political defence, opening the way for Albany to mount his invasion (expressed in soliloquy at the close of the scene: 5.1.1479–517). His title of Duke of Albany was distinctly topical in 1565, because in that year on 22 July Henry Stuart (Lord Darnley) – the maternal great-grandson to Henry VII, and therefore blood relative to Elizabeth I – was made Duke of Albany by Mary Stuart, Queen of Scots. Seven days later he would marry Mary (his first cousin), and realise the worst fears of the Elizabethan regime. The first printed edition of *Gorboduc* was issued exactly two months later (22 September) – at a time when rumours of Mary becoming pregnant were undoubtedly rife. News of her actual pregnancy followed soon enough, and the British political world paid close attention to this conception. If Elizabeth did not marry, the child would almost certainly become the next English monarch; and, so it transpired, because Mary was pregnant with James (her only child) who would inherit the English throne in 1603. Whether or not the narrative and character of the fictional invading Albany were used in the play's 1561–2 performances (they might not have been), their place in the September 1565 edition undoubtedly alludes to the Scottish king-consort.[13] In sum, no 1565 English reader could read about an invasion at the hands of the Duke of Albany without recourse to the events unfolding in the contemporary North.

Regardless of the disdain that Elizabeth's supporters and advisors held for Mary and Darnley's marriage, no one could have predicted the further political adjacencies (between Gorboduc's past, and their present) that *Gorboduc* would throw up in the subsequent period of Mary's pregnancy. Darnley was unhinged and over-ambitious, and his paranoia and impatience with Mary escalated wildly. Then, three months before James' birth on 9 March 1566 at Holyrood Palace, Darnley staged an elaborate and gruesome execution of Mary's Italian private secretary David Riccio. Riccio was stabbed over fifty times, with Darnley himself issuing the final blow. According to Alan Stewart, '[e]ach account tells how Riccio, terrified, moved away from [Lord] Ruthven and tried to take refuge behind the Queen, clasping his arms around her pregnant belly'.[14] It was this occasion that James himself recalled to parliament, stating:

> Kings, as being in the higher places like the high Trees, or stayest Mountains and steepest Rocks, are most subject to the daily tempests of innumerable dangers; and I amongst other Kings have ever been subject to them, not only ever since my birth, but even as I may justly say, before my birth: and while I was yet in my mother's belly.[15]

Queen Mary swore revenge upon her husband, and the infamously mysterious circumstances of Darnley's murder followed on 9–10 February 1567: Darnley's strangled body was found in Kirk o'Field in the periphery of an apparent explosion. Rumours of Mary's complicity abounded.

The bloody circumstances of James' gestation are, of course, legendary – and *Gorboduc*'s interest in northern blood and imagery of unnatural maternity can hardly be separated from them – especially if we think about this play as a source of influence over Shakespeare's later Jacobean plays. Jacqueline Vanhoutte reads Queen Videna as 'a foil for mother England', shaped by 'Elizabeth's maternal posturing and evident also in current rumours that cast the queen as the murderer of her own illegitimate children'.[16] This is certainly plausible, but it is also likely that readers of the play, including Shakespeare, might relate her to Elizabeth's northern cousin Mary – whose marriage and pregnancy carried immediate implications for the English throne. Norton and Sackville's play registers a distinct preoccupation with unnatural maternity through, for instance, the figure of Medea in the dumb show before the fourth act: here Medea (mythological priestess of Hecate who marries Jason and then murders their children in an act of revenge) forms part of the procession of kings and queens who 'unnaturally had slain their own children' (4.0.8). Indeed, Seneca's *Medea* is itself echoed by the Chorus' line 'Ne dreads his hand in brother's blood to stain' (3.1.958), from a line Medea speaks at the close of Seneca's first act: 'In blood to bathe thy bloody hands / and traitorous lives to waste'.[17] Elsewhere in *Gorboduc*, the crimes of Medea are mediated through Queen Videna's concentration of womb imagery.[18] And the final act's insistent repetition of the phrase 'strangling cord' (three times in

55 lines: 5.2.1526, 1569 and 1581) accompanies a matrix of 'motherland' referents which inform Eubulus' warnings of the advancing mercilessness of Albany's northern soldiers:

> Even thou, O wretched mother, half alive,
> Thou shalt behold thy dear and only child
> Slain with the sword while he yet sucks thy breast!
> ...
> Thus wreak the gods, when that the mother's wrath
> Nought but the blood of her own child may suage. (5.2.1738–40; 1757–8)

The realm's descent into civil war calls forth and depends upon maternal corruption, weakness and culpability. In relation to Videna's murder of Porrex, it occurs offstage (like Shakespeare's infamous depiction of regicide in *Macbeth*), and is reported to King Gorboduc by Marcella, lady of the queen's privy chamber:

> *Enter Marcella*
> O where is ruth, or where is pity now?
> Whither is gentle heart and mercy fled?
> Are they exil'd out of our stony breasts,
> Never to make return? Is all the world
> Drowned in blood, and sunk in cruelty?
> If not in women mercy may be found –
> If not, alas, within the mother's breast
> To her own child, to her own flesh and blood –
> If ruth be banished thence, if pity there
> May have no place, if there no gentle heart
> Do live and dwell, where should we seek it then? (4.2.1219–29)

Marcella's double use of 'ruth' (meaning compassion, but also an ironic abbreviation of 'truth') not only exemplifies the play's wider preoccupations with North-South rumour and distortion, it also carries Old Testament links to maternity via Ruth (great grandmother of David), who was read by early modern exegetes as proto-mother to Christ. Ruth embodied a typology of divine maternity (and we might remember that Videna's name – Norton and Sackville's creation – is an anagram or corruption of *devina*, i.e. divine). Ruth's metaphorical absence ('O where is ruth …? … ruth be banished') underscores the unnaturalness of Videna's crime – and heightens connections between northern topography, errant maternity, and filicide. (Though this is taken from the portion of the play claimed to be by Sackville, Norton's experience in translating Calvin's *Institutes* just months before writing *Gorboduc* surely encourages a biblical reading.) Given the emphasis on maternity and blood here, Marcella's use of the phrase 'drowned in blood' possibly also echoes Ezekiel 16.6, where the prophet envisages God's care of Jerusalem as a bloody infant, rescued from a field. Raised to be a queen, Jerusalem proves to be a harlot, who 'used your fame to become a prostitute' and 'lavished your favours on anyone who passed by and your beauty became his' (16.15). Invested as Queen of Scotland six days after her birth, Mary Stuart is again a likely political analogue – and was likened by polemicists to the Whore of Babylon.[19]

From the remainder of Marcella's account, the emphasis on Porrex's blood is worth quoting at length:

> We then, alas, the ladies which that time
> Did there attend, seeing that heinous deed,
> And hearing him oft call the wretched name
> Of mother, and to cry to her for aid,
> Whose direful hand gave him the mortal wound,
> Pitying, alas – for nought else could we do –
> His ruthful end, ran to the woeful bed,
> Dispoiled straight his breast, and all we might,
> Wiped in vain with napkins next at hand,
> The sudden stream of blood that flushed fast
> Out of the gaping wound. Oh, what a look,
> Oh, what a ruthful, steadfast eye methought
> He fix'd upon my face, which to my death
> Will never part from me ...   (4.2.1262–75)

The blood flow that the maids attempt to stem is that of Brutus and Aeneas – the mythological Trojan purity that connected the Tudors to the ancient world of gods and warriors, of the cultural and political majesties of Greece and Rome. In the graphic way that it invites us to imagine Porrex's gushing wound and fading expression, we could read Marcella's account in relation to wider anxieties concerning the Tudor line. Porrex's death prompts a civil war and an invasion from the North – and the association of his mother Videna with northern words and unnatural maternity could certainly be read as a political echo of the threat posed by Mary Stuart. That the invasion is led by a duke of Albany *is* a certain echo of Mary's husband, Lord Darnley. The final spattering of Trojan (Tudor) blood is viscerally imaged to emphasise the political threat of the North, and perhaps to anatomise what an unruly North could do to a politically divided England and Britain.

Textual Transfusions: *Macbeth* and *Cymbeline*

Shakespeare had evidently read and been influenced by *Gorboduc* from an early stage of his career because *Titus Andronicus* demonstrates some notable borrowings from it, and clearly *King Lear* emulated its major narrative and thematic interests.[20] Given *Gorboduc*'s investment in northern political scandal and the bloodline of the Stuarts, it makes sense that he would draw from it again in his only Scottish play (written at around the same time that he was working on *King Lear*). *Macbeth* is, of course, the play in which Shakespeare comments most directly on the Stuarts, because King James claimed descent from the historical Banquo (and his son Fleance); and the influence of James' obsession with witchcraft is well known. And *Cymbeline*, a play in which Shakespeare critically confronts the Brutus myth and the origins of ancient Britain, has been argued as something of a sequel to *Macbeth*.[21] For in Shakespeare's main source for *Cymbeline* (the *Chronicles* of Raphael Holinshed), Fleance flees from Macbeth's Scotland into Wales, where he marries a Welsh princess (Nesta) and then fathers the first of the Stuart line (Walter). According to Holinshed's account, Walter fled to Scotland after murdering a man who slandered him a bastard ('begotten in unlawful bed').[22] Furthermore, Hopkins reads *Cymbeline*'s villain Giacomo as a satirical 'version of James'; and the play's wicked mother (the unnamed queen) as a recollection of Mary Queen of Scots.[23] Elsewhere, Donna B. Hamilton reads the play as patterned by a concentration of Jamesian iconography.[24] Furthermore, we might consider it more than a stylistic quirk that both *Macbeth* and *Cymbeline* are bookended by allusions to blood: in *Macbeth*, after the witches exeunt, the opening line of the former is King Duncan's 'What bloody man is that?' (1.2.1), spoken as he observes a wounded captain returning from the battlefield; and the play draws to a close with Lennox's promise that the blood of Macbeth and his followers will 'dew the sovereign flower and drown the weeds' (5.2.30).[25] *Cymbeline* also uses the word in its opening and closing lines.[26] Drawing upon these connections, the rest of this chapter will consider a further point of interaction between these plays and *Gorboduc*: their blood-soaked preoccupations with unnatural maternity, the Stuart family line, and fractured British histories of northern invasion and violence.

Rather than list from the many instances of blood imagery in *Macbeth*, a more arresting starting point might be how, like *Gorboduc*, the play foregrounds infanticide and the trope of the bloody child. In 1.7 Macbeth personifies his pity for Duncan 'like a naked newborn babe / Striding the blast, or heaven's cherubim horsed / Upon the sightless couriers of the air' (22) in a speech that is cut short by Lady Macbeth's entrance; and in 4.3 we learn that Macduff's 'babes' have been 'Savagely slaughtered' (205). In 4.1 the Third Witch also lists the 'Finger of [a] birth-strangled babe' (30) in the contents of the cauldron, eight lines before the entrance of Hecate. In the subsequent apparitions, Macbeth is shown '*a bloody child*' (4.1.92), and then '*Thunder . . . a child crowned with a tree in his hand*' (4.1.102). Macbeth responds to it: 'What is this / That rises like the issue of a king, / And wears upon his baby-brow the round / And top of sovereignty' (102–4). There are a number of ways that we (and, for that matter, Macbeth) can read the image – but two of them certainly relate to both Mary and James Stuart, who were both crowned as infants. Furthermore, the play's fascination with witchcraft – and the persistent connections of witchcraft to its villainess – force similar connections to the energies of the Book of Ezekiel's bloody infant motif echoed in Marcella's account of Porrex's murder (quoted in the previous section). The bloody circumstance of Mary's marriages and James' youth join eerily here with the arborescent metaphor – a potent signifier of familial lineage. Furthermore, the response of the Third Apparition (the crowned child) instructs Macbeth to 'Be lion-mettled' (4.1.106), invoking the heraldic animal that emblazoned the royal arms of Scotland, which James, from a very young age, obviously bore. The image of drowning in blood is elsewhere invoked by Macbeth's 'All causes shall give way: I am in blood / Stepped in so far that, should I wade no more' (3.4.135–6), and in the Sergeant's report that the opening battle hangs in the balance: 'As two spent swimmers, that do cling together / And choke their art' (1.2.7–9). Moreover, if we accept the symbolic relevance and application of *Macbeth*'s blood to the Stuart family, we might also read instances such as Macbeth's vision of the bloody dagger as specific to these concerns. He claims to see 'on thy blade and dudgeon *gouts* of blood' (2.1.46, my emphasis), which could well instance one of James' many rumoured physical inadequacies. The noun 'gout' was used, after 1598, to mean a 'channel of water' or 'sluice' (*OED n*.2); but the word held much older definitions with the hereditary disease 'characterized by painful inflammation of the smaller joints' (*n*.1) – with which James infamously suffered throughout his life.[27]

Much of *Macbeth*'s blood-Stuart imagery hinges upon the figure of Medea who, while not directly alluded to by the language of play, has been recognised as a clear prototype for Lady Macbeth (just as she was for Queen

Videna): 'The language of Lady Macbeth's blood-curdling invocation to be unsexed echoes the opening speech of Seneca's *Medea*, where Medea calls "with cursed throate" upon spirits of darkness and Hell as she prepares to murder her "Babes"'.[28] And just as Videna's crime evoked the macabre circumstances of Mary Stuart's marriage to Darnley and pregnancy with James, her separation from her son is itself, it seems, viscerally imagined:

> I have given suck, and know
> How tender 'tis to love the babe that milks me.
> I would, while it was smiling in my face,
> Have plucked my nipple from his boneless gums
> And dashed the brains out, had I so sworn
> As you have done to this. (1.7.54–9)

Maternal instinct conjoins with murderous impulse and abandonment – a connection entirely in keeping with contemporary rumours about Mary and the infant James. For example, a letter written to Cecil recorded that on 21 April 1567, the last time that Mary saw her son, '[s]he offered him an apple, but it would not be received of him, and to a greyhound bitch having whelps was thrown, who eat it, and she and her whelps died presently'.[29] Two months later Mary allegedly miscarried a five-month pregnancy (possibly twins) fathered by her third husband, the Earl of Bothwell (then Duke of Orkney).[30] Her public image was saturated by instances of maternity and untimely and/or violent death, so the notion of both her literal (biological) and abstract (political) bodies being poisonous and corrupt stuck – with serious implications for the reputation of James, the only surviving issue of her womb. In relation to Lady Macbeth's breast-feeding, this again borrows from *Gorboduc*. In her most Medea-like speech, Queen Videna swears revenge on Porrex:

> Thou never sucked the milk of woman's breast
> But from thy birth the cruel Tiger's teats
> Have nursed, nor yet of flesh and blood is
> Formed is thy heart, but of Iron wrought (4.1.1044–7)

All of this is relevant to the plays' shared interest in Stuart blood because, according to Janet Adelman, 'breast milk itself was believed to be a derivative of menstrual blood – "nothing else but blood whitened" – which was still held by some to be poisonous'.[31] And the anxious association with Mary Queen of Scots' poisonous milk raised questions about exactly what the king of England may have inherited from his mother.

Shakespeare advances these interests (and his recycling of *Gorboduc*) in the later play, *Cymbeline, King of Britain* (c.1611). Set in Roman Britain at the time of the birth of Christ, *Cymbeline* is, like *Gorboduc*, fixated by origins. Despite the play's Welsh setting, it also discloses sharpened interest in the Scottish roots of Britishness – most specifically, in Scottish chronicle history. For, according to Mary Floyd-Wilson, *Cymbeline* plays 'fast and loose with its primary [English] historical source' (Holinshed's *Chronicles*), by 'tap[ping] into the uncertainties already present in Holinshed – the discrepancies between the English and Scottish histories of ancient Britain'.[32] It creates an anarchic collage of English, Welsh, Irish and Scottish chronicles and identities, most strongly portrayed when the action of the play moves to Milford Haven (in Wales). Here Welsh topography and history are synthesised with broader interests in Stuart blood – and, again, this borrows from Norton and Sackville's Inns of Court tragedy.

To start with, *Cymbeline* and *Gorboduc* are bridged by two characters who share the name of Cloten. The word 'clot' (noun and verb) had been associated with coagulation since the Middle Ages, but the name also carries chronicle significance to the Stuarts. In *Gorboduc*, Cloten is the name of the Duke of Cornwall, on stage in the play's penultimate scene (noted above) wherein the rulers of Britain unite to shut down the common rebellion. But the historical and geo-political symbolism of Cloten's name is more capacious than meets the eye, because of the Welsh political localities that name provokes. While English annals record a Cloten, Duke of Cornwall, the name also instances Welsh territorial annexation and division through King Cloten of Dyfed (in South Wales), whose marriage to Princess Ceindrech of Brycheiniog in c.650 AD temporarily united two powerful Welsh families and southern topographies.[33] Cloten was among the dynasty of Irish kings who ruled in South Wales from the third to tenth centuries (the Goedels). Sharing the same genealogical line as the Tudors, King Cloten's control of Dyfed and Brycheiniog mirrored the fusion of the houses of Lancaster and York under Henry VII. This is relevant to James because it was from Henry VII that his claim to the English throne originated. And during the reign of Cloten's heir, Rhain ap Cadwgan (in the eighth century), an opportunistic northern invasion, not unlike that of *Gorboduc*'s Duke of Albany, by King Seisyll of Ceredigion, saw Dyfed invaded and annexed to the territories to the North.[34] Because of the Brutus and Arthurian mythologies, Welsh space was an important site of origins for nationalistic writers at this time – and was, moreover, a space through which much discussion concerning the Union of the thrones of Scotland and England was being triangulated. So, in *Gorboduc*, the staged presence of Cloten alongside the Welsh Gwenard

(Duke of Camberland) embodies an important history of North–South Welsh division, with potent analogues to the threat of northern violence and annexation associated with the Stuarts, who had for generations been associated with violent political intrigue in Scotland.[35]

Cymbeline's Cloten is the stepson of the king (Cymbeline), and his villainous narrative comes to a bloody end at Milford Haven. Favoured child of another unnatural queen, Cloten stalks his banished half-sister Princess Innogen to Wales, planning to abduct and rape her. Disguised as her husband (Leonatus Posthumus), Cloten meets and quarrels with Polydore (actually Prince Guiderius), and is beheaded. The sleeping Innogen is woken by the melee, and discovers Cloten's body (which she takes to be that of Leonatus Posthumus) after Guiderius has left the stage:

> *Innogen awakes*
> Yes, sir, to Milford Haven. Which is the way?
> . . .
> *She sees Cloten*
> But soft, no bedfellow! O gods and goddesses!
> These flowers are like the pleasures of the world,
> This bloody man the care on't. I hope I dream;
> For so I thought I was a cave-keeper,
> And cook to honest creatures: but 'tis not so;
> 'Twas but a bolt of nothing, shot at nothing,
> Which the brain makes of fumes: our very eyes
> Are sometimes like our judgements, blind. Good faith,
> I tremble still with fear; but if there be
> Yet left in heaven as small a drop of pity
> As a wren's eye, feared gods, a part of it!
> The dream's here still. Even when I wake it is
> Without me as within me; not imagined, felt.
> A headless man? The garments of Posthumus?
> I know the shape of's leg; this is his hand,
> His foot Mercurial, his Martial thigh,
> The brawns of Hercules; but his Jovial face –
> Murder in heaven! How? 'Tis gone. Pisanio,
> All curses madded Hecuba gave the Greeks,
> And mine to boot, be darted on thee!
> . . .
> *she smears her face in blood* (4.2.297–310; 327)

This is a scene dense with imagery relating to the Stuarts and animated by borrowings from both *Gorboduc* and *Macbeth*. To start with, Innogen's name is significant because it is the same name that Geoffrey of Monmouth gives to the wife of Brutus, the Trojan founder of Britain. The location is of similar symbolic import, because Milford Haven was the original landing point of Brutus' ships. (So it is important to remember that the scene invites us to imagine *the origins of Britain*, at a moment in time *in which Christ was born*.) In relation to the Stuarts, the name of the husband for whom Innogen believes herself to be grieving is important, because it literally couples the meanings of 'a lion' and 'a child born after the death of his father'. James' father (Darnley) died eight months after his birth, but many rumours held that he was in fact Riccio's son (the man Darnley murdered while James was still in his mother's womb). The lion, as noted, was the heraldic animal emblazoned upon the royal arms of Scotland and England. These references to James surround Innogen's confusion – and the scene certainly emphasises misperception and illusion as she mistakes Cloten's body for that of her husband. Innogen's weary dream-like state enhances the play's emphasis on misinterpretation here, for just as she cannot find the way to Milford Haven, she cannot tell the difference between the blood of Posthumus and his pretender: 'our very eyes / Are sometimes like our judgements, blind'. Having already echoed *Macbeth*'s famous line 'This bloody man', she then soaks herself in the corpse's blood. Thus, *Gorboduc*'s motif of the bloody infant (as Jerusalem in the field) is reinforced when Innogen is discovered by the Roman Captain and Lucius later in the scene. When she is asked her name, Innogen (who is disguised as a boy) replies 'Richard du Champ', that is, Richard of the Field.[36] Far from embodying the birth of a mighty nation, which we might expect from a play so doggedly concerned with British (and Stuart) origins, Innogen's borrowing from *Gorboduc* assumes a grotesque inversion of the origins story that her name precipitates. After she smears blood on her face and faints, her unconscious bloody body (lying beside the decapitated Cloten) is like a monstrous miscarriage, born of a headless traitor.

The imagery of these lines is rich and ambiguous, but whatever else we might take them to mean, the most infamous beheading in recent memory was certainly that of James' mother Mary. And the emphasis here on illusion and misperception, and the groggy uncertainty of Innogen's half-conscious, barely-awake shock, casts a warped shadow over this complex retelling of Britain's origins. Where we might expect the context of the birth of Christ, the origins of the Stuart family line, and the various nods to Brutus to prompt an emphasis on a promising future, what we find is a bloody miscarriage laid out beside (and wallowing in the blood of) a pretender – whose name (Cloten) remembers a failed union, and subsequent northern territorial annexation. In these moments of Innogen's confusion, *Cymbeline* grotesquely reshapes the chronicle history of Britain, dissecting and distorting the mythic beginnings of Britishness; in so doing, it does not find glorious or noble origins, but violence, discord and illusion.

Conclusion

King James' blood lineage is figured throughout these plays as inherently corrupt and stained. When Shakespeare felt moved to write about the Stuarts, he looked to a recent history of dramatic writings, and borrowed from *Gorboduc* a thematic interest in blood politics that his audiences and readers could well have connected with England's new king. That *Macbeth* was performed before James himself might seem remarkable; yet this too was a precedent that *Gorboduc*'s performances at Elizabeth I's court had already broached. So what else might this tell us about Shakespeare's writings and the political North more broadly? To begin with, he was influenced by a greater range of texts than is generally accounted for; and while Shakespeare's political loyalties are often seen as elusive, he was, in these case studies, persistently critical of the Stuart bloodline. *Macbeth* and *Cymbeline* display a staunch resistance to mythologies that serve nationalistic ends, particularly (in this period of his career) in terms of the relationship between Scotland and England – which forms an unnatural and unsettling backdrop to both plays. The borrowings from *Gorboduc* provide a useful lens through which to observe how politically motivated literatures decode and oppose power structures, and how – for literature scholars and students – intertextuality functions in enabling ways within tense political circumstances of change. The geo-political bloodwork of *Gorboduc* provided Shakespeare with an important language of critique, and understanding this demonstrates something meaningful and important. Literature is always political, and literary histories of political resistance can enable intellectual expressions of political agency in formidable ways. Now, as political forces continue to negotiate the alignment of these islands to each other and the world, literary and other forms of artistic expression (and the histories therein) form a crucial backstop.

Notes

1. According to Simon Palfrey, 'Public theatre fills in for the belatedness of political institutions: playing in the gap between desire and achievement, it can be the auditorium of disappointment, but equally of legitimate expectation'; see *Late Shakespeare: A New World of Words* (Oxford: Clarendon Press, 1999), 38.
2. For an overview of the central critical perspectives and debates see Henry James and Greg Walker, 'The politics of *Gorboduc*', *The English Historical Review*, 110: 435 (1995), 109–21; Mike Pincombe, 'Robert Dudley, *Gorboduc*, and 'The masque of Beauty and Desire': a reconsideration of the evidence for political intervention', *Parergon* 20: 1 (2003), 19–44; and Dermot Cavanagh, *Language and Politics in the Sixteenth-Century History Play* (Basingstoke: Palgrave Macmillan, 2003), 36–57.
3. See Patrick Collinson, *Birthpangs of Protestant England: Religious and Cultural Change in the Sixteenth and Seventeenth Centuries* (Basingstoke: Palgrave Macmillan, 1998), ix; and Alec Ryrie and Peter Marshall (eds), *The Beginnings of English Protestantism* (Cambridge: Cambridge University Press, 2002), 1–13.
4. For plausible speculation that the 1565 print edition might well have been a substantially different text to the one actually performed before Elizabeth, see Norman Jones and Paul Whitfield White, '*Gorboduc* and royal marriage politics: an Elizabethan playgoer's report of the premiere performance', *English Literary Renaissance*, 26: 1 (1996), 3–17.
5. Geoffrey of Monmouth, *Historia Regnum Britanniae*, II.16. Quoted in 'Appendix: the sources of *Gorboduc*', in William Tydeman (ed.), *Two Tudor Tragedies* (London: Penguin, 1992), 345. All quotations from *Gorboduc* (hereafter cited in-text) are from this edition, unless otherwise stated.
6. Andrew Hadfield, *Shakespeare, Spenser and the Matter of Britain* (Basingstoke: Palgrave Macmillan, 2004), 59, 155.
7. Homer, *Chapman's Homer: The Iliad, The Odyssey and the Lesser Homerica*, George Chapman (trans), Allardyce Nicoll (ed.), 2 vols (London: Routledge & Kegan Paul, 1957), I: 217.
8. Plutarch, *Plutarch's Lives: The Dryden Translation*, John Dryden (trans), Arthur Hugh Clough (ed.), 2 vols (New York: Modern Library, 2001), I: 44.
9. Both Robert Fabyan's 1516 *Prima pars conecarum* and Edmund Spenser's accounts of the Matter of Britain evoke Gorboduc as the end of the line of the Trojan-British genealogical line. See excerpts in the 'Appendix: the sources of *Gorboduc*' in Tydeman's *Two Tudor Tragedies*, 344–7.
10. Jaecheol Kim, 'The North-South divide in *Gorboduc*: fratricide remembered and forgotten', *Studies in Philology* 111: 4 (2014), 691–719.
11. Peter C. Herman, '"He said what?!?": Misdeeming *Gorboduc*, or problematizing form, service and certainty', *Exemplaria* 13: 1 (2001), 285–321.
12. Lisa Hopkins, *From the Romans to the Normans on the English Renaissance Stage* (Kalamazoo: Medieval Institute Publications, Western Michigan University, 2017), 33; see also 50, n.13.

13. See note 4 above.
14. Alan Stewart, *The Cradle King: A Life of James VI and I* (London: Chatto & Windus, 2003), 9.
15. King James I and VI, *Political Writings*, Johann P. Sommerville (ed.) (Cambridge: Cambridge University Press, 1994), 148.
16. Jacqueline Vanhoutte, 'Community, authority, and the motherland in Sackville and Norton's *Gorboduc*', *Studies in English Literature, 1500*–1900, 40: 2 (2000), 227–39; see also Carole Levin, *The Heart and Stomach of a King: Elizabeth I and the Politics of Sex and Power* (Philadelphia: University of Philadelphia Press, 1994), 65–90.
17. Lucius Annaeus Seneca, *The Seventh Tragedy of Seneca, Entitled Medea*, trans. John Studely (London: 1566; STC 22224), sig.4r. A similar line is repeated in *Gorboduc* by Videna at 4.1.1015–16: 'to stain thy deadly hands / With blood deserv'd, and drink thereof thy fill?'.
18. On *Gorboduc*'s womb imagery see Sara Petrosillo, 'A microhistory of the womb from the N-Town Mary plays to *Gorboduc*', *Journal of Medieval and Early Modern Studies*, 47: 1 (2017), 121–46.
19. See, for instance, Susan E. Krantz's 'Thomas Dekker's political commentary in *The Whore of Babylon*', *Studies in English Literature, 1500–1900*, 35: 2 (1995), 271–91, especially 282, and 290–1, n.43.
20. See James D. Carroll, '*Gorboduc* and *Titus Andronicus*', *Notes and Queries* 51: 3 (2004), 267–9; and Barbara H. C. Mendonca, 'The influence of *Gorboduc* on *King Lear*', *Shakespeare Survey* 13 (1960), 41–8.
21. Donna B. Hamilton considers the possibility that the plays formed a natural pairing because of their appearance, one after the other, in Simon Forman's diary accounts of the play's plotlines; see the chapter on *Cymbeline* and the Oath of Allegiance in *Shakespeare and the Politics of Protestant England* (Lexington: University Press of Kentucky, 1992), 128–62.
22. Raphael Holinshed, *The Second Volume of Chronicles: Containing the Description, Conquest, Inhabitation and Troublesome Effect of Ireland* (London: 1586; STC 13569), 173.
23. Lisa Hopkins, *The Cultural Uses of the Caesars on the English Renaissance Stage* (Aldershot: Ashgate, 2008), 120, 123.
24. Hamilton, *Shakespeare and the Politics of Protestant England*, 129.
25. All Shakespeare quotations from Stephen Greenblatt et al. (eds), *The Norton Shakespeare: Based on the Oxford Edition* (New York and London: Norton, 1997). Hereafter cited in-text.
26. 'You do not meet a mean but frowns. Our bloods / No more obey the heavens than our courtiers' (1.1.1–2); 'Never was a war did cease, / Ere bloody hands were washed, with such peace' (5.6.484–5).
27. Stewart, *Cradle King*, 38. See also Frederick Holmes, *The Sickly Stuarts: The Medical Downfall of a Dynasty* (Stroud: Sutton Publishing, 2003; rpr. 2005), 80–1.

28. See, for instance, Jenijoy La Belle, '"A strange infirmity": Lady Macbeth's amenorrhea', *Shakespeare Quarterly*, 31: 3 (1980), 381–6.
29. 'Drury to William Cecil', 20 May 1567, cited in Stewart, *Cradle King*, 29, 357, n.38.
30. Stewart, *Cradle King*, 31; Antonia Fraser, *Mary Queen of Scots* (London: Weidenfeld & Nicolson, 1969; rpr. London: Phoenix Press, 2002), 410.
31. Janet Adelman, *Suffocating Mothers: Fantasies of Maternal Origin in Shakespeare's Plays, Hamlet to The Tempest* (London and New York: Routledge, 1992), 7; Adelman cites James Guillimeau, *The Nursing of Children*, affixed to *The Happy Delivery of Women* (London: 1635), 'Preface', I.i.2.
32. Mary Floyd-Wilson, 'Delving to the root: *Cymbeline*, Scotland, and the English race', in David J. Baker and Willy Maley (eds), *British Identities and English Renaissance Literature* (Cambridge: Cambridge University Press, 2002), 101–18, 101. See also Emrys Jones, 'Stuart *Cymbeline*', *Essays in Criticism*, 11 (1961), 84–99.
33. See Melville Richards, 'The Irish settlements in South-West Wales: a topographical approach', *The Journal of the Royal Society of Antiquaries of Ireland*, 90: 2 (1960), 133–62.
34. According to Timothy Venning, Seissyl had 'presumably profited from the ravaging of his Southern neighbour and potential rival Dyfed by the Mercians in the 780s'; see *A Chronology of Medieval Europe: 450–1066* (Abington and New York: Routledge, 2018), 288.
35. The most complete recent account of the remarkable Stuart/Stewart family history is Oliver Thompson's *The Rises and Falls of the Royal Stewarts* (Stroud: The History Press, 2011).
36. Jean E. Howard notes that the name could be an allusion to Richard Field (the printer), who was well known to Shakespeare, having printed *Rape of Lucrece* and *Venus and Adonis*. Field was also from Stratford-upon-Avon; see *The Norton Shakespeare*, 3022, n.7.

2

'Here are strangers near at hand': Anglo-Scottish Border Crossings Pre- and Post-Union

Steven Veerapen

On 6 April 1603, James VI of Scotland crossed the border to succeed his late cousin, Elizabeth I. The 37-year-old Scotsman was not the only contender for the throne, and his (and his Borders chieftains') very visible greeting by Sir John Carey and the officials of Berwick was designed to smooth over decades of uncertainty that had resulted from Elizabeth's stout refusal to name a designated heir. James, like his mother, had been championed by some, and rejected by others.[1] Yet due to the likelihood (if not the absolute certainty) of a Scottish succession, any late-Elizabethan plays, such as Robert Greene's *The Scottish History of James the Fourth* (1599) which portrayed Scotland and its people, had been perforce succession plays. Similarly, plays depicting Scotland which emerged in the aftermath of the Union of the Crowns, including *Macbeth* (1606), undoubtedly cast a critical eye on the advantages and disadvantages of ever-greater union, and what the continuing existence of the independent nation with an absentee monarch meant for England.

In the spindly-legged, modestly-dressed king existed an entirely personal union between two historically belligerent kingdoms.[2] The relationship between England and its northern neighbour had, however, undergone significant changes throughout the sixteenth century. Henry VIII and Edward VI's bellicose and covetous policy towards Scotland, which promoted an ancient belief in English suzerainty, had given way to an uneasy stalemate under the preoccupied Mary I, and ultimately to a quasi-maternal amity under the Protestant Elizabeth. It is something of an historical irony that Elizabeth achieved a greater degree of control over Scottish affairs than her proprietorial father. Yet through the dangling of the English succession, first to Mary Queen of Scots and latterly to James VI, and intermittent financial inducements, she had managed to keep England's northern border largely secure. It is this border, and theatrical representations of those who crossed it before and after the Union of the Crowns, that will be the focus of this chapter.

Though its parameters and territories shifted, the border marked out England's northern periphery. Yet if the border was the kingdom's periphery, looming – and actual – Scottish advances across it invited playwrights to consider what lay beyond. Accordingly, critical consideration of the Borders as represented in literary works have not been ignored. David J. Baker's '"Stands Scotland where it did?" Shakespeare on the march' provides a useful study of both the historiography of the border and contends that the *Henriad* presents a 'history [of the border] that can be traced from the older conception' of England to the newer in a way that 'is uneven and multidirectional'.[3] To Baker, the Marches are possessed of an interminable history that endured beyond 1603. As will be seen, this persistence was anticipated by Robert Greene. Lisa Hopkins' seminal studies, *Renaissance Drama on the Edge* and *Shakespeare on the Edge*, dealt likewise with the dramatic representation of border crossings; to Hopkins, the northern Borders were the most 'politically charged' of England's frontiers – areas which themselves were on their way to becoming 'simply parts of the landscape'.[4]

When James crossed into his newly acquired kingdom, it was with a definite and, as it turned out, quixotic plan in mind. The self-styled King of Great Britain sought nothing less than full political integration, with the borderlands rebranded as the 'middle marches' of a single country.[5] Poets' pens scratched out verses in favour, with Samuel Daniel writing:

> Now thou art all Great Britain and no more;
>   No Scot, No English now, nor no debate:
> No borders but the Ocean and the shore;
>   No wall of Adrian serves to separate
> Our mutual love, nor our obedience
>   Being subjects all to one Imperial Prince.[6]

Daniel's sanguine assessment of the prospect of union was destined to remain unfulfilled. In fact, it was only in the Borders that 'March law', that judicial system peculiar to the Anglo-Scottish Borders, was formally disestablished, as the king sought to efface difference. However, concerns about union harming 'the very name of England', which had existed at least as early as Mary Tudor's marriage, were reignited – and roundly resisted by the English parliament – on the Jacobean succession.[7] Indeed, as James Shapiro notes, as animated polemicists penned tracts and debates on the subject of England's national identity in the light of a proposed British identity, it is therefore unsurprising that *Macbeth*, written in the wake of James' accession, should investigate the prospect of 'ever greater union' in a typically non-committal fashion.[8]

In considering the presentation of Scots who ventured into England (and English characters who ventured into Scotland) in the present plays, it is worth noting, finally, the relative paucity – and sudden explosion – of Scotsmen and women available to London-based playwrights as models. A 1570 census records only forty Scots living in the capital, which was dolefully expected to become a problematic influx in the event of regnal union.[9] It is as a result of this lack of widespread familiarity that Shapiro contends that Elizabethans, in particular 'got their sense of Scottishness second-hand':

> [F]rom long-circulating stereotypes, from books like Raphael Holinshed's *Chronicles*, from memories of James' mother, and from the stage (where Marlowe's *Edward the Second* recalled how the Scots humiliated the English at the Battle of Bannockburn, and Shakespeare's more recent *Henry the Fifth* casually alluded to their neighbours to the north as the 'weasel Scot' [1.2.170]). The arrival of many Scots in James' entourage in 1603 . . . only stoked English xenophobia.[10]

Although examples can readily be found of negative presentations of Scottish border crossers, it should also be noted that Greene and Shakespeare were not simply xenophobic English nationalists. Available to each playwright were more nuanced texts, including Hector Boece's *History of Scotland* (published in Paris in 1526, and replete with heroic and fanciful tales of valiant Scots), William Stewart's *The Buik of the Cronicles of Scotland* (1531–5) and Holinshed's *History of Scotland to 1571* (1571). We must not therefore expect the plays to present unambiguously hostile Scots as Shakespeare and his contemporaries looked northwards to see who was coming and going. Instead we should consider the ways in which these playwrights considered, in turn, the prospect of being governed by a northern border crosser, what the new sovereign's personal union might mean for England's identity, and the dangers of a northern kingdom whose independent identity was embodied by a monarch now ensconced south of the border.

Before the Union: Greene's *The Scottish History of James the Fourth*

The Scottish History of James the Fourth, dated by Norman Sander as likely written in 1590, is, in many ways, a perplexing play. As Kirk Melnikoff notes, it moves from tragedy to tragicomedy prior to its peaceful denouement.[11] It also, however, has obvious if ironic pretensions to the textual authority of a history, being 'associated ... with the conventions and intentions of the genre'.[12] One might therefore usefully think of the play itself as being somewhat on the borders of genre, revelling in its status as a gallimaufry of popular theatrical modes. Its main narrative, drawn from Cinthio, is claimed to have taken place in 1520, a date meaningless to the historical James IV (who had been slain, as the play's subtitle notes, at Flodden, though in 1513). Although bearing no relevance to Anglo-Scottish historiography, it does playfully resonate as the year of one of history's most famous border summits: the largely ineffectual Field of the Cloth of Gold, which took place at Guisnes, near the Anglo-French border. In a tacit way, *James the Fourth* thus acknowledges and foreshadows the short-lived nature of monarchical alliances forged by cross-border meetings and primes the audience to distrust the effusive affection demonstrated by each monarch in the first act. Via an accordioning of history, the play's king of Scots is simultaneously James IV, James V, James VI, and none of these kings. Instead, he is a figure invested with qualities associated with each – lust, callowness, wiliness, and youth. Likewise, the English king is an amalgam of the qualities Greene associates with English kingship: bluster, strength, and mercurial bonhomie.

It is interesting to note that the play's framing narrative is situated in the Borders, and its first speaker the mysterious Scot, Bohan, 'attired like a Rid-stall [or Redesdale] man' and woken from a magical slumber by Oberon. First noted in the emendation of W. L. Renwick, this allusion has been expanded upon by J. A. Lavin, who notes that 'a Redesdale man would have a wild, ferocious appearance'.[13] Redesdale, the 'epitome of all the wild border', was a liberty within England's middle march.[14] Bohan, therefore, is a stranger, wearing the garb of a southern-based Border Reiver, the troublesome, semi-autonomous class of the Marches. However, he presents a peculiarly noble and civilised attitude towards the play's events, lamenting 'lust and lawless will', and 'treasons 'gainst the innocent'.[15] It would thus be a mistake to assume that the borderer's costume simply denotes ferocity; the play, indeed, is keen to impart a surprising amount of Bohan's life prior to his awakening:

> I was born a gentleman of the best blood in all Scotland, except the king; when time brought me to age, and death took my parents, I became a courtier, where though ay list not praise myself, ay engraved the memory of Bohan on the skin-coat of some of them, and revelled with the proudest. (Induction, 40–5)[16]

He is, then, a figure familiar with the court and courtly life, and by his own claims a magnate. Via his choral commentary, full as it is of astute observations and noble sentiment, the play refuses to make any unambiguously negative assessments about the Scottish nobility, but neither does it seek to soothe anxieties about them and their potential appearance in London society. In *James the Fourth*, the Scottish noble is uncomfortably wild, while admirable, and comfortable even in the Marches south of the Tweed.[17]

Bohan's opening line ('Ay say, what's thou') is singled out by J. O. Bartley as worthy of criticism: 'Bohan's dialect', he argues, 'is well marked, though not consistent . . . None of the other Scottish characters is distinctly nationalised, and there is nothing further that could be taken as intended for typically Scottish about Bohan or Sir Bartram'.[18] Bartley is correct, yet he neglects to acknowledge the function of Bohan's slippery linguistic style. From the outset, the borderer's prose is singled out as different, even, as becomes clear, from the play's other Scots. That his language is unstable is significant: as a liminal figure, he is occasionally comic and othered, and occasionally familiar and grave, with his Scottishness waxing and waning unpredictably. The first appearance of his sons, who slip into his border retreat, coincides with his desire that they 'haud their clacks', with the more ominous warning, 'Prattle an thou darest ene word more, and ay's dab this whinyard in thy womb' (Induction, 82, 86). Bohan's language has, indeed, proven problematic even for Lavin, who erroneously emends the line, 'Do not more glee to make the fairy greet' to 'to salute (?) qy. Gree; cf. 'to make gree' (to give satisfaction)'.[19] A more sensible emendation of this line, given the context, is 'to weep': a meaning which survives in modern Scots, and represents one of many textual moments in which the language spoken on stage has itself crossed the border.

The language of the Borders marks out the region as a between-space: between the political nations of Scotland and England, which, within the play's parameters, share the common language of diplomacy and intrigue. In this way, Bohan's lack of a concise speech pattern – and his presentation as a violent figure prone to perdurable slumber rather than death – is best understood less as a London playwright's uncertain grasp of vernacular and more as a nod to the unpredictability of a region seen as being, in Anna Groundwater's phrasing, 'on the road to pacification', but nevertheless a 'region of special concern'.[20]

Lisa Hopkins argues that Bohan's costume carries a political statement, pointing to borderers, 'whom James VI and I tried so hard to suppress, with mixed success'. The play, she suggests, 'draws attention to the changing role of the Borders'. To accept this claim is not to gift Greene too much prescience. If one accepts the 1590 dating, the king of Scots' irenic intentions with regard to the Borders had been developing for decades.[21] Bohan the Border Reiver's appearance at the start of the play and his continued interludes at the close of each scene provide further evidence that the play itself is intensely interested in the status of the Borders.[22] In *James the Fourth* they become a space for animated discussion, separate from the events of the play proper both temporally and physically. They are, as Hopkins suggests, an enduring location, which, despite the play's 'insistent glances' towards Jacobean succession, serve 'to gesture towards a world in which the Border itself will be undone', whilst retaining the 'very different logic of the magical'.[23] Hopkins is certainly correct in that the play glances forwards; but so too does it glance backwards, and surveys Greene's present – and in each, the same heavily distorting lenses are employed. One might go further. By virtue of Bohan's slumber, and the magical nature of his environs, the border can be read as curiously persistent, and resistant to any suggestion of political and national union. As Bohan appears to confuse and collapse his history – playfully so, as he claims his mythical tale is 'much like our court of Scotland this day'– the Border Reiver retains his aloof autonomy, critical of his ostensible leaders, and magically elusive (Induction, 105). In this way the Borders function, as they would later do for Walter Scott, as sites of mystification, with the celebration of magic and unreality a tool in their preservation.

The first border crossers seen in the play's main narrative come in the form of the king of England and his daughter, Dorothea. Both have bypassed the land border and its notoriously dangerous marches for a sea crossing, as, at their first meeting, the Scottish king advises his new bride and attendants to 'Attend to see our English friends at sea' (1.1.68); Dorothea soon confirms that 'My royal father is both shipped and gone' (1.1.141). Following the play's induction, the narrative thus shifts from the borderland realm of the magical to that of the political. The two border crossers, having arrived by ship, are separated by ship, and yet their role in the play is clear: those whom the audience first witness crossing the border have done so for the diplomatic reason of marriage between the political nations. Given the recent incursion of the Spanish Armada, and the Tudors' history of attacking and garrisoning Scottish ports, it is a striking choice (and, in terms of historiography, a distancing one, given that James IV's wife, Margaret Tudor, arrived overland), but it makes dramaturgical sense.[24] Throughout, the play strives to identify and examine different means of crossing the border, and the various reasons for doing so. Diplomatic visits, and especially the transportation of brides by ship, were certainly grist for the political mill, Greene's contemporary king of Scots having recently imported a bride from Denmark.

Allusions to the contemporary political landscape pepper the play, with Dorothea serving as a wise, dual-gendered peacemaker to a reckless young Scottish king.[25] It is difficult not to see in their relationship the shadow of Elizabeth's own quasi-maternal, financially backed, and occasionally exasperated relationship with her putative successor, even without Bohan's overt encouragement.[26] However, it is more difficult to identify a contemporary for a character like Dorothea's father, the king of England. Following his departure, he remains offstage until 5.3., whereupon he appears at the gates of Dunbar. Since Dunbar lay some twenty-eight miles from the border north of Berwick-upon-Tweed, the king is thus shown to have crossed the border offstage at the head of an army. Douglas, the castle's keeper, cries out,

> What, though the lion, king of Brutish race,
> Through outrage sin, shall lambs be therefore slain?
> ...
> O English king, thou bearest in thy breast
> The king of beasts, that harms not yielding ones,
> The roseal cross is spread within thy field,
> A sign of peace, not of revenging war:
> Be gracious then, unto this little town (5.3.19–27)

Typically, the king shows mercy, 'eagle-like' choosing to 'disdain these little fowls' (5.3.41). It is here that his function becomes clear. Greene's king of England is a symbolic presence, and his appearance is thus marked by symbols: the lion, England's national animal, the cross, its flag, and the eagle, the chief of birds.[27] The king of England's overland border crossing – surprising and frightening the cowed Scots – is also symbolic, of England's military capacity and might over its northern neighbour.

With the settling of diplomatic alliance and the violence of war thus a prerogative of royal border crossers, the play also puts under the theatrical lens another type of crossing: that brought about by friendship and the sharing of news. In 1.3., the English lord Sir Eustace meets with his northern counterpart in Scotland, and the two exchange pleasantries, followed by gossip about the court. Eustace and his attendants are 'booted' for travel, and Sir Bartram, after welcoming his 'ancient friend', recalls the 'merkist night, when we the borders track' (1.3.10). Although the comedy of the scene derives from Bartram's ignorance of Eustace's private life, the two nevertheless represent another incursion of Englishmen into Scotland: that brought about by amity between neighbours. It is still, however, coloured by the political, as the pair discuss the respective conditions of their countries' monarchs (1.3.21–30). In this way, *James the Fourth* again offers multiple interpretations, refusing to be drawn on either advocating or supporting border crossings. Although the scene appears innocuous, it nevertheless depicts the border as permeable, allowing for subjects to form their own alliances and exchange news irrespective of (and without the knowledge of) the play's main political players.

Sir Eustace is noteworthy not only for his friendship with his northern counterpart, but for what he brings across the border with him. Visiting the countess of Arran, the mother of the king of Scots' would-be lover, he reveals his mission:

> The county Countess of Northumberland
> Doth greet you well, and hath requested me
> To bring these letters to your ladyship. (2.1.33–5)

In the countesses, Greene again encourages a kaleidoscopic reading. The earls and countesses of Arran had historically been the Hamiltons, the first noble family in Scotland. At the time of Greene's writing, however, there was only one living holder of the title of countess of Arran: Elizabeth Stewart, the much-gossiped-about wife of James' disgraced minister, James Stewart (d. 1595), the former Earl of Arran, who had been accused of complicity in the Borders murder of Francis Bedford, the incident which had threatened the incipient alliance between the kingdoms in 1585.[28] His fall at that time had brought about the restoration to the title of the insane, unmarried James Hamilton (d. 1609).[29] If the nod to the Arran earldom is politicised, so too is the countess' friend, the 'county Countess of Northumberland'. In 1590, there were two living holders of the title: the exiled Anne Percy (d. 1596), who had fled to Scotland after the 1569 Northern Rebellion, there to seek refuge with Borders outlaw Hector Armstrong of Harlaw; and Katherine Percy (d. 1596), widow of the 8th Earl of Northumberland, who had died in the Tower under mysterious circumstances after having been imprisoned for illicit correspondence with Mary Stuart and her agents.[30] Greene is careful, of course, to present his fictitious countesses as modest, and the letters they exchange as harmless. Nevertheless, the historical echoes are present, and the depiction of noble ladies exchanging letters across the border presents a potential risk as much as a means of exchanging news. As the countesses can be either innocently fictitious or historical threats to the state, so too can letters, which might cross a porous border at the behest of interested factions and via overly friendly northern couriers. London audiences, then, were both reminded of amity between those in northern England and Scotland – likely a source of comfort for those anticipating a monarchical union – and the risks of that friendship in the form of unchecked correspondence and intrigue.

Greene's play, ultimately, considers a variety of border crossers – from language to royals to couriers to letters. However, each is marked by a doubling technique, for which the obfuscation of history and fiction serves as a tool, making innocuous or well-intended events within the fictional world take on more sinister or dangerous complexions when they cross the border into the real world. The act of crossing the border is, it will be noted, invariably offstage. Despite the Borders featuring as Bohan's mysterious home (and thus the site of the play's commentary), those characters who cross from England to Scotland – and Greene always looks northwards, at those crossing in that direction – are always seen *after* having done so, further distancing the border itself from the recognisable worlds of court, country house, and town. This refusal to portray the act of crossing over was to be shared by Shakespeare in *Macbeth*.

In the Wake of the Union: Shakespeare's *Macbeth*

Julian Goodare and Michael Lynch have convincingly argued that 1603 has been overstated as a 'turning point', at least in terms of Scottish polity.[31] However, the arrival in England of a foreign ruler with a bevy of attendants invited those working in the political arena of the stage to consider not only that they had acquired a new king, but that their northern neighbour had exported theirs. Further, James had let it be known that he intended to visit Scotland every three years (a pledge he would ignore), leading to the possibility of England sharing sovereignty with its northern neighbour, and also looking forward to extended periods of absentee monarchy. This prospect can only have added to the uncertainty aroused by the narrow escape of the king and his family in the failed Gunpowder Plot of 1605. It is in this context that Shakespeare opted to present the tragic history of Macbeth, mining the historical record and adding to it – a comparatively safe choice, given the suppression of his company's theatrical representation of more recent events in *The Tragedy of Gowrie* (1604).

Shakespeare's *Macbeth* has often been considered as having been written to please the recently installed James. Rightfully, this notion has been problematised.[32] After all, given James' notorious terror of naked steel, his fears of assassination, and his beliefs in the divinity of monarchy, it would be odd for any playwright to seek to panegyrise him with the depiction of a king dispatched in his bed with daggers. Nevertheless, the occasional concessions the play makes to celebration of the Stuart dynasty do not require rehearsal.[33] Unlike Greene, who could only look forward ambivalently to a king who had crossed the border, Shakespeare wrote from the vantage point of the succession having been won by the Stuarts. Like Greene, however, Shakespeare refuses to either approve or overtly criticise the recent *fait accompli*, as he refuses wholly to support or condemn James' ongoing quest for fuller union.[34] Like Greene, too, Shakespeare was to play somewhat loose with Scottish history in exploring the northern kingdom, its inhabitants, and those who travelled between it and England.[35]

If *Macbeth* is less pronounced in its exploration of the border and those who cross it than *James the Fourth*, it nevertheless shows an interest. The first reference to a border crossing comes early, and is mentioned only by allusion, as the witches discuss their recent activities. Immediately the prevalence of magic is apparent, with the witches, like Bohan, beginning the play on a supernatural note, openly avowing their border crossing while situated ambiguously in 'a desert place'. Though elusive in terms of gender, the witches are undoubtedly Scottish characters – tempest-raising witches having been something of a bugbear to James during his reign in Scotland, and a focal point of his *Daemonologie* (1597).

As they recount their recent adventures, the Third Witch enquires as to her sisters' whereabouts, which elicits this response from the First Witch:

A sailor's wife had chestnuts in her lap,
And munch'd, and munch'd, and munch'd:
'Give me,' quoth I:

> 'Aroint thee, witch!' the rump-fed ronyon cries.
> Her husband's to Aleppo gone, master o' the Tiger:
> But in a sieve I'll thither sail,
> And, like a rat without a tail,
> I'll do, I'll do, and I'll do. (3.1.4–10)

The ship referenced has aroused scholarly interest, with Marion A. Taylor favouring the identity of the unfortunate sailor as Sir Edward Michelbourne who had, in 1606, arrived from a voyage in a ship called the Tiger.[36] Others, as Taylor notes, consider the 'master o' the Tiger' a reference to Ralph Fitch, a well-known sailor who had served aboard another Tiger. Whichever candidate is correct (if either), it remains clear that in order for the witch to have menaced the wife of a sailor aboard an English ship called the Tiger, she would have perforce have crossed the border into England and back into Scotland between her first and second appearances in the play (both candidates being English ships). Further, she must have crossed temporal borders, which renders her a threat both in the fictitious history of the play and to the audiences of London's playhouses.[37] In the first act we therefore learn of an offstage border crossing, which might well have been designed to thrill audiences via a metatheatrical topical allusion (in much the same way that modern horror films pursue collective shivers by exposing the terror lurking in the familiar). The horror comes not only from the imagined proximity of the witch, but also her crossing a variety of borders: gender, geographical and temporal.

The witches' meeting place is, furthermore, a place outside of the political nation: a heath near Forres (3.1). This joins a number of similarly liminal spaces: an anteroom in the castle; a camp near Forres; the country near Dunsinane; before Macbeth's castle; outside Macbeth's castle; the country near Birnam Wood. Shakespeare's eleventh-century Scotland is a divided land, mapped onto the geography of the play by its internal borders and bordering spaces. It is possessed of its own North, South, East and West, and therefore the loss of its king invites a political vacuum – which Macbeth is led or walks into – and the disorders attendant upon his rule.

In discussing the *Henriad*, Baker poses the provocative question: what is Scotland, then?[38] This question arguably was more difficult to resolve in 1606 than it had been in the 1590s. For centuries, Scotland's autonomy and independence had been defined by separate monarchy, the incumbents of which alternately sought, withstood or fiercely rejected the political will of England's monarchs. As Goodare points out, 'that the "country" might be something different from the court and government was a new idea'.[39] After James had relocated to England, Scotland's status as a country was – with the king's own encouragement – questionable, and it is significant that following his successful bid for the crown, Macbeth is only seen cloistered within his fortresses, and in the desolate cavern in pursuit of the supernatural, until his appearance on the battlefield. *Macbeth* certainly depicts a disorderly nation, and the play does not compromise on Scotland's need for strong kingship.[40] Yet, in effect, the state of semi-subjection which Scotland's monarchs had exhibited during Elizabeth's reign (in the hope of winning her crown) had been lost with the Jacobean succession. Although James famously boasted that his northern realm was governed as well by his pen as it had once been by the sword, *Macbeth* serves as a reminder of the complexities of Scottish politics even as it offers a celebration of the Stuart line.[41] Once James had acquired Elizabeth's office, he was arguably in a more troublesome position, having the governance of Scotland in his hands, but no deferential ruler serving his interests in a kingdom which, as the play suggests (albeit via fictional tinkering), has a volatile history and politically charged peripheries.[42] An equally pertinent question, and one with which *Macbeth* engages in a variety of its permutations, is 'what is a border?' The borders north of the Borders are, in Shakespeare's play, sites of trouble, especially without an effective governor present.

If the Scotland of *Macbeth* is fragmented and fractious, and descends into chaos, the play's treatment of its other featured nation is somewhat less nuanced. In another offstage border crossing, Macduff and Malcolm are seen before Edward the Confessor's palace. Here the play is circumspect, arguably celebrating the idea of a nation being defined by a strong centralised monarchy, while keeping its border crossers on its fringes. The country into which the pair have crossed is a political nation in the old sense alluded to by Goodare, with Macduff and Malcolm immediately placed at the gates of a king's palace; but they remain at its gates, thus allowing the audience's glimpse of England to show it, too, as possessed of something wider than the national model of king and court. Before they can penetrate the heart of the nation – the king's presence – Macduff encounters a cultural barrier:

Macduff: What's the disease he means?
Malcolm: 'Tis called the evil.
A most miraculous work in this good king,
Which often, since my here-remain in England,
I have seen him do. (4.3.146–50)

Though it captures an historical moment – Edward the Confessor's introduction of 'the king's touch' as a cure for scrofula – Shakespeare's reasons for including the exchange are at first puzzling. As Richard McCoy has noted, further, the 'treatment of the royal touch . . . is somewhat wan and oblique because Edward remains offstage . . . the audience never actually sees the miraculous work in this good king'.[43] Yet the reference also alludes to King James' own scepticism over the efficacy of the centuries-old cure, and it is this moment of cultural confusion which Shakespeare chooses to incorporate.[44] The inclusion thus serves to depict the difference in cultural practices faced by border crossers. The rights and wrongs of the alleged cure notwithstanding, Shakespeare's interest here lies in the intangible barriers standing between the northern kingdom and its neighbour.

The reason behind Malcolm and Macduff's visit to England is also noteworthy. When placed against an historical context of prospective political union, the play presents the Scots as seeking (and receiving) from 'Gracious England . . . ten thousand men' (4.3.190–1). As Lorna Hutson has pointed out in her discussion of *Henry V*, Shakespeare wades into the war of Anglo-Scottish historiography, to 'efface the historical idea of Scotland as a nation'.[45] *Macbeth*, on the other hand, presents Scotland as a nation whilst depicting the English forces' crossing of the border as an entirely acceptable intervention rather than an invading foreign army. Macduff therefore champions Scotland's nationhood – lamenting its disgrace – as he crosses the border, only to efface that autonomy as he re-crosses it with an English army. Scotland, in *Macbeth*, is both an historic nation, and a client of England.

Perhaps wisely, Shakespeare neglects to portray the Scots' arrival with the same comical exasperation for which Ben Jonson was briefly imprisoned following his *Eastward Ho* (1604); but, nevertheless, they are supplicants, looking to take from their benevolent neighbour. Inescapably, the acquisition of Scotland via monarchical union – or more pointedly via James' favoured political union – is, under Shakespeare's pen, the acquisition of a burdensome state, despite the desirability of the unity, peace and order offered by English intervention. That the ultimate victory over Macbeth comes with English assistance provides a counterbalance, allowing the play its satisfying dramatic conclusion: the restoration of order. Yet it is a resolution which again highlights the need for a Scottish ruler, subservient to but separate from the political nation of England. Shakespeare cannot resist making this plain, as Malcolm, standing before the severed head of the previous head of Scotland, declares:

　　　　　　　　　　what needful else
That calls upon us, by the grace of Grace
We will perform in measure, time, and place.
So, thanks to all at once and to each one,
Whom we invite to see us crowned at Scone. (5.8.71–5)⁴⁶

The 'Grace' of Malcolm, a reference to his monarchical styling, is, by his own admission, willing to perform in 'place'. 'Place' in Scotland, as the play earlier suggests, is multifaceted: from the 'western isles', to the 'rich east' (1.2.12; 4.3.37). Closing on the ancient site of Scottish coronations, too, links Scottish kingship with a strong sense of place, and invites audiences to consider the dangers of a Scotland which has exported its king, yet retains a problematic nationhood, cultural differences, and geographical complexity. While Lisa Hopkins makes the persuasive claim that the play 'does not so much engage with the idea of a border as lament the lack of one', it might be fairer to say that the play instead seeks to uncover a plethora of alternative, remaining borders and peripheries.⁴⁷

'No borders but the ocean and the shore'

James VI and I re-crossed the border northwards only once, in 1617. By that time, his project for union between the two kingdoms had all but foundered, and although his disestablishment of March law had been effective, the Borders as a distinct region themselves remained, as Greene had anticipated, resistant to elision within a unified Great Britain. Despite the king's hopes, those Borders did not 'become the centre [rather than] the margins'.⁴⁸ Further, the prospect of renewed Anglo-Scottish hostilities was to rise again in the seventeenth century, and James' death, and his son's separate coronations north and south of the border, were to reignite questions about having a permeable northern gateway to an historically antagonistic neighbour.

Thus, it should not surprise us that in the 1630s plays such as John Ford's *Perkin Warbeck* (1634), and *The Valiant Scot* (1639), would turn attention to historical moments of conflict. *The Valiant Scot* presents the Scots positively, condemning the English – a swipe at Charles I's unpopular policies.⁴⁹ *Perkin Warbeck*, as Hopkins has convincingly argued, engages with another succession crisis, in addition to portraying a dangerously convincing border crosser in Warbeck, and a source of trouble in his surviving Scottish wife's presence in the English court.⁵⁰ As in *James the Fourth* and *Macbeth*, the crossing of the border northwards and southwards provided a means of interrogating politics from the marginal space of the stage.

England's northern border might have been less attractive as a setting for playwrights than their own capital, and continental and foreign settings, precisely because it continued to be a disputed site, haggled over by a king who wished it to be refashioned, yet which was nevertheless a porous gateway to a separate kingdom. What remains to be considered, therefore, is the persistent tendency of playwrights to have their border crossers do so offstage. To account for this, one must, ultimately, understand the nature of the Marches. While Scotland – with or without its king – remained a northern kingdom, and thus a political nation, the Borders remained between-spaces: buffer zones which did not fit the recognisable model typified by king and court. It should not surprise us that such murky, liminal spaces provided useful metaphors for playwrights interested in sites which were politicised and grappled over: sites for staging conflict, negotiation, and supernatural prophesying outside the centres of two political nations.

Notes

1. For an account of the complexities and debates surrounding the Jacobean succession, see Leanda de Lisle, *After Elizabeth: How James King of Scots Won the Crown of England in 1603* (London: Harper Collins, 2004).
2. Anthony Weldon, *The Court and Character of King James* (London: Howlett and Brimmer, [1650] 1817), 55.
3. David J. Baker, '"Stands Scotland where it did?" Shakespeare on the march', in Willy Maley and Andrew Murphy (eds), *Shakespeare and Scotland* (Manchester: Manchester University Press, 2004), 20–36.
4. Lisa Hopkins, *Shakespeare on the Edge: Border Crossings in the Tragedies and the Henriad* (Aldershot: Ashgate, 2005), 57, 7.
5. Although it is often stated that James' plan eventually came to fruition in 1707, it must be noted that even the Treaty of Union did not quite meet his lofty political goals. Under the terms of the treaty, Scotland was incorporated into a new kingdom, but nevertheless retained preserved interests in the form of Scots Law and the Scottish Kirk. James' motto for union was 'Unus Rex, unus Grex, & una Lex': one king, one flock, one law. He further exhorted the 'Common Law of England' as 'the best law of any in the world', yet Scots Law was to endure; see James I, *The Workes of the Most High and Mightie Prince, James* (London: Miscellany Press, [1616] 2008), 512.
6. Samuel Daniel, 'A panegyric congratulatory', in Robert Anderson (ed.), *A Complete Edition of the Poets of Great Britain, Volume the Fourth* (London: J. and A. Arthur Arch, 1793), 196.

7. Christopher Hibbert, *The Virgin Queen: A Personal History of Elizabeth I* (London: Tauris Park Paperbacks, 2010), 38.
8. James Shapiro, *1606: William Shakespeare and the Year of Lear* (London: Faber and Faber, 2015), 58; Sarah Waurechen, 'Imagined polities, failed dreams, and the beginnings of an unacknowledged Britain: English responses to James VI and I's vision of perfect union', *Journal of British Studies*, 52: 3 (2013), 575–96.
9. Lori Anne Ferrell, *Government by Polemic: James I, the King's Preachers, and the Rhetorics of Conformity, 1603–1625* (Stanford: Stanford University Press, 1998), 184. For a Scottish perspective, see Roger Alexander Mason, 'Debating Britain in seventeenth-century Scotland: multiple monarchy and Scottish sovereignty', *Journal of Scottish Historical Studies*, 35: 1 (2015), 1–24. Despite the relative small number of Scots living in London in 1570, it should be noted that the 1593 census records that 'the inhabitants of St. Martin's liberty were chiefly French, Germans, Dutch, and Scots'; see Thomas Allen, *The History and Antiquities of London: Westminster, Southwark, and Parts Adjacent* (London: Cowie and Strange, 1839), 51.
10. Shapiro, *1606*, 44.
11. Kirk Melnikoff, 'Robert Greene and the authority of performance', in Melnikoff and Edward Gieskes (eds), *Writing Robert Greene: Essays on England's First Notorious Professional Writer* (London: Routledge, 2016), 39–54, 49.
12. Kristin M. S. Bezio, *Staging Power in Tudor and Stuart English History Plays: History, Political Thought, and the Redefinition of Sovereignty* (London: Routledge, 2015), 76.
13. J. A. Lavin (ed.), *James the Fourth* (London: New Mermaids, 1967), 5, n.d.
14. Alan Hall, *The Border Country: A Walker's Guide* (Milnthorpe: Cicerone, 2012), 104.
15. Robert Greene, *The Scottish History of James the Fourth* (London: New Mermaids [1599] 1967), Chorus 1.11; Chorus 3.5.
16. The 'ay' for 'I' usage might imply pronunciation or a misunderstanding of Scots language.
17. In a curious twist of history, this was a sentiment to be shared by Elizabeth herself some years later. In 1596, the Borders' premier nobleman, Walter Scott of Buccleuch, nearly sparked war between the two kingdoms when he invaded England to free Willie Armstrong of Kinmont. On later being brought before the queen of England, Scott gave a spirited defence of his incursion, to which the queen replied, 'with ten thousand such men, our brother of Scotland might shake the firmest throne in Europe'; see J. S. Roberts, *The Legendary Ballads of England and Scotland* (London: Frederick Warne and Co., 1868), 120.
18. J. O. Bartley, *Teague, Shenkin and Sawney* (Cork: Cork University Press, 1954), 85.
19. Javier Ruano-Garcia, *Early Modern Northern English Lexis: A Literary Corpus-Based Study* (Oxford: Oxford University Press, 2010), 384.
20. Anna Groundwater, *The Scottish Middle March 1573–1625: Power, Kinship, Allegiance* (Chippenham and Eastbourne: Boydell Press, 2010), 176.

21. Ibid. 173–6.
22. The correct placement of the play's interludes is debated; see Melnikoff, 'Robert Greene and the authority of performance', 48.
23. Lisa Hopkins, *Renaissance Drama on the Edge* (London: Routledge, 2014), 64–5.
24. See Childs, *Tudor Sea Power: The Foundation of Greatness* (Barnsley: Seaforth Publishing, 2010), particularly 237, for England's seafaring interventions in Scotland; for the historical Margaret's land crossing see George Goodwin, *Fatal Rivalry, Fatal Rivalry: Henry VIII, James IV and the Battle for Renaissance Britain* (London: Hachette, 2013), 43–8. Lisa Hopkins has suggested that the overland crossing might be excused by the narrative; the king and Dorothea might well have wished to avoid Bohan's lawless borders. Whilst this might be the case, it also allows Greene to contrast the peaceful sea crossing with the later military invasion; see Hopkins, *Renaissance Drama on the Edge*, 64.
25. See Steven Veerapen, '"What think you of this present state?" Representations of Scotland and Anglo-Scottish Union in Greene's *The Scottish History of James the Fourth*, and John Ford's *Perkin Warbeck*', *Early Modern Literary Studies*, 20 (2017), 1–12.
26. The relationship between Elizabeth and James was an interesting one. Though she was to condemn him as a 'false Scotch urchin' in 1581, he was to receive a pension (or, as James preferred, an 'annuity') from England from 1586 onwards in order to cement the Anglo-Scottish league, and to alternately address her as 'sister', 'mother', and 'cousin'; see J. Bruce (ed.), *The Letters of Queen Elizabeth and James VI of Scotland* (London: Camden Society, 1849).
27. E. M. W. Tillyard, *The Elizabethan World Picture* (Harmondsworth: Penguin, 1974), 38.
28. An account of the Stewart Earl and Countess of Arran can be found in Steven J. Reid, 'Of bairns and bearded men: James VI and the Ruthven raid', in Miles Kerr-Peterson and Steven J. Reid (eds), *James VI and Noble Power in Scotland: 1578–1603* (London: Routledge, 2016), 32–56, 37. At the time of the historical James IV's marriage, the 1st Earl of Arran was married to the childless Elizabeth Home. This marriage was dissolved, and he remarried the relatively little-known Janet Bethune (or Beaton) in 1516.
29. This Earl of Arran had once been considered a match for Elizabeth I in her younger years.
30. K. J. Kesselring, *The Northern Rebellion of 1569: Faith, Politics and Protest in Elizabethan England* (Basingstoke: Palgrave Macmillan, 2007), 93.
31. Julian Goodare and Michael Lynch, *The Reign of James VI* (East Linton: Tuckwell Press, 2000), 22.
32. Olga L. Valbuena, *Subjects to the King's Divorce: Equivocation, Infidelity, and Resistance in Early Modern England* (Indiana: Indiana University Press, 2003), 80.
33. Marjorie Garber provides a particularly germane reading of the alleged genealogical line of descent from the legendary Banquo to James VI and I depicted

in the play via mirrors, noting that 'the "glass" is another transgression of the inside/outside boundary, crossing the barrier that separates the play and its spectators'; see Garber, *Shakespeare's Ghost Writers: Literature as Uncanny and Causality* (London: Routledge, 1997), 116. Thomas Kullmann argues that the play's presentation of Fleance and Banquo is not intended to be a celebration of the Stuart dynasty, but 'about the relationship between England and Scotland'. There is no reason that both cannot be correct; see Kullmann, 'Shakespeare and peace', in Ros King and Paul J. C. M. Franssen (eds), *Shakespeare and War* (Basingstoke: Palgrave Macmillan, 2008), 43–55, 49.

34. The first Jacobean English parliament, convened in 1604, was to reveal James' plans; see Andrew D. Nicholls, *The Jacobean Union: A Reconsideration of British Civil Policies under the Early Stuarts* (London: Greenwood, 1999), 30–3.
35. For discussion of Shakespeare's sources, see Kenneth Muir, *The Sources of Shakespeare's Plays* (London: Routledge, 2014), 208–17.
36. Marion Taylor, 'He that did the Tiger Board', *Shakespeare Quarterly*, 15 (1964), 110–13.
37. For discussion of the play's relationship with time, see D. W. Foster, 'Macbeth's war on time', *English Literary Renaissance* 16: 2 (1986), 319–42.
38. Baker, '"Stands Scotland where it did?"', 22.
39. Goodare, 'Scottish politics in the reign of James VI', 44.
40. Scotland's status as a country and nation – 'Poor country'; 'O nation miserable' – is pointed out by Macduff, who seeks aid from England (4.3.32, 104).
41. Goodare and Lynch, *The Reign of James VI*, 21–2.
42. In fairness, it should be noted that although James did not institute a deputy, governor, or lieutenant in Scotland, the Scottish Privy Council was to be relatively successful in continuing to govern and build the nation (which was to lead to anxieties surrounding an independent, militaristic Scotland, as seen in Ford's *Perkin Warbeck*). Nevertheless, this was impossible to predict at the time of *Macbeth*'s creation. Indeed, James himself lamented only a year after Shakespeare's play that he did not 'know the one half' of his former countrymen by face.
43. R. C. McCoy, '"The grace of grace" and double-talk in *Macbeth*', in Peter Holland (ed.), *Shakespeare Survey 57: Macbeth and its Afterlife* (Cambridge: Cambridge University Press, 2004), 27–37, 30.
44. Arthur F. Kinney, *Lies Like Truth: Shakespeare, Macbeth, and the Cultural Moment* (Detroit: Wayne Street University Press, 2001), 97–8.
45. Lorna Hutson, 'Forensic History: Henry V and Scotland', in Lorna Hutson (ed.), *The Oxford Handbook of English Law and Literature, 1500–1700* (Oxford: Oxford University Press, 2017), 687–708, 695, 704.
46. The 'head' is a familiar topos in discourses of kingship, forged into gory literalism in the play's climax. It should be noted also that James was known for declaring himself the 'head' of his kingdoms. In 1604 he declared, 'I am the head, and it is my body . . . I hope, therefore, that no man will be so

unreasonable as to think that . . . I being the head, should have a divided and monstrous body'; see Keith M. Brown, 'The vanishing emperor: British kingship and its decline, 1603–1707', in Roger A. Mason (ed.), *Scots and Britons: Scottish Political Thought and the Union of 1603* (Cambridge: Cambridge University Press, 2006), 58–87, 60–2, for discussion of James' failed attempts to convince the English political community of arguments via heavy-handed parliamentary interventions.

47. Hopkins, *Renaissance Drama on the Edge*, 83.
48. Neil Rhodes, 'Wrapped in the strong arms of the Union: Shakespeare and King James', in Willy Maley and Andrew Murphy (eds), *Shakespeare and Scotland* (Manchester: Manchester University Press, 2004), 37–52, 42.
49. A useful account of the little-known *The Valiant Scot* can be found in Siobhan Keenan, *Acting Companies and their Plays in Shakespeare's London* (London: Arden, 2014), 157–64.
50. See Lisa Hopkins, *Drama and the Succession to the Crown* (London: Ashgate, 2011), 139; Gilles Monsarrat, 'John Ford's substantive accidentals in *Perkin Warbeck*', *The Library*, 16: 4 (2015), 446–57; and Steven Veerapen, 'European unions: The Spanish wife and the Scottish widow in Shakespeare and Fletcher's *Henry VIII* and Ford's *Perkin Warbeck*', *Early Modern Literary Studies*, 27 (2017), 1–12.

3

Shakespeare, King James and the Northern Yorkists

Richard Stacey

This chapter explores the influence of the House of York upon Shakespeare's most trenchant response to the Stuart accession, *Macbeth*. At first it may seem like a strange connection. James VI was a Scottish monarch at the head of a nation that had endured numerous assaults by the Yorkist regime in the previous century, most notably the invasion of 1482, which attempted to install a puppet king on the throne and seize large swathes of land south of Edinburgh for the English state.[1] The aggressive behaviour of the Yorkists was chronicled by Scottish historians, and the memory of their ruthless expansion into the North lingered on well into the sixteenth century.[2] Yet the competition for the English crown occasioned by the impending death of Elizabeth I necessitated a revision of long-held suspicions and prejudices. James was himself part-Yorkist, tracing his heritage through the maternal line of Margaret Tudor. His proximity to Elizabeth in the order of succession was a significant element of the Stuart claim, and helped in part to ensure the smooth and surprisingly conflict-free transfer of power in 1603. As part of his engagement with the new political establishment, Shakespeare chose to rework a number of tropes from his earlier plays, particularly those from the 1590s which debated the succession question. *Macbeth*, first performed in 1606, is notable for its use of the imagery and theatrical rhetoric previously associated with the House of York, a northern dynasty which, like the Stuarts, had a circuitous claim to the throne. Focusing on *Macbeth*, the following argument will trace the complex relationship between James and the House of York in polemical literature, before considering the use of Yorkism more broadly as a basis to fashion an Anglo-Scottish conception of statehood. A careful examination of these topics will reveal that there was often more white than red in the Tudor rose inherited by James.

Yorkism and the Stuart Accession

In an introduction to a 1616 verse translation of John Barbour's medieval poem on the reign of Robert the Bruce, the printer Andro Hart distances the work from the politicised reading practices which had come to define much historiographical output in the first decades of the seventeenth century:

> There be some who hold the opinion that the publishing of those bookes is hurtfull, as embers of consumed discord, but it is not the publishing of the simplicitie of our predecessours that can divide us, or cause any discord, but rather our owne too great subteltie, ambition & avarice, & the turning the pages of *Tacitus* & of Secretar *Machiavell* that can breed an ague in our state. Can the reading of the warres betwixt *Longcaster* & *Yorke* separate the red & white Roses? I thinke no.[3]

According to Hart it is not the act of memorialising the past that can breed dissension, but the wilful identification of motives which might only be half-articulated in the text. To abuse the 'simplicitie' of previous ages by forging a precedent for ambition is a practice which directly leads to factionalism and division. In order to demonstrate his point, and place Tacitus and Machiavelli in a more local intellectual context, Hart uses the example of the warring Houses of York and Lancaster, whose rival claim to the throne was successfully unified by the marriage of Henry Tudor and Elizabeth of York, and whose eldest lineal heir currently ruled as James VI and I of Scotland and England.[4] Teasing out the primacy of the Yorkist claim over the Lancastrian, for example, would be to probe too deeply into current politics and run the risk of sowing discord in an only recently consolidated state.

It might seem that the allusion to the Yorkists and Lancastrians was a chance for a Scottish printer based in Edinburgh to draw attention to the lack of stability in recent English political history. Yet throughout the 1590s, Hart had been employed by William Cecil as a spy to offer information on James and his court in relation to the Stuart claim to the throne, and provide him with details of the succession literature being surreptitiously printed on the continent. A cursory glance at the work of polemicists such as Robert Persons, Peter Wentworth and Irenicus Philodikaios reveals that the identification of competing blood-claims – separating the 'red & white Roses', in England and in other countries such as Spain and Portugal – was a defining trope of the genre, and one liable to provoke the ire of the Elizabethan establishment. Hart's preface in 1616, then, reveals a more conciliatory position, in which he aims to distance himself from his earlier activities in print by disavowing the heightened scrutiny encouraged by English succession literature, thereby endorsing the rule of James VI and I and his twin monarchies. It is also a subtle attempt to align himself with his subject, John Barbour, who wrote the original poem *The Bruce* in the 1370s to commemorate his patron, the first Stuart monarch Robert II.[5]

As a subject of James VI, Hart does not seem to define his political and cultural identity in exclusively Scottish terms. Rather, he uses the image of the English blended rose to associate internal stability with a fundamental lack of 'division'. In this, he is possibly offering a further sign of his obedience to James by gesturing to an extended metaphor that the king often used to promote a Unionist agenda; in one of his earliest speeches to the English parliament, for example, James stated that 'the Union of these two princely Houses', through which he is 'justly and lineally descended', is 'nothing comparable to the Union of two ancient and famous Kingdoms, which is the other inward Peace annexed to my Person'.[6] Yet in practice, James often favoured his Yorkist heritage, exploiting the association of the House of York with the North to inculcate his policies within a largely resistant populace on both sides of the border; to quote David Womersley, 'the stricter primogenitural basis of the Yorkist claim to the throne made them in their turn a proxy for the succession of James VI of Scotland'.[7] Although Andro Hart cautioned his readers against teasing out the different claims of the Yorkists and Lancastrians, this was one of the chief pleasures of the form. In the small body of succession literature which did manage to trickle through the censorship restrictions of the late-Elizabethan regime, readers in the 1580s and 1590s had a rare opportunity to weigh the respective merits of different claimants. The House of Stuart had several advantages, including their dominant place in a strict model of male-preference primogeniture. As the eldest heir of Margaret Tudor, the senior daughter of Henry VII, James bypassed the Suffolk line of the younger daughter Mary, and claimed primacy over English peers such as the Earl of Derby and the Seymour brothers. However, there were serious impediments in the form of the Henrician Succession Acts of the 1530s and 1540s, which barred the heirs natural of the Stuart line from ascending the throne on the death of Henry VIII and his children without issue. Such a process placed the succession in the prerogative of the monarch and opened the possibility that the endorsement of a new ruler was dependent, to an extent, on the acquiescence of parliament.[8] Elizabeth was notoriously silent on this complex issue, however, and the Stuarts were tacitly regarded as the strongest claimants in the years leading up to her death.[9]

This schema was strongly challenged in succession tracts with an anti-Stuart agenda. The most influential of these was *A Conference upon the Next Succession* by Robert Persons, which cast aspersions on James' twin claim by positing that he was merely the successor of the House of York rather than both royal lines. Persons' reasoning was derived from the writings of an obscure figure named Robert Highington, who used Henry VII's descent from John of Gaunt's third wife Katherine Swynford, and the status of their children as retrospectively legitimised bastards, to posit that the Tudor-Lancastrian claim was weak and highly suspect in relation to inheritance law:

> this man (I meane Highington) maketh the king of Spayne to be the next and most righful pretender by the house of Lancaster, for proofe wherof he holdeth first that king Henry the 7. had no title in deede to the crowne by Lancaster; but only by the house of York, that is to saye; by his marriage of Queene Elizabeth elder daughter to king Edward the fourth, for that albeit himselfe were discended by his mother from Iohn of Gaunt duke of Lancaster, yet this was but by his third wife Catherin Swynford.[10]

If the reader is tempted to turn a blind eye to this loophole, Persons makes the point clear: 'I meane aswel the line of Scotland'.[11] As a Yorkshire Catholic who was compelled to flee England after his role in the Rising of the North in 1569, Highington's strategy was designed to relegate the Stuart claim to that of the Portuguese royal family on the continent. The reason for this was rooted in religion. It was assumed that James' Protestant beliefs would encourage him to adopt harsh measures against his Catholic subjects, so a more sympathetic ruler was sought through the descendants of Blanche of Lancaster. Persons argues, via Highington, that Henry VII's rule was unlawful as he had little right to claim a position of primacy in the Lancastrian succession. As Henry's heirs were therefore illegitimate, the next logical step would be to invite a Catholic monarch with purer blood to assume the throne; to quote Rei Kanemura, 'it was not the King of Scots but the Spanish Infanta who was the real Lancastrian heir'.[12] A host of Catholic pamphleteers used the Lancastrian claim as a basis to denigrate the Stuart cause and promote the candidacy of other figures, such as Philip II. William Allen, a prominent Catholic with Yorkshire roots, suggested that the Protestant faith practised in both Scotland and England had reduced 'so florishing and auncyent a commonwealth' to 'destruction' and called upon the king of Spain to restore the English to 'their auncient liberty of lawes' under papal control.[13] Persons observed that 'the king [i.e., James] is tossed and tumbled by troublesome people' due to the engorged role of the Kirk in internal Scottish politics, and Richard Verstegan warned the Elizabethan Protestant establishment to be mindful of vengeance for 'injuries ... so great, as the cutting of of his owne mothers head'.[14] The Highington line of argument therefore had several implications which shaped the popular perception of James in the English political imaginary: as insular rather than continental; as doggedly Protestant with the potential to upend international relations; and bent on revenge for the execution of Mary Queen of Scots.

However, the pejorative associations of Yorkism articulated by Persons (and Highington) could swiftly be turned by James' supporters to his advantage. Like Elizabeth, the 'line of Scotland' advocates were adherents to Reformed faith. Paulina Kewes observes that '*A Conference* paradoxically boosted the chances of the main hereditary contender, James VI of Scotland. Vilified by a papist, James became more attractive to Protestants of all hues'.[15] Yet there were other representations of the House of York within English culture which were more problematic. Although the Yorkists claimed superiority over the Lancastrians in the succession, this was displaced through the female line twice. By sheer coincidence, James traced his Tudor heritage in the same way, calling male-preference primogeniture, and even Salic conceptions of inheritance, into question, and threatening to bring about the same fissures which had dogged the country in the late fifteenth century.[16] There was also the issue of parliament. Both Edward IV and Richard III had ambiguous routes to power which rested, to an extent, on the endorsement of the commons, as Peter Wentworth indicated:

> if the crowne might be lawfully given at the pleasure of a Parliament, what reason is there to call Rich. 3. or any such others, usurpers? ... unles the right of succession were a thing impregnable by any Parliament, by what reason, or with what face could the Duke of Yorke or Edward the fourth, so boldly & confidentlie have claimed the crown in the verie Parliament it self?'[17]

The two Yorkist monarchs are explicitly identified as co-opting parliament to ratify a tenuous blood claim, thereby challenging the supposed inviolability of hereditary right by reinforcing it with a type of elected mandate. James ran a similar risk of compromising his own position by the necessary repeal of the Henrician Succession Acts, thus subverting his superior claim even as it was publicly recognised. In tandem with this point, the North had accrued an association throughout the Tudor period with the twin evils of rebellion and recusancy. Yorkshire in particular had rebelled three times in the preceding century, and Catholicism was widely practised throughout the shire.[18] If James was perceived to be a pure Yorkist rather than a mixed Plantagenet, as suggested by Highington and Persons, then his political reputation in English circles was oddly commensurate with the persona espoused by his detractors, centring as it did on suspected Catholic sympathy and an estrangement from the traditional centres of English power. The Stuart apologist Henry Constable was compelled to defend James from a charge of excessive tolerance due to 'the favour that he hath shewed to some Catholickes', for example, and John Colville wisely reminded his readers that 'Scotland is no more secluded' than other fringes of the British island, such as 'Wales & Cornewall'.[19]

James' association with the North was further complicated by the issue of ethnicity. The turn towards antiquarian studies in the late sixteenth century had shed light on the ethnic composition of the northern British archipelago to reveal an intricate patterning of different groups. Historiographers either side of the border such as Hector Boece and William Camden were keen to stress that the Scottish nation comprised 'thre syndry pepyll'.[20] These were the Scots who, to quote Camden, '[came] out of Ireland' and 'planted themselves in this Isle the North side of Cluid'; the Picts, who settled in the East after a westward migration from Denmark; and the Britons, who travelled north from Galicia in Spain and settled in Brittany, Cornwall, Wales and the Scottish lowlands around Galloway.[21] James' identification as a Briton would have been strongly reinforced by his genealogy, which traced the Stuart line back to Brittany and accounted for its presence in Scotland as part of the widespread political diaspora during the Norman Conquest.[22] He was also, of course, half-English; Henry, Lord Darnley, was a Yorkshireman, born and raised in Temple Newsom a few miles outside of Leeds.[23] As the Darnley heir, James could demonstrate his Englishness not only through his Plantagenet roots but by his paternity, supplanting any doubts regarding his suitability to inherit the throne twice over. But it is here that the situation becomes more complex. As a Yorkshireman, Darnley may not have had such an easy claim to an Anglo-Saxon identity. To quote the statesman Samuel Lewkenor, in a travel guide to Santiago de Compostela:

> This cittie of ancient historiographers was called in time passed Brigantium, from whence the Irish nation, the Scots in Galloway, & our Northerne Yorkshire men, called in old authors Brigantes, glory & boast, that they have received the first originall of their race.[24]

Rather than dilute James' Celtic ethnicity, Darnley's status as a Yorkshireman, with its Galloway affiliation, had the potential to effectively double it. This provided a potent context within which to situate Highington's conception of James as a Yorkist. The House of York was deeply rooted in the history and cultural identity of Yorkshire. Not only did it take its ducal title from the second largest city in the country and own most of the county land, it was tied to a range of smaller fiefdoms; Richard of Gloucester, for example, was raised at Middleham castle near Wensleydale and held the Honour of Richmond, a semi-autonomous region of the North which Michael Drayton characterised as a 'shire' that was 'subject' to the 'mightie king' of Yorkshire.[25] The City of York famously opened its gates to Edward IV, and according to Philip Schwyzer maintained 'an enduring attachment to Richard's memory' long after his defeat at Bosworth.[26] The Yorkshire – and Yorkist – blood of James was liable to accentuate the suspect allegiances of the 'line of Scotland' rather than ameliorate them.

James' identity, then, provided him with a number of problems in his attempt to promote his candidacy for the English throne. As a Scot with Yorkshire roots he was ethnically distinct from a swathe of the English population, particularly those clustered in the South and East; as a Stuart barred by statute, he risked reducing his monarchy to a conciliatory office. Rather than let these impediments stand in his way, however, James used them to articulate his vision for a unified state, exploiting his position as a Yorkshire Briton to embody a conception of Britishness which traversed Scottish and English divisions. In his early political rhetoric, James effected a subtle shift whereby the names of his two kingdoms were changed to 'our native and ancient countrey of North Britaine' and 'the Estates of South Britaine' respectively; as someone whose British heritage traversed both polities, and who could claim to be northern in both English and Scottish terms, he was in a perfect position to propose the dissolution of distinctions between the two nations.[27] It is no coincidence that the word 'Britain' in pro-Union literature was sometimes spelt 'Brittanie'.[28] Francis Bacon rejoiced that 'this Iland of great Brittanie is now joyned in Monarchie for the ages to come'.[29] The Scottish divine John Gordon echoed this sentiment, stating 'what a great benefit God hath powred foorth vpon this Iland of great Brittannie, in choosing it to be the holy place, wherein this admirable vnion of God and man is conioined in the person of a Britaine King'.[30] Gordon used the analogy to associate James with 'Constantinus Magnus' who 'mysticallie' arrived in 'Britannie' to convert the island to Christianity; tellingly, he reminded the reader that Constantine 'died at Yorke' and transferred sovereignty to his son from this location.[31]

Such allusions were cultivated by pro-Union apologists such as Bacon and Gordon to emphasise the indigenous aspects of James' heritage, and stress his ability to heal division not only between the states of Scotland and England but other areas of early modern intellectual life, such as the Church.

The literary community in London was quick to respond to the new set of circumstances. Panegyrics in praise of James often define his northern identity in relation to his embryonic Britishness and potential to establish a nascent empire. In a poem celebrating the Stuart accession through the figure of Cadwallader, William Herbert, 3rd Earl of Pembroke drew on his Welsh heritage to reflect on the creation of the new British state:

> All haile great Monarch of the greatest Ile,
> The Northerne worlds vnited lawfull King,
> Pardon my rudest reede vndecent stile,
> Though I want Skill in thy new Empires spring,
> Yet doe I loue, and will thy prayses sing.[32]

Herbert constructs James as a 'Northerne' monarch whose origin provides him with a unique propensity to facilitate a 'vnited' state. The reference to the North and the 'empire' recur in a panegyric by Herbert's former tutor Samuel Daniel; in his own poem, Daniel states that James has 'Unbarr'd the North' and will 'make this Empire of the North to shine' through his munificence.[33] Herbert and Daniel use this strain of rhetoric to allude to the biblical figure of Jacob, who was told in a dream by God that his 'seed' would spread to 'the North, and to the South, and in thee and in thy seed shall all the families of the earth be blessed'.[34] The theological controversialist James Maxwell later employed this analogy to praise James in political terms: 'oft did I thinke of Almighty Gods raising of you our Jacob from the North . . . among your owne ununiformed [ie. diverse] Britaines'.[35] A raft of intellectuals, spanning the aristocracy, clergy and cultural elite, were therefore attuned to a project which associated James' northern origins with the fomentation of a British state predicated on imperial expansion southwards, bolstered by a recognisably Protestant mandate. Significantly in this context, Herbert opens his oration with a paean to the House of York: 'You that did euer with your swords maintaine, / The vndoubted title of the whiter Rose'.[36] As a Welsh aristocrat, Herbert may have wanted to stress his own Celtic origins to benefit from the favour being extended to peers with Yorkist credentials. On entering York, for instance, James selected to carry the ceremonial sword George Clifford, 3rd Earl of

Cumberland, an aristocrat whose stepmother was descended from Henry VII through the Suffolk line and was, according to Highington, a Yorkist. The king also appointed Edmund Sheffield, 3rd Baron Sheffield as Lord President of the Council of the North, a conciliar body established by Richard III; Sheffield's mother Douglas Howard had recently married Sir Edward Stafford, who was also a hereditary Yorkist. For Herbert, James appeared to be using his cultural and ethnic association with the North to cultivate the support of a group of aristocrats who were connected by family ties to this specific facet of his complex English heritage. By associating a British poem with the House of York, Herbert is therefore inculcating himself within an emergent coterie that married a type of political nativism to a small Celtic oligarchy as a prelude to the hoped-for implementation of a unified state.

The trend of poeticising James as a northern imperialist is also evident in a little-known poetic miscellany from 1603 titled *Northerne poems congratulating the Kings majesties entrance to the crowne*. The anonymous poet dedicates the work to Edmund Sheffield in the hope that 'as you are the worthy President of the North countrey, so it will please you to bee the honourable Patrone of these Northerne poems'.[37] The collection is an attempt to articulate the Stuart accession from a northern perspective for a primarily London-based clientele:

> Al evill from the North saith proverbe olde,
> But we may saye, the North sends us most good,
> Our gratious king with offspring manifold
> From thence derives his stocke and royall bloud.[38]

The poet begins by revising the proverb 'Out of the North all ill comes forth' to offer a view centred on the restorative potential of the Stuart dynasty.[39] The use of pronouns is finely calibrated to position the speaker, and the intended reader, between both sides of the border; although the depiction of the North as a location from which James originates suggests that it is a fundamentally separate space from the English court, the inclusive phrase 'our king', and the explicit association of the collection with the North in the prefatory material, serve to obfuscate any barriers that are evoked. The reference to James' 'stocke' is also complicated by his Yorkshire heritage, which is presumably shared by the poet and the countrymen for whom he speaks, evoking a Yorkist context which emphasises James' ethnic similarity to his new northern subjects as opposed to his cultural or political differences. There may even be a covert allusion to the Yorkist context of James' accession later in the collection through a reference to '*Allin* of Rome by title Cardinall, / The scourge & shame of England'.[40] William Allen, of course, worked closely with Robert Persons to investigate the English succession and disseminate his conclusions in print through a network of recusant coteries; as someone who favoured a Lancastrian successor, and even wrote to Philip II of Spain to encourage the 1588 Armada, it is almost certain he subscribed to the Highington view of the Tudor-Stuart line as Yorkist in nature alongside the other Catholic pamphleteers.[41] *Northerne poems* can be placed alongside the work of more celebrated figures such as William Herbert and Samuel Daniel to offer an insight into the complexities attendant on James' assumption of power at a crucial juncture. It is part of a poetic trend in the years 1603–4 which celebrates the new regime through a special identification between the Stuart dynasty and the English North, centred on ethnic affiliation and political sympathy via the Yorkist inheritance.

This is the cultural context, then, within which Shakespeare wrote *Macbeth*. As part of its examination of contemporary politics, the play dramatises the overlap between spatial boundaries, particularly those which coalesce around the border between Scotland and England; it also blurs the line between hereditary right and public assent through the sequential rule of Duncan, Macbeth, Malcolm and, later, the heirs of Banquo. Although many Londoners would have viewed the Scottish king with suspicion, Shakespeare weighs the merits of Jacobean kingship proposed by his supporters, centring on due right of inheritance and a less threatening, even native, ethnicity. However, there is also an attempt to draw attention to the suppleness of Yorkist politics, which often couches itself in the seductive rhetoric of shared affiliation as a method of ensuring its own survival.

Macbeth and the Yorkist Influence

When Simon Forman noted his observations on a performance of *Macbeth* that he saw at The Globe, he made a small but telling error in his recreation of the plot:

> And so they departed & cam to the Courte of Scotland to Dunkin king of Scotes, and yt was in the dais of Edward the Confessor. And Dunkin bad them both kindly welcome, And made Mackbeth forth with Prince of Northumberland.[42]

Macbeth was not made the Prince of Northumberland, of course, but the Thane of Cawdor. Forman has probably confused this moment with

Duncan's decision to offer Malcolm the title of 'the Prince of Cumberland' (1.4.39), which occurs a few scenes later in the printed Folio text; both Northumberland and Cumberland were border shires, and Northumberland appears as a prominent character in the latter half of the play. However, it also points to the increasing fluidity with which the spatial polity of the British Isles was regarded in a play which anticipated the merging of the two crowns. As prince of Northumberland, Macbeth is interpreted, or even constructed, as a proto-Anglo-Scot, with an endowment that collapses the difference in territorial sovereignty which had defined political and diplomatic relations throughout the previous Tudor era. In Scottish politics, the Prince of Cumberland was the title of the heir apparent to the throne, so Macbeth is even positioned as an elected heir, whose insertion in the succession exerts a claim which binds, rather than separates, the two nations either side of the border. It is impossible to fully account for Forman's misreading of the plot, yet it certainly offers an insight not only into the political context in which the play was initially received, centring on Unionist anxieties, but also into the crucial role of the English North as a revised, unstable marker of statehood in the changing landscape of the 1600s.[43]

Macbeth appeared on the London stage in 1606, when the English succession was no longer in doubt. At this time, we find a small resurgence of theatrical material on Yorkist themes, such as Shakespeare's *Richard III* and Heywood's *The first and second parts of King Edward the Fourth*, which were both reissued in quarto editions in 1605.[44] In detailing the exploits of the two most prominent monarchs of the House of York, these plays from the 1590s would have spoken to a readership whose new king shared a particular association with the Yorkists through his bloodline and his northern origin. Like his forebears, James held fast to a strict interpretation of primogeniture which necessitated the co-operation of parliament in order to ratify his claim. *Macbeth*, in its depiction of a figure who appears to be elected yet lives in fear of his sceptre being 'wrenched to an unlineal hand' (3.1.62), was part of this theatrical trend.[45] Although the play is not set in the late fifteenth century, and does not represent anyone associated with the House of York, its treatment of inheritance, right to rule and regionalism was coloured by debates on Yorkism in political literature, particularly in the succession tracts which explored the dynastic merits of the Stuart line. A theatre-goer with an interest in contemporary politics could effectively use *Macbeth*, alongside the print reissues of *Richard III* and *King Edward the Fourth*, to construct a miniature Yorkist canon of works debating the complex intersection between James' northern heredity and the strength of his claim to the English crown.

Succession pamphleteers sympathetic to James were keen to distance his monarchical identity from the worst excesses of the House of York, even as they stressed the legitimacy of his genealogical descent. This was because the Yorkists were seen as familicides who allowed personal ambition to destroy the natural order of succession by repeated acts of kin-slaying. The writer who adopted the pen name Irenicus Philodikaios constructed an image of the House of York as a defective dynasty cursed by a fatal flaw - the inability of its members to stop murdering each other:

> The trueth heereof is manifest by the example of King Edward the fowrth, and Richard the third: who both not onlie destroied, and bannished their enemies of the house of Lancaster, with their adherents; but also the former of them put to death his own brother, George Duke of Clarence, and the other murthered his young nephues, Edward the fift, and his brother.[46]

Philodikaios' vision of a successful House corrupted by the rupture of familial bonds is part of the 'mirror for princes' tradition, in which James is tacitly warned of the dangers of paranoia.[47] The depiction of the Yorkists as kin-slayers is almost an allegorical shorthand for bad government, predicated on the wilful disruption of lineal descent by the fear of overly ambitious minor royals once a power base has been established. *Macbeth*, and the other Yorkist plays which were reissued in the years 1605–6, feature this trope obsessively. Once Duncan has been killed, Macbeth caricatures Malcolm and Donalbain as treasonous subjects who have committed the double sin of regicide and patricide:

> We hear our bloody cousins are bestowed
> In England and in Ireland, not confessing
> Their cruel parricide, filling their hearers
> With strange invention. (3.1.29–32)

Macbeth's use of the word 'invention' evokes the rhetorical practice of the careful selection of material in the construction of an argument.[48] Macbeth warns his listeners to be on their guard against the persuasive arguments fashioned by Malcolm and Donalbain, which are designed to castigate Macbeth as a tyrant and excuse their own murderous behaviour. However, this is itself a masterly example of 'strange invention' (3.1.32), drawing on the popular perception of the House of York as familicides to condemn the two lawful heirs with the twinned crimes of kin and king killing. If a reader felt inclined to consult the recently reissued version of *Richard III* in 1605, they would encounter the Duchess of York describing her own progeny as 'mak[ing] war upon themselves, brother to brother, / Blood to blood, self against self' (2.4.63–4). *Macbeth* uses the trope of internecine bloodshed in Yorkist dramaturgy to produce a narrative whereby Duncan's line is unfit to rule through a similar propensity to destroy itself from within. In the context of election, Macbeth is presented as the best candidate for the throne because he cannot by definition commit 'parricide' (3.1.31), allowing him to morally castigate the severance of heredity by Duncan's heirs even while the succession is upended by his own machinations. Donalbain recognises the persuasiveness of such oratory as he leaves Scotland for his safety, stating 'the near in blood, / The nearer bloody' (2.4.140–2). Condemnation of ambition via kin-killing in theatrical discourse is thus a method through which that ambition can be paradoxically fostered, enacting the 'dissembling' (1.1.19) of stage Yorkists such as Richard at the level of inference and historical analogy. Macbeth's use of the memorable phrase 'bloody cousins' (3.1.29) may also have evoked the complex inter-relations between the various claimants to the English throne prior to the accession. Elizabeth and James often used the word 'cousin' to refer to each other, as did Elizabeth and James' mother Mary Queen of Scots, who were both cousins of James' father, Darnley, himself another claimant.[49] The internecine assaults committed by these figures, including the murder of Darnley on Mary's orders, and her own public execution by Elizabeth, would have had a distinctly Yorkist flavour. In Holinshed, one of Shakespeare's source texts, Macbeth's and Duncan's mothers are described as sisters; Duncan's mother Beatrice was the sister of Macbeth's mother Doada, who were both the younger sisters of the reigning king Malcolm. As Duncan traced his claim through the maternal line, there is, of course, a striking correlation between the familial structure of the ancient Scottish succession and the Stuart claim via Henry VIII's eldest sister Margaret Tudor.[50] It is possible that Shakespeare's decision to excise this familial connection in his own narrative is an attempt to deflect the transference of power between Duncan and Macbeth from the matrilineal line of descent, which of course characterised both Stuart and Yorkist heredity.

There are other moments whereby a theatre-goer may have used the small number of Yorkist plays in current circulation to establish textual or metaphorical parallels across texts. When Macbeth sees the ghost of Duncan, he marvels at the lack of fear exhibited by the other guests: 'you can behold such sights / And keep the natural ruby of our cheeks / When mine is blanched with fear' (3.4.112–14). The image of white offset against red, especially in body parts, is a recurring trope used to delineate the different factions of York and Lancaster in Shakespearean dramaturgy.[51] In *Richard III*, the vision of a white face is used when the surviving Yorkists learn that Richard has arranged for his brother Clarence to be murdered: 'no man in the presence / But his red colour hath forsook his cheeks' (2.1.85–6). In a similar manner, Shakespeare uses the colour white to associate Macbeth's horror at his act of regicide with the severance of lineal hereditary succession. There may have also been a subtler inference at work here. Throughout his reign James was associated with the white topoi of the House of York, particularly in charged contexts which necessitated the use of a code-image to question the validity of the Stuart claim. For example, in a disputation with the Catholic preacher Thomas Percy, popularly known by the pseudonym 'Fisher', James appears to have been publicly dismissed as a 'White Rose'. The only evidence available to account for this odd personification is a written denunciation of Percy's arguments after the fact by the divine Francis White, who states that 'the White Rose you speake of, by your malice, might againe turne Red'.[52] No transcript was made of the disputation, so we are obliged to infer that Percy characterised James as a 'White Rose' as an insult, necessitating White's use of paradiastole, and a pun on his own name, to turn the metaphor to a more threatening end. As Percy was a Jesuit who preached in Yorkshire, and was therefore receptive to a Lancastrian intervention from the Spanish and Portuguese claimants on the continent, it is likely that he was subtly alluding to the Highington controversy to cast aspersions on James' lineage and right to rule. There are other uses of white and red corporeality in *Macbeth* which would have evoked northern culture. Near the end of the play Macbeth describes his servant as a 'cream-faced loon' who should 'o'er red' his 'fear' with blood (5.3.11, 14). A. R. Braunmuller glosses the word 'loon' as a Scotticism but the *OED* traces its etymology to the Old Norse word 'lúenn', citing it as the source of an insult in the dialect of the English North.[53] Macbeth's image is intricately located in the vernacular of the borderlands, directly associating red and white affective responses with spatial – and lexical – slippage in a context of Anglo-Scottish regime change between monarchs. Shakespeare's uses of this thread of imagery, and the triggering of its attendant political associations, therefore construct Macbeth as the potential embodiment of a contemporary strain of Yorkism which is fundamentally pejorative in import. James, like Macbeth, is a northern Scot who uses his suspect allegiances to establish a power base which could be interpreted as expansionist in nature, and which is pursued at the expense of individuals with an arguably stronger claim, such as Malcolm and Donalbain, or the Spanish Infanta.

However, there are other conceptual strains at work in *Macbeth* which embody the alternative model of Yorkism founded on proto-British Union explored earlier. When the play opens, Macbeth and Banquo have just returned from a Highland revolt by the Thane of Cawdor and Sweno the 'Norwegian lord' (1.2.31), who are both supported by 'kerns and galloglasses' from the 'Western Isles' (1.2.12–13). In this figuration, the nobility are positioned in opposition to an antagonistic force entrenched in a northern hinterland, comprised of marginal groups with a distinct Scottish and Pict ethnicity; correspondingly, the Scots with which the audience are encouraged to identify occupy a southern vanguard, which mimics an English battalion. Willy Maley has alluded to the propensity of the English state to implement imperialist policies within British borders to replicate, in miniature, the expansion of Catholic continental powers: 'The Reformation put Union high on the agenda, as England began the retreat into Britain, a retreat from Europe that was also a westward and northern expansion of Englishness'.[54] If the play was read through the lens of Yorkism, we can see an intriguing parallel, even at this early stage, between James' desire to emphasise his similarity to his English subjects, and Shakespeare's presentation of a British state in fomentation. Macbeth is fighting to quell a revolt which is positioned as the North in geographical relation to the court, which is largely comprised of Lowland Britons. In this schema, Shakespeare's version of Scotland is fashioned as a civilising force tasked with bringing the unstable, barbaric fringes into line; Sweno's Scandinavian ethnicity would have recalled the Pict migration from Denmark, and the 'galloglasses' (1.1.13) were understood to be Highland mercenaries descended from the Irish. The war in the opening scene replicates the larger English project to civilise Celtic nations such as Ireland in the late sixteenth and early seventeenth centuries, defined by Edmund Spenser as a process of 'reducing [the] salvage nations' to 'better goverment and civillity'.[55] The suggestion of an Anglicised force battling a group of rebels on the edge of the nation is a recurring trope in the spatial organisation of the English state in Yorkist drama. In Heywood's 1605 edition of *King Edward the Fourth*, for example, the play opens with a rebellion 'from euerie part of Sussex, Kent, and Esier' (sig.A2v). Edward is described as an 'emperiall maiestie' (sig.A2r) who must save the state from the 'hedge-bred rascals' and 'filthie frie of ditches' (sig.B3v) who are threatening to topple his rule. Both *Macbeth* and *King Edward the Fourth* present a polity in which rebellion is pushed to the literal margins of the state, revealing a centralised view of power which appears to be positioned squarely in the middle of the Isle – not North as in the Highlands, not South as in Kent, but somewhere which traverses both liminalities.[56]

Crucially, it is not Macbeth who is placed at the centre of this conception of Scotland but Malcolm, who states: 'This is the sergeant, / Who like a good and hearty soldier fought / 'Gainst my captivity' (1.1.3–5). Malcolm, as critics have noted, is an Anglo-Scot; according to Sharon Alker and Holly Faith Nelson, he is a political figure 'whose actions imply consent to an English hegemony', using the support of his maternal uncle Northumberland to foreshadow Scotland's submission to the authority of England.[57] Yet from a Yorkist perspective this argument is slightly too neat. Malcolm's position as both Scottish and English would not only have prefigured an ideal confluence of ethnic Britishness but recalled James' dual Celtic ancestry through the Darnley line. Rather than being an architect of Scottish decline, as argued by Alker and Nelson, Malcolm appears to embody a concept of Unionism through his ability to tie the English North via Seward to a political body of Britons, distinct from the isolated and unresponsive 'skipping kerns' (1.1.30). In the milieu of renewed interest in Yorkism, this is likely to have evoked James' complex relationship to his own heritage. The rhetoric of James' supporters such as Francis Bacon and John Gordon, writing in the mid-1600s, used the Briton origin of the king to stress his shared Yorkist affiliation with much of the English population in the North. As Malcolm has a similar mixture of northern English and Scottish blood in his genealogy and is regarded by his peers as the future hope of Scotland, he is positioned as the head of a state, which appears to correlate national stability with ethnic and political mingling. Shakespeare's depiction of the Scottish court is therefore reflective of some of the tenets of pro-Stuart apologia in the early years of James' reign, which used his Yorkist blood as a basis to posit Union as a necessary prelude to social cohesion, something that other claimants lingering in the public consciousness, such as the Lancastrian candidates on the continent, could never feasibly achieve.

Malcolm would have evoked other conceptions of Yorkism at various points in the play. When testing the loyalty of Macduff, he constructs himself as a model 'bad' king in a manner which offers the audience an unambiguous parody of Edward IV, familiar through popular drama and chronicle literature:

> I grant him bloody,
> Luxurious, avaricious, false, deceitful,
> Sudden, malicious, smacking of every sin
> That has a name. But there's no bottom, none,
> In my voluptuousness. (4.3.57–61)

Edward IV was often depicted as a voraciously sexualised epicure, known for his affair with Jane Shore and unconstitutional marriage to the commoner Elizabeth Woodville which fatally compromised his royal authority; to quote Edward Hall, 'vnaduised wowyng, hasty louyng, and to spedy mariage, were neither meete for him beyng a kyng, nor consonant to the honor of so high an estate'.[58] Heywood adopts these criticisms in the 1605 quarto of *King Edward the Fourth*, to the extent that Edward boasts of his 'proud, saucie roauing eye' (sig.D4r) to his supporters. The pervasiveness of Edward's reputation for lechery is the reason Shakespeare's Richard III is able to cast aspersions on his fitness to rule so easily, imploring Buckingham to 'urge his hateful luxury / And bestial appetite in change of lust' (3.5.80–1). When Malcolm is testing the loyalty of Macduff, he obviously uses the perception of Yorkist intemperance to associate sexual profligacy with bad kingship. Yet this is couched in irony. As a scion of pro-Stuart Yorkism, Malcolm is displacing his vision of bad rule onto a political stereotype which is culturally redolent of Yorkist royal conduct. This subtle use of rhetorical displacement effects a purgation of 'bad' Yorkism by associating 'voluptuousness' with defective kingship, leaving him to emblematise an alternative model which stresses shared ethnicity and an unimpeachable heritage – Macduff recognises Malcolm's 'royal father' (4.3.108) – as the prelude to a successful union between the Scottish and English states.

This line of argument is pursued in the closing moments of *Macbeth*. In an almost paradoxical denouement, Macbeth is forced to employ the services of the 'wretched kerns' (5.7.18) who he successfully destroyed in the first act. Against an Anglo-Scottish coalition, comprised of 'Siward's son, / And many unrough youths, that even now / Protest their first blush of manhood.' (5.7.9–11), Macbeth cannot hope to succeed; he occupies, in effect, an isolationist, non-Union position which is defined equally by its military weakness as its descent into tyranny. In contrast, Malcolm's familial alliance with the South is almost supernatural in its effectiveness, to the extent that the 'English force' (5.3.18) appear to push the rooted 'Wood of Birnam' (5.4.3) northwards into Scottish territory. Once again, Macbeth is constructed as a receptacle of 'bad' Yorkism as espoused by James' detractors in the succession literature of the 1590s; isolated, and without support. An inability to mingle with or embrace allies of a different ethnicity is a trope used in Yorkist drama to denote unsuccessful kingship. One of the reasons Shakespeare's Richard III is unable to secure victory at Bosworth is that he is contemptuous of Richmond's Celtic heritage; he is derided as 'the Breton Richmond' (4.3.40) who leads a

'Breton navy' (4.4.521) peopled by 'bastard Bretons' (5.3.333). As stated earlier, Brittany was regarded in early modern ethnography as indistinct from Yorkshire and Galloway, as well as being the ancestral home of the House of Stuart, so a quarto reader in 1605 could easily draw an analogy between the false Yorkist Richard, with his xenophobic attitudes, and the true Yorkist Richmond, who would marry Elizabeth of York and diffuse his bloodline into the Tudor – and Stuart – lines. As *Macbeth* concludes in a victory for the Anglo-Scottish alliance, we see a similar process enacted on stage in 1606; the modification of the internal political order as ambitious, quasi-feudal Scottish 'thanes' are turned into deferential English 'earls' (5.9.28–9), and the cultivation of an approach to co-operative statehood that prefigures the hoped-for transformation of the two nations into the aggregated state of Britain.

Conclusion

Shakespeare's use of Yorkist thinking throughout *Macbeth* is a pervasive, under-explored element of his most complex response to the Stuart succession. Theatre-goers with even a cursory interest in James' genealogy would have been able to discern connections between the two Scottish kings which went far beyond their shared northern origin. In some ways the play acts in the service of a pro-Stuart agenda, regarding Union as an unambiguous force for progress; Malcolm is restored to his rightful place as ruler, and the aberration of Macbeth's intervention in the state is exacerbated by its rejection of English support. Yet this reading is too neat a note to end on. Although Malcolm can be read as the embodiment of a version of Yorkism which traverses ethnic and cultural boundaries, he is, of course, not James' direct ancestor; that honour goes to 'blood-boltered Banquo' (4.1.122), a figure who will end up fathering a 'line of kings' (3.1.59) in a parallel, separate path of descent to James' English forebears, such as the Yorkists. An audience member in possession of knowledge of Scottish history may not have been able to trace the exact point at which the Stuart, or Stewart, line was founded. If this was the case, and it is a lacuna which is supported in Shakespeare's text, then we see the source of an aetiology which is curiously Yorkist in import; Banquo initiates a lasting bloodline resulting in the accession of James, but he must, at some point, have been elected. This bifurcation in the issue of the right to rule takes us back to the start of the chapter, and also to the complexities inherent in Yorkist ideology. Is it a political concept which is reliant for its impetus on a strict interpretation of primogeniture, or does it require, even encourage, parliamentary intervention? The answer is not neat, but then neither is a claim which can use the senior Yorkist position to flout the prohibition of the Henrician Succession Acts in the 1530s, yet still require a form of assent in order to institute itself as an accepted form of government. In providing a discourse for his dramatic treatment of hereditary rule in the charged context of regime change, Shakespeare turned to the pragmatism of Yorkist political thought, which exploited and adapted its ostensible conservatism to fit a beguilingly broad range of circumstances.

Notes

Thanks are extended to Paulina Kewes for generously sharing her work with me pre-publication, and to Willy Maley and Adrian Streete for their incisive notes and comments during the drafting of this chapter.

1. For a clear exploration of the 1482 invasion, see John Sadler, *Border Fury: England and Scotland at War 1296–1568* (Abingdon: Routledge, 2005), 380–405.
2. Scottish chronicles which detail the 1482 invasion include Robert Lindsay, *The historie and cronicles of Scotland* (c.1570s); John Leslie, *The historie of Scotland* (1578); and George Buchanan, *Rerum Scoticarum Historia* (1582).
3. John Barbour, *The actes and life of the most victorious conquerour, Robert Bruce, King of Scotland* (Edinburgh: Andro Hart, 1616), sig.B4r. For further discussion of the culture of Tacitean historiography in early modern culture, see Peter Burke, 'Tacitism, scepticism and reason of state', in J. H. Burns (ed.), *The Cambridge History of Political Thought 1400–1700* (Cambridge: Cambridge University Press, 1991), 479–98.
4. For further discussion of the succession context surrounding James' claim in the 1590s see Susan Doran, 'James VI and the English succession', in Ralph Houlbrooke (ed.), *James VI and I: Ideas, Authority, and Government* (Aldershot: Ashgate, 2006), 25–42; and Jane E. A, Dawson, 'Anglo-Scottish relations: security and succession', in Robert Tittler and Norman L. Jones (eds), *A Companion to Tudor Britain* (Oxford: Oxford University Press, 2004), 167–81.
5. *Oxford Dictionary of National Biography*, 'Andro Hart', A. J. Mann (2004); *Oxford Dictionary of National Biography*, 'John Barbour', A. A. M. Duncan (2004).
6. James VI and I, *The Kings Maiesties speech, as it was delivered [. . .] on Munday the 19. day of March 1603 being the first day of this present Parliament* (London: Robert Barker, 1604), sig.B1r. For a more thorough debate on the political circumstances surrounding the projected union of the Scottish and English states, see Jenny Wormald, 'The Union of 1603', in Roger Mason (ed.), *Scots and Britons: Scottish Political Thought and the Union of 1603* (Cambridge: Cambridge University Press, 1994), 17–40; and Conrad Russell, 'The Anglo-Scottish Union, 1603–1643: a success?', in Anthony Fletcher and Peter Roberts (eds), *Religion, Culture and Society in Early Modern Britain* (Cambridge: Cambridge University Press, 1994), 249–51.
7. David Womersley, *Divinity and State* (Oxford: Oxford University Press, 2010), 247.

8. For a complex discussion of the role of parliamentary assent in the accession of James, see Rei Kanemura, 'Kingship by descent or kingship by election? The contested title of James VI and I', *Journal of British Studies*, 53 (2013), 317–42. For a detailed engagement with James' literary output, see Jane Rickard, *Writing the Monarch in Jacobean England: Jonson, Donne, Shakespeare and the Works of King James* (Cambridge: Cambridge University Press, 2015); and Jane Rickard, *Authorship and Authority: The Writings of James VI and I* (Manchester: Manchester University Press, 2007).
9. John Guy writes that James' succession occurred because 'he was the most realistic alternative, and because fifteen nobles and councillors signed the warrant that ordered proclamation of his style'; Elizabeth's silence could have been a pragmatic attempt to avoid a potential coup, even as she worked in tacit agreement with the Cecil faction to ensure a smooth succession. See *Tudor England* (Oxford: Oxford University Press, 2000), 445–54.
10. Robert Persons, *A conference about the next succession to the crowne of Ingland* (Antwerp: A. Conincx, 1595), 7. For further discussion of the political context in which the *Conference* appeared, see Peter Holmes, 'The authorship and early reception of a conference about the next succession to the crown of England', *Historical Journal*, 23 (1980), 415–29.
11. Persons, *Conference*, 8.
12. Kanemura, 'Kingship by descent', 320.
13. William Allen, *An Admonition to the Nobility and People of England and Ireland* (Antwerp: A. Conincx, 1588), 22, 50.
14. Robert Persons, *Newes from Spayne and Holland* (Antwerp: A. Conincx, 1593), sig.E3v; Richard Verstegan, *A declaration of the true causes of the great troubles* (Antwerp: J. Trognesius, 1592), 48.
15. Paulina Kewes, 'The idol of state innovators and republicans: Robert Persons's *A Conference about the Next Succession* (1594/5) in Stuart England', in Paulina Kewes and Andrew McRae (eds), *Literature of the Stuart Successions* (Oxford: Oxford University Press, forthcoming), 250–313, 252.
16. The Suffolk line was traced through the issue of Mary Tudor's second marriage to Charles Brandon, Duke of Suffolk, and arguably resulted in the most visible cluster of claimants through the Clifford and Stanley families. For further detail on the succession question in early modern culture, see Lisa Hopkins, *Drama and the Succession to the Crown, 1561–1633* (Farnham: Ashgate, 2011).
17. Peter Wentworth, *A pithie exhortation to her Majestie for establishing her successor to the crowne* (Edinburgh: Robert Waldegrave, 1598), 55–6.
18. Yorkshire was at the centre of three rebellions in the Tudor era: The Yorkshire Rebellion (1489); The Pilgrimage of Grace (1536–37); and the Rising of the North (1569). For a discussion of the religion and political context of Yorkshire during these moments of volatility, see Bruce Campbell, 'North-South Dichotomies, 1066–1550', in Alan R. H. Baker and Mark Billinge (eds), *Geographies of England: The North-South Divide, Material and Imagined*

(Cambridge: Cambridge University Press, 2004), 140–153; M. A. Hicks, 'The Yorkshire Rebellion of 1489 Reconsidered', *Northern History*, 22 (1986), 39–62; and K. J. Kesselring, *The Northern Rebellion of 1569: Faith, Politics and Protest in Elizabethan England* (Basingstoke: Palgrave Macmillan, 2007).
19. Henry Constable, *Discoverye of a counterfecte conference* (Collen: S.N., 1600), 85; John Colville, *The palinod of John Colvill* (Edinburgh: Robert Charteris, 1600), sig. A8v.
20. Hector Boece, *Heir beginnis the hystory and croniklis of Scotland* (Edinburgh: Thomas Davidson, 1540), sig. B2r.
21. William Camden, *Remaines of a greater worke, concerning Britaine* (London: George Eld, 1605), 8; and Boece, sigs. B2r-D2v. For a complex examination of the ethnographical debates surrounding the English and Scottish races, see Mary Floyd-Wilson, *English Ethnicity and Race in Early Modern Drama* (Cambridge: Cambridge University Press), 48–66.
22. Interestingly, John Barbour composed a long genealogical poem on the origin of the Stewart line entitled *The Stewartis Oryginalle* (c.1378). Unfortunately it is lost, but as a plea for royal patronage it testifies to the central importance of genealogy as part of the wider political identity of the Stuart dynasty in the Scottish court.
23. *Oxford Dictionary of National Biography*, 'Henry, Lord Darnley', Hans Eworth (2004).
24. Samuel Lewkenor, *The situation and customes of forraine cities* (London: Humfrey Hooper, 1600), 63. Lewkenor may have been influenced by Boece, who stated that the Briton people migrated 'out of Brigance ye toun of Spanye (quhilk is now namit Compostella)'; such a reference traces a line not only from Galicia to the Lowlands via Yorkshire, but positions the process within a tradition of Scottish historiography; see Boece, sig. B1v.
25. Michael Drayton, *The second part, or a continuance of Poly-Olbion* (London: Augustine Mathewes, 1622), 146. For a detailed exploration of the northern context of Yorkist rule, see A. J. Pollard (ed.), *The North of England in the Age of Richard III* (New York: St. Martin's Press, 1996).
26. Philip Schwyzer, *Shakespeare and the Remains of Richard III* (Oxford: Oxford University Press), 61. The most well-known dramatisation of this moment occurs in William Shakespeare's *Henry VI Part 3*, where Edward demands entry through the city gates by asserting a form of regional sovereignty via his title: 'if Henry be your king, / Yet Edward, at least, is Duke of York' (4.7.20–1). Such a moment establishes York as a metropolis which recognises local ties over a centralised power based in the South, and further establishes the region as a separate hinterland, both culturally and administratively, from the rest of the country; see John D. Cox and Eric Rasmussen (eds), *Henry VI Part 3* (London: Arden, 2001).
27. James VI and I, *By the King whereas wee have ever since it pleased God to establish vs in the imperiall crowne of Great Britaine* (London: Robert Barker, 1605), sig. A1r.

28. Philip Schwyzer has skilfully explored the graphological slippage between the word 'Britain' and its cognates 'Britons' and 'British' as part of a detailed exploration of Yorkist isolationism in *Richard III*; however, the pun in pro-Unionist literature is a specific example of paronomasia designed to collapse the distinction between James' supposedly alien ethnicity and the unified nation he aims to rule over; see Schwyzer, 'A scum of Britons? *Richard III* and the Celtic Reconquest', in Willy Maley and Rory Loughnane (eds), *Celtic Shakespeare: The Bard and the Borderers* (Farnham: Ashgate, 2013), 25–34.
29. Francis Bacon, *The twoo bookes of Francis Bacon* (London: Thomas Purfoot and Thomas Creede, 1605), 12.
30. John Gordon, *Enotikon or A Sermon of the Union of Great Brittannie* (London: George Bishop, 1604), 44.
31. Ibid. 27, 45.
32. William Herbert, *A prophesie of Cadwallader, last king of the Britaines containing a comparison of the English kings* (London: Thomas Creede, 1604), sig.H1v.
33. Samuel Daniel, *A panegyrike congratulatorie to the Kings Majestie* (London: Valentine Simmes, 1603), sig.A2v.
34. Genesis 28:14, *Geneva Bible* (1599).
35. James Maxwell, *A new eight-fold probation of the Church of Englands divine constitution* (London: John Legatt, 1617), sig.A2r.
36. Herbert, *Cadwallader*, sig.F3r.
37. Anon., *Northerne poems congratulating the Kings majesties entrance to the crowne* (London: John Windet, 1604), sig.A2r.
38. *Northerne poems*, sig.A4v.
39. Morris Palmer Tilley, *A Dictionary of the Proverbs in England of the Sixteenth and Seventeenth Century* (Ann Arbor: University of Michigan Press, 1950), 501.
40. Anon., *Northerne poems*, sig.C3v.
41. For a comprehensive examination of the polemical interactions between Allen and Persons, see T. H. Clancy, *Papist Pamphleteers: The Allen-Persons Party and the Political Thought of the Counter-Reformation in England, 1572–1615* (Chicago: University of Chicago Press, 1964), 14–43.
42. Simon Forman, *Bocke of Plaies* (1611), quoted in E. K. Chambers, *William Shakespeare: A Study of Facts and Problems* (Oxford: Oxford University Press, 1930), II: 337.
43. There is a wealth of critical material exploring the various political contexts of *Macbeth*. For further discussion, see Arthur Kinney, 'Scottish history, the union of the crowns and the issue of right rule', in Jean R. Brink and William F. Gentrup (eds), *Renaissance Culture in Context* (Aldershot: Scolar Press, 1993), 18–53; David Norbrook, '*Macbeth* and the politics of historiography', in Kevin Sharpe and Steven M. Zwicker (eds), *Politics of Discourse: The Literature of Seventeenth Century England* (London: University of California Press, 1987), 78–116; and Michael Hawkins, 'History, politics and Macbeth', in John Russell Brown (ed.), *Focus on Macbeth* (Abingdon: Routledge, 1982), 155–88.

44. Shakespeare, *The Tragedie of King Richard the third* (London: Thomas Creede, 1605). Interestingly, the prefatory material on the title page alludes to the trope of the Yorkists as familicides, explicitly mentioning the 'treacherous Plots against his brother Clarence' and 'the pittifull murther of his innocent Nephews' (sig.A1r). The publisher Thomas Creede printed Herbert's poem on Cadawaller the previous year, so he may have had a small line in literary material which responded to an audience eager to engage with the revived interest in Yorkist politics on the accession of James. See also Thomas Heywood, *The first and second parts of King Edward the Fourth* (London: Nathaniell Fosbrooke, 1605).
45. Sandra Clarke and Pamela Mason (eds), William Shakespeare, *Macbeth* (London: Arden, 2015).
46. Irenicus Philodikaios, *A treatise declaring, and confirming against all obiections the just title and right of the moste excellent and worthie prince, Iames the sixt, King of Scotland, to the succession of the croun of England* (Edinburgh: Robert Waldegrave, 1599), sig.D3v.
47. For perhaps the most lucid discussion of the 'mirror for princes' tradition in intellectual history, see Quentin Skinner, *The Foundations of Modern Political Thought* (Cambridge: Cambridge University Press, 1978), I: 118–28. See also Harriet Archer, *Unperfect Histories: The Mirror for Magistrates, 1559–1610* (Oxford: Oxford University Press, 2017).
48. To quote the rhetorician Thomas Wilson: 'The findyng out of apte matter, called otherwise Invencion, is a searchyng out of thynges true, or thynges likely, the whiche maie reasonably sette furth a matter, and make it appere probable'; see Wilson, *The arte of rhetorique* (London: Richard Graftus, 1553), sig.A3v. The *OED* defines the word in the following manner: 'The finding out or selection of topics to be treated, or arguments to be used'; "invention, n.1d."; *OED Online* (last accessed September 2018).
49. For a detailed account of the familial structures used by James and Elizabeth to frame their correspondence, see Janel Mueller, '"To My Very Good Brother the King of Scots": Elizabeth I's correspondence with James VI and the question of the Succession', *PMLA*, 115 (2000), 1063–71; and Rayne Allinson, '"These Latter Days of the World": the correspondence of Elizabeth I and King James VI, 1590–1603', *Early Modern Literary Studies*, 16 (2007), 1–27.
50. According to Raphael Holinshed, Duncan's mother Beatrice was the sister of Macbeth's mother Doada, who were both the younger sisters of the reigning king Malcolm; as Duncan traced his claim through the maternal line, there is, of course, a striking correlation between the familial structure of the ancient Scottish succession and the Stuart claim via Henry VIII's eldest sister Margaret Tudor; see Holinshed, *The Second volume of Chronicles* (London: F.T., 1586), 168.
51. The most well-known example is Henry VI's arbitrary choice of the different roses in *Henry VI Part 1* to define the competing factions for the crown,

in which white roses are characterised as 'cheeks' which are 'pale ... with fear' (2.4.63–4); see Edward Burns (ed.), *Henry VI Part 1* (London: Arden, 2000). Other examples in the first tetralogy include the phrases 'The red rose and the white are on his face, / The fatal colours of our striving houses' (*3H6*, 2.5.97–8), and the contrast between the 'alabaster arms' of the two Yorkist princes and the 'red roses' of their 'lips' (*RIII*, 4.3.10–13). It is no exaggeration to say that this strain of imagery is one of the most consistent and finely developed in the Shakespearean corpus, recurring as it does over different plays within the cycle; see Cox and Rasmussen (eds), *Henry VI Part 3*; and James R. Siemon (ed.), *Richard III* (London: Arden, 2009).
52. Francis White, *A replie to Jesuit Fishers answere to certain questions propou[n]ded by his most gratious Matie: King James* (London: Adam Islip, 1624), 591.
53. A. R. Braunmuller (ed.), *Macbeth* (Cambridge: Cambridge University Press, 1997); "loon, n. etymology"; *OED Online* (last accessed September 2018).
54. Willy Maley, *Nation, State and Empire in English Renaissance Literature* (Basingstoke: Palgrave, 2003), 13.
55. Andrew Hadfield and Willy Maley (eds), Edmund Spenser, *A View of the State of Ireland* (Oxford: Blackwell, 1997), 10.
56. Kent was also a fringe of the English state which was associated with rebellion on stage; it had been the setting of Jack Cade's insurrection as dramatised by Shakespeare in *Henry VI Part II*, and was also the location for Jack Straw's rebellion in the anonymous play *Life and Death of Jack Strawe*. For a more detailed exploration of Kentish dissent in early modern culture, see Peter Clarke, 'Popular protest and disturbance in Kent, 1558–1640', *The Economic History Review*, 29 (1976), 365–82.
57. Sharon Alker and Holly Faith Nelson, '*Macbeth*, the Jacobean Scot, and the politics of the Union', *Studies in English Literature 1500–1900*, 47 (2007), 379–401, 382.
58. Edward Hall, *The vnion of the two noble and illustrate famelies of Lancastre [and] Yorke* (London: Richard Grafton, 1548), sig.fl95r. Another Yorkist text detailing the sexual exploits of Edward IV, and acting as a major source for Heywood's play, is the anonymous 1595 poem *A merrie pleasant and delectable historie, betweene King Edward the fourth, and a tanner of Tamworth* (London: John Danter, 1595). It may have been slightly too early to directly inform the use of Yorkist rhetoric in *Macbeth*, but it is a nice example of the persistent association of Edward IV with licentiousness in early modern popular culture.

4

North by Northwest: Shakespeare's Shifting Frontier

Lisa Hopkins

In the long-running TV series *Doctor Who*, Christopher Eccleston's ninth Doctor is asked by Rose how come, if he's an alien, he sounds as if he's from the North, to which he replies that lots of planets have a North. In this chapter, I am going to argue that there is indeed a plurality of Norths, and that the answer to *Macbeth*'s question 'Stands Scotland where it did?' (4.3.164) is 'It depends'. I aim to show two related things: first, that the North stands in a charged and vibrant relationship with the West, and second that where England's own North begins and ends is at least partially conditioned by the other countries which lie to the north of it, particularly Denmark, since successive Viking invasions changed England's sense of its own cultural geography. The two plays on which I shall spend most time are Anthony Brewer's *The Lovesick King* (1617?) and Richard Brome's *The Queen's Exchange* (1633-4?), which are neither by Shakespeare nor particularly well known in their own right. However, both of them move Britain about, and both of them use Shakespeare to help them do it.[1] For the playwrights I shall be considering, Shakespeare can be used to do cultural work, and one of the things he can do is help to trouble and destabilise the idea of the North.

Shakespeare himself, though, also moves the North about, and I want to start by considering how he does that. Shakespeare's career can in a sense be seen as structured by twin geographical poles. Pembroke and Montgomery, the incomparable brethren to whom the First Folio was dedicated, were marcher lords, whose territory and titles were both associated with the area where England marched with Wales. Lord Hunsdon, for whose playing company Shakespeare acted and wrote, was a Border warden, and

Catherine Loomis has recently suggested that the 'bloody man' in *Macbeth* (1.2.1) may well have been directly influenced by a pamphlet account of his son Robert Carey's ride to Edinburgh to inform James VI of the death of Elizabeth.[2] England's North and West may seem to be very different places, but there were systemic links between them. Oswald, first king of Northumbria, died at Oswestry in the Welsh Marches; his skull, initially displayed on a pike there, later became a relic of Durham Cathedral, connecting him to both North and West. The Battle of Shrewsbury, shown by Shakespeare in *Henry IV*, features Border lords fighting on the Marches and seals the fate of the North.

Above all, the march and the Border both marked the interface between Englishness and Britishness, for beyond them lay the Celtic fringe to which the Britons had been pushed back by the invading Saxons and Danes. This made for a link between North and West; it is not by accident that the *Gododdin*, the great lament for a lost battle which we now identify as being in medieval Welsh, tells a story of a battle fought at Catterick in Yorkshire. Both *The Queen's Exchange* and *The Lovesick King* tell stories about tensions between different parts of early medieval Britain, and to do so they make use of the fact that three of Shakespeare's greatest plays, *Hamlet*, *Macbeth* and *King Lear*, are also set in periods when the internal boundaries of Britain were still in flux. Lear should logically be pre-Roman, but the reference to 'a century' as a military unit invites us to associate it with the period between the Romans and the Normans.[3] *Macbeth* is set during the reign of Edward the Confessor, and *Hamlet* refers to the Danish occupation of England.

Moreover, if there is one story Shakespeare must have known it is that of Guy of Warwick.[4] To us, Guy may seem a rather anticlimactic sort of hero, since his most famous deed was fighting the not very fearsome-sounding Dun Cow. However, it has been suggested that beneath the seemingly ridiculous Dun Cow may lurk the words *Dena Gau*, the Danes' kingdom, and that this may encode a reminder that the border of the Danelaw was not far from Stratford. We may rarely think now of the internal borders of England, but they were hugely important. It was well understood that the England of the past had been separated into different internal jurisdictions. Drayton in *Poly-Olbion* declares that 'it appears that there were three sorts of lawes in the Saxon Heptarchy'.[5] Likewise, Samuel Daniel speaks of 'the Saxons, encroching vpon each others parts, or States (which neuer held certaine boundes)'.[6] There was also a strong sense of physical demarcations between these different territories, which for Daniel are:

Intrenchments, Mounts and Borroughs raised for tombes and defences vpon all the wide champions [champains] and eminent hils of this Isle, remayning yet as the characters of the deepe scratches made on the whole face of our country, to shew the hard labour our Progenitors endured to get it for vs.[7]

It was, then, well understood that England retained the traces of ancient physical borders which had once divided the territory of different tribes from each other.

Borders and Walls

In the question of where England began and ended, the question of where the North began and ended was crucial. Stuart Laycock notes that 'The element Merc in Mercia refers to a border, so essentially the name Mercia means "borderland"', something of which early modern linguistic enquiry is likely to have increased awareness.[8] One specific area of tension came between Mercia and the Danes. Aethelflaed, Lady of the Mercians, daughter of Alfred the Great, instituted from her seat at Tamworth a building programme which essentially plotted a border between Mercia and the Danelaw; she also built the first known fortification at Warwick in 914 as a defence against the Danes. When Elizabeth visited Kenilworth in 1575, the inhabitants of Coventry asked her to reinstate the locally popular play *The Conquest of the Danes*, which although devoid of 'ill exampl of mannerz, papistry, or ony superstition', 'had recently been suppressed by "the zeal of certain theyr Preacherz"': perhaps the popularity of the play reflected a memory that the Danes had once been a real presence in and around Coventry.[9] This idea that the men of the North were pressing on Coventry reminds us that the North had historically possessed more than one frontier, many of them physical boundaries erected as ways of defining and demarcating the very concept of northness: one of the most notable features of the Border is that it is not systematically defended, but the Stanegate, Hadrian's Wall, the Antonine Wall, and the Scots Dyke followed one after the other.[10] As the northern border moved, so did centres of power: York gradually gave way to Newcastle as the northernmost fortified city of England, before Newcastle itself gave way to Berwick-upon-Tweed, whose massive walls represented one of Elizabeth I's rare building programmes. To a certain extent there were strategic interests in play in such shifts – Hadrian built the Wall where he did because it straddles the gap between the Tyne and the Solway – but there were also strong economic considerations: Berwick-upon-Tweed protected valuable fishing rights, and both the Wall and the city of Newcastle protected mining rights. As Max Adams argues:

> It is no coincidence that the most lasting permanent border structure of the Western Empire was built just a few miles beyond the most northerly state-controlled lead mines in Britain, in Weardale and Allerdale. The Roman road system, strategically linking forts and signal stations, created a web of fast communications far into what is now Scotland. If the Romans failed to permanently conquer these lands it was probably not because they couldn't but because the game was not worth the candle. Their mineral prospectors knew where the most northerly exploitable ores were and decided that nothing beyond the frontier of Hadrian was worth their permanent attention.[11]

As mining operations in the region extended to coal as well as lead, the region took on even greater importance, and needed better defences than could be offered by distant York. Moreover, York's loyalty was not beyond question; its strong association with the House of York had led it not only to lament the death of Richard III but to declare support for Lambert Simnel, terming him 'King Edward VI', with the result that when Simnel was defeated at the Battle of Stoke Henry VII had *Te deum* sung in York Minster in order to make quite sure they understood his to be a lost cause.[12]

We can see this growing importance of both Newcastle and mineral resources very clearly in Anthony Brewer's play *The Lovesick King*, which plots the changing limit of the North. As the play opens, Osbert, duke of Mercia, has sided with the Danes and betrays Winchester to them, leading to the death of the character whom the *dramatis personae* identifies as 'Etheldred King of England'. Given that Etheldred is based at Winchester and is presented as the brother of Alfred the Great, he is in fact more properly king of Wessex, but calling him king of England and reducing the ruler of Mercia to the status of a mere duke obviously makes it easier to deal in concepts of nation rather than of locality, and this is what *The Lovesick King* does. The story of the main plot is almost comically simple: at the beginning of the play the marauding Danes have chased the English all the way down to the south coast, leaving them only Winchester (and they take that in the first scene); by the end of it, the English have chased them all the way back again, reclaiming the country for a securely English identity.

As the men of the North retreat, the northern edge of what is understood as England is pushed progressively further. The reason for this extraordinary reversal is partly that the Danish king Canutus allows himself to be distracted by the beauties of Cartesmunda, the fair nun of Winchester, and so stops bothering about fighting, but it is also partly attributable to the growing importance of Newcastle, as we see when at the end of the play King Alfred declares 'your Newcastle strength set England free' (sig.G1v).

The Lovesick King is therefore a play that is deeply concerned about Englishness. Just before he is killed, King Etheldred (referring to himself in the third person) notes that 'in nine set Battels against the conquering Danes hath Etheldred with various fortunes fought, to rescue you and England from the spoyls of War and Tyranny' (sig.A2r), and it is made repeatedly clear that what is at stake is the survival of England, not merely of Wessex. Canutus orders his followers 'Who bears the name of English strike him dead' (sig.A3r) and tells them to 'Whip out this English Race, with iron rods' (sig.A3v). It seems that Etheldred is right to warn his followers that if they are not victorious they will have to see 'Your Wives and Daughters slaves to Danish lust' (sig.A2r) and Edmund is equally right to add that the result of losing the battle will be

> The names of English torn from memory;
> Oh let your valors in one chance be buil'd,
> Or quite extirpe a Nation from the World. (sig.A2r)

Canutus himself, by contrast, is initially at least utterly un-English. In several early modern plays, the Danes pose a religious as well as a sexual threat. In *The Tragical History, Admirable Atchievments and various events of Guy Earl of Warwick*, Swanus, king of Denmark, invades Athelstane's England and the Danes appear, curiously enough, to be Muslim, since they invoke Mahound (Mohammed), and in Henry Burnell's *Landgartha* the Norwegian heroine Landgartha has a cousin called Fatyma. Canutus and his Danes certainly conform to this stereotype. The Danes enter crying 'Kill, kill' (sig.A2v), and Alured presents them as acting directly contrary to the will of Heaven: 'See noble Edmond what the Danes have done, a King, by Heaven created for a crown, . . . betrayd to death and slaughter pittiless' (sig.A2v). Most notably, as Robert W. Dent points out, the story of *The Lovesick King* is 'an Anglicized version of a frequently dramatized story, that of Mahomet and the fair Irene at the fall of Constantinople'.[13] This implicitly connects Canutus to the Prophet Mohammed, and he certainly sounds oriental enough when he says to the beautiful Saxon Cartesmunda 'vail thy face my love, we must not have thee seen too much by slaves' (sig. F3r), and when he echoes Tamburlaine by vowing to the dead body of Cartesmunda that 'Canutus arms, a while shall be thy Tomb, / Then gold inclose thee till the day of Doom' (sig.F4r). Finally, Alured refers to 'the usurped Temples of Canutus' (sig.G1v), again associating him with non-Christian worship. Canutus is also blasphemous: as far as he is concerned, it is fine to kill all the English because 'The vanquish'd are but men, the Victors, gods' (sig.A3v).

Soon, however, something odd starts to happen. Canutus' sister Elgina falls in love with Alured, the future Alfred the Great (who in fact lived over a century before Canute); we are spared the sight of a Saxon icon in love with a Dane by the fact that Elgina is accidentally killed, but not before she has uttered a resounding defence of her own identity when, pleading for Alured to be spared, she argues that

> If all the English perish, then must I, for I (now know) in England here was bred, although descended of the Danish blood, [the] King my Father, thirty years governed the one half of this famous Kingdom, where I, that time was born an English Princess. (sigs B2r-v)

Even Canutus starts sounding like a king of England when he says of Cartesmunda 'Were Hellen now alive, this Maid alone would stain her beauty and new Troy should burn, Paris would dye again to live to see her' (sig.B1r): the allusion to the tale of Troy implicitly figures him as an inheritor of the *translatio imperii* in the same way as more unequivocally English kings are often figured as being. The play is after all aware that the Danes, paradoxically, are both others and mothers; having started as alien, they have become English.

Kings, Queens, Merchants and Peddlers

One reason for the play's sensitivity on the question of the Danes is that it was almost certainly specially written for a visit to Newcastle by a Scottish-born king of England who had a Danish wife and whose pet project was to instantiate a blended identity for his two previously separate kingdoms. Although *The Lovesick King* was not published until 1655, M. Hope Dodds argues that it was certainly written for one of James I's two visits to Newcastle in 1603 and 1617 and that the likelier is the 1617 visit, since there would not have been time to prepare it in 1603 when he was there from 9 to 13 April on his way southwards after the death of

Elizabeth.[14] It is however impossible to rule out either that it *was* ready for 1603, given that James had long been a likely heir, or that it was written very shortly after, since the citizens of Newcastle would have had every reason to expect that James' duties as king of Scotland as well as of England would bring him back to the city much more frequently than in fact they did. One of James' pet projects was to abolish the Border and have the Border counties renamed 'The Middle Shires'; he declared that they were now 'the verie hart of the cuntry', and at one point even proposed to set up his own capital at York in imitation of Constantine, who had been proclaimed emperor there.[15] *The Lovesick King* implicitly opposes this idea. It goes out of its way to present York as both tainted by its long association with Danes and also dangerously vulnerable to attack, and reads to a large extent like Newcastle's bidding document for the title of Top City in the North. The Danes put all their faith in York, but it is misplaced: despite the strength of its Roman walls, York falls to the Scots, who threaten to level it with the earth unless the Danes yield the city (sig.E4r). Newcastle, however, is presented as never conquered. Alured tells its civic leaders that 'your true Allegiance hath proclaim'd it self that never yeelded yet to foreign Scepter, you have fortified your walls 'gainst all invasions' (sig.F2r), and stresses that for the last twenty-five years the Danes have been 'planting here your selves in Norfolk, Suffolk, and in Cambridgeshire' (sig.Fr4), reminding the audience that despite Danish encroachments at their edges, such as a settlement in Tynemouth, the Northumbrian heartlands remained unconquered. It is a neat irony that at one point Grim the Collier should hear shouting and observe 'I think there's some Match at Foot-bal towards' (sig.F1r), because the note is indeed that of an English North East derby between Newcastle and York, in which Newcastle emerges as the triumphant winner.

In Act Two of *The Lovesick King*, when we first move to Newcastle, we also apparently leap forward several centuries to focus on the story of merchant Roger Thornton, an historical figure but one who did not live until the fifteenth century. The two parts of the play at first seem wholly disconnected. However, they come together not only at the end but also when Thornton promises to rebuild Allhallows Church (where he was in fact buried), and to build a tomb for his late master, offering a parallel to Canutus' resolve that Cartesmunda should be buried in gold (sig.E4r). They need, then, to be read together, and the story of the rise of Newcastle needs to be understood as part of the story the play tells about Englishness.

When we first meet him, Thornton is a poor peddler, but a witch has assured him that if he can get himself taken on as a servant in Newcastle he will make his fortune. This duly happens, and he proceeds to show his gratitude by giving the city walls:

> *Thornton.* How many Towers of strength may be erected, dividing each distance by a hundred pace.
> *Workman.* 'Tis cast already, and the compass falls,
> A hundred fourscore Towers to grace the Walls.
> *Thornton.* How high de'you raise the Walls?
> *Workman.* As you directed sir, full a hundred foot.
> *Thornton.* Right, and twelve in breadth.
> *Workman.* Just so, sir, 'twill be a pleasant walk to view the Town:
> *Thornton.* So I wo'd have it; And therefore from the highest erect a Battlement above the Platform four foot high a' both sides, both to secure, and make the place more pleasant; See it rais'd so. (sig.E3r)

John Leland said of Newcastle that 'the strength and magnificens of the waulling of this town far passeth al the waulles of the cities of England, and most of the townes of Europe', but it was not only the strength of walls but also their age that was a sign of prestige.[16] In *A Survey of London* Stow had claimed extraordinary antiquity for those of the capital, declaring that 'Helen, the mother of Constantine, was the first that inwalled this city, about the year of Christ, 306' and also quoting the twelfth-century William Fitzstephen as claiming that there had been walls on the southern bank too: 'London was walled and towered in like manner on the south, but the great fish-bearing Thames river which there glides, with ebb and flow from the sea, by course of time has washed against, loosened, and thrown down those walls', which for Stow is 'proof of a wall, and form thereof, about this city, and the same to have been of great antiquity as any other within this realm'.[17] The building of the walls of Newcastle is usually credited to William Rufus, looking to consolidate his grip on the area after his father's Harrying of the North in 1069–70: according to Harding's *Chronicle*, William Rufus 'buylded the Newcastell upon Tyne The Scottes to gaynstande'. Some parts seem to predate this, and indeed to include elements of Roman fortification, but the play is probably right in ascribing the construction of the West Gate, which was pulled down in 1811, to the wealthy merchant Roger Thornton. Its covert implication that the Thornton subplot is contemporary with the main plot preserves this tradition, but also makes the walls older than they really are, and thus metaphorically as well as literally more venerable.

Partly as a result of his munificence, the Newcastle in which Thornton lives is an extremely prosperous one. The merchant Goodgift says,

> I, I, Wife, thy Brother Randolfe here is known a famous Merchant for Newcastle Coals, and England holds the circuit of his traffick, but we that are Adventures abroad, must fame our Country through all Christendom, nay far beyond our Christian Territories, to Egypt, Barbary, and the Tauny Moors, Where not indeed? if Sea and wind gives way unto our dancing Vessels; nay, nay, Brother, your merchandize compar'd with us, I tell you, is but a poor fresh-water venture. (sig. A3v)

There is another piece of historical elision at work in that Goodgift here shares the concerns of seventeenth-century English traders rather than fifteenth-century ones, but more pertinent is that Randolfe himself puts his faith not in the results of overseas trade but in home-grown sources of wealth:

> Well, brother, well, pursue your Foraign gain, I rest content at home, at the years end wee'l cast the difference 'twixt your far-fetch'd treasure, and our Newcastle home-bred Minerals, you shall perceive strange transformation, black coals turn'd to white silver, that's my comfort sir. (sig. A3v)

This is echoed in the scene in which Thornton discovers that metal which he had bought as iron is in fact gold, making him the richest subject in the kingdom, and the importance of Newcastle's underground wealth is confirmed when Grim the Collier offers to march his seven hundred miners underground to London, a journey which he affirms will take no more than six days. Newcastle is thus presented as in no sense marginal to London but directly connected to both it and the wider world of international sea trade, and also a power in its own right as the strongest city in the North.

Shakespeare in *The Lovesick King*

In order to tell the story that it wants to, *The Lovesick King* finds that it needs both *Macbeth* and *Hamlet*. *Macbeth* is evoked primarily in order to register this play's difference from it. The play features a king of Scots called Donald and another Scot called Malcolm, but these apparent nods to *Macbeth* are counteracted by the fact that it is the Scots who help civilise England rather than *vice versa*, an obvious compliment to James. The Scots aid Alured to march as far as York, which they threaten with destruction if it does not yield, but they are very pointedly dissociated from the pillage and devastation which historical cross-Border raids traditionally entailed, as we see when Alured says,

> I came now with my best Hors-manship from the Scotch Army, whose Royal King in Neighbor amity, is arm'd in my just cause, has past the Tweed with prosperous forrage through Northumberland, all Holds and Castles taken by the Danes restore themselves to his subjection in our behalf. (sig. F2r)

These are no Border Reivers or marauding half-savages but well-mannered and well-behaved troops who 'forage' prosperously rather than despoil, do not appear to have destroyed any property, and promptly pass over to English hands any cities that they take. It seems only fitting that Alured at the close of the play should repay their help by gifting them some of England:

> Great King of Scotland, we are yet a debtor to your kind love, which thus we 'gin to pay, all those our Northern borders bounding on Cumberland, from Tine to Tweed, we add unto your Crown, so 'twas fore-promised, and 'tis now perform'd; Most fit it is that we be ever lovers;
> The Sea that binds us in one Continent,
>   Doth teach us to imbrace two hearts in one,
> To strengthen both 'gainst all invasion. (sig. G2r)

Even this, though, does not have the feel of a genuine reduction in English territory since Alured is so insistent on the essential territorial integrity of the British mainland, a theme that would have been very familiar to Jacobean audiences.

This civilising of the Scots does not, however, quite disguise the fact that *Macbeth* tells a story about Northumbria as well as about Scotland. A website on the history of Viking Northumbria offers a slightly unexpected perspective on the events of Shakespeare's play:

> In 1054 Siward, the Earl of Northumbria, defeated the Scots under King Macbeth and Siward's nephew Malcolm Canmore was appointed Lord of Strathclyde and the Lothians. It was an attempt to bring the Scottish lowlands once more under Northumbrian control.[18]

Macbeth certainly does not privilege such a perspective on events, but it does allow for it, reminding the audience both of Siward's status as Earl of Northumberland and the fact that Malcolm is his nephew, and Shakespeare was probably aware of it through his sources: in Caradoc of Llancarvan's *The historie of Cambria, now called Wales*, the section about Macbeth, Banquo and Fleance is immediately preceded by the information that:

> Oswald Earle of Northumberland, when he heard that his sonne was slaine in Scotland, whither his father had sent him to conquere it, asked whether his deaths wound was in his brest or in his backe; and they said in his brest: and he answered, I am right glad thereof, for I would not wish me nor my sonne to die otherwise.[19]

Macbeth reuses this anecdote and has Malcolm assure Macduff that even before he arrived, 'Old Seyward with ten thousand warlike men / Already at a point, was setting forth' (4.3.144–5), making it quite clear that the invasion of Scotland is a specifically Northumbrian rather than more generally English enterprise, and later Malcolm addresses Siward as 'worthy uncle' (5.6.2). It is also suggestive that Malcolm should close the play by saying to his followers, 'Henceforth be earls, the first that ever Scotland / In such an honour named' (5.7.92–3).[20] Scotland may not have had earls as such, but it had had jarls, such as Macbeth's cousin Thorfinn Sigurdsson who ruled not only Orkney but Caithness, and the climate of philological enquiry in the early seventeenth century would not have made it hard to perceive that the two words were cognate. When Malcolm converts his thanes to earls, he borrows the title of his Northumbrian uncle and extends it to Scotland, and by refusing to acknowledge the existence of jarls he again implicitly dissociates Northumbria from any tainting element of Danishness. *The Lovesick King* may show the English having to be helped by the Scots, but alluding to *Macbeth* allows it to remind audiences that there have also been occasions when the Scots have had to be helped by the English, and specifically by Northumbria.

Hamlet, too, is a presence in *The Lovesick King*, in the subplot concerning the hasty remarriage of Randolfe's widowed sister. When Randolfe first suggests to her that she could now marry the wealthy Thornton, she demurs, 'Hey, ho, Hee's a very honest man truly, and had my husband dyed but two months ago, I might ha' thought on't' (sig.E3r). After a little persuasion, however, she consents to marry him the same day. This looks pointed, as too does the inclusion of a character with the name Osric;

it works to connect the inhabitants of Newcastle to the Danes in the same way as does Thornton's Tamburlainian interest in gold, confirming the sense that there is contact between the two ostensibly disparate plots. However, *Hamlet*, too, is interested in walls and battlements, and understanding *The Lovesick King* as in dialogue with *Hamlet* helps us see things not only about Brewer's play but also about Shakespeare's. At an early stage of *The Lovesick King*, Osbert reminds Canutus that 'an hundred thirty years the English Kings have paid just tribute to the conquering Danes' (sig.A3r). That *Hamlet* is explicitly set during this period is signalled by the fact that Claudius dispatches him to England 'for the demand of our neglected tribute', and that the country he is expected to visit is one whose 'cicatrice looks raw and red / After the Danish sword' (4.4.63–4).[21] Like *The Lovesick King*, too, *Hamlet* is notably interested in underground activity: the Ghost is a 'mole' who works fast in the earth (1.4.170), and Hamlet reflects that

> 'tis the sport to have the enginer
> Hoist with his own petard, and't shall go hard
> But I will delve one yard below their mines
> And blow them at the moon. (3.4.208–11)

As the Arden 2 edition notes, 'a *petard* was an explosive device, recently invented, for breaking through gates, walls, etc.', so this is a passage which has in mind exactly the kind of warfare which the walls of Newcastle were able to withstand. *The Lovesick King* is thus not simply recalling *Hamlet*, but intelligently considering the ways in which the play speaks to the history of England, and to the history of the North of England in particular.

For *The Lovesick King* to point to *Hamlet* enables it to suggest a number of things without having to articulate them directly. In both *Hamlet* and *The Lovesick King*, the crown changes hands. In *Hamlet*, it has been acquired by Claudius and is expected to pass to Hamlet, but in fact devolves on Fortinbras. In *The Lovesick King*, the crown of England is brought to Canutus after the death of Etheldred, but subsequently passes to Alured. In both cases, a Dane is the loser, and in both plays wives are fickle, which may have expressed some unease about Anna of Denmark. More fundamentally, though, both plays suggest that crowns may be lost as well as won, and *Hamlet* explicitly declares that the Danish crown is elective, a matter of some debate among political theorists.

Moreover, both plays posit an England which is subject to a foreign power, but in both cases the audience is implicitly or explicitly invited to remember that such a state of affairs was only temporary. Newcastle, so long a bulwark against the Scots, was prepared to extend only a provisional welcome to its new Scottish king, and reference to *Hamlet* helps it inject that note of caution, and to remind the audience that today's Middle Shires might yet revert to being tomorrow's northern border.

Another play which talks both about the North and about Shakespeare is Richard Brome's *The Queen's Exchange*.[22] This opens at the court of the West Saxons, the people whom Camden understood as living beyond Wansdyke, whose queen, the fictional Bertha, is proposing to marry yet another Osric, the king of Northumbria (the name is also found in the anonymous *A Knack to Know a Knave*, published in 1594 and featuring King Edgar and St Dunstan). The proposed marriage is opposed by Segebert, the favourite counsellor of Bertha's father, on the grounds that there are fundamental and irreconcilable differences between Northumbria and Wessex:

> I know, and you, if you knew anything,
> Might know the difference twixt the Northumbrian laws
> And ours. And sooner will their king pervert
> Your privileges and your government,
> Than reduce his to yours. (1.1.116–20)

Segebert implicitly connects Osric to Tamburlaine, who also uses 'reduce' in relation to his project of world domination: 'and with this pen reduce them to a map'.[23] However, Bertha dismisses Segebert's advice and receives the Northumbrian ambassador Theodric (Theodric was historically the name of a king of Bernicia, a kingdom eventually subsumed into Northumbria under Oswald), who is no blunt northerner but in fact honey-tongued, leading the West Saxon lord Elwin to lament that 'howe'er the laws may go, our customs will / Be lost: for he, methinks, out-flatters us already' (1.1.222–3). Plans for the marriage proceed apace – except that once again a subplot takes a hand.

The play which *The Queen's Exchange* most obviously remembers is *King Lear*. Segebert, like Lear, has three children, except that in this case there are two sons, Offa, a name which obviously speaks of boundaries, and Anthynus, and one daughter, Mildred. Anthynus is the eldest, but the least favoured, and when Segebert on the point of being exiled conducts a love test, Anthynus fails it miserably:

> *Segebert.* Now there rests, of all my children, but you
> To resolve me how you have found my love?
> *Anthynus.* You ask me last, sir, I presume, cause you
> Have had me longest, to crown their testimony.
> *Segebert.* Yet you seem, Anthynus, by your leave, the
> Least to know me, but like a stranger look
> Upon me when these give me due respect.
> *Anthynus.* Less than due I dare not give you; and more
> Were to abuse you. Though I do not applaud,
> I must approve you are a right good father. (1.2.75–84)

Segebert is not impressed with this qualified rapture, and decides to punish it by disinheriting Anthynus insofar as he is able to:

> Though you are eldest, and my lawful heir,
> And must be lord, at my decease, of all
> My large possessions, yet, it is my will
> That, till my death, my Offa have the sway
> And government of all, allowing you
> That yearly stipend formerly I gave you. (1.2.116–21)

Nevertheless, the loyal Anthynus follows his father into exile in Northumbria, where he is able to defend the old man from a murderous attack by outlaws. The presence of outlaws in the woods of Northumbria might suggest that it is a lot wilder than Wessex, and Anthynus does indeed term it 'this wild desert' (2.3.15), but in fact the supposed outlaws have been suborned and paid by the wicked Offa, who wants his father dead so that he can inherit his estate, which suggests that Northumbria is really not all that different from Wessex. We even find the Lear plot cropping up there too, since Osric, the king of Northumbria, has a fool called Jeffrey who wants to stay with him during his self-imposed absence from court. Most strikingly, the West Saxon lord Anthynus and the Northumbrian king Osric turn out to be absolutely identical, for no particular reason that the play ever troubles to give us. Their interchangeable bodies lead to an ending which keeps the two kingdoms technically separate when the West Saxon queen Bertha marries the West Saxon lord Anthynus, but since the Northumbrian king Osric marries Anthynus' sister Mildred, a marriage alliance has been forged which will presumably lead to much closer ties between the two lands. The play thus ends by evoking both separation and unity.

Where Northumbria does differ from Wessex is that it is haunted. When Anthynus goes to sleep in a Northumbrian wood, he has either a vision or a genuine supernatural experience:

> *Enter* six Saxon kings' ghosts, *crowned with sceptres in their hands, etc. They come one after another to* Anthynus, *then fall into a dance; loud music sounds. After the dance, the first leads away the second, he the third, and so on; the last takes up* Anthynus *and leaves him standing upright.* (3.2.39 s.d.)

This is a bit surprising in that *King Lear* is the only one of Shakespeare's four pre-conquest plays to include no supernatural material, but of course what is being recalled here is *Macbeth* (in case we miss that, Alfrid says shortly afterwards to Edelbert, 'A witch could not guess righter / Than thou hast done' (3.2.80–1).[24] Anthynus correctly interprets what has passed as a prophecy about future rule:

> If now I be awake, and am Anthynus, ...
> Then did I see, in apparition,
> The ghosts of our six last West Saxon kings, ...
> Of which, the last, Kenwalcus, our late king,
> And father to the tyraness that banished
> Mine, seemed to take me up to his succession. (3.2.45–52)

The North is a holy place: Max Adams notes that the first stone structure built after the departure of the Romans was York Minister and Hexham Abbey the second.[25] This made them, according to Stow, older than the Tower of London, since he rejects the idea that it was built by Julius Caesar and declares it to be built 'of stone brought from Caen in Normandy, since the Conquest'.[26] Another great religious centre, Lindisfarne, brought literacy to the area, and Northumbria's greatest king, Oswald, killed the pagan king Cadwallon at a river helpfully called Devil's Water and became a saint after his victory at the even more resonantly named Heavenfield, fought only yards from Hadrian's Wall.[27] This was remembered by Geoffrey of Monmouth, who wrote that 'Oswald was besieged by this Penda in a place called Hevenfield, that is, the Field of Heaven', and in the early modern period by Foxe, who called him Oswald 'last king of the Britanes', by Holinshed and in *The*

Faerie Queene; as late as the seventeenth century coins showing Oswald were being minted in Switzerland.[28] Suggestively, *The Queen's Exchange* appears to have been in some form of intertextual dialogue with the now lost *Play of Oswald*, whose eponymous hero, heir to Mercia, has been sent to Northumberland in infancy to escape from his murderous uncle. Part of the very small fragment which remains has Oswald saying, 'brother I am glad you cozen'd / me of a wife; sister I am glad you call'd / me not husband', suggesting an incest motif similar to that found in *The Queen's Exchange* where the villainous Offa tries to persuade his sister Mildred to sleep with him.[29]

In *The Queen's Exchange*, the border between worlds seems almost as porous as at that victory at Heavenfield which gave Oswald both an earthly and a heavenly kingdom, for the apparently dead do not stay dead.[30] The murderers sent by Offa convince him that they have indeed killed his brother and father, and the reader or audience member might well be deceived into thinking that Segebert is indeed dead. However, Offa struggles to believe it, asking successively, 'You are sure they both are dead?' (4.1.2), 'but are they dead indeed?' (4.1.7), 'But he's dead too, y'are sure?' (4.1.15) and 'They are both dead you say?' (4.1.22), before disposing, as he thinks, of the murderers themselves by pushing them through a trap-door into a cellar. In fact neither Anthynus nor Segebert is dead, and the murderers are inadvertently liberated from the cellar by a gang of would-be jewel thieves. By contrast, though the supernatural is twice gestured at in the West Saxon scenes, it is not real on either occasion: when Anthynus asks those attending him: 'What fiends or fairies are ye?' (4.2.32), the rather prosaic answer is that they are a physician and his attendants, and when a group of men dressed as devils appear on the stage they turn out to be jewel thieves wearing costumes which they hope will frighten away anyone who might see them. The king of Northumbria might be physically indistinguishable from the future king of the West Saxons, but their two territories are subtly different.

The Queen's Exchange is difficult to date precisely, but Richard Wood has suggested that as well as its obvious debt to Ford's *'Tis Pity She's a Whore* it is also in dialogue with his *Perkin Warbeck* (published in 1634 but probably composed in 1633), and 1633 or 1634 does indeed seem a likely date, because the play appears to reflect on the Scottish coronation of Charles I in 1633.[31] I have argued elsewhere that this second coronation for Charles, coupled with the fact that the arrival of Prince James gave the reigning king two male heirs for the first time since the death of Prince Henry, prompted speculation about whether England and Scotland should remain joined under one monarch or whether the two sons of the king might each inherit one of his two kingdoms. This is a question which *The Queen's Exchange* addresses head on, since as Richard Wood suggests its introduction of a fool named Jeffrey makes it look like a glance at Henrietta Maria, who had a fool named Jeffrey Hudson, and it evokes *Lear*, the ultimate succession play, and *Macbeth*, as part of its strategy for doing so. *Lear* itself is indecisive about whether power passes to the midlands-based Edgar or the Scottish Albany. *The Queen's Exchange* proposes that two separate scenes of power shall continue, one in the North and one in the West, and though it does hint that the initially threatening Northumbria might ultimately become more closely aligned with Wessex, Wood is surely right to suggest that 'the happy failure of Bertha to marry the northern king, Osric (thus not uniting their kingdoms) would be seen as a comment on the union'. Once again, then, a play set in the North invokes the West to suggest a less than total commitment to the Stuarts, and once again it uses Shakespeare to do so.

Notes

1. Anthony Brewer, *The love-sick king, an English tragical history with the life and death of Cartesmunda, the fair nun of Winchester* (London: Robert Pollard, 1655); hereafter cited in the text. Only England and Ireland were invaded by Vikings, and I am not concerned here with Ireland; however, the whole of mainland Britain was affected by England's understanding of its northern and western borders. I am thus using 'England' and 'Britain' advisedly rather than treating them as interchangeable.
2. Catherine Loomis,'"What bloody man is that?": Sir Robert Carey and Shakespeare's bloody sergeant', *Notes and Queries*, 246 (September 2001), 296–8.
3. R. A. Foakes (ed.), William Shakespeare, *King Lear* (London: Thomas Nelson and Sons, 1997), 4.4.6.
4. On the prominence of the Guy of Warwick story in Warwickshire see Helen Cooper, 'Guy of Warwick, Upstart Crows and Mounting Sparrows', in Takashi Kozuka and J. R. Mulryne (eds), *Shakespeare, Marlowe, Jonson: New Directions in Biography* (Aldershot: Ashgate, 2006), 119–38, 121.
5. Michael Drayton, *Poly-Olbion: A Chorographicall description of tracts, riuers, mountains, forests, and other parts of this renowned isle of Great Britain* (London: John Marriott, John Grismand, and Thomas Dewe, 1622), 126.
6. Samuel Daniel, *The first part of the historie of England* (London: Nicholas Okes, 1612), 29.

7. Ibid. 25–6.
8. Stuart Laycock, *Britannia the Failed State: Tribal Conflicts and the End of Roman Britain* (Stroud: The History Press, 2008), 228.
9. Beatrice Groves, *Texts and Traditions: Religion in Shakespeare 1592–1604* (Oxford: Clarendon Press, 2007), 39, 55.
10. Max Adams remarks that the Stanegate 'at its inception was probably intended as a frontier in its own right'; see *The King in the North: The Life and Times of Oswald of Northumbria* (London: Head of Zeus, 2013), 150.
11. Adams, *The King in the North,* 211–12.
12. John Ashdown-Hill, *The Dublin King* (Stroud: The History Press, 2017), 208.
13. Robert W. Dent, 'The Love-sick King: Turk Turned Dane', *The Modern Language Review*, 56: 4 (October 1961), 555–7, 556.
14. M. Hope Dodds, '"Edmund Ironside" and "The Love-Sick King"', *The Modern Language Review* 19: 2 (April 1924), 158–68, 164.
15. J. G. A. Pocock, 'Two kingdoms and three histories? Political thought in British contexts', in Roger A. Mason (ed.), *Scots and Britons: Scottish Political Thought and the Union of 1603* (Cambridge: Cambridge University Press, 1994), 293–312, 307.
16. Quoted in Eneas Mackenzie, 'Fortifications and buildings: town walls and gates', in *Historical Account of Newcastle-Upon-Tyne Including the Borough of Gateshead* (Newcastle-upon-Tyne, 1827), 105–17.
17. John Stow, *A Survey of London written in the year 1598* (London: The History Press, 2009), 28, 16, 31.
18. See <http://www.englandsnortheast.co.uk/VikingNorthumbria.html> (last accessed 12 April 2018).
19. Caradoc of Llancarvan, *The historie of Cambria, now called Wales*, trans. Humphrey Llwyd (London: 1584), 97.
20. Sandra Clark and Pamela Mason (eds), William Shakespeare, *Macbeth* (London: Bloomsbury, 2015).
21. Harold Jenkins (ed.), William Shakespeare, *Hamlet* (London: Methuen, 1982), 3.2.172.
22. Richard Wood (ed.), Richard Brome, *The Queen's Exchange*. Available at: <http://extra.shu.ac.uk/emls/iemls/renplays/qexchcontents.htm> (last accessed 17 July 2019); hereafter cited in the text.
23. Mark Thornton Burnett (ed.), Christopher Marlowe, *Tamburlaine: Part One*, in *The Complete Plays* (London: Everyman, 1999), 4.4.84.
24. *Hamlet* has the ghost of Hamlet's father, *Cymbeline* has Posthumus's vision, and *Macbeth* has the witches and Banquo's ghost.
25. Adams, *The King in the North*, 295.
26. Stow, *Survey of London*, 58, 46.
27. Max Adams, *In the Land of Giants: Journeys through the Dark Ages* (London: Head of Zeus, 2015), 205.

28. Geoffrey of Monmouth, *The History of the Kings of Britain*, trans. Lewis Thorpe (Harmondsworth: Penguin, 1966), 277.
29. See David McInnis, 'Play of Oswald (BL MS Egerton 2623)', *Lost Plays Database* <http://www.lostplays.org/index.php/Play_of_Oswald_(BL_MS_Egerton_2623)> (last accessed 17 July 2019).
30. Another instance of eschatological resonances accruing to a northern border can be found in Anon., *A Knack to Know a Knave* (London: Richard Jones, 1594), where the bailiff of Hexham is carried away by the devil.
31. See Richard Wood, 'Introduction' to Brome, *The Queen's Exchange*. On dating *Perkin Warbeck*, see Peter Ure, 'A pointer to the date of Ford's *Perkin Warbeck*', *Notes and Queries*, 215 (1970), 215–17.

II

Performing Shakespeare in the North

5

The People's Shakespeare: Place, Politics and Performance in a Northern Amateur Theatre

Adam Hansen

In 1933, J. B. Priestley visited Newcastle upon Tyne as part of his journey around an England in the grip of economic depression. A local friend and amateur actor took him to The Bridge Hotel, where the People's Theatre – an amateur company founded in 1911 on socialist principles – was rehearsing Euripides' *The Trojan Women*. This is how Priestley described the scene:

> In the shadow of an enormous ebony bridge, which looked as if it stretched into the outer spaces of the universe, we found a large but almost deserted pub. But vague noises came from upstairs, and I was steered in their direction . . . When we crept in, a spectacled young man in a raincoat was declaiming with passion some lines about Greek gods and Trojan heroes . . . Then . . . about a dozen women . . . slowly moved forward . . . and in far-away voices began chanting verses that prophesied woe . . . If you were writing a story about a large pub in Newcastle, you would never have the impudence to fill its first-floor front with people rehearsing Greek drama. . . . we sneaked out, and down the stairs I muttered: 'What's Hecuba to them or they to Hecuba?'[1]

Priestley's question relies on a sense of incongruity (just, perhaps, avoiding patronising), which works to heighten the People's significance to but also its distinction from the city of which it is a part: this isn't the sort of place you'd expect a theatre like this; this isn't the sort of thing you'd expect such a theatre to produce; yet this theatre is undeniably here.

Beyond noting the incongruity it evokes, though, we can see how Priestley's question echoes Hamlet's beguilement by the passion of the players visiting Elsinore (in 2.2.). In turn, that question might be repurposed in a way that relates directly to this collection's concerns: what's

Shakespeare to them, or they to Shakespeare? Or, more expansively, what did and does Shakespeare mean to a local, amateur, politicised theatre in northern England, and how might such a theatre use him? Significantly, Priestley's question is similar to ones that the People's Theatre has asked itself, in various ways, in the years since its inception in 1911. This means that answering it, and my own questions, involves exploring debates that have played out over several decades within the People's itself (and beyond) about Shakespeare's place at the People's, and in Newcastle; about Shakespeare's political resonance (or lack of it); and about what local amateur theatre is for. The People's has itself also long self-consciously poked fun at the notion that Shakespeare and the non-professional stage are not meant to mix. In William Scott's 1963 play written for the People's, *No Women, Mr Shakespeare*, Shakespeare accepts five guineas from an aristocrat to interpolate lines into a performance of *The Merchant of Venice*, but whinges: 'I am nothing but a paid hack, writing common stuff for damned amateurs to recite'.[2] These words, of course, were recited by 'damned amateurs', helping keep Shakespeare alive. Accordingly, this chapter is in part a contribution to the ongoing (global and local) effort to rethink where, why, and by whose graft and energy Shakespeare is sustained and 'happens', outwith the 'metropolitan bank of Shakespeare knowledge'.[3] Equally, too, this chapter is part of the move to redress the way amateur Shakespeare has been 'substantially overlooked' by scholars.[4] As Michael Dobson notes, this redressing raises other important questions:

> [T]he long history of how Shakespeare has been performed by amateurs is a story of how successive groups of people have committed themselves to incorporating these plays into their own lives and their own immediate societies, and it makes visible a whole range of responses to the national drama which other reception histories have missed . . . How have different instances of amateur performance negotiated between Shakespeare's plays as expressions of high or at least national culture and the lived everyday local cultures in which they have been mounted?[5]

Though Dobson does not mention the People's in his study, there can be no question that as an amateur theatre the People's contributed to, and indeed still helps constitute, the 'lived everyday local cultures' of which it was, and *is*, a part. Writing in 1950, Sir Charles Trevelyan, husband of Lady Mary Trevelyan (the Theatre's president), former minister for education, Labour MP for Newcastle Central (1922–31), and Lord Lieutenant of Northumberland (thus a man with impeccable northern credentials), asserted: 'To hundreds of us Northerners, the People's Theatre in Newcastle is a big element in our lives. It has become an enduring part of Tyneside society'.⁶ Trevelyan confidently predicted that the Theatre would 'not only survive but play a leading part in the dramatic and cultural life of the north of England'.⁷ This involved performing Shakespeare, as a review of *Othello* in the same year affirmed: 'Tyneside always has reason to be grateful to the People's Theatre for bringing . . . "difficult" plays to the north-east'.⁸ By the 1940s, the People's was self-consciously aware that its reputation was attracting audiences from the greater North, 'from Sheffield . . . from Berwick . . . from Carlisle . . . from Middlesbrough and Sunderland, from Morpeth and Alnwick . . . and many more regularly from the Tyneside districts outside the city boundaries'.⁹

However, in a key instance of the People's ambiguous and complex relationship to Shakespeare, this northernness did not always mean that the People's members and audiences expected to see or hear their region reflected in productions of his plays. A review of a 1926 *Troilus and Cressida* observed that 'defects of enunciation' were 'worse than the occasional inflection of Tyneside accent which crept into the voices of one or two of the Greeks and Trojans'.¹⁰ It would seem to some that both should be guarded against.

When northernness *was* evoked in Shakespearean productions, especially in vocal delivery, there was not necessarily any sense of association or sympathy with a character (quite the opposite). For example, a 1976 *Twelfth Night* featured 'old sourpuss Malvolio, portrayed here complete with clipped northern accent'.¹¹ Nonetheless, the People's could sometimes not be beyond reproducing old stereotypes about regional accents and their association with stupidity or low comedy in productions of Shakespeare. So, in a 1987 *Much Ado*, Christopher Goulding offered a 'show-stopping performance as a foolish constable with a strong Geordie accent'.¹² When productions did touch on regional locations, effects were mixed for some local reviewers. A 1974 production of *Macbeth* could not, we're told, match 'the atmosphere of . . . [Roman] Polanski's [1971] film', much of which was shot in Northumberland; but, nonetheless, a distinctly regional feel was aimed at: 'Huge whirling clouds scud crazily in the background, sombre northern hills loom menacingly'.¹³ Some productions sought to establish what was seen as an authentic rendering of local identity, as they tried to negotiate issues like accent in ways that emphasised the complexity of that identity's history:

> Contrary to usual tradition John Barber who takes the part of the Duke of Northumberland and John Shepherd who plays young Hotspur, his

son, in the People's production of *Richard II* are not using a Northumbrian accent . . . Producer Nicholas Whitfield thinks that accents in the area were probably more Scots than Northumbrian in the 14th century.[14]

Furthermore, reviewers have sometimes understood productions in relation to 'everyday local cultures', including a terrace in the stands at St James' Park, the ground of Newcastle United Football Club: 'The assembled horde on stage for the start of "Julius Caesar" seems to be of Leazes End proportions'.[15] While this raises questions about how to perceive the assembled citizens on match-day, this was a canny image to use to describe a theatre who could count Colin Veitch, a former Newcastle United FA Cup-winning Captain, and 'committed socialist', as a founder member.[16]

Shakespeare and Socialism at the People's: To Be or Not to Be?

Colin Veitch's politics bring into play another significant set of ambiguities and complexities regarding Shakespeare at the People's. In 1911, along with the Clarion Cycling Club and Clarion Vocal Union, The Clarion Dramatic Society grew up out of and alongside Newcastle's branch of the British Socialist Party, 'united' by 'a Fabian outlook on politics and the pursuit of a healthy and intellectually stimulating way of life':

> A love of culture was a fundamental part of the socialism practised by the Clarion movement . . . What could be better than the formation of a drama group to bring culture to the masses?[17]

Such aspirations were common across the North in the period, as Alice Foley's account of her coming of political and cultural age in Bolton attests:

> As a member of a group of young socialists I hoarded my scanty pocket-money, amounting at that time to one penny in the shilling of factory earnings, so that I could afford with them the luxury of a monthly matinée. With a cheap seat in pit or gallery we saw most of the early Shaw and Galsworthy plays, followed by tea in the Clarion café in Market Street . . . If the café was crowded, we hived off to the Art Gallery and over tea, brown bread, peaches and cream we animatedly argued and discussed the philosophy, art or satire of the productions. The whole outing cost about five shillings each, but we returned home like exultant

young gods, tingling and athirst with the naïve faith that if only sufficient human beings could witness good drama and comedy it might change the world.[18]

By doing what it did when it did, the People's was continuing what Dobson sees as 'the radical heritage of the early nineteenth-century "spouting clubs" and their politicized Chartist descendants'.[19] The Dramatic Society and the Socialist Party were both working to provide funds to 'meet the rent of the premises' they shared:

> If, we asked, money was needed to keep the wolf from the door of our faith, why not use the drama both to collect funds and to propagate our truths? Let us . . . bring in the money with one hand and deal out our doctrines with the other . . . All the collections went to the British Socialist Party.[20]

From the off, this drive to create a self-sufficient and financially sustainable union of politics and playing produced some radical performances, and some tensions and conflicts. Radical performances included the first staging 'in Britain on September 23rd, 1911', of George Bernard Shaw's *The Shewing-up of Blanco Posset*, a play 'recently . . . forbidden by the Censor'.[21] Equally, though, the tensions and conflicts which attended on aligning performance and politics complicated responses to the types of plays produced, with even a financially successful production like 1913's version of W. S. Gilbert's *Pygmalion and Galatea* (1871) criticised by those involved because it had 'none of the propaganda of social betterment we thought a play should have'.[22] And if this union was meant to have a bettering effect on *audiences*, it could sometimes be hard to discern. Describing a 1916–17 season staging of J. M. Barrie's *The Admirable Crichton* (1902) in which the players 'resisted the temptation' to turn the production 'into an entertaining piece of Socialist propaganda', Norman Veitch reflects:

> We had always received letters of encouragement and criticism from our audiences, including many which denounced the introduction of 'insidious Socialist propaganda' into the plays we performed, but during the run . . . we received more of these denunciatory letters than we had ever received before.[23]

Ironically, the production team had decided against changes to the text which would have 'enhanced the socialist nature of the play's message'.[24]

As the 1910s progressed, tensions within the theatre, and between players and audiences, mirrored conflicts between the People's and its political hosts:

> From our original intention to produce plays for the purpose of keeping the British Socialist Party's head above the financial breakers, we had gone on to the idea of propagating Socialism, firmly believing that if our audiences could be compelled to ponder the ills of our times they would discover that the only remedy was a Socialist one. There can be no doubt, however, that interest in the drama for its own sake was growing; and ... some members of the British Socialist party both saw and resented it.[25]

By March 1917, one of a set of new rules sought to insist that the Clarion Dramatic Society had as its object "'the propaganda of Socialism and financial assistance to the Socialist movement'"; this was 'immediately' amended to affirm "'That all plays be applicable to Socialism or other advanced subjects.'" Another new rule stated that no member could hold office unless they were "'an avowed Socialist'"; this was not amended despite the heterogeneous politics of those comprising the People's even at this stage.[26] Crucially, one month later (and one year after the 1916 Shakespearean celebrations), 'it was decided to put on a Shakespearean production during the next season'.[27] In his history of the People's, Veitch describes 'the fact that we had chosen to do a Shakespeare play at all' in 1917 as 'significant'.[28]

Sadly, Veitch doesn't elaborate at that point why it might have been. Perhaps, though, it was in part because this dating puts the People's slightly ahead of the game in the North – as Dobson reports, Middlesbrough Little Theatre staged its first Shakespearean play in 1935 (*The Merchant of Venice*), and Bolton Little Theatre put on *Much Ado About Nothing* in 1937.[29] Equally, the significance of a socialist-inclined theatre group deciding to do Shakespeare might have been increased because, around the same time, some were arguing for the incommensurability of Shakespeare and socialism. As numerous scholars have shown, it is possible (and important) to evince 'Shakespeare's complex embeddedness in Communism and socialism'.[30] But in part because of Shakespeare's status as 'representative of "bourgeois" artistic traditions', his usefulness in advancing left-wing politics has at times been far from assured.[31] Hence, to Edward Salmon, writing in 1916, Shakespeare was 'superior to any mere party or class feeling', and showed that the 'craving for equality' was as 'chimerical as all Socialistic experimenters, if not Socialistic theorists, know it to be'.[32]

If Shakespeare could be seen as antagonistic to socialism, why should a theatre group with socialist roots perform him?

Later in his history, though, Veitch does offer some further comments which provide insights into the theatre's burgeoning relationship with Shakespeare from 1917 onwards:

> When *Twelfth Night* was performed in the season of 1922–23 it was done in our extremity because of the difficulty of obtaining licences, and in fifteen seasons we had only produced two Shakespearean plays. The fact seems to be that we were still under the spell of 'Socialism or other advanced objects', even though we had dropped the words as expressing our object as a theatre; and the 'merely poetic' drama was frowned on . . . The desire for Shakespeare, however, had been growing and could not now be entirely disregarded.[33]

Such comments suggest that we cannot discount the financial and logistical benefits – which were clearly considerable at a time of 'diminishing funds'– of putting on a play that needed no licence, and would draw in crowds.[34] These reflections do not, however, explain the delay in producing Shakespeare between that decision to stage him in 1917 and the eventual staging in 1921 (beyond the obvious pressures of the war), or explicate whose 'desire' it was to see or perform Shakespeare. But it may or may not be coincidental that as the Theatre's explicitly political imperatives became more contested, so the 'desire' to offer Shakespeare – lucrative, but '"merely poetic"'– increased. Indeed, it was in 1921 that the Theatre's big break with its past was formalised, reflected in the name change from the Clarion Dramatic Society: '[The] People's Theatre . . . sounded more democratic, more all-embracing than the old name'.[35] The same year witnessed a new constitution, which stated the 'object of the Society, more tersely than before, was to be "the production of plays applicable to Socialism or other advanced objects"'.[36] Building on the flexibility allowed by that critical 'or', by 1924 another new set of rules stated that '"the object of the Society shall be the furtherance of Art by the production of plays, the development of players and the founding of a People's Playhouse"'.[37] This 'got rid of that avowal of Socialism . . . as desired by some of our members', but 'it brought repercussions' from the (itself now renamed) Newcastle Socialist Society, with whom 'relations . . . became more and more strained'.[38] By the middle of the 1920s, those relations were 'deteriorating rapidly', as the Socialist Society saw the 'financial value' of the Theatre, but also wanted more control over its assets and resources.[39]

However, so as not to denude Shakespeare's political potential, or the Theatre's, it is important to contest the idea that the People's was committing 'apostasy' by steadily turning its back on politically improving, socially conscious drama.[40] As Veitch triumphantly declares, productions in 1924–5 continued to present 'a season of propaganda, of religion, of pacifism, of sociology and of ethics preached by authors who meant what they said'.[41] Fittingly, in 1926 the People's staged *Troilus and Cressida*, the programme for which stated that Shakespeare, 'alone of all dramatists', gave 'to the world . . . a picture so vivid of the desolation wrought by human conflict', proving 'that in every war there is an element of irredeemable shame and misery'.[42] This tradition continued with 1981's inaugural production at the Theatre's Studio Upstairs, *Henry V*, the programme for which noted 'it is . . . a play about war and especially peace'.[43]

Indeed, to later, geographically removed, outside observers of the People's, there was no contradiction between Shakespeare and socialism either. The Irish playwright Sean O'Casey contributed 'A Message' to the Theatre's in-house magazine in 1947, drawing on Shakespearean imagery to celebrate what he foresaw as social emancipation, as well as the Theatre's role in achieving it, as 'a University of the Arts in Newcastle':

> Don't forget your folk-lore, folk-song, and folk-dance. England must come back to England . . . Bottom is the real hero in "Midsummer Night's Dream", and the ass's head is fading away from the workers' and the peasants' body. More and more are we workers becoming worthy to lie beside the fair Titania.[44]

While the atavism and cultural regression O'Casey expresses here arguably runs counter to socialism's internationalist outlook, his idealism nonetheless offers a vision in which Shakespeare and amateur productions of him are part of a radically liberating 'folk' movement with a long heritage and bright future.

In reality, though, life at the People's was not entirely in accord with O'Casey's exultant imaginings, though it remained sympathetic to their aims. In an open letter in the theatre's in-house magazine that same year, Inez Scott addressed a column by William Poulton (in the *Newcastle Journal*, 1 December 1947) which reported that a certain '"W. G. of South Shields . . . sees the setup [at the People's] as a sub-political propaganda organisation"'. In a judicious appraisal of the Theatre's past, and the situation at the time, Scott retorts:

> It is, of course, perfectly true that the dramatic club which founded our theatre was born in a socialist club. I have always been a little ashamed of the fact that, as soon as it was able to afford other premises, it apparently shook the dust of the socialist off its feet ... Since that time, the theatre has no official politics ... I have met both socialists and communists at the theatre ... at least one Irish Home Ruler ... however, the only subscription for season tickets ... comes from a local Conservative association.[45]

Recognising a comparable heterodoxy, one historian of the theatre notes that eventually, by the middle of the 1900s, it was only those 'who were unfamiliar with our ways' who 'regarded' the People's as a 'nest of communists' with a 'hotline to Stalin'.[46] Further evidence for this perspective comes from noting that, for some, heterodoxy had gone too far, as can be seen in a letter published in the Theatre's in-house magazine in 1950. The author acknowledged what some referred to as 'the unfortunate skeletons of a disreputable past' of the People's socialist reputation, but averred 'I am not at all sure that the past was so disreputable', and lamented that 'I have seen little manifestation of that revolutionary spirit', because 'audiences' have 'too much in them of the season ticket and the bourgeoisie'.[47]

This history of engagements with Shakespeare hopefully shows how the People's was grappling with 'the problem of how to produce and act Shakespeare ... for a modern audience' in a 'progressive theatre' trying to extricate itself from ossified dramatic practices and ideological positions.[48] The theatre's often heated debates about its identity and politics were informed as much by its members' perceptions of what theatre – including Shakespeare – was for, as they were by shifts in what socialism was for during the century. But one key theatrical figure had a part to play in arguments about the People's Shakespeare: George Bernard Shaw.

Chafing with its Shaw

In their earliest days, and for many years after, the People's was in awe of Shaw, 'almost the patron saint' of the theatre.[49] He made it easy to stage performances 'of the best drama ... being written at the time' that were also 'sympathetic to the cause of socialism'.[50] He provided their 'first full-length play' (*Major Barbara*, 1912), and the vast majority of their plays in the Theatre's early years.[51] After some persuasion, he attended a performance of his own play *Candida* in 1921, and gave 'his last speech in public' at the Theatre in 1936.⁵² So awed and Shawdolatrous were the actors of the People's that putting on their 'first Shakespearean production', *The Merry Wives of Windsor*, just after Shaw's first visit in 1921, felt like light relief after an 'occasion' that was 'too big for us': 'into it we put all the gaiety and buoyancy we felt after our emergence from a great ordeal'.⁵³ As this comment intimates, because Shaw was integral to the People's identity, and just as his creative output dominated the repertoire, so, at times, his simultaneously dogmatic and accommodating view of Shakespeare provided a model of ambivalence for the Theatre's own approaches.

On the one hand, writing 'countless passages of hyperbolic denunciation', Shaw made no secret of his revolutionary solution to the problems he saw in Shakespeare, and the oppressive and 'superstitious veneration' in which he was held: 'Shakespeare ... is to me one of the towers of the Bastille, and down he must come'.⁵⁴ Shaw thought one would have a vain 'search for statesmanship, or even citizenship' in Shakespeare's works.⁵⁵ Shakespeare had, railed Shaw, 'no politics, no conscience, no hope, no convictions of any sort'.⁵⁶ On the other hand, however, over his career, Shaw's response to Shakespeare was more ambiguous and complex than such denunciations would suggest, and the People's replicated these ambiguities and complexities at various points in its history.

In his 'Preface' to *The Dark Lady of the Sonnets* (1914), George Bernard Shaw suggested that Shakespeare 'regarded himself as a gentleman under a cloud ... and never for a moment as a man of the people'.⁵⁷ Or, we might say, as a man of the People's; indeed, the Theatre staged this play demythologising Shakespeare as part of an 'Oriental Carnival' in 1923. That said, in the same season the People's put on a hugely successful *Twelfth Night*. When presenting 'a sequence of plays from the time of Queen Elizabeth to the present day', in 1934–5, the People's did not include any Shakespeare, because 'there are many excellent plays other than Shakespeare's'.⁵⁸ Nonetheless, in the same season they did put on *King Lear* and 'attendances ... were really good'.⁵⁹

As Shaw put it in the 'Preface' to what he deemed 'in all actuarial possibility ... my last play', the irreverent and punchy, in all senses, *Shakes Versus Shav* (which the People's produced along with Joe Ging's parody of an equally irreverent song about Shakespeare in 1953's *Kiss me Kate*, 'Brush up your Shavian', in 1988): 'Nothing can extinguish my interest in Shakespear [*sic*].'⁶⁰ In *Shakes Versus Shav*, a puppet 'William Shakes' mocks the 'ecstasy of self-conceit' of the 'shameless fraud' that is 'G. B. S.' (also a puppet), and '*They spar.*' Shav responds by ridiculing Shakes' verse with unflattering comparisons, and resolves, in the end 'We are both mortal'.⁶¹

Some accommodation has been reached: 'Shaw can delight in the best things in Shakespeare because he does not pretend to perpetual awe.'[62]

The People's subscribed to this anti-bardolatrous perspective. The programme for a 1932 *Macbeth* noted how 'the opening of the Stratford Memorial Theatre on April 23rd' had occasioned a widespread hero worship in 'the general mind' that 'embalmed' Shakespeare, like some mummy. The People's independent-minded production, however, had 'no thought of joining in this pious adoration' or contributing to 'the pomp of ritual on a state occasion' in staging 'the glorious exciting delightful plays of the lovable enigmatic man who was Shakespeare'.[63] Comparably, People's members pulled no punches when critiquing Shakespeare as they offered in-house reviews of the Theatre's productions:

> Considering the author, the play [*Measure for Measure*] is not up to much, with fewer 'immortal' lines in the verse than in any other I recall, and with a narrative that degenerates into a terrible scrappiness towards the end.[64]

When Shaw criticised Shakespeare, he emphasised the Bard's compromising commercial instincts, noting that 'Shakespeare found that the only thing that paid in the theatre was romantic nonsense', and that, for Shakespeare, 'all inquiry into life began and ended with the question, "Does it pay?"'[65] At times it seemed that the People's saw Shakespeare the same way. Discussing the Stockport Garrick amateur theatre, Michael Dobson suggests an appeal for other amateur theatres that contradicts this:

> As pillars of an alternative theatre repertory otherwise dominated by Ibsen and Shaw, Shakespeare's defiantly outmoded plays were identified not just as uncommercial but potentially as anti-commercial into the bargain . . . and it is clear from the archives of the [Stockport] Garrick and other societies like it that the underlying ideal of twentieth-century amateur Shakespeare, derived ultimately from John Ruskin and William Morris, was the restoration of the organic society, the return to an imagined collective artisan life of unalienated labour . . . a short-cut back to Merry England.[66]

For the People's, however, whatever the function of other dramatists, during that transition through and from socialist ideals, Shakespeare was a commercial means to an end. As we have seen, in 1922, 'diminishing funds' meant that that 'we turned – such was our extremity – to Shakespeare and selected *Twelfth Night*'.[67] This behaviour repeats itself. Closing the season in 1932 with *Macbeth* 'started off a series of Shakespearean productions . . . which were real money-makers'.[68] Later directors of the People's would confidently assert that 'Shakespeare . . . will fill the house, whatever the season, whatever the weather and, mercifully, whatever the play'.[69] But for the theatre in its earlier days, productions that were 'financially disastrous', like 1927's *Troilus and Cressida*, or *Love's Labour's Lost* ten years later, made some opine that '[i]t is questionable whether the lesser works of great writers ought to be laboriously kept alive'.[70] Shakespeare's stature was, therefore, conditional.

Nonetheless, linking Shakespeare and financial success – or survival – influenced the schedule of productions. In the 1930s, members of the Theatre militated against putting on a pantomime, despite (or perhaps because) it would be useful 'from a money point of view', with some arguing that 'the People's Theatre did not exist for that sort of thing'; that is, commercial, low-brow fluff.[71] However, in time, giving Shakespearean productions an air of panto's cheap thrills was a way to square the circle, to both make money and offer something aesthetically nourishing if not always ideologically respectable. Of a winter 1961 staging of *As You Like It*, one in-house commentator observed 'The production . . . put me . . . in the right mood for Christmas'.[72] The local press agreed, with one reporter noting 'Many a modern pantomime producer would be glad to provoke so many laughs'.[73]

As Shaw's cultural power waned in these post-war years (as did, unfortunately, progressive socialism's political valency in the world), so Shakespeare's waxed at the People's. A lengthy discussion of the merits (and failings) of *Cymbeline* (as a play, not a production) a year before Shaw's death, and perhaps influenced by his later outlook, noted 'Shakespeare is our master-dramatist; the influence of his writings is immeasurable'.[74] And then, in the very year of Shaw's death, and in an issue of *The Tyneside Phoenix* titled the 'Bernard Shaw Number' (featuring a lengthy piece celebrating the recently deceased playwright, and emphasising how much the Theatre owed to him), this: 'Shakespeare home again at the Old Vic. His birthplace alive this summer . . . Othello at the "People's". All should be well for those who, like the writer, consider Shakespeare more worth acting and seeing than . . . I would say a trio of Shaws!'[75] Shawconoclasm, indeed.

By 1954, it appeared to those involved that the People's ventured to offer something approaching a consistent method for engaging with Shakespeare: 'The People's Theatre policy with regard to Shakespeare usually is to perform . . . lesser known . . . plays'.[76] By 1958, the People's was making 'yearly obeisance to Shakespeare'.[77] By 1964, buoyed by this familiarity, and to celebrate the 400th anniversary of Shakespeare's birth, a programme for *King Lear* indicated that the company was no longer merely 'content to sport among the foothills of Shakespeare' as it took on that intense tragedy.[78] In the eyes of the Theatre itself, the ambition paid off, certainly with regard to this production:

> this was an amateur production, but the term could not be applied in any derogatory sense. Where previous 'People's' Shakespeare productions have often lacked cohesion and smoothness . . . here the overall feeling was one of pace, polish and sheer professionalism.[79]

Ultimately, based on such ambitions, facility, and success regarding Shakespeare, by 1979, reviewers could confidently claim of the Theatre that 'A Shakespearian play is always in its repertoire'.[80] Shakespeare was – and is – still regarded as something special, and somewhat apart, amid the array of dramatists whose work is staged by the Theatre. The director Chris Heckels recalls how 'you'd have to be one of the great and the good' to be offered the opportunity to direct a Shakespeare play.[81]

Nothing voices this ambivalence, if not endorsing it, better than Scott's *No Women, Mr Shakespeare*. Set at The Globe in 1600, the play begins with Shakespeare's friends and contemporaries about to celebrate his 36th birthday, but with the man himself too lovelorn and depressed to write again. This prospect upsets some more than others:

WEBSTER: There are other playwrights.
BURBAGE: None like him. He's more than a man – he's a portent – he's the prop of the stage – he's the spinner of words – he's the king of the theatre –
KEMP: (drily from the door) He's coming.[82]

When staged in December 1963, the production allowed the Theatre to offer a 'light-hearted curtain raiser' prior to a 'serious tribute to the fourth centenary of Shakespeare's birth' in 1964.[83] With this 'hilarious' commemorative tribute, the People's was both celebrating and de-mythologising the Bard, in a manner that accorded with its history (and Shaw's methods) of handling Shakespeare.[84]

Topical Theatre

Even after the People's protracted divorce from doctrinaire socialism, a commitment remained to staging drama that spoke to and about the concerns of the locality and period – what we might call *topical* art, for and from a particular place and time. And despite Shakespeare's problematic place in the arguments surrounding that divorce, as being '"merely poetic"' (or just *not* Shaw), this urge to make topical art sometimes involved him too. Sometimes, but not always, and not always successfully to some. Veitch dismissed 'producing Shakespeare in modern dress' in 1930's *Two Gentleman of Verona* as 'largely a stunt': 'while we found it certainly novel, we did not find it attractive'.[85] Comparably, the 1964 *King Lear* eschewed modernising at all, and sought to evoke a 'timelessness' in its staging, which offered an 'orthodox reading of the play' and did not try to 'emulate [Peter] Brook's strikingly original production'.[86]

Part of the reticence about 'modernising' Shakespeare might have been related to what (paying) audiences would take. To one reviewer in 1958, Shakespeare offered respite from anything modern, or challenging intellectually or aesthetically, 'a rest-cure for audiences after the heavy, searching works of Green, Williams, Miller and Tchekov we have seen during the last months'.[87] When modernising did happen, not all reviewers approved, as with a 1966 production of *The Taming of the Shrew*, which was an 'experiment in modern, with-it dress' and 'hipster slacks'.[88] One opined that they were 'all for making Shakespeare modern in a powerful, social way' (without specifying what this might mean), but also grumbled at how modernising productions unsettled expectations about both Shakespeare and gender identity: 'Tight trousers make minces where swaggers should be.'[89]

Even these reservations indicate that the People's has a long and rich tradition, which still continues, of trying to make Shakespeare meaningful for modern audiences, and in socio-political terms. During and just after the Second World War, other dramatists, including early modern ones, were read by the Theatre's members as having contemporary resonances. A review of a 1946 production of Marlowe's *Doctor Faustus* in the in-house magazine *The Tyneside Phoenix* observed as much:

> In view of current history it is difficult to avoid comment on the subject matter of a play about a clever German who in exchange for a few years of unlimited power sells his soul to the devil ... The World has progressed since the 16th Century and, if [Faustus'] spirit was allowed off the coals for a visit to the Court-room of Nuremburg, he would, I am sure, acknowledge that the modern art of wickedness has moved out of his class.[90]

Nonetheless, at this time, and in something of a contrast that again seems to emphasise Shakespeare's '"merely poetic"' qualities, the theatre favoured Shakespearean comedies and other plays of reconciliation and recovery (reviving *Twelfth Night*, as well as premiering *The Winter's Tale*, *The Comedy of Errors*, *The Tempest*, *As You like It*, and *A Midsummer Night's Dream*). Some of these productions, such as the 1946 *Dream*, sought to cast Shakespeare as 'purely decorative, as we . . . have tried to be'.[91] This need not be interpreted as escapism, however, rather a desire to offer light amid, and while acknowledging, the darkness of the times. Indeed, the programme for the 1942 *Comedy* explicitly situated the production in relation to the paranoia and discriminations of the conflict:

> TIME:
> The present
> SCENE:
> THE PORT OF EPHESUS
> NO SYRACUSANS ADMITTED
> DEFENSE D'ENTRER AUX SYRACUSIENS
> Syrakusanern ist der Eintritt verboten
> SYRACUSANI VETANTUR INTRARE[92]

Mid-century concerns about violent bigotry certainly informed other, non-Shakespearean productions. A 1937 staging of *Professor Bernhardi*, Arthur Schnitzler's account of anti-Semitism (translated into English in 1927), was ideologically sound given the climate in Europe at the time, but commercially unsuccessful: 'A play with a moral, indeed, but . . . the audiences were the poorest of the whole season'.[93] Choosing to stage *The Merchant of Venice* in 1943 (a play which is a comedy really only in generic terms) could be seen as an attempt to remedy that failure, while maintaining the message, though one reviewer wanted more: Inez Branson (as Jessica) 'was hardly Oriental and fiery enough', suggesting the play's staging of othering deserved a stronger showing.[94] The first post-war Shakespearean *tragedy* put on by the People's, in 1948, was *Coriolanus*. This is a play that can be seen to expose the depredations of arrogant, heedless autocracy, and the desperation of rationing and dearth, where citizens (however compromised) find their voices: the perfect work, perhaps, for life under the nationalising Labour government of 1945–51. War, and the effort of rebuilding a nation fit for heroes, cast a long shadow: the permanent set for 1955's *Antony and Cleopatra* featured 'bomb-tail-like decorations' and 'festival of Britain scaffolding'.[95]

Later directors and productions at the People's – by Eric Peel, Tony Childs, and Chris Heckels – have sought to be even more explicit in attaining Shakespearean topicality. In this, while they might not have been overtly socialist, they have come close to the cause celebrated by some Shakespearean critics in the 1980s, whose work sought to manifest a 'commitment to the transformation of a social order which exploits people on grounds of race, gender, and class'.[96] Accordingly, Peel identified Shakespeare's simultaneously vital and unsettling resonance amid modern cultural faultlines, with his *Othello* in 1999:

> Is there a play more contemporary than Shakespeare? . . . I have never read a more contemporary play than 'Othello' . . . 'Ebony and Ivory live together in perfect harmony' Wrong! . . . The Lawrence report[97] has just been published. I find it difficult to take while doing this play.[98]

Similarly, reviving *The Winter's Tale* in 1994, Tony Childs emphasised how the play's 'miracles' of 'human forgiveness and reconciliation' provoked questions for post-conflict environments now: 'Is it too fanciful to think of Ireland [the Downing Street Agreement had been signed between the British and Irish governments in 1993, and in August 1994 the Provisional IRA proclaimed a cessation of violence], or South Africa [where Nelson Mandela had been inaugurated as president on 10 May 1994], at this moment?'[99] And when commenting on *Measure for Measure* in 2002, Childs (co-directing with Sue Hinton) suggested that the play's questions about 'public and private morality . . . the nature of justice, and the role of the state and the church in sexual behaviour' were 'very much of our time'.[100]

Peel, directing *Henry IV Part I* in 1991, recommended and acclaimed the play as 'the most accessible to twentieth-century readers and audiences'.[101] Discussing the aspiration to make Shakespeare topical in her own productions, Heckels asserts 'I do if I can'; that is, where 'immediacy' means audiences can 'relate' to the text, when it 'helps understanding of the play', and if it provides answers to the question 'What's the play about?'[102] For Heckels, this requires not changing the language (apart from expeditious cuts), while also affirming, like Peel, that a staging has to be 'accessible'.[103] For the People's in recent years, on the one hand this accessibility has involved 'being less traditional with Shakespeare' than some previous directors in terms of sets, costume and stage imagery, but also simply ensuring that a cast works 'like mad on voice and language', focusing on clarity, diction and projection.[104]

Following these principles, Heckels' large-scale 1987 *Much Ado* included a magazine about the characters, and TV news footage describing their relationships, to help situate the play in a world of contemporary celebrity and recent conflicts: 'I did it modern', she asserts now.[105] The production's image of the return of the 'main protagonists' from a successful military campaign offered 'a strong analogy of the Falklands conflict'.[106] Furthermore, the lovers were, to several commentators, 'in the role of Andy/Fergie [Prince Andrew and Sarah Ferguson, married in 1986]'.[107] For some reviewers, in contrast to earlier concerns about 'modernising' Shakespeare, this method was only partially successful, either because it didn't go far enough, or not clearly enough. While acclaiming Heckels' 'thoughtful direction', one reviewer suggested that the contemporary 'connection' was 'never fully exploited', and concluded that the audience was 'left wondering whether they've missed some subtle political message', suggesting that 'it's doubtful whether dragging this play into the 20th century has added anything to it'.[108]

Yet Heckels developed her methods, and explicated the political potentials of playing Shakespeare, with 2005's *Henry V* at the 'height of the Iraq war'.[109] Noting that 'the modernity of this play is staggering', Heckels interpreted 'Shakespeare's "Wooden O"' as 'the Media Circus which both surrounds and is embedded in modern warfare' and the production featured a mixed-media montage of contemporary military hardware and footage from the conflict, as Henry's troops advanced on the audience in combat gear.[110]

The politicality and contemporaneity of Heckels' 2013 *King Lear* can be seen to bring productions at the People's full circle back to something close to socialist roots in a nation and a region subsisting in an age of government-ordained austerity. Her staging focused on 'the difference between the fantastically rich and powerful and those who have nothing – neither hope, money, nor future . . . who, to the "haves", are both invisible and insignificant'. Heckels' programme notes quoted Gloucester's lines about 'distribution' undoing 'excess' until 'each man has enough', to make this point: 'Politicians, please take note!'[111] Colin Veitch would have been proud.

Stratford upon Tyne?

If the People's Shakespeares have engaged over many years in different ways with critical moments in the remaking of national identity and political culture, so the theatre has had a complex relationship with the institutions of national (not to say international) Shakespeare, such as the

Royal Shakespeare Company, based in Stratford-upon-Avon. In the theatre's earlier days, it was at times dependent on the larger, professional company's resources for prestige: discussing the use of outfits borrowed from the RSC in 1956, one reviewer opined 'the Stratford costumes gave a finish to the picture that, alas, is often missing from productions at this theatre'.[112] Even for some sympathetic commentators, then, it was hard for the People's to compare to the RSC on its annual visits to Newcastle's Theatre Royal:

> The RSC has clearly spoiled the North-East with Shakespeare. We've come to expect impeccable acting, beautiful sets, imaginative lighting and the rest, almost as a right. Fine for the RSC – but how to adjust to the efforts of others – to something like the Newcastle People's Theatre account of *King Lear*? A Shakespearian play is always in its repertoire, but even on its own level, which is by no means inconsiderable, the results have not always been successful. *King Lear*, however, scrapes in as an exception.[113]

Occasionally, the People's internalised these ambivalent feelings. The RSC would use the Theatre as a host space for its own productions in 1987–8 and 2005, performing *Titus Andronicus* and *Thomas More* - lesser-performed texts with which to be experimental in a low-risk, unusual setting. But the first arrival of the august company did not go unremarked by the Theatre's members. In December 1986, *Offset*, the latest incarnation of the Theatre's in-house magazine, reported the concerns felt within the People's, under a banner citing *Timon of Athens* '"O! THE FIERCE WRETCHEDNESS THAT GLORY BRINGS US"'. It is hard to tell whether the glory was reflected from the RSC's presence (which would confirm the inferiority and wretchedness of the People's), or already inherent in the People's (which had attracted the RSC and which their presence would simply burnish). *Offset* acknowledges that the potential of hosting the RSC has provoked 'reservations', because it 'affects and influences so many areas' of the People's, and would cause 'considerable disruption' to the Theatre's spring season in 1987; there is, then, a strong sense of the question of keeping the People's identity intact as they accommodate the Stratford theatre rolling into town: 'Could we do it? Should we do it?'. At the same time, *Offset* appreciates those voices who want to 'minimise any potential disadvantages' and 'make the most of the opportunities offered', for revenue, expertise and exposure.[114] The same issue of *Offset* featured a playful vignette which sought to both air concerns about what the RSC's arrival might do to the People's status as an amateur, non-commercial theatre, and also satirise them. A 'young playwright' clutching a script passes 'the [fictional] Stella Theatre' in Newcastle (patronised by those 'reeking of vulgar wealth') and is appalled to see it 'blazing' with 'neon lights' advertising 'RSC COMING SOON! ... TV STARS! DESIGNER COSTUMES! ... REAL MONKEYS!'. The idealistic dramaturge passes by in disgust, en route to a place where he could 'bring real theatre to the people', untainted by commercial bourgeois affectation; the socialist roots of the People's would thereby be honoured. To his horror, though, on arrival at the People's (where else?) he sees it too gaudily lit up 'like an amusement arcade': 'RSC COMING SOON! ... Oh no! They were everywhere!' As if to emphasise the prostituting of art for or by money, the Corner House pub next to the Theatre on the Coast Road was 'bedecked' with 'flashing lights' inviting punters to the 'ANNE HATHAWAY PIZZA LOUNGE', with 'ROMEO 'N' JULIET'S BAR INSIDE!!' As the rain falls, the young man's script for a 'forgotten play' inevitably dissolves.[115] Comparably, an *Offset* edition for April 1987 featured a hand-drawn cover image showing someone in the process of pasting 'R. S. [C.]' over 'THE PEOPLE'S', suggesting both the potentially effacing but also transient nature of the relationship.[116] The self-deprecating humour and hyperbole in these responses both set up and undo oppositions between amateur and professional, big business show business and small-scale, local production, North and South, 'them' and 'us', at once making and mocking the People's distinctness. As it was, by February 1987, the People's was explicitly extending 'a warm welcome' to the RSC.[117] Little wonder, since the profit from the hire was almost '£8000', and the RSC praised the 'knock-out effort' of the People's members, affirming 'We want to come back'.[118]

They were true to their word. Their 2012 performance of *Quick Bright Things*, a play by a local dramatist Alison Carr inspired by *A Midsummer Night's Dream*, was a site-specific promenade production, beginning in the Theatre's green room bar and ending in the dressing rooms. Because this play was produced as part of the RSC's 'Open Stages' initiative, it not only made manifest Shakespeare's integration within the very fabric of the People's theatre, but also a new accommodation made with the more powerful, professional company.[119] More recently still, the People's was one of only a few regional amateur theatres selected through a competitive process to participate in the RSC's 2016 national touring production of *A Midsummer Night's Dream: A Play for the Nation* (directed by Erica Whyman).[120] Heckels directed her group of 'rude mechanicals' auditioned via the People's – Reg White, Mike Smith, Stuart Douglas, Jo Kelly, Pete McAndrew and Gordon Russell – through a series of intensive workshops with the RSC in a staging at Newcastle's Northern Stage theatre, becoming part of both a play and a process working to integrate (while also maintaining the idiosyncrasy of) amateur actors.

Conclusion: Why Shakespeare?

Speaking in 2018, Tony Childs affirmed that the People's did, and should do, Shakespeare 'because he's very good'; staging him has 'nothing to do with cultural heritage' and everything to do with the ways the plays can 'speak to a modern audience'. That said, Childs notes of his production choices that 'probably the reason wasn't to say something about modern politics'. Nonetheless, he was guided by a principle of trying 'to allow people to connect' Shakespeare 'to themselves'. This could mean suggesting contemporary resonances, but it could also mean costume or design choices that 'remove barriers' without 'imposing a reading'.[121] Comparably, Chris Heckels' recent observation that Shakespeare helps put 'bums on seats' shows that some of the imperatives behind staging his work that held sway in the theatre's earliest incarnations still do today.[122] Heckels notes other drivers, too, for the amateur stage: Shakespeare is good for actors, good for the theatre, and good for the locality. His plays allow for a good mix of roles by age and gender, and big productions can require large casts, thus contributing to 'community feeling' in the theatre, where everyone has a part to play.[123] As Dobson notes, in this we can see 'the societies which Shakespeare's plays . . . help convene'.[124] Shakespearean roles are good for actors because they help develop 'craft and voice', and, because they are based on complex texts, they hone analytical skills. And while Heckels notes that community engagement 'has not been a big part of our brief' as the People's seeks to be a 'good, old-fashioned repertory theatre', in recent years, due in part to the requirements of funders and of accessing grants, the Theatre has made much 'clearer statements' about its 'responsibility to the community' and 'outreach'.[125] This, again, sustains amateur theatre's role in fostering 'social inclusiveness'.[126]

Partly this responsibility has involved working with the next generation of actors, audiences and writers through education. Time was, engaging with schools at the People's (and other amateur theatres) understandably meant little more than ensuring paying audiences for Shakespeare productions, even if, as in 1934, 'admission of school children' was 'at reduced prices', or, as in 1974, schools were 'shunted to [*Macbeth*] in obligatory hordes'.[127] As ever, however, the urge to stage the People's Shakespeare went beyond ensuring mere survival. One reviewer of the 1969 *Hamlet* hoped that '[p]erhaps the schoolchildren who will see the People's version will begin to see something living in Shakespeare'.[128]

The urge, and the success, live on. By 2005, Chris Heckels notes, she recognised that 'we should do more with local schools', and was true to her word. Developing work undertaken as part of the national Shakespeare for Schools programme during the 1990s, and until school budgets were cut, Heckels engaged with six primary schools in Newcastle's Heaton area to stage a Shakespeare play in four days in the People's Studio. More recently, in 2016, Heckels worked with teachers in the local Hotspur Primary School to help their pupils put on a play featuring the characters whose names grace the 'Shakespeare streets' in Heaton: *Richard II*. Always, evidently, the emphasis is on involving new people, and Shakespeare is a vital medium for doing so. As this chapter has tried to show, this does not mean the theatre's approach is reverential, parochial or partial, rather that while they are doing Shakespeare, its members remain mindful of why and *where* they are doing the People's Shakespeare.

Notes

This chapter would not have been possible without the insights, patience and good offices of Martin Collins, who manages the People's Theatre Archive (PTA) at the theatre in Heaton, in which the majority of resources cited here can be located, and other researchers interested in the topics touched on here would be well-advised to contact him; gratitude is also due to Chris Heckels, Tony Childs, and Monika Smialkowska.

1. J. B. Priestley, *English Journey* (1934; Ilkley: Great Northern Books, 2009), 253–4. For another contemporary account of the theatre, see Keith Armstrong, 'People's Theatre: People's Education', *North East History* 39 (2008), 144–52.
2. William Scott, *No Women, Mr Shakespeare* (Newcastle upon Tyne, 1963), archive of the People's Theatre, 7.
3. Martin Orkin, *Local Shakespeares: Proximation and Power* (London and New York: Routledge, 2005), 1.
4. Michael Dobson, *Shakespeare and Amateur Performance: A Cultural History* (Cambridge: Cambridge University Press, 2011), 1.
5. Ibid. 1–2, 11.
6. Sir Charles Trevelyan, 'Foreword', in Norman Veitch, *The People's: Being a History of the People's Theatre Newcastle upon Tyne 1911–1939* (Gateshead on Tyne: Northumberland Press Limited, 1950), v–vii, v.

7. Ibid. vi.
8. 'W. O. R', 'People's "Othello" courageous', *Newcastle Evening Chronicle* (11 December 1950), 7.
9. Veitch, *The People's*, 166.
10. 'Review: *Troilus and Cressida*: Defects and delights of a Newcastle production', *Newcastle Evening Chronicle* (22 November 1926), n.p.
11. Peter Mortimer, 'Knockabout time with the Bard', *Newcastle Journal* (24 November 1976), 3.
12. Ian Whittell, 'Shakespeare worth seeing', *Newcastle Evening Chronicle* (7 October 1987), 2
13. Peter Mortimer, 'Success for super Macbeth', *Newcastle Journal* (3 April 1974), 2.
14. Preview of *Richard II*, *Newcastle Evening Chronicle* (8 December 1960), 4.
15. Peter Mortimer, 'Not so noble Romans . . .', *Newcastle Journal* (2 November 1977), 3.
16. See <http://www.colinveitch.co.uk> (last accessed 18 July 2018).
17. Chris Goulding, *The Story of the People's* (Newcastle: Newcastle upon Tyne City Libraries, 1991), 7. For one history of such clubs, see Denis Pye, *Fellowship is Life: The Story of the National Clarion Cycle Club, 1895–1995* (Scarborough: National Clarion Publishing, 2014).
18. Alice Foley, *A Bolton Childhood* (Manchester: Manchester University Extra-Mural Department and the North Western District of the Workers' Educational Association, 1973), 66.
19. Dobson, *Shakespeare and Amateur Performance*, 18. In the 1800s, a 'spouting club' was a group of apprentices or other workers aggregating to rehearse and perform plays.
20. Veitch, *The People's*, 1, 4, 9.
21. Ibid. 4.
22. Ibid. 13.
23. Ibid. 39.
24. Goulding, *Story of the People's*, 15.
25. Veitch, *The People's*, 18–19.
26. Ibid. 30–1.
27. Ibid. 31.
28. Ibid.
29. Dobson, *Shakespeare and Amateur Performance*, 108.
30. Irena R. Makaryk and Joseph G. Price, 'Introduction: Shakespeare and Communisms', in Irena R. Makaryk and Joseph G. Price (eds), *Shakespeare in the Worlds of Communism and Socialism* (Toronto and London: University of Toronto Press, 2013), 3–10, 7; in the same excellent collection see also Werner Habicht, 'Shakespeare and the Berlin Wall', 157–76; Lawrence Guntner, 'In search of a Socialist Shakespeare: Hamlet on East German stages', 177–204; and Xiao Yang Zhang, 'The Chinese vision of Shakespeare (from 1950 to 1990): Marxism and Socialism', 270–82. More generally, seminal studies of Shakespeare's implication in Marxist, Communist, and socialist

thought and action include Jean E. Howard and Scott Cutler Shershow (eds), *Marxist Shakespeares* (London: Routledge, 2001), and Gabriel Egan, *Shakespeare and Marx* (Oxford: Oxford University Press, 2004).
31. Makaryk and Price, 'Introduction', 4.
32. Edward Salmon, *Shakespeare and Democracy* (London and New York: McBride Nast & Co., 1916), 2, 28. I am grateful to my colleague Monika Smialkowska for drawing Salmon to my attention, and the characteristic acuity and diligence of her responses to earlier versions of this chapter.
33. Veitch, *The People's*, 84–5.
34. Ibid. 57.
35. Ibid. 48.
36. Ibid.
37. Ibid. 63.
38. Ibid. 64.
39. Ibid. 71.
40. Ibid.
41. Ibid. 70.
42. 'Prefatory Note', Programme for *Troilus and Cressida* (November 1926), n.p.
43. Programme, *Henry V* (May–June 1981), n.p.
44. Sean O' Casey, 'A Message', *The Tyneside Phoenix* (Spring 1947), 8.
45. Inez Scott, 'Dear Mr. Poulton', *The Tyneside Phoenix* (Spring 1948), 2.
46. Goulding, *Story of the People's*, 32.
47. Brian Redhead, 'A Letter to the Editor', *The Tyneside Phoenix* (Summer 1950), 23.
48. Margot Heinemann, 'How Brecht read Shakespeare', in Jonathan Dollimore and Alan Sinfield (eds), *Political Shakespeare: Essays in Cultural Materialism*, second edition (Manchester: Manchester University Press, 1994), 226–54, 234.
49. Review of *St. Joan*, *The Tyneside Phoenix* (Autumn 1951), 8.
50. Goulding, *Story of the People's*, 9.
51. Veitch, *The People's*, 6.
52. Ibid. 162.
53. Ibid. 47.
54. Robert B. Pierce, 'Bernard Shaw as Shakespeare critic', *SHAW: The Annual of Bernard Shaw Studies*, 31 (2011), 118–32, 118; Felix Grendon, 'Shakespeare and Shaw', *The Sewanee Review*, 16: 2 (April 1908), 168–83, 168; Christopher St. John (ed.), George Bernard Shaw, *Ellen Terry and Bernard Shaw: A Correspondence* (London, 1931), 149.
55. George Bernard Shaw, *Dramatic Opinions and Essays*, 2 vols (New York, 1906), II: 143.
56. George Bernard Shaw, 'Bernard Shaw abashed', *London Daily News* (17 April 1905), 12.
57. George Bernard Shaw, 'Preface', *The Dark Lady of the Sonnets* (perf. 1910, publ. 1914), in *Selected One Act Plays*, vol. 2 (Harmondsworth: Penguin, 1965), 19.
58. Veitch, *The People's*, 147, 149.

59. Ibid. 152.
60. George Bernard Shaw, 'Preface' to *Shakes Versus Shav: A Puppet Play* (1949), in *Buoyant Billions, Farfetched Fables, & Shakes Versus Shav* (London: Constable and Company, 1950), 135–7, 136.
61. *Shakes Versus Shav: A Puppet Play* (1949), 139–43.
62. Pierce, 'Bernard Shaw as Shakespeare critic', 130.
63. Programme Notes, *Macbeth* (May 1932), n.p.
64. Tom Armstrong, review of *Measure for Measure*, *The Tyneside Phoenix* (Spring 1948), 7.
65. George Bernard Shaw, 'Bernard Shaw abashed', *London Daily News* (17 April 1905), 12.
66. Dobson, *Shakespeare and Amateur Performance*, 101–2.
67. Veitch, *The People's*, 57.
68. Ibid. 131.
69. Clive Hilton, Programme note, *Measure for Measure* (February 1973), n.p.
70. Veitch, *The People's*, 178.
71. Ibid. 175.
72. Tom Armstrong, review of *As You Like It* (December 1961), Programme notes for *The Family Reunion* (January 1962), n.p.
73. A. M. B., 'Shakespeare – the Pantoman's dream', *Newcastle Journal* (11 December 1961), 5.
74. 'CALL BOY', review of 'Cymbeline', *The Tyneside Phoenix* (Spring 1950), 4.
75. Charles James, 'Othello', *The Tyneside Phoenix* (Spring 1951), 9.
76. 'C.C', review of *Much Ado About Nothing* (24 April – 1 May 1954), Programme notes for *Bacchus* (15 May 1954), n.p.
77. Review of *A Midsummer Night's Dream* (November 1958), Programme notes for *The Strong are Lonely* (December 1958), n.p.
78. Preview of *King Lear*, *Newcastle Life* (April 1964), n.p.
79. Marshall Gray, review of *King Lear* (April 1964), Programme for *Doctors of Philosophy* (May 1964), n.p.
80. David Durman, review of *King Lear*, *Newcastle Journal* (31 October 1979), 3.
81. Interview with the author (9 July 2018).
82. William Scott, *No Women, Mr Shakespeare* (1963), archive of the People's Theatre, 2.
83. 'A note on the play', Programme for No *Women, Mr. Shakespeare* (December 1963), n.p.
84. John Ardill, 'Wry Bard fresh and so witty', *Northern Echo* (11 December 1963), n.p.
85. Veitch, *The People's*, 113.
86. 'Moving Lear amid the thunder', *Northern Echo* (8 April 1964), n.p.
87. P. D. 'First-rate Shakespeare by People's', *Newcastle Evening Chronicle* (17 November 1958), 3.
88. AMB, 'Taming the Shrew in mod gear', *Newcastle Journal* (14 November 1966), 5.

89. Philip Norman, 'When a swagger becomes a mince', *Northern Echo* (14 June 1966).
90. Review of *Doctor Faustus*, *The Tyneside Phoenix* (Spring 1947), 4.
91. I. B., 'A note on the play', Programme for *A Midsummer Night's Dream* (February 1946), n.p.
92. Programme, *The Comedy of Errors* (December 1942), n.p.
93. Veitch, *The People's*, 173.
94. 'The Merchant was worthy finale', *Newcastle Journal and Northern Mail* (30 April 1943), 3.
95. W. N. Shields, review of *Antony and Cleopatra* (October 1955), Programme for *The Trojan Wars* (12 November 1955), n.p.
96. Jonathan Dollimore and Alan Sinfield, 'Foreword to the first edition: Cultural Materialism', vii-viii, in *Political Shakespeare*, viii.
97. The Lawrence report is also known as the Macpherson Report, which detailed 'institutional racism' in the police and other public bodies, and was commissioned following the mismanaged investigation of the murder of Stephen Lawrence by racist thugs in 1993.
98. Eric Peel, Programme note, *Othello* (March 1999), n.p.
99. Tony Childs, 'Director's note', Programme notes, *The Winter's Tale* (November 1994), n.p.
100. Tony Childs, Programme note, *Measure for Measure* (November 2002), n.p.
101. Eric Peel, Programme note, *Henry IV Part I* (November 1991), n.p.
102. Interview with the author (9 July 2018).
103. Ibid.
104. Ibid.
105. Ibid.
106. Ian Whittell, 'Shakespeare worth seeing', *Newcastle Evening Chronicle* (7 October 1987), 2.
107. David Whetstone, 'Much Ado makes for a fun evening', *Newcastle Journal* (7 October 1987), 3.
108. Ian Whittell, 'Shakespeare worth seeing', *Newcastle Evening Chronicle* (7 October 1987), 2.
109. Interview with the author (9 July 2018).
110. Chris Heckels, Programme notes, *Henry V* (April 2005), n.p.
111. Ibid.
112. Louis Herrick, review of *The Merchant of Venice* (December 1956), Programme for *The Wild Duck* (12 January 1957), n.p.
113. David Durman, review of *King Lear*, *Newcastle Journal* (31 October 1979), 3.
114. *Offset*, 7 (December 1986), 1.
115. 'Just a nightmare...', *Offset*, 7 (December 1986), 4
116. *Offset*, 10 (April 1987), 1.
117. 'RSC AT THE PEOPLE'S', *Offset* (February 1987), 3.
118. '"I AM GOING TO CARRY THE CAPTAINS A RECKONING"', *Offset* (11 May 1987), 1; William Wilkinson, letter, *Offset* 11 (May 1987), 3.

119. See <https://www.rsc.org.uk/open-stages> (last accessed 18 July 2018).
120. See <https://www.rsc.org.uk/a-midsummer-nights-dream> (last accessed 18 July 2018).
121. Interview with the author (11 October 2018).
122. Interview with the author (9 July 2018).
123. Ibid.
124. Dobson, *Shakespeare and Amateur Performance*, 2.
125. Interview with the author (9 July 2018).
126. Dobson, *Shakespeare and Amateur Performance*, 1.
127. 'Study of Falstaff', *Newcastle Evening Chronicle* (24 February 1934), 7; Peter Mortimer, 'Success for super Macbeth', *Newcastle Journal* (3 April 1974), 2.
128. Phil Penfold, 'Hamlet bounces along', *Newcastle Evening Chronicle* (2 December 1969), 5.

6

Only Northerners Need Apply? Northern Broadsides and No-nonsense Shakespeare

Caroline Heaton

Northern Broadsides is a well-known touring company based in Halifax, West Yorkshire, which was founded by Hull-born Barrie Rutter in 1992, in part to offer 'no-nonsense' Shakespeare.[1] In 2012, Rutter told *The Guardian*'s Andrew Dickson that, while playing walk-on parts at the *Royal Shakespeare Company* as a young actor, 'I kept thinking I should be playing that part, but then I'd remember the actor doing it was posh'.[2] The impression he received at the time was that British actors with northern voices would struggle to be accepted as serious contenders for classical roles in the British theatre. Indeed, he was reportedly informed directly: 'I could never play a king, because I had an accent'; Rutter's response was defiant: 'so I founded my own company and played a bloody king'.[3] That king was Shakespeare's *Richard III*, in Rutter's first *Northern Broadsides* production in 1992, performed in Hull's Marina Boatshed, on a shoe-string budget, featuring an all-northern cast, and using props salvaged from local scrap. Thus began Rutter's journey to fulfil his vision of establishing a company which would incorporate a range of classical and modern dramatic works, with the 'spellbinding' nature of Shakespeare's iambic pentameter representing the 'formal heartbeat' of classical theatre.[4] The company would become known for what their website describes as a 'distinctive northern voice, strong musicality and a clear narrative journey'.[5] In 2000, when Rutter won first prize in the 'Creative Britons' awards, the then deputy prime minister John Prescott commented: 'Barrie's northern-accent, fast-action, factory-floor Shakespeare is as far from elitism as can be, though it has never, never dumbed Shakespeare down'.[6] Prescott also praised the fact that Broadsides were offering 'the real thing, but with a northern vigour; an energy which connects people and holds their attention'.[7] This chapter explores how this connection and vigour have been made possible for so long (and what yet may threaten them), by considering the beginnings of Northern Broadsides, the company's role as a forum for performers with northern English voices, and the challenges it faces in securing its future in an age of austerity.

Rough Beginnings

Rutter's concern about the lack of or limits on northern English voices in theatre was personal, but also historically specific. Roy North, actor, and one of what Rutter has often referred to as the Northern Broadsides 'Old Stagers', highlights the fact that the 1960s was an era when 'a lot of working class kids went to drama school. Not long before that it simply wasn't possible. We could afford to go through grants'. In this fresh era, which appeared to welcome a broader section of society into the acting profession, there was 'a new generation of working-class actors coming through. They were pioneers – people like Tom Courtney (also from Hull), Albert Finney, and Ian McKellen too . . . and of course, the writers were writing parts and plays about working class people'.[8]

However, although the mid-twentieth century saw an increase in the popularity of northern voices (largely through their association with the working classes), Edward Pearce, author and columnist for *The Guardian*, reflects on the fact that this did not necessarily translate directly into an increase in available work for northern actors. Southern actors would sometimes assume a northern accent for a role as a gritty northerner and would tend to follow the generally accepted view that 'a northern voice implied a northern type, loud, brazen, truculent, thumping from overdone stress'.[9] There was little room for subtlety, tenderness or the nuances of northern identities in these portrayals.

Perhaps somewhat surprisingly then, despite Northern Broadsides being established as a company driven by its determination to foreground northern voices in classical roles, the inaugural production of *Richard III* was warmly received by the national press, with *The Independent on Sunday* describing it as a 'thrilling departure in classical performance'. *The Guardian* referred to the production as a 'revelation' and *The Daily Mail* found it to be 'totally accessible'.[10] Other than a few critics who saw it as an attempt by an upstart actor to worm his way into performing 'royal Shakespeare' by choosing a Shakespearean king who could reasonably be categorised as northern, on the whole the UK press seemed to grasp and welcome Rutter's intentions.[11] *The Independent*'s Jeffrey Wainwright was able to appreciate the difference between Shakespeare in a northern *accent*, and Shakespeare in a northern *voice*, 'with all the bodily depth, personal and cultural rootedness the word implies'.[12] Even the *Telegraph*'s Charles Spencer had to reluctantly concede: 'I confess I thought it sounded dotty, but the weird thing is, it works . . . the flattened vowels, dropped aspirates, and use of words like 'owt' and 'thee' . . . give the language a real immediacy and speed'.[13]

The unusual venue for their first production of *Richard III* was an early indication of the Broadsides' well-known flexible approach to identifying and utilising performance spaces to suit a modest budget. North, who has appeared in many Broadsides productions, recalls:

> For a long time Rutter didn't want to do theatres. He wanted to play a swimming baths in Warrington, a marina, a bus museum in Bradford, cattle markets, stables, tram sheds, mills. It was all 'non-velvet' venues and the costumes were from Oxfam and he'd pick up props from the places we were working. Gritty northern actors swinging chains from mills. It was terrific.[14]

This straightforward, practical approach to theatre was exemplified by the company's experience when performing *A Midsummer Night's Dream* at the newly opened Shakespeare's Globe, as part of the *Prologue* Season in 1996. Arriving directly from a tour of Brazil, the company had just a couple of hours to familiarise themselves with the new auditorium, while rehearsing alongside the builders, and Rutter was content to shout out to unsuspecting tourists in the gallery 'Can you hear that?' before setting about the business of staging 'a party for sixteen hundred people, courtesy of Will Shakespeare', without the aid of the actors' costumes, which had been mislaid en route.[15] For Rutter, the emphasis has always had to be on the performance, rather than the expensive sets and costume. In an interview in 2018, he pointed out Northern Broadsides' employment record: '16 actors on stage regularly, five crew, on the smallest grant in the middle-scale touring department'.[16] The emphasis has therefore long been on a lack of pretension, and a lot of grit.

In 1995, Northern Broadsides found a home underneath a viaduct at a former carpet factory in Halifax. When Sir Ernest Hall turned Dean Clough into an arts space, Broadsides created an auditorium within the underground space between two buildings, and offered a production of *Antony and Cleopatra* which made the most of the reverberations produced by the viaduct walls, through the use of oil drums as percussion for the battle scenes. The cavernous Viaduct Theatre is characterised by flexible seating, portable electric heaters, uneven stone floors, trailing wires, the sound of running water and very clear acoustics. It continues to provide a base for the company, but all of the Broadsides productions have also toured to a wide variety of venues, leading Rutter to advise that a director should always 'utilise your location – use the vistas, the size, shape and tone of the space'.[17] In a sense, this is a ringing endorsement, and exemplification of, the notion of a company rooted in a particular, northern English location.

With the Broadsides' gradual rise in popularity and increase in funding, Rutter became less averse to performing in purpose-built theatres, and the company graduated from stables, cattle markets, factories and school sports halls to warmer and more traditional venues, with more audience-friendly facilities. Even though Rutter initially claimed that he 'didn't want to play in velvet theatres',[18] he now jokes: 'even Skipton cattle market has been tarted up a bit, although they do still have sheep'.[19]

Northern Voices

In the nineteenth century, the 'dialect map' of England 'became a guide to a cultural hierarchy', putting 'the South of England and its cultural institutions at its apex'.[20] Not much has changed. As Graham Holderness and Andrew Murphy assert, there has been huge institutional investment in aligning Shakespeare and non-regional accents: 'The ability to speak and write, clearly and confidently, standard English; and the capacity to demonstrate an acceptable level of understanding *vis-à-vis* Shakespearian drama, are in the National Curriculum regarded as interdependent.' But as Murphy and Holderness explain, this ignores a reality (that the Northern Broadsides do not): namely that 'there is not of course only one English, but many: class and regional dialects; all the Englishes of the large anglophone world'.[21] Nonetheless, despite the Broadsides' successes, Rutter's appreciation of the obstructions faced by northern actors wishing to take on major classical roles has been echoed by Carol Chillington Rutter, in her observation that, since the emergence of Public School Pronunciation (the precursor to Received Pronunciation, abbreviated to RP), accent has been heard not simply as 'a regional marker but as an index of class' which marks those regarded as socially inferior as also fit for social exclusion.[22] This view was shared by the Lancastrian actor and writer Maxine Peake, who explained: 'Northern means assumptions being made, including class, education and background. We are still battling the prejudice about what being "northern" means.'[23]

In defiance of this, Rutter has made no apologies for the company's northern slant, despite the occasional inclusion of southern venues in their performance schedule. In the 2016 production of *The Merry Wives* (the company's third in its then twenty-five-year history), Rutter set Shakespeare's play not in Windsor, but in an unspecified semi-rural northern location in the 1930s, complete with local cricket pitch and a handy forest from which young lovers can elope to Skipton (rather than Eton). The production featured flat caps, flat vowels, a 'Fat Woman of Ilkley', a very practical Mistress Quickly with housecoat and feather duster, plenty of physical comedy, and a northern 'make do' attitude which was reflected in the creation of the local gents' 'fairy' outfits from their wives' nightwear. Rutter himself offered a bumbling, but largely harmless tweed-suited Falstaff, who could take a joke with the best of them and even joined in with the feel-good Charleston dance at the end. The northern stereotypes were light-heartedly drawn, but recognisable to both northern and southern audiences, contributing to a mix of energy, humour, charm and celebration, to which audiences seemed to warm.

However, when responding to Emma Rice's invitation to stage a production at the Sam Wanamaker Playhouse, and setting the 2018 reimagining of John Dryden's *The Captive Queen* in the late twentieth century, during the last days of the great woollen mills of the England's North, Rutter received some criticism for the localised frame setting, which was regarded by some as incongruous with the play's substantive location in Mughal India. The mill scenes were interpreted by Peter Viney as 'there only to justify the use of Northern accents', when 'the battle on accents was won decades ago . . . it is really no longer an issue'.[24] However, this is the view of someone who also suggests, in a review of Northern Broadsides' *The Merry Wives*, that northern accents 'reference the sit-com / farce elements of the play', since 'any regional accent always helps comedy'.[25] Clearly the assumptions – not to say prejudices – identified by Peake and Chillington Rutter, and against which Rutter has positioned himself, still have power.

That said, since and arguably because of the inception of the Broadsides in 1992, there has been a noticeable, though sometimes subtle, shift towards the larger popular classical theatre companies employing a wider diversity of actors, which has sometimes necessitated (and even encouraged) the inclusion of those with 'accents'. In 2008, David Tennant used his native Scottish accent for his portrayal of Berowne in the *Royal Shakespeare Company*'s production of *Love's Labour's Lost*, although there is, potentially, special licence for well-known actors with huge popularity, who are likely to attract audiences, whichever accent they use. And perhaps, as Viney inadvertently intimates, the perceived norms are different for comedy than for tragedy. Tennant's *Hamlet* of the same year was firmly entrenched in the world of RP. As demonstrated in numerous Royal Shakespeare Company productions of *A Midsummer Night's Dream* (for example 2005-8, directed by Gregory Doran), and in their 2016 touring *Play for the nation* version of that play, northern (and Midlands) accents were often confined to supporting comedic roles and clowns, such as the mechanicals, while Shakespeare's thugs and villains regularly sound as though they've just emerged from an episode of *EastEnders*. Just occasionally, *Henry IV* (Part 1)'s Hotspur might sound as though he has actually spent some time in the North East, and *Twelfth Night*'s Feste might have picked up a slight hint of something regional while on his travels but, as John Morrish points out, accents are often used to denote character traits, which can change over time: 'It is not long since Scouse meant native wit and charm: now it is associated with fecklessness. Brum sounds miserable. Cockney sounds devious and aggressive. West Country speakers . . . sound like simpletons.'[26]

As we will now see, characters of high social status, and/or those with emotional depth such as Richard II, King Lear, Macbeth, Othello, Rosalind, Juliet and Beatrice, are therefore still generally considered to be too sophisticated, eloquent, intelligent, and high-born to have more than a very vague trace of anything other than Received Pronunciation in our national theatre companies. It was noticeable that Ian McKellen's 2007 King Lear, Patrick Stewart's 2006 Prospero, and even Sean Bean's 1986 Romeo seemed to suggest that, while you might be proud of the fact that your roots are firmly fixed somewhere outside the reach of the M25, it might nevertheless be regarded as inappropriate to foist your regional accent on an unsuspecting (and perhaps predominantly middle-class) audience, who might regard it as incongruent with a character of high status, and, instead, may equate a northern accent with stupidity, or lack of emotional depth. In preparation for his 2018 portrayal of Macbeth at the Royal Shakespeare Company, Salford-born Christopher Eccleston stated that his desire to take on Shakespearean roles has been hampered by his northern accent, since he is 'never offered Shakespeare', due to the assumption: 'people like me can't be classical'.[27] Indeed, even as a well-known and highly experienced actor, Eccleston had been unable to secure a major Shakespearean role on a national stage. Despite the warm critical reception of his portrayal of Hamlet at the West Yorkshire Playhouse in 2002, he was only able to win the Stratford role by writing an 'old fashioned letter' to artistic director Gregory Doran asking to be allowed to play the part. Maxine Peake's portrayal of Hamlet at the Manchester Royal Exchange was particularly notable in having the eponymous tragic hero portrayed by a woman, but this, too, was staged in a northern city, where we might assume her accent might be more palatable to the audience. As Peake pointed out in an interview with *The Telegraph*: 'you can get away with doing posh all the time but if you do Northern a lot, they say, "Oh, are you doing Northern again?" like you're playing the same character continually. But nobody says to Judi Dench, "Oh, Judi, love, you're not going to do that RP again?"'.[28]

Despite these assertions, assumptions remain, colouring how a company like the Broadsides functions and is perceived. In 2009, the actor and writer Eileen Atkins famously commented that the 'fashion in drama schools now not to get rid of your basic accent' was leading to young actors being 'pretentious' and setting 'a bad example'.[29] Atkins suggested that, as a consequence of retaining a regional accent, actors would 'never get classical leading parts'.[30] What seems like pragmatism can soon disclose prejudice: *The Telegraph*'s Michael Simkins also laments the 'demise of Received Pronunciation', which he regards as commensurate with a 'marked deterioration in the quality of our language.'[31] Comparably, Ronald Harwood has criticised the rise of 'kitchen sink' stars, the 'terrible' declining emphasis on standard English, and the associated 'problem of poor language skills'.[32] Prunella Scales, in turn, may have claimed that her dissatisfaction with the decline of the use of 'posh English' is about 'the accuracy of playing a part' and not about 'social snobbery'.[33] Chris Hastings seems to sum up all these concerns: 'scripts have had to be rewritten to accommodate the actors' limited vocal skills' and producers 'have difficulty casting parts for children who speak properly', being forced to 'bypass stage schools in favour of private schools where standards of English are higher'.[34] It sometimes seems as if the battles fought and gains made by the Broadsides have been in vain.

But all these concerns beg the question: who determines or polices a performer's accuracy, and why? Moreover, what do we mean by speaking 'properly', and why might it be considered more acceptable to speak with a regional accent (and hence not speak 'properly') in a comedic role than in a tragic one? Furthermore, how do the prejudices which seem to prevail in relation to northern British accents stand up to scrutiny amid the spread of 'Estuary English', global migration, and social or ethnic diversity? We might also reflect that while the judgements we make in relation to regional voices are influenced by the inequalities of our current class system, they do not necessarily correspond with social norms of the era in which Shakespeare and his contemporaries were writing and performing. Edward Pearce suggests that a northern voice is actually quite close to a Shakespearean one: 'Almost certainly the short vowels and strong endings, within which northern speech varies like quicksilver, approach the speech of Shakespeare's time'.[35]

In this regard, David Crystal's observations about his experience of transcribing Shakespeare's text for performances at Shakespeare's Globe in Original Pronunciation (OP) are significant. While recognising that 'every attempt at an "original practice" is an experiment', since 'so little is known about theatrical practice in Shakespeare's time', Crystal himself did not seek to establish a uniformity of pronunciation.[36] He did so in recognition of the fact that 'actors on the Elizabethan stage came from many parts of the country, and would have brought their accents with them'.[37] Received Pronunciation did not emerge until the beginning of the nineteenth century and 'there was no drama-school system to teach actors how to enunciate. Diversity would have been the norm on the Elizabethan stage'.[38] Surely it should be now. Indeed, echoing Rutter and Peake, *The Guardian*'s Daniel Bye promotes the use of regional accents, particularly within regional theatres, which he regards as having 'some responsibility to hold a mirror up to nature', by reflecting their local environment, since 'more than half the work I see around the country . . . features people who speak in received pronunciation' and 'there's something missing when an accent spoken by less than 5% of the population is so prevalent'.[39]

Fulfilling the Vision

Whatever the assumptions, demands and challenges, the Broadsides continue to work in their own way. Just as Broadsides' audiences return year after year, so do many of the performers, most of whom tend to originate from UK locations north of Birmingham: Rutter himself has commented that, for him, a northerner is 'everyone from Geordies to people from Nottingham', and his audiences seem to identify with this.[40] However, the venues in which the company performs still vary greatly and, when planning for the company's 2016 production of *The Merry Wives*, designer Lis Evans was conscious that: 'we open the play in the round, but it tours to many different configurations, such as end-on, thrust stage, proscenium arch and traverse'.[41] Their usual haunts now also include the West Yorkshire Playhouse, Harrogate Theatre, the New Vic, the Lawrence Batley Theatre in Huddersfield, the Liverpool Playhouse, and Stephen Joseph Theatre in Scarborough, among others. And whatever the assumptions of some about what is proper for Shakespearean theatre, the Broadsides have even been as far south as the Everyman in Cheltenham and the Rose in Kingston. However, as if in response to those negative, limiting assumptions, their focus on northern voices has been retained, unwaveringly. As Rutter told the BBC's Ian Youngs in 2015, he had clarified his views in an email to his fellow actors in the King Lear company, stating 'Look, you know what I think. We're called Northern Broadsides. There's a clue in both bloody titles. Stick to it'.[42] Given that emphasis, much was made in the press of Lenny Henry's big theatrical break in the Northern Broadsides 2009 production of *Othello*. Could a famous comedian and Open University graduate from the West Midlands who was formerly 'allergic to Shakespeare' carry off such a serious Shakespearean role?[43] With some reservations, the critics generally seemed to think so. Although some found the production competent but unexciting, the London Theatre guide was fairly typical in its description of a 'surprisingly successful performance, that shows Henry has the necessary acting capability and understanding of the text', as well as physical presence, a mellow rich voice and the ability to portray both the 'child-like whimperer and the raging bull'.[44] Despite Peter Brown's comments on 'some odd variations in the northern accents', the production was successful enough to transfer to London's Trafalgar Studios.[45] This demonstrated the Broadsides' commitment to showing that non-RP actors can deliver classical lines with clarity and depth, but also that not only northern audiences welcome the opportunity to hear intelligent drama in accents, encouraging actors to 'speak authentically, in their natural voices'.[46]

Through this steadfastness and such developments, of course, Broadsides have acquired a loyal following among theatre-goers, and Rutter has enjoyed welcoming back old faces into the auditorium, and occasionally asking whether there are any 'Broadsides virgins' among the audience. Productions are usually vibrant, musical and accessible. As *The Whitby Gazette*'s Mike Tilling observed, in his review of the 2015 production of *The Winter's Tale,* 'you get value for money with Northern Broadsides: a big cast, a play with a big theme and music as well as dancing'.[47] Set alongside this festive performativity, though, the company is known for an emphasis on 'plainness', which is perhaps partly what has appealed to audiences over the years. The clarity of speech arguably carries over into a straightforward performance style, which is what attracted Jonathan Miller to direct Rutter in the 2015 Broadsides production of *King Lear*. Miller explained: '*King Lear* and *Hamlet* are two of the plays that I've enjoyed doing several times precisely because it's possible to do them without being poetic and simply being realistic'.[48] It was clear that Miller felt his interest in seeing these plays performed 'very naturally' could be compatible with the Broadsides' commitment to directness, especially Rutter's aversion to paying slavish attention to the stylistic construction of the language, as he preferred to free Shakespeare's words from any artificially imposed constraints, thereby rejecting what he describes as 'toothpaste acting' – characterised by 'squeezing it out as if every actor is constipated'.[49] Rutter has always instead placed great emphasis on clarity and audibility of delivery throughout his tenure – suggesting that his epitaph might read: 'They heard me at the back'.[50]

Like John Barton, Rutter believes there is a tendency within modern productions to over-emphasise punctuation, adjectives and adverbs, which does not reflect what he perceives to be natural speech patterns. Indeed, he insists:

> Elizabethan and classical plays are delivered via their construction, not in spite of it. These plays were written before Freud and the camera. Often it's about the music of the lines, the music of the rhythm, the music of the content.[51]

In his review for *The Telegraph* of Rutter's performance as Lear in Miller's 2015 production, Dominic Cavendish made no mention of accents, and made no suggestion that northern voices might present a barrier for audiences or hinder understanding. Instead, bearing out Rutter's thoughts above, he focused on the simplicity of tone, the lack of scenic grandeur, the production's clarity, and the touching portrayal of Lear and Cordelia's relationship.[52] Rutter himself pointed out: 'delivering the script in a Yorkshire accent may give the words a "guttural rasping roar", but it will not otherwise change the play'.[53] Such interpretations suggest a middle way in the accent wars, one also articulated by Sarah Mann, director of the London Language and Drama School, who, in a 2002 article in *The Economist*, noted that there had been a dramatic rise in the number of individuals signing up for elocution lessons, as part of a growing demand for 'better' speech from people wishing to 'soften or dilute regional accents to the point that they will be readily understood by people from elsewhere'; yet Mann also pointed out: 'so long as the speaker learns to eliminate "lazy" speech . . . you can get away with even quite a marked accent if you are an interesting enough speaker, with pitch and pace and pause in your delivery'.[54] Perhaps this ability to think and hear both with and beyond accent has been part of what the Broadsides have done from the start. Indeed, a review of the 1996 *A Midsummer Night's Dream* at Shakespeare's Globe in *The Independent* made this point, relatively early in the company's history: 'Northern Broadsides are claiming Shakespeare for their own voice and, as previously, they make their point. To hear 'I know a bank where the wild thyme blows' in the scoops of Rutter's Yorkshire is not an exciting novelty. It just sounds right'.[55]

Trouble at Mill

Despite the efforts of Northern Broadsides to tackle perceived social and linguistic prejudices in the theatre, and the support they have received for doing so, in a 2015 interview, Rutter remained concerned about the lack of opportunities in the arts for people from diverse backgrounds, and suggested that the disparity in arts funding between London and the rest of the UK, together with the high cost of a drama school education, means that acting will continue to have a London-centric focus and therefore that 'you're probably going to get a very middle-class drama school intake'.[56] So, perhaps there is still a place for a Northern Broadsides which is just for northerners (and Midlanders, like Lenny Henry)? The Arts Council may still need to be convinced of the argument though. Rutter suggested that it wasn't until he won his award in 2000 that: 'the Arts Council had to give us proper funding'.[57] However, the company has continually had to fight for its grants, and as Andrew Dickson noted in 2012, 'Rutter is unrepentant, and unashamed of wanting it both ways: one moment he's boasting of the company's fearless independence; the next he's complaining loudly about other people's funding'.[58] Another funding crisis arose in 2016, which was highlighted in *The Telegraph* in September 2016, when Rutter explained: 'We need to pay the actors more. I'm running out of their good will. I'm running out of my own good will.'[59] Reporting on this, Dominic Cavendish described Rutter as 'the last of the great northern theatrical chieftains' since Alan Ayckbourn left Scarborough's Stephen Joseph Theatre and John Godber stepped down from Hull Truck.[60] Despite noting Rutter's continuing passion for the work, and his unwavering sense that 'the act of reclaiming the Bard for the regional voice still feels radical', Cavendish reflected on Rutter's air of 'weary resignation', due to his frustration at the apparent ongoing North–South divide in relation to the funding of smaller touring theatre companies.[61] To Rutter, and observers, these differences in financial support are long-standing and significant. For example, just one year after the Broadsides was founded, the London-based English Touring Theatre was set up to offer traditional productions of English classical theatre in Received Pronunciation and immediately received public funding, whereas Broadsides had begun with just £15,000 from the City of Hull, the loan of a free rehearsal space and support from the Bradford Alhambra.[62] English Touring Theatre badges itself as 'England's National Theatre of Touring' and receives sufficient funding to be able to lay claim to being 'the only touring company with public investment, to produce work for larger theatres in England'.[63] Cavendish also points out that Headlong Theatre, which, like Northern Broadsides, stages a mixture of classical and contemporary texts, receives £679,000 in Arts Council funding.[64] The Broadsides' offer has always had competition, but with changes in the landscape of arts funding in the mid-2010s, the struggle for resources has become even harder.

Rutter stated that he would leave the company if the funding was not increased and his frustration at the continual struggle led to the response: 'You don't want us? Fine! Kiss my a**e and goodnight Vienna'.[65] This forthright, insistent attitude was perhaps characteristic of Rutter's own approach to performance; he began acting while at school, after an English teacher suggested 'you've got a big gob in class Rutter. Why not put it to use?'[66] Yet, after overseeing more than seventy productions for the Broadsides, and having received an OBE in 2015, in July 2017 Rutter announced that he would be leaving his role as artistic director in April 2018, having been told that Arts Council England would not be increasing its annual funding from the usual £255,287 until 2022. He informed the press: 'I have decided that after 25 wonderful years it is the right time for me to stand down'.[67] When considering his decision back in 2016, Rutter expressed concern for the future of northern Shakespeare, and asked: 'who else will take sixteen-handed Shakespeares to Scarborough if Northern Broadsides don't get any money?!'[68] It would seem his appeal – and what it represented – fell on deaf ears.

New Broom?

Funding challenges aside, other developments will affect the Broadsides' journey. Following Rutter's departure, Conrad Nelson assumed more responsibility within the company, as the resident (associate) director, as well as a leading actor and composer. Nelson has a very long association with Broadsides. He's been Richard III and Henry V, was the Iago to Lenny Henry's *Othello*, and appeared as Leontes in the 2015 modern-dress production of *The Winter's Tale* which he also directed (and composed for). In an interview with the *Yorkshire Post*, Nelson stated:

I have been involved in every production we have done since 2004. At two a year, that's 28 productions. I have either directed, written the music for, been in or choreographed every single one. Barrie was only involved in the ones he directed.[69]

Nick Ahad clams that Nelson has 'defined the style of the company at least as much (and arguably more) than Rutter. Clog dances and rousing music? Nelson . . . the performance of *Richard III* which formed the centrepiece of the Wars of the Roses productions in 2006? Nelson'.[70]

Nelson's rise reflected the extent of his creative involvement: in April 2018 it was announced that he had been appointed as artistic director and joint CEO until April 2019. However, Nelson stood down at that point and in 2020 the company is under the charge of Laurie Samsom; a new broom originally from Peckham, and formerly Artistic Director of the National Theatre of Scotland. Perhaps he and his colleagues will continue the fight for national recognition for Northern Broadsides and the funding which accompanies it. Although Rutter claimed that 'I leave the supporters of Northern Broadsides in the hands of a robust and creative staff', without him at the helm the company's future perhaps seems uncertain, not simply because Rutter has been such an influential character but because the company is still situated within an era of austerity, where there is reduced funding for actors from lower socio-economic backgrounds, and a clear predominance within our national culture of performers from London and the South East, with financial cushioning.[71] As theatre companies continue to compete with each other for ever-decreasing funds, we can only hope that there will still be a place for productions in northern voices. Given the Broadsides' history, and what they have brought to and from Shakespeare, it would be a disaster if audiences and actors lost the opportunity to realise and demonstrate that the 'iron consonants and short vowels' of a northern voice are 'ideally suited' to Shakespeare.[72] As Rutter notes: 'wrapping your gob around great, wonderful – often rhyming – language is one of life's great pleasures'.[73] Long may it prove to be so.

Notes

1. See Robert Butler, 'Barrie Rutter runs a theatre company with a difference: only Northerners need apply', *The Independent* (19 June 1993) <http://www.independent.co.uk/arts-entertainment/theatre-regional-variations-barrie-rutter-runs-a-theatre-company-with-a-difference-only-northerners-1492762.html> (last accessed 17 July 2019).

2. Andrew Dickson, 'Barrie Rutter: a life in the theatre', *The Guardian* (9 March 2012). Available at: <http://www.theguardian.com/culture/2012/mar/09/barrie-rutter-life-in-theatre> (last accessed 17 July 2019).
3. Barrie Rutter, guest lecture, *British Shakespeare Association* Biennial Conference, personal comment (10 September 2016).
4. Barrie Rutter, 'Extracts from CP Taylor Lecture', *British Theatre Guide* (2005). Available at: <http://www.britishtheatreguide.info/otherresources/interviews/BarrieRutter.htm> (last accessed 17 July 2019).
5. Northern Broadsides, 'About Us', Northern Broadsides website (2018). Available at: <https://www.northern-broadsides.co.uk/about-us> (last accessed 17 July 2019).
6. BBC, 'Top prize for factory floor Shakespeare' (28 June 2000). Available at: <http://news.bbc.co.uk/1/hi/uk/810139.stm> (last accessed 17 July 2019).
7. Ibid.
8. Northern Broadsides, 'Education pack: the Merry Wives', Northern Broadsides website (2015). Available at: <https://www.northern-broadsides.co.uk/wp-content/uploads/2015/03/The-Merry-Wives-Education-Pack.pdf> (last accessed 17 July 2019).
9. Edward Pearce, 'Edward Pearce on Northern Voices', Northern Broadsides website (2018) <https://www.northern-broadsides.co.uk/test3/edward-pearce-on-northern-voices> (last accessed 17 July 2019).
10. Butler, 'Barrie Rutter', *The Independent*.
11. Carol Chillington Rutter, 'Rough magic: Northern Broadsides at work, at play', *Shakespeare Survey*, 56 (2003), 236–55, 239.
12. Jeffrey Wainwright, 'Review of Northern Broadsides' The Merry Wives', *The Independent* (25 June 1993) Available at: <http://www.independent.co.uk/arts-entertainment/theatre-its-right-grand-jeffrey-wainwright-relishes-barrie-rutters-northern-falstaff-1494042.html> (last accessed 17 July 2019).
13. Charles Spencer, 'Review of Northern Broadsides' *Richard III*', *The Daily Telegraph* (14 December 1992).
14. Northern Broadsides, 'Education pack: The Merry Wives'.
15. Northern Broadsides, 'Past productions: A Midsummer Night's Dream', Northern Broadsides website (2018). Available at: <http://www.northern-Broadsides.co.uk/past-productions/a-midsummer-nights-dream> (last accessed 17 July 2019).
16. Liz Hoggard, 'Barrie Rutter: I'm not everybody's cup of tea', *The Observer* (4 February 2018). Available at: <https://www.theguardian.com/stage/2018/feb/04/barrie-rutter-not-everybodys-cup-of-tea-interview-northern-broadsides-the-captive-queen> (last accessed 17 July 2019).
17. Rutter, *British Shakespeare Association*.
18. Rutter, *British Theatre Guide*.
19. Rutter in Hilary Whitney, 'Q&A: director Barrie Rutter', *The Arts Desk* (29 January 2012). Available at: <http://www.theartsdesk.com/theatre/theartsdesk-qa-director-barrie-rutter> (last accessed 17 July 2019).

20. Stuart Rawnsley, 'Constructing "the North": space and a sense of place', in Neville Kirk (ed.), *Northern Identities: Historical Interpretations of 'the North' and 'Northernness'* (Aldershot: Ashgate, 2000), 3–22, 8.
21. Graham Holderness and Andrew Murphy, 'Shakespeare's England: Britain's Shakespeare', in John J. Joughin (ed.), *Shakespeare and National Culture* (Manchester: Manchester University Press, 1997), 19–41, 22–3. Good surveys of the socio-politics of northern English dialects can be found in Dave Russell, *Looking North: Northern England and the National Imagination* (Manchester and New York: Manchester University Press, 2004), 111–46; and Simon Featherstone, *Englishness: Twentieth-Century Popular Culture and the Forming of English Identities* (Edinburgh: Edinburgh University Press, 2009), 140–58.
22. Chillington Rutter, 'Rough magic', 243.
23. Bernadette Hyland, 'Sally Wainwright, Maxine Peake and others consider the state of northern drama', *Contributoria.com* (4 June 2014). Available at: <https://www.prolificnorth.co.uk/broadcasting/featured/2014/06/sally-wainwright-maxine-peake-and-others-consider-state-northern-drama> (last accessed 17 July 2019).
24. Peter Viney, 'Review of *The Captive Queen* at the Sam Wanamaker Playhouse', *Peter Viney's Blog* (11 February 2018). Available at: <https://peterviney.wordpress.com/stage/the-captive-queen> (last accessed 17 July 2019).
25. Peter Viney, 'Review of *The Merry Wives* at Yvonne Arnaud Theatre, Guildford', *Peter Viney's Blog* (12 May 2016). Available at: <https://peterviney.wordpress.com/stage/the-merry-wives-northern-broadsides> (last accessed 17 July 2019).
26. John Morrish, 'The accent that dare not speak its name', *The Independent* (21 March 1999). Available at: <https://www.independent.co.uk/life-style/focus-the-accent-that-dare-not-speak-its-name-1082144.html> (last accessed 17 July 2019).
27. Christopher Eccleston, 'Christopher Eccleston: northern accent held me back', BBC (21 February 2018). Available at: <http://www.bbc.co.uk/news/entertainment-arts-43139805> (last accessed 17 July 2019).
28. Anita Singh, 'Maxine Peake: regional accents are taken less seriously', *The Telegraph* (12 June 2014). Available at: <https://www.telegraph.co.uk/culture/theatre/10861268/Maxine-Peake-regional-accents-are-taken-less-seriously.html> (last accessed 17 July 2019).
29. Eileen Atkins, 'Eileen Atkins voices concern at Lenny Henry's accent', *The Telegraph* (17 February 2009). Available at: <http://www.telegraph.co.uk/news/newstopics/mandrake/4681368/Eileen-Atkins-voices-concern-at-Lenny-Henrys-accent.html> (last accessed 17 July 2019).
30. Ibid.
31. Michael Simkins, 'Standard English still has a part to play', *The Telegraph* (30 June 2010) <https://www.telegraph.co.uk/comment/personal-view/7862596/Standard-English-still-has-a-part-to-play.html> (last accessed 17 July 2019).

32. Cited in Chris Hastings, 'Estuary English is destroying British drama', *The Telegraph* (31 October 2004). Available at: <https://www.telegraph.co.uk/news/uknews/4194086/Estuary-English-is-destroying-British-drama.html> (last accessed 17 July 2019).
33. Ibid.
34. Ibid.
35. Pearce, 'Northern Voices'.
36. David Crystal, *Pronouncing Shakespeare* (Cambridge: Cambridge University Press, 2005), 7.
37. Ibid. 26.
38. Ibid. 27.
39. Daniel Bye, 'Vernacular spectacular: why theatre speaks louder with regional accents', *The Guardian* (6 October 2010). Available at: <https://www.theguardian.com/stage/theatreblog/2010/oct/06/theatre-english-pronunciation-apples-accent> (last accessed 17 July 2019).
40. Rutter in Whitney, *The Arts Desk*.
41. Northern Broadsides, 'Education pack: The Merry Wives'.
42. Ian Youngs, 'Barrie Rutter on giving King Lear a Yorkshire accent', BBC (27 February 2015). Available at: <http://www.bbc.co.uk/news/entertainment-arts-30937165> (last accessed 17 July 2019).
43. Lenny Henry, 'Comedian Henry tackles Othello', *BBC* (3 October 2008). Available at: <http://news.bbc.co.uk/1/hi/entertainment/7650432.stm> (last accessed 17 July 2019).
44. Peter Brown, '*Othello* Review', *London Theatre* (18 September 2009). Available at: <http://www.londontheatre.co.uk/londontheatre/reviews/othello-09trafalgar.htm> (last accessed 17 July 2019).
45. Ibid.
46. Northern Broadsides, 'Company history', Northern Broadsides website (2018). Available at: <https://www.northern-broadsides.co.uk/about-us/company-history> (last accessed 17 July 2019).
47. Mike Tilling, 'Review of Northern Broadsides' *The Winter's Tale* at the Stephen Joseph Theatre Scarborough', *Whitby Gazette* (22 October 2015). Available at: <http://www.whitbygazette.co.uk/what-s-on/out-about/review-northern-broadsides-the-winter-s-tale-at-stephen-joseph-theatre-scarborough-1-7530026#ixzz3zPksy7GN> (last accessed 17 July 2019).
48. Jonathan Miller, 'Education Resource Pack: King Lear', Northern Broadsides website (2015). Available at: <https://www.northern-broadsides.co.uk/wp-content/uploads/2018/01/King-Lear-Education-Pack.pdf> (last accessed 17 July 2019).
49. Rutter, *British Shakespeare Association*, 2016.
50. Ibid.
51. Rutter in Whitney, *The Arts Desk*.
52. Dominic Cavendish, 'King Lear, Viaduct Theatre, Halifax, review', *The Telegraph* (3 March 2015). Available at: <https://www.telegraph.co.uk/culture/theatre/

theatre-reviews/11454060/King-Lear-Viaduct-Theatre-Halifax-review-sends-out-little-splinters-of-insight.html> (last accessed 17 July 2019).
53. Barrie Rutter, 'My Yorkshire', *Yorkshire Post* (6 February 2009). Available at: <http://www.yorkshirepost.co.uk/news/analysis/my-yorkshire-barrie-rutter-1-2334012> (last accessed 17 July 2019).
54. Sarah Mann, 'We want to talk proper', *The Economist* (5 December 2002). Available at: <https://www.economist.com/britain/2002/12/05/we-want-to-talk-proper> (last accessed 17 July 2019).
55. Northern Broadsides, 'Past productions: A Midsummer Night's Dream'.
56. Youngs, 'Barrie Rutter', BBC.
57. Rutter, *British Shakespeare Association*.
58. Dickson, 'Barrie Rutter', *The Guardian*.
59. Cited in Dominic Cavendish, 'Barrie Rutter: there's still the feeling that all these bloody northerners should just shut up', *The Telegraph* (11 September 2016). Available at: <http://www.telegraph.co.uk/theatre/actors/barrie-rutter-theres-still-the-feeling-that-all-these-bloody-nor> (last accessed 17 July 2019).
60. Ibid.
61. Ibid.
62. Butler, 'Barrie Rutter', *The Independent*.
63. Cavendish, 'Barrie Rutter', *The Telegraph* (2016).
64. Ibid.
65. Ibid.
66. Rutter, *British Theatre Guide*.
67. Georgia Snow, 'Barrie Rutter to leave Northern Broadsides after 25 years', *The Stage* (20 July 2017). Available at: <https://www.thestage.co.uk/news/2017/barrie-rutter-leave-northern-broadsides-25-years> (last accessed 17 July 2019).
68. Rutter, *British Shakespeare Association*.
69. Nick Ahad, 'Conrad Nelson and Deb McAndrew on life after Barrie Rutter at Northern Broadsides', *The Yorkshire Post* (10 February 2018). Available at: <https://www.yorkshirepost.co.uk/news/analysis/conrad-nelson-and-deb-mcandrew-on-life-after-barrie-rutter-s-at-northern-broadsides-1-9009801> (last accessed 17 July 2019).
70. Ibid.
71. Chris Wiegand, 'Barrie Rutter resigns from Northern Broadsides due to stagnant funding', *The Guardian* (20 July 2017) Available at: <https://www.theguardian.com/stage/2017/jul/20/barrie-rutter-resigns-from-northern-broadsides-25-years> (last accessed 17 July 2019).
72. Rutter, *British Theatre Guide*.
73. Rutter in Whitney, *The Arts Desk*.

7

Shakespeare and Blackpool: The RSC's *A Midsummer Night's Dream* (2016): A Play for the Nation?

Janice Wardle

This chapter explores a production of a Shakespeare play in the North of England, namely *A Midsummer Night's Dream* staged by the Royal Shakespeare Company at the Blackpool Grand Theatre in April 2016. It will investigate how this canonical Shakespearean comedy is shaped by, and interacts with, the North West of England, and the particular northern phenomenon which is Blackpool. This production was part of the RSC tour which, following a two-week residency in both Stratford-upon-Avon and Newcastle, visited another ten venues across the UK, before it returned to Stratford in June 2016 for a month.[1] The significant factor which characterised this production was not necessarily that it toured so many venues, but rather that at each theatre it incorporated a local amateur cast. Across the twelve productions it eventually utilised nineteen professional actors, eighty-four actors from fourteen amateur companies, and 580 child performers drawn from local schools near the theatrical venues. The final performances in Stratford offered the amateur groups an opportunity to reprise their performances at the Royal Shakespeare Theatre. The scope and range of the production was challenging and ambitious, with the amateur groups at each theatre performing the three scenes involving the 'rude mechanicals' (3.2.9) and the children expanding Titania's fairy band. This touring production was seen by the RSC as a significant commemorative event in the year of the 400th anniversary of Shakespeare's death and billed as a 'Play for the Nation', a phrase which was utilised in all promotional material, including video 'trailers', theatre programmes, and on the RSC website.[2] This billing raises an interesting and complex issue about how precisely this idea of 'nation' was to be constructed from a series of 'local' performances. As we will see, the abiding interpretative structure for the production was provided by the RSC, with interventions from local voices. This in itself is a significant dramatic experiment, and one with which Shakespeare's touring companies may have been familiar. Yet my focus here is on how the production in Blackpool located itself in this specific place, represented and engaged with the North West, and with ideas associated with the North.

Blackpool, Past and Present

First a few words about Blackpool itself, which is a town about which there has been much debate. Described by John Walton as 'still by far the most popular British resort', Blackpool's 'career' attracted 'over three million visitors per annum by the 1890s and over seven million by the 1930s' with recent figures identifying a peak of seventeen million visitors in the 1990s dropping to about ten million per annum since.[3] It was, as Walton notes, the world's first working-class seaside resort. Blackpool owes its conception to Victorian ingenuity (particularly the railway) and social change, which saw the formalisation of industrial workers' holiday patterns. It owes its success to the staggering of these different holidays, in so-called 'wakes weeks', taken in a range of towns across the industrial North West including Preston, Wigan and Burnley. Blackpool provided its visitors with a version of those same Lancashire towns, with accommodation in small hotels in streets not dissimilar to those at 'home'. But, in addition, it offered 'fun', 'medicinal' sea air, and an escape from 'normal' life. In *The Delicious History of the Holiday* Fred Inglis offers an evocative description of the range of entertainments available, and goes on to note '[Blackpool] was not genteel. It was intensely gregarious. Its population came from skilled labour and repeated in its play assorted negations of its work: crowded non-productivity; collective unself-protectiveness; joint indolence; financial carelessness; unrewarded effortlessness.'[4] All this in time, of course, meant Blackpool seemed to offer, according to Walton's reading of Tony Bennett's work, a 'northern counter culture' that is in opposition to the 'dominant southern (and especially metropolitan) ethos, based on aristocracy and high finance, . . . pallid and effete'.[5] Moreover, as Featherstone notes, Blackpool 'represented the transformation of the conflicts of northern traditional custom and industrial discipline into a distinctive kind of mass culture', and by the beginning of the twentieth century had 'come to be represented as a place of nostalgia, a representation of an older North'.[6] The elements of that nostalgic representation are still familiar – the Tower, the donkeys on the beach, fish and chips on the prom, the annual illuminations. All these features have been aided and abetted by what John Urry calls the 'collective tourist gaze', and are further reinforced by representations in the media, and supplied by the industry to fulfil a perceived need.[7] Such activities, deemed 'industrial saturnalia', are part of collective performative rituals, which are often carnivalesque in mood, and sexual in preoccupation, and which may be illustrated by the town's fondness for risqué seaside postcards, phallic-shaped confectionery, or transvestite drag cabaret acts.[8]

Yet there are other sides to Blackpool. It is worth noting that initially it was the playground not of the working people of the North West but of the wealthy middle classes. As the town developed it relied on capital from these same groups as they built their palaces of entertainment. The iconic Tower and its massive entertainment complex featuring a ballroom, a circus and a zoo was built in 1894, the Winter Gardens and Opera House in 1889, and, of course, the Grand Theatre in 1894. Like the three piers that were also constructed, these buildings were both places of entertainment and objects of wonder and spectacle in themselves, with their elaborate gilded stucco designs echoing those of the leading theatre and opera houses in London. Some of these buildings marked the cultural aspirations of the middle classes. The Grand Theatre (where *A Midsummer Night's Dream* was performed in 2016) has an impressive nineteenth-century Thomas Matcham interior. Vanessa Toulmin notes that the original theatre was 'neither designed to be nor programmed as a variety house in its original incarnation', and in fact opened with a production of *Hamlet*.[9] The current programme of The Grand is more diverse, with its interweaving of opera, ballet and theatre with popular music and comedy performances. The RSC's production of *A Midsummer Night's Dream* was book-ended by *Jackie – the Musical*, and *Let it Be*, a concert performance of Beatles' hits. Such mixed programming incorporating high and popular culture is the staple of many contemporary theatres, but it does also reflect something specific about the varied and itinerant nature of audiences in Blackpool.

We need also to note that modern Blackpool has particular social and economic challenges as a result of the decline in visitor numbers in the twentieth and early twenty-first century. Walton notes that 'by the 1991 census it was already occupying high places in league tables of multiple deprivation, especially in the central wards which had been the core of the traditional holiday industry'.[10] In 2013 a report on Blackpool for the Centre for Social Justice was headlined 'the problem-family capital of the North', and continued:

Blackpool, by far the largest town considered in this report with a population of 142,000, is an example of a community blighted by family breakdown and the wider social problems which can be associated with it. In tandem with the town's economic decline as the tourism industry has receded, families in Blackpool have come to face some of the most pronounced problems in the UK today. The social problems Blackpool faces are not only economic, but also familial, and supporting vulnerable families will be key to tackling Blackpool's difficulties.[11]

The report goes on to propose that unemployment and a transient population has led to one of the least settled school populations in the UK, high levels of domestic abuse, and high levels of alcohol and drug abuse in the town, with the highest alcohol mortality rates for men in the UK. Blackpool therefore represents not only a nostalgic 'representation of an older North', but the very real problems of the contemporary North.[12] A key question is thus: what place does Shakespeare have in this particular complex and ambiguous northern locale?

A Midsummer Night's Dream as a 'Play for the Nation'?

Before analysing the Blackpool RSC production, it is important to unpack some of the ideas around the concept of a 'Play for the Nation', and the choice of *A Midsummer Night's Dream* as that play. The idea of a 'Play for the Nation' appears to have had its foundation in the Royal Shakespeare Company's long-term aspiration to stage all of Shakespeare's plays as an act of prolonged national celebration. Gregory Doran, the Royal Shakespeare Company's artistic director, noted as a preface to the 2014 season:

> Under the banner *Shakespeare Nation*, we will lead a truly nationwide celebration of our greatest playwright beginning next summer [2014] and culminating in 2016 [the 400th anniversary of Shakespeare's death].[13]

Peter J. Smith explores how this focus on nation is a narrowing from the focus on Global Shakespeare of two years earlier during the London Olympics' cultural celebrations.[14] In addition, we should also note that the idea of 'nation' itself is a much-contested term. In literary criticism the debate about the extent of the engagement of Shakespeare's texts with aspects of nationhood remains a key question. Political theorists similarly continue to explore the development and ideological assumptions of this term. Shiv Visvanathan, summarising some of that debate, comments:

> The history of debates on nationalism and the nation-state described in such classic texts as Gellner and Hobsbawm unravel the ambivalence of the idea of nation and its duck-rabbit status. In its early phases, nationalism was seen as primordial, something objective, a link between community, a culture, and a territorial map. But attempts to establish objective criteria for nation failed. Such a congruency between people, history and territory was easy at the level of definition but problematic at the level of reality.[15]

As Doran's statement quoted earlier seems to suggest, the RSC's understanding of 'nation' is linked to this idea of a shared – or *to be shared* – culture, which in this instance is Shakespeare's plays. While not quite a 'territorial map' in Visvanathan's terms, the UK tour scoped the constituent parts of the nation and at the same time engaged in cultural exchange. The RSC's presentation of the tour in its publicity was also somewhat nostalgic, with a poster design harking back to a more old-fashioned age of cultural engagement, depicting a vintage motor-coach, a kind of charabanc, decorated with festive bunting, trees and a moon on its roof, with a donkey at the wheel. This depiction of the tour as an unthreatening, jolly outing around the UK draws on a nostalgic idea of a 'nation' of shared values and experiences.

If we look to the reason behind the selection of *A Midsummer Night's Dream* as the 'Play for the Nation', we will find other clues related to this idea. The director, Erica Whyman, indicates that the choice was partly due to the play's perceived universal relevance and accessibility. She explains:

> [it] is an enchanting play, full of wisdom, mischief and joy, but it is also about community, about people coming together from all walks of life and congregating in the name of peace and stability. It is full of beautiful poetry, almost no difficult language and themes known to every single one of us, such as how to love, how to grow up, and that allowing ourselves to believe in fairies, even just for an evening, is very good for the soul.[16]

This reference to the play's thematic interest in 'community' (albeit in the play one which emerges from discord) is again significant. The idea of 'community, about people coming together from all walks of life' demonstrates that there are parallels being drawn between the play's content and the theatrical practice of the production, with the mixture of amateur and professional performers. Moreover, the play was selected as it is accessible and projects an idea of nation which is community based and founded in shared life-affirming values. Similar positive explanations for the choice of play were offered by the assistant director, Kimberly Sykes, in a post-performance discussion in Blackpool. Again highlighting nostalgic associations, she commented upon the audience's familiarity with the play from school days, noted that it was a play about identity, and also part of a national memory about Shakespeare.[17] Other reasons were given on the RSC website suggesting that the choice of play was related to the RSC Open Stages project which had for two years given amateur companies across the UK access to RSC rehearsal techniques and support.[18] As the website noted, the production was 'inspired directly by the experience of Open Stages', which meant, in the RSC's words, that 'we are producing a large-scale production of *A Midsummer Night's Dream* Shakespeare's love letter to amateur theatre'.[19] In addition one might add that *A Midsummer Night's Dream* is a play which, possibly because of its familiarity, often invites experimentation – from Peter Brook's 1970 production of the play to the RSC's *Midsummer Night's Dreaming* Project with Google+ in 2013. It also featured prominently in different kinds of celebratory projects for the 400th anniversary of Shakespeare's death (including CBBC's fifty-minute version for young children filmed at the Everyman Theatre, Liverpool; the Globe's 2016 production; and the BBC TV production directed by Russell T. Davies). Moreover, the extent and range of these different engagements attests to the play's currency across contemporary media and provided another reason why this particular play was chosen as a 'Play for the Nation'.

The Production in Blackpool

The planning of the RSC's 'Play for the Nation' production of *A Midsummer Night's Dream* began at least fifteen months before the performance date, when the host theatres were asked to identify amateur groups who would be invited to apply to be involved in the project. There were two stages of auditions culminating in final auditions in Newcastle over two days for the so-called 'Northern section', with amateur groups from Glasgow, Newcastle, Blackpool and Bradford.

The successful group for the Grand Theatre in Blackpool was Poulton Drama, which has been established since the 1940s. In terms of location,

Poulton, and its local theatre at Thornton, is about six miles from Blackpool in a rather middle-class hinterland of Blackpool itself. The school children involved in the production were recruited from nine local schools including schools such as Larkholme School, Fleetwood, in a more socially deprived area of the North West, seven miles north of Blackpool in the Wyre area. This school, like others, had been involved with the RSC for two years as part of the Learning Performance Network through which the RSC was teaching the children both in and out of the classroom to engage with the work of Shakespeare, and thirty children performed during the run in Blackpool. The 'local' amateur element was thus established before the professional actors began their rehearsals, and the amateurs, playing the mechanicals, rehearsed mostly at a distance in their home towns and communicated with the so-called 'mother ship' via a sophisticated Skype link. This also enabled them – technology willing – to see and work with the other companies across the UK. However, Tony Stone, the Poulton amateurs' director, has noted that they were 'virtually self-contained', and they were initially encouraged to develop their own interpretation of the mechanicals scenes, although they had to take account of staging practicalities such as the size of the set.[20]

Nevertheless, it is clear that the overall interpretation of the play and production was established by the RSC. In December 2015, the 1940s period for the production was established, and the design for the set, as a post-war bombed-out theatre, was finalised. The choice of the 1940s was, as Erica Whyman noted, 'to get a sense of place . . . one we could remember – within living memory'.[21] In a programme note she added 'I have set the play in a Britain reminiscent of the 1940s because, like Shakespeare's remembered Athens, it was a place and time of great change'.[22] She goes on to indicate that the time was a moment of hope during a period of austerity, as well as commenting that in this decade the 'founding of the Arts Council in 1949 was visionary but it also marked a fundamental split between the amateur and professional worlds'.[23] The implication was that this production aimed through its practice, temporarily at least, to bring those worlds back together.

The theatre set presented an image of a post-war bombed-out shell of a theatre building, where the interior and floors had been obliterated. In front of this was a dusty grand piano, and an area allocated to the on-stage musicians. Above the stage hung what appeared initially to be large sandbag scenery weights. The performance space also had its surreal aspects, with a large staircase and two door frames at stage level which were moved around during the performance to suggest the magical confusion of the wood. On a practical level this rudimentary set ensured that the touring production was adaptable to a variety of venues. Yet as Pete Kirwan notes:

> Pleasingly, given the tour's use of the country's network of grand Theatre Royals and the foregrounding of theatre making, the production itself was set in a run-down 1940s theatre. Costume baskets, ladders, tatty red curtains and floorboards demarcated a space of play and celebration of the groups meeting in it.[24]

As identified here, the placing of this 'run-down 1940s theatre' set within the elaborate interiors of some of the country's stately theatrical houses drew attention to the play's, and the production's, fascination with the idea of theatre-making. Paradoxically, perhaps, the representation of a literally deconstructed theatre within Matcham's elaborate interiors at The Grand Theatre seemed to pull together various constituent parts of this 'Play for the Nation'. The juxtaposition of the meta-theatrical set with the grand physicality of the host theatre worked to synthesise and celebrate the theatrical history, architectural spaces, and maybe even geographical places that have contributed to the nation's play-making. It is significant that publicity photographs of the amateur groups involved in the tour were framed against a background of the various beautifully presented theatre auditoriums.[25] The similar framing and lighting of the photographs appears to be an attempt to join the various locales into a united national venture. While signalling the innovative linking of professional and amateur performance in the production, the photographs also serve to acknowledge the rich theatrical heritage of those spaces which the company hoped to incorporate into their forthcoming 'Play for the Nation'.

The set, along with costume, was also utilised to make distinctions between the mortal and fairy worlds. After an opening establishing scene where Puck seeks applause after a bathetic performance of 'chopsticks' on the grand piano, two red carpets are rolled out and Theseus and Hippolyta enter ceremoniously. The 1940s costumes were used to mark out social distinctions with Egeus' RAF officer's uniform showing him to be part of an old world order, contrasted with the fashionable 1940s clothing of the leisured aristocratic couple, Theseus and Hippolyta, and the lovers in period dresses and casual suits. The mechanicals' initial scene took place in the same setting, with them in work clothes of the period – overalls, aprons, and for the female 'Peter Quince' a turban. As the mechanicals exited, the supposed scenery weights dropped and revealed long red pillars of material. These, together with the moveable stairs and doors, were utilised to create a surreal 'wood outside Athens' which confused the mortal visitors with false entrances and exits and created visual humour in the scenes with the lovers. Titania (Ayesha Dharker) was linked to the red of the wood with her full-length red dress, decorated in gold and with a sari-like train. Her senior fairies wore a punkish mix of tight jackets and full skirts. The children who made up the rest of the group wore 1940s dresses, shorts and school blazers 'like returning second world war evacuees'.[26] All of the fairies (except Oberon) were splattered with brightly coloured paint which Gardner identified as 'the vivid colours of the Hindu festival Holi'.[27] This festival, during which bright coloured powder paints and water are thrown, represents a moment of creation and renewal, the beginning of spring, and the triumph of good over evil, as well as achieving a temporary suspension of power relationships within caste and gender.[28] Arguably all these have a resonance with the themes and festive structure of Shakespeare's play. The performative quality of Holi also chimes with the activities in the comedy's festive 'green world' as well as, one may argue, with the festive activities outside the Blackpool theatre, which share this temporary suspension of the 'normal' world. The incorporation of this particular festival appears to be an attempt to create a diverse and inclusive 'Play for the Nation'. However, given that this aspect was only mentioned in a few of the reviews, it seems likely that references to this Hindu festival were not recognised by all audience members. Nevertheless, the production certainly tried to make the contrast between the 'dust left by bombs' and the physical transformation within the wood brought about by the Holi colours.[29] In some ways, the inclusion of these particular festive qualities alongside the multi-ethnic casting challenged the potential Anglocentric nostalgia of the 1940s' post-war setting. Whyman commented in the theatre programme that the 'late 40s also heralded a long but revolutionary struggle for new equalities'.[30] Whyman's remarks focus more on gender politics, but arguably the 1940s setting, the casting, and the festivity of Holi identify the post-war period also as a time of increasing immigration and multiculturalism. This Shakespearean 'Play for the Nation' argues for an inclusive multi-cultural sense of national identity and a celebration of the diverse community of that 'nation'.

Yet the Hindu festival is also supposed to be high-energy and fun, and overall this seemed lacking in the fairy world of this production. It was almost as if the party was over, and had taken place off-stage, so the audience instead saw the rather melancholic aftermath of a festival. Perhaps the idea was that the disagreement with Oberon had curtailed the festivities signalled by the way in which his pristine white suit remained unsullied by Holi colours, whereas Titania's red dress with traces of Holi paint indicated her participation and aligned her with ideas of love and fertility. This rather melancholic Oberon was served only by Puck, an impish androgynous figure played by Lucy Ellinson in a black suit and top hat. She was variously described by critics as 'Vesta Tilly', 'Liza Minelli in *Cabaret*', and 'part crossing-dressing music-hall male impersonator'.[31] Ellinson engaged the audience in the manner of a self-conscious mime artist – using her hat to strike rakish poses, encouraging applause at the beginning and end of the play, as well as ushering in the performers for the next scene. As Kirwan notes:

> The action was orchestrated by Lucy Ellinson's Puck, a variation on *Cabaret*'s Emcee . . . her energetic performance established a presentational, pageant-like quality to the play – characters are brought on and displayed or introduced . . . the adventures of the forest . . . a series of pageants, orchestrated by Puck for the pleasure of Oberon.[32]

Puck was thus central to the production's idea of playing and also playfulness. This last trait was very much part of her relationship with the audience. At one point she made an exaggerated slow process of clambering over the audience in the stalls, 'stealing' sweets along the way. This comic stylised performance served to endear her to the audience, and with her energy and empathy helped to draw the various groups in the production and play together. Nevertheless, despite the fact that her clothes gradually showed signs of her engagement with the festivity of Titania's fairy band, with Holi colours dusted on the shoulder of her jacket, her melancholy was on occasions also made apparent to the audience. At the end of 2.2., during the scene featuring 'I know a bank where the wild thyme blows' (248), she sat on the staircase with Oberon who gradually leaned back against her. As, unseen by Oberon, she moved to stroke his head, he moved away, leaving her looking rather mournful, before she quickly slipped back into her clownish childlike mode by placing the flower in her mouth, which distracted her from Oberon's instructions about the Athenian youth, and prompted his comment 'effect it with some care' (2.1.265).

It is tempting perhaps to ascribe the performance of this vaudeville Puck to some northern archetype of comedy, engaging with a local audience, in a style such as that espoused by Ken Dodd, who appeared many times at the Grand Theatre. However, the interpretation of Puck was grounded in a much broader cabaret tradition, and, more importantly, the interpretation was offered at all venues across the UK, not just in Blackpool. The same applies to the physical comedy of the lovers' scenes, complete with the conventional visual gag of Hermia held back by a hand on her head, as she tries to hit Demetrius. These recognisable comic turns may be part of a shared national understanding of different types of comedy, but they are not distinctively northern.

Yet a concern to root the production in its northern setting did feature in the casting. Erica Whyman, in an interview following the final audition stage, commented on the Poulton group that they had really caught her eye and she 'really found them very entertaining as you'd expect from that bit of the world. Very strong sense of humour and they properly made us laugh'.[33] The 'as you'd expect from that bit of world' is intriguing and does seem to place humour as a defining feature of Blackpool and the North. Dave Russell in his work *Looking North* certainly includes 'humour' in his list of attributes of the North although he notes how northerners see themselves as 'humorous/witty' whereas from an external viewpoint this might be viewed as 'humorous if crude'.[34]

Consequently, given Whyman's comments, one might have expected to find evidence of 'northern' humour in the mechanicals' scenes. Paul Morley, describing Lancashire humour, notes:

> [A. J. P.] Taylor concluded that there was 'something in the air'. You could actually connect Lancashire's defiant sense of humour with the wind coming in from the south-east, from beyond British shores, bringing traces of distant difference, encouraging a certain edgy whimsy, jittery dreams of otherness, a glorious blend of silliness and wisdom, and a general belief that one way of beating the odds, outwitting fate and rising above social inequity was with a gag. Lancashire was where the world's antic mental energy eventually drifted to, and was absorbed and dispersed with a ruthless sense of timing rooted in fierce centuries of hard labour, defiant love and constant loss.[35]

And yet in this production, perhaps somewhat disappointingly given Whyman's remarks, this exuberant comic energy was deliberately discounted. Tony Stone, the director of the Poulton amateurs, reported that the group were given some initial freedom to devise their own style for the scenes. They decided not to go for 'slapstick' as, according to Stone, it easily 'moves from quality humour to pantomime dame', and because the mechanicals 'are funny not because of contrived jokes, but because they were inept'.[36] Moreover, it seems likely that despite the celebration of localness, these rude mechanicals scenes had to fit a basic template. For example, the group received broad parameters for the Pyramus and Thisbe scene – the chink (following Jonathan Bate's reading in the text used by the RSC) drew out the sexual references and became the gap between the legs of 'Wall'. In the Poulton version, Snout, as Wall, seemed initially rather over-confident in his role, only becoming slightly more perturbed as the lovers move to kiss through the chink. There were variations to this in other productions' reading of the scene – some Walls were portrayed as being more anxious and uncomfortable with the sexual innuendo of their required performance, anxiously looking over their shoulders as the lovers approached. Others played it very straight (no pun intended). The death of Pyramus and Thisbe also revealed variations in interpretation. The Poulton group gave both characters extravagant and prolonged deaths – both 'dying' to both sides of the stage before eventually collapsing. They included some business with the already 'dead' Pyramus passing a small wooden sword to Thisbe in response to 'come, trusty sword' (5.1.337). The Poulton Thisbe (Gary Houghton) gave a sensitive nuanced performance, which drew out the emotional aspects of the tragedy (as in Michael Hoffman's film version) and almost seemed to be defying the audience to laugh (which, perhaps unfortunately, they did).[37] She/he was also portrayed as rather fastidious, and upon seeing that she would have to lie across Pyramus's lower regions, she moved carefully so that she was just touching his chest. Other versions of this scene drew out the slapstick humour and made more of the positioning of Thisbe's head across the lower body of Pyramus.

Compared to other productions of the play, such as Peter Brook's or the concurrent Globe production, the Kottian sexual interpretation of Bottom's transformation into an ass, where the ass overtly represents sexual potency and desire, a reading which might have chimed well with the sexual frisson of Blackpool popular culture, was not pursued.[38] Perhaps this is understandable given that in other locations on this tour Bottom was played by women (Nottingham and Canterbury). Also, while the Blackpool Bottom was an amateur actor, he was also a professional primary school teacher, and so further moral constraints in his interpretation may have been appropriate. Quince, on the other hand, was here played by a female actor. This gender switching seems to have been encouraged across all the amateur groups, with female actors taking the parts of the various mechanicals in different permutations across the groups. Here the female Quince worked well as a post-war new woman within the 1940s setting, and, as a female director of the on-stage acting troupe, mimicked the RSC's own all-female directorial team. Whyman commented that the Blackpool mechanicals were 'a hard working group with an endearing humility, they are perfect casting . . . people for whom theatre is evidently a life-affirming joy'.[39] There might, however, have been more opportunity to introduce some regional variations into these scenes, given that the Bottom at Glasgow's Citizens Theatre appeared in the 'Pyramus and Thisbe' play wearing a kilt and carrying a large wooden claymore. Nevertheless, the Blackpool scene was very funny, without resorting to clichés of northernness, and perhaps, more so than some other venues' versions, their interpretation chimed well with the melancholic thread which ran through the production.

However, the key contribution of a local voice in all of the productions was quite literally in the local accents of the actors. Erica Whyman, commenting on the amateur casting in the production, indicated:

> In every single region the cast we have chosen has a distinctive voice and a strong sense of connection to the place where they will perform. I think it will be a real treat for audiences everywhere to see Shakespeare's most magical play with a proper local flavour.[40]

While the Poulton group had a connection to the Grand Theatre itself, having performed at the theatre in amateur productions, the 'proper local flavour' was for the most part conjured up by the actors' accents. All the actors in the Poulton group (apart from a Welsh Huw Rose playing Moonshine) have accents from the North West although not all are Blackpool accents. For local audiences this serves to create a sense of affinity with the speakers, to hear their own voices 'speaking words and experiencing words'.[41] Arguably, the audience in Blackpool, and other local audiences with their own groups, championed and supported their local amateur group because of the familiarity of accent and the implied connection to the shared sense of place. Certainly Katherine Brockaw in her review of the Poulton group's later performance at the Royal Shakespeare Theatre thought the amateurs not as good as the professionals, and commented on the audience's 'awkward chuckles', which suggests that the empathetic, and possibly compensatory, sense of a shared locale had been disrupted in the transfer to Stratford.[42] Somewhat ironically perhaps, this dislocation of the local, and the apparent consequent removal of some empathy, parallels the courtiers' response to the 'Pyramus and Thisbe' interlude in the play. Nevertheless, Brockaw goes on to praise 'the use of amateur performance [which] made one aware of an actorly humanity and theatrical love (going to the etymological roots of "amateur") that one doesn't always feel at the glossy RSC'.[43]

Arguably when creating a 'Play for the Nation' the utilisation of local accents is potentially significant. David Russell, discussing the work of the Northern Broadsides Company, who predominately cast actors with northern voices, emphasises how this 'plac[es] its accents and intonation at the absolute heart of the national culture'.[44] Perhaps in productions such as this *A Midsummer Night's Dream*, where local northern accents are only used by amateurs for the humorous, but somewhat foolish, lower-class mechanicals, there is a danger of simply reinforcing certain regional clichés and stereotypes. Yet in this production, this did not appear to happen – at least not in the performances in Blackpool, probably due in part to the multi-racial casting of Ayesha Dharker (Titania), Chu Omambala (Oberon) and Mercy Ojelade (Hermia). This deliberately and significantly brought other linguistic patterns and nuances to the production, and the northern voice became part of that national fabric.

Identity and Community

This fabric of voices and identities is perhaps what ultimately substantiates the production's claim to be a 'Play for the Nation'. Whyman, returning to the idea of community in a programme note, says '*A Midsummer Night's Dream* is an enchanting play . . . but is also about community, about overcoming prejudice, looking to new horizons'.[45] The production, as discussed here, utilised professional and amateur actors, local children, an actor of restricted height (who attacked Demetrius for calling Hermia a 'dwarf') and multi-ethnic casting – all representing a conscious and laudable attempt to create an inclusive sense of a diverse community. Interestingly, though, in the nine BBC TV documentaries *Best Bottoms in the Land*, broadcast on different local television channels corresponding to the location of the amateur groups, the narratives constructed were very different and much more about a rather distorted sense of 'localness'. In the BBC Northwest programme which featured the Blackpool cast, the footage of the amateur group showed them walking down the promenade, rehearsing in a social club while downstairs the clientele played Bingo, and improvising a dance routine wearing 'kiss me quick' cowboy hats.[46] Anthony Henry (Bottom) was interviewed on the beach learning more about the donkeys (this storyline was also used in other episodes with Norwich and Black Country companies visiting a donkey sanctuary). As they neared the opening night, the Blackpool group were seen enjoying a rather staged moment of relaxation at the Pleasure Beach on the 'Alice in Wonderland' ride. This was followed by the actor playing Bottom utilising one of the traditional funfair face-in-the-hole photograph boards, and, in an interesting reversal, sticking his head through a cardboard cut-out of a donkey. No cliché was left unturned! This television programme, presumably, was designed to be a celebratory account of the interaction of the local with the national, and to create a record of the input of the various regions in the production. Nevertheless, its portrayal of northernness was crafted to reinforce a series of high/low culture oppositions, which the theatre production largely avoided. It also reveals some of the possible complexities and pitfalls involved in the interaction of local identities with the construction of a 'Play for the Nation'.

In attempting to create a 'Play for the Nation', the production, as well as navigating the various identities of places, as discussed here, was also negotiating various aspects of its historical context. Primarily, as we have seen, the tour was designed to commemorate the 400th anniversary of Shakespeare's death. However, this tour should also perhaps be seen within the context of the Coalition government's austerity programme, which had led the RSC to cut back on its annual sojourn in Newcastle. Whyman herself noted of the RSC's former Newcastle season that '[t]he relationship is unlikely to return to its "golden age"'.[47] The 2016 'Play for the Nation' tour could thus be seen as an attempt to fulfil the RSC's flagging (and/or refocused) touring policy. Noting, in 2016, the still extant 'special relationship' with Newcastle, Whyman added 'We are in a constant state of evolution and a lot has changed since 1977. We just have to make sure that the kind of relationship we have is one that is fit for the 21st century environment'.[48] The 'Play for the Nation' tour provided the RSC with an opportunity to revisit destinations with which it had a prior association, such as Newcastle and Blackpool, perhaps to refresh and extend the interests and loyalties that had previously existed.

Nevertheless, during the course of the tour, different political debates came to the fore when questions about the UK's future as part of the European Union became a significant historical moment in terms of issues around 'the nation'. Arguably, given the long preparation time for the production there was no intention to overtly address this issue. The referendum was not announced until 20 February 2016, and the decision to leave the EU was not declared until 23 June 2016. Nevertheless, one might argue that presenting a version of the nation as one centred on the cultural richness of one of its canonical writers, while embracing a diverse assembly of audiences and theatrical performers, may have implicitly raised questions in the minds of its viewers about the coherence and integrity of those ideas of nation, and perhaps that nation's future. In April 2016 in Blackpool, the nostalgic 1940s setting helped suggest a positive reference point in the interpretation of the play, to illustrate how ideas of community could be influential in resolving social discord. Later, in June 2016 in Stratford, after the referendum result, a reviewer saw the production very differently:

> [I]ts simultaneous nostalgia for the more unified Britain of wartime yore belied the notion that the RSC was truly producing a 'play for the [current] nation'. Watching the professional actors of Britain's best bank-rolled company play Athenians who mock provincial actors (played by provincial actors) because they don't toil enough in their heads was, in the immediate aftermath of Brexit, an unintentionally disquieting reminder that there is much that separates Britons.[49]

This is a crucial observation, which usefully alerts us to the variables of time (as well as of place) in any performance. In late June 2016 in Stratford, the production was in a different place, where its northernness was estranged, and also a different time, where ideas of nationhood had taken a different turn.

To conclude, I would propose that the value of this interaction between the local and national, between Shakespeare and the North, ultimately lies beyond this specific Brexit moment. The Grand Theatre reported that audience numbers exceeded expectations, and that they had drawn in people, partly those supporting family members and communities, from a wider-than-usual catchment area. The production, together with its accompanying educational projects, appears to have made a significant intervention in the lives and aspirations of a community challenged by a range of social issues. Shakespeare's *A Midsummer Night's Dream* suggests that transformation is possible in the Athenian and forest communities it depicts. It seems that Blackpool, long associated with carnivalesque festivity and sites of spectacle and wonder, found that the topsy-turvy holiday world of the Shakespearean comedy provided an occasion to stimulate the revival and reinvigoration of its own communities.

Notes

1. The RSC tour included performances at the following in 2016: Northern Stage, Newcastle upon Tyne (16–26 March), Citizen's Theatre, Glasgow (29 March–2 April), Grand Theatre, Blackpool (5–9 April), Alhambra Theatre, Bradford (12–16 April), Marlowe Theatre, Canterbury (19–23 April), Theatre Royal, Norwich (26–30 April), Theatre Royal, Nottingham (3–7 May), Hall for Cornwall, Truro (10–14 May), Barbican Theatre, London (17–21 May), New Theatre, Cardiff (24–28 May), Grand Opera House, Belfast (31 May–4 June), Royal Shakespeare Theatre, Stratford-upon-Avon (15 June–16 July).
2. Royal Shakespeare Company, 'Erica Whyman 2016 production'. Available at: <www.rsc.org.uk/a-midsummer-nights-dream/past-productions/erica-whyman-2016-production> (last accessed 27 June 2018).
3. John K. Walton and Jason Wood, 'Reputation and regeneration: history and the heritage of the recent past in the re-making of Blackpool', in Lisanne Gibson and John Pendlebury (eds), *Valuing Historic Environments* (Abingdon: Routledge, 2016), 115–38, 126. See also Jill Fernie-Clark, 'Contemporary carnival: Blackpool and the symbolic suspension of real life', in Roger Spalding and Alyson Brown (eds), *Entertainment, Leisure and Identities* (Newcastle: Cambridge Scholars Publishing, 2007), 36–49.
4. Fred Inglis, *The Delicious History of the Holiday* (London: Routledge, 2000), 52.
5. John K. Walton, *Blackpool* (Lancaster: Carnegie Pub Ltd, 1998), 173.
6. Simon Featherstone, *Englishness: Twentieth-Century Popular Culture and the Forming of English Identity* (Edinburgh: Edinburgh University Press, 2009), 97–8.
7. John Urry, *The Tourist Gaze* (London: Sage, 2002), 94.
8. Gary S. Cross, 'Crowds and leisure: thinking comparatively across the 20th century', *Journal of Social History*, 39: 3 (Spring 2006), 631–50, 632.
9. Vanessa Toulmin, '"Bid me discourse, I will enchant thine ear": Frank Matcham in Blackpool (1889–1920)', *Early Popular Visual Culture*, 12: 1 (2014), 37–56, 42.
10. Walton and Wood, 'Reputation and regeneration', 122.
11. *Turning the Tide: Social Justice in Five Seaside Towns*, The Centre for Social Justice, August 2013. Available at: <www.poverty.ac.uk/editorial/deprivation-seaside-towns> (last accessed 29 May 2016), 25.
12. Featherstone, *Englishness*, 97.
13. Royal Shakespeare Company brochure, *Summer 14 March – October 2014 Stratford upon Avon* (2014), 2.
14. Peter J. Smith, 'Inaugurating the complete works (again): Shakespeare Nation, Doranism and literalism in the Royal Shakespeare Company's 2014 summer season', *Cahiers Elisabéthains: A Journal of English Renaissance Studies*, 89: 1 (2016), 58–73, 59.
15. Shiv Visvanathan, 'Nation', *Theory, Culture and Society*, 23 (2006), 533–49, 533.

16. Erica Whyman, 'A Play for the Nation', *Arts Professional* (14 January 2016) www.artsprofessional.co.uk/magazine/article/play-nation> (last accessed November 2017).
17. Kimberley Sykes, Post-performance audience and cast discussion. The Grand Theatre, Blackpool (6 April 2016).
18. Royal Shakespeare Company, '*A Midsummer Night's Dream*: A Play for a Nation' <http://www.dream2016.org.uk> (last accessed 17 February 2016).
19. Ibid.
20. Tony Stone, interview with author (May 2016).
21. *Best Bottoms in the Land*, television programme, produced by Sally Williams. UK: BBC Northwest (20 May 2016).
22. Whyman, 'A national passion', *A Midsummer Night's Dream – Play for the Nation*, the Grand Theatre Blackpool, Programme (April 2016).
23. Ibid.
24. Peter Kirwan, '*A Midsummer Night's Dream*: A Play for the Nation (RSC/Lovelace Theatre) @Theatre Royal, Nottingham'. Available at: <blogs.nottingham.ac.uk/bardathon/2016/05/07/a-midsummer-nights-dream-a-play-for-the-nation-rsclovelace-theatre-theatre-royal-nottingham> (last accessed 30 May 2016).
25. Royal Shakespeare Company, 'Erica Whyman 2016 production'.
26. Lyn Gardner, '*A Midsummer Night's Dream* review – RSC's delightful "play for the nation"', *The Guardian* (24 February 2016). Available at: <www.theguardian.com/stage/2016/feb/24/midsummer-nights-dream-review-royal-shakespeare-theatre-stratford-upon-avon-rsc-ayesha-dharker-chu-omambala> (last accessed 20 May 2016).
27. Ibid.
28. Society for the Confluence of Festivals in India, 'Holi – let the colour shower joy' <www.holifestival.org> (last accessed 27 June 2018).
29. Gardner, '*A Midsummer Night's Dream* review'.
30. Whyman, 'A national passion'.
31. William Stafford, 'A way with the fairies' (June 2016). Available at: <bumonaseat.wordpress.com/2016/06/16/a-way-with-the-fairies> (last accessed 27 June 2018); Kirk McElhearn, '*A Midsummer Night's Dream*' (25 February 2016). Available at: <www.mcelhearn.com/theater-review-a-midsummer-nights-dream-by-the-royal-shakespeare-company> (last accessed 27 June 2018); Gardner, '*A Midsummer Night's Dream* review'.
32. Kirwan, '*A Midsummer Night's Dream*'.
33. *Best Bottoms in the Land*, BBC TV Northwest.
34. Dave Russell, *Looking North: Northern England and the National Imagination* (Manchester: Manchester University Press, 2004), 27.
35. Paul Morley, *The North (and almost everything in it)* (London: Bloomsbury, 2013), 293.
36. Stone, interview with the author.

37. Michael Hoffman (dir.), *A Midsummer Night's Dream* (USA: Fox Searchlight Pictures, 1999).
38. See Jan Kott, *Shakespeare Our Contemporary* (New York: Norton, 1974), 183.
39. Whyman, 'Amateur actors from Poulton cast in the Royal Shakespeare Company's production of *A Midsummer Night's Dream*: A Play for the Nation'. Available at: <https://www.visitblackpool.com/latest-news/amateur-actors-from-poulton-cast-in-the-royal-shak> (last accessed 27 June 2018).
40. Whyman, 'RSC Dream Team 2016' (1 October 2015). Available at: <www.blackpoolgrand.co.uk/rsc-dream-team-2016> (last accessed November 2017).
41. Sykes, 'Post performance discussion'.
42. Kathryn Steele Brockaw, '*A Midsummer Night's Dream* by The Royal Shakespeare Company with Poulton Drama at the Royal Shakespeare Theatre, and *A Midsummer Night's Dream* by Shakespeare's Globe at Shakespeare's Globe, and *A Midsummer Night's Dream* by Pendley Shakespeare Festival at Pendley Manor (review)', *Shakespeare Bulletin*, 35: 1 (Spring 2017), 148–56, 153.
43. Ibid. 153.
44. Russell, *Looking North*, 173.
45. Whyman, 'A national passion'.
46. *Best Bottoms in the Land*, BBC TV Northwest.
47. BBC, *Shakespeare 2016 on Tour*, 'Newcastle's special relationship with Shakespeare'. Available at: <www.bbc.co.uk/programmes/articles/49CPwpV9TktfzyHFD6qMlWs/newcastle-s-special-relationship-with-shakespeare> (last accessed 27 June 2018).
48. Ibid.
49. Brokaw, 'A Midsummer Night's Dream', 156.

8

William the Conqueror: The Only Shakescene in a Country

Richard Wilson

The Grafton Shakespeare Portrait, owned by the John Rylands Library in Manchester, which represents an 'angelic-faced' young man 'Aged 24' in 1588, was definitively declared to be 'a fake' by the National Portrait Gallery at the launch of its own 2006 'Searching for Shakespeare' exhibition, on the grounds that at 24 the dramatist 'would have been unable to afford the sumptuous silk jacket' displayed in the painting, 'having recently become a father of twins and joined a travelling theatre troupe'. Tarnya Cooper of the NPG explained that the painting had been 'looked at in a systematic way', and analysis proved 'there was no evidence' it was of Shakespeare. Indeed, the only authentic extant representation of the Bard, apart from the Folio frontispiece, was declared to be the Chandos Portrait, which the London gallery owned. This self-promoting stunt thus raised more questions than it answered. For if Cooper's research had been as 'expensive and timely' [*sic*] as she claimed, it would have involved some investigation of the provenance of the Manchester picture. But instead the NPG event typified metropolitan resistance to the idea of a 'Northern Shakespeare', and demonstrated why the story of the young dramatist's non-Stratford connections needs to be ceaselessly retold.[1]

The portrait Cooper described as showing 'a Joseph Fiennes lookalike' was purchased in 1909, in the Durham village of Winston-on-Tees, near Darlington, from the Misses Alice and Florence Ludgate. The elderly sisters told how 'about the year 1876' the oil painting 'came into the possession' of their mother from their grandfather, a farmer of Grafton Regis, Northamptonshire, but that their family had long ago received it from 'a rich old uncle', together with a belief that it 'represented Shakespeare'. Because of this reputed likeness their father branded the back of the panel, 'W. S.'.[2] Yet, as Katherine Duncan Jones huffs in her *Portraits of Shakespeare*, 'Even if some genuine provenance lies behind this "old family tradition", it brings us no closer to Shakespeare', as it is 'not clear where Shakespeare was in 1588. He was probably a recruit to one of the playing companies then touring . . . [but] it seems highly unlikely that he had already acquired a patron willing to fund such a work'.[3] This objection seems persuasive; *except* that it overlooks one intriguing fact, which is that the village of Grafton abuts Easton Neston, seat of the Hesketh family, who relocated there, precisely in 1876, from Rufford Old Hall in Lancashire, where a matching oral tradition has long held that in 1588 Shakespeare was employed as an actor by Sir Thomas Hesketh.[4] And this link gains interest from the fact that Hesketh's cousin, Thomas Savage, also from Rufford, was a Globe trustee.

Since English theatre history orthodoxy is violently allergic to a 'Northern Shakespeare', no one examining the Grafton Portrait makes the Hesketh connection. Yet the Heskeths moved from Lancashire to Northamptonshire in circumstances that suggest the possibility of a different, equally plausible narrative to that of the 'rich old uncle' as to how the picture might have been acquired by a Grafton tenant farmer. The Heskeths inherited Easton Neston in 1867 but leased out this mini-Versailles (to the Empress Elizabeth of Austria, no less), until the then Thomas Hesketh succeeded in 1876. Shortly after transferring his seat, the 7th baronet organised a sale to fund the construction of his luxury yacht, *Lancashire Witch*, in which he then sailed around the world. During this cruise he met the Californian heiress he married in 1880, who ordered further drastic modernisation of Hawksmoor's building. The Heskeths have form in offloading what they deem 'old junk'.[5] Whether or not that included the 'old papers' in which the name 'Shakeshafte' had been 'changed to Shakespeare' which their solicitor claimed to have glimpsed between the wars, a battered Elizabethan panel might well have been banished, to make way for sporting trophies, just as the Hesketh Renaissance library was flogged off at Sotheby's in 2010.[6] But however it got there, its emergence in the adjacent village, at the exact moment of the transfer of the contents of Rufford to Easton Neston, is a coincidence that provides the Grafton Portrait with a plausible alternative provenance to the one offered by the Miss Ludgates. This chapter will argue that there are far too many such coincidences connecting the dramatist to the political landscape of the North for the 'Lancastrian Shakespeare' to be dismissed as contemptuously as it is by the gatekeepers of early modern English drama. It therefore proposes that it may be time to revisit the idea that the stylish young sitter with expensive sartorial tastes, depicted in what might be renamed the Manchester Portrait, is William the Conqueror of Lancashire.

In Furthest Lancashire

In 1592 what is thought to be the first recorded comment on Shakespeare described him as an 'absolute *Johannes factotum*', who 'is in his own conceit the only Shake-scene in a country'. Though it was transcribed and published by Henry Chettle, the attack on this know-all, as 'an upstart Crow, beautified with our feathers', is now increasingly accepted as the dying curse of Robert Greene; and it had evidently been provoked by a bruising encounter on some provincial estate with a retainer who had been allowed to get above himself, and to steal the thunder by imagining he was 'as well able to bombast out a blank verse as the best'.[7] The incident must have been like the one in *The Taming of the Shrew* when the actors arrive expecting 'to play a pleasant comedy' (Induction 2.125), only to discover that their host instead wants them to perform 'a kind of history' (135) to disarm a troublesome guest, and the Lord's co-opted page Bartholomew then steals the show. If the Manchester picture did originate at Rufford, it would therefore record a time when the dramatist was indeed being 'beautified' above his station; and some biographers infer this was because by 1588 he was also appearing regularly before Henry Stanley, Earl of Derby, in his Lordship's nearby residences at Knowsley and Lathom, where it would pay to look spruce, as the guests there included family relations like George Carey, who would eventually succeed his father Lord Hunsdon, as lord chamberlain and patron of Shakespeare's theatre troupe.[8]

On 20 September 1589 the governor of Carlisle, Lord Scrope, notified William Asheby, the English emissary in Edinburgh, that upon learning of King James' 'earnest desire to see Her Majesty's players repair unto Scotland to His Grace, I did forthwith despatch a servant unto them where they were in the furthest part of Lancashire'.[9] The Queen's Men had been at Knowsley, where they played on 5, 6, and 7 September, and again on Sunday, 13 September, 'the Queen's players played in the afternoon', the Malvolio-like steward William Farrington recorded, 'and my Lord of Essex's at night'.[10] David George notes that Farrington clocks thirteen gigs by five companies between 1587 and 1590: Leicester's, Hesketh's, the Queen's, Essex's, and Strange's, the troupe of Ferdinando, Lord Strange, the earl's son and heir.[11] But as James VI appears to have been informed, the 1589 Knowsley theatricals were grander than anything yet seen in

Lancashire, with the Queen's and Essex's Men playing back-to-back, afternoon and evening, in a ten-day residency. And that constellation of thespian talents implies that 'the great desire the king had to have the same come unto his grace' was not unanticipated, and that it may have been to meet his command that the earl's local fixer, Richard Harrington, ordered the construction of the indoor playhouse at the gates of the estate, in Prescot, which is known to have existed in the 1590s.[12] Lawrence Manley and Sally-Beth MacLean are curtly dismissive of this venue in their 2014 study, *Lord Strange's Men and their Plays*, objecting that 'it would have been a major fall from grace' for any professional company to perform in this 'improbable location'.[13] But there the actors could have conveniently rehearsed, prior to performing up at the great house, on the royal road to their future Scottish patron.

The 1589 festivities were exceptional for Knowsley, in being staged outside a holiday; and directly the order came from Carlisle the party broke up, as 'my Lord and all went away'. So, when on 14 September 'Mr Towneley came in the evening to have seen my lord', he found the house empty.[14] The players were presumably seizing the moment of James' most star-struck theatre craze, when his betrothal to the fourteen-year-old Anne of Denmark inspired the king to compose a wedding masque for his favourite, the Earl of Huntly, in which he performed as Hymen's 'patron', and to pen a set of Marlovian poems trumpeting his role as a new Leander.[15] His 'Hero' set sail for Scotland on 1 September; and it seems that the actors were hailed from 'furthest Lancashire' to grace the nuptials 'with pomp, with triumph, and with reveling' (*A Midsummer Night's Dream* 1.1.19).

The Danish royals hosted the pick of Leicester's Men at Elsinore in 1586. Speculation therefore centres on whether Shakespeare now rushed further north himself, to play the Scottish court. And a clue to this mystery lies in Greene's hostility to the Jack-of-all-trades who eclipsed him, and an episode that perhaps caused their rift, when the professional and the provincial may have been forced to team up on a drama that seems designed for Lancashire, yet with one eye on opinion 'down south' and the other on opportunities north of the border. The anonymous 1591 *A Pleasant Comedy of Fair Em the Miller's Daughter of Manchester: With the love of William the Conqueror, as it was sundry times acted in the honourable City of London by the right honourable the Lord Strange his servants* was attributed in the seventeenth century to Greene, the established playwright, but this has always looked dubious because he satirised some of its speeches and derided their author.[16] Manley and MacLean think the play gave offence by simply 'drawing on the work of Greene'.[17] Yet unless he had a hand in it, his emotional investment in the work seems excessive. And once the high stakes are grasped, the possibility of Greene's competitive co-authorship of 'the one play with an unambiguous title-page attribution to Lord Strange's Men' adds a new dimension to the Lancastrian story.[18]

Because debate focuses on its authorship, little is said about the topicality of *Fair Em*. Yet the opening of this 'kind of history', which the 'University Wit' was perhaps forced to co-write with some household tutor, poses a riddle that also puzzles historians: 'What means fair Britain's mighty Conqueror / So suddenly to cast away his staff, / And all in passion to forsake the tilt?'[19] Putting the question otherwise, why did James suddenly entertain 'the possibility of falling in love with a woman'?[20] For these lines wink at the king's homoerotic 'tilting' with his 'Castalian Band' of poets, and the dilettantism that made him a dream patron of English writers such as Marlowe, who would 'persuade men of quality' to go to Scotland, where he 'meant to be'.[21] The only extant Elizabethan play about William the Conqueror, and possibly the 'william the conkerer' played at the Rose on 4 January 1593-4, yet long dismissed as more old junk, this fantasia about what John Kerrigan terms 'the British problem' in fact reflects James' cult of his ancestor, 'The Bastard of Normandy' who 'gave the law, and took none', as his descendant loved to say, when the bold Northman 'came into England' and 'made himself king by force'.[22] James' belief that the Conqueror's heirs were thereby 'absolute owners' of England provoked parliamentarians into fabricating an opposing myth of Anglo-Saxon liberty, as Christopher Hill related.[23] *Fair Em* thus seems at first sight to belong to a genre of 'Medieval Conquest' plays that resist a centralising monarchy, and fits the 'demonstrable interest of Strange's Men' in Saxon history.[24] Yet by having the Viking invader 'turn his conquering eyes', and 'Disclose himself thrall'd to unarm'd thoughts' (1.1.14–15), the play works to quell fears of 'The Norman Yoke'. And its subplot spins its marital surprise as a special favour conferred by the king upon his loyal subjects in Lancashire: 'I amorously do bear to your intent, / For thanks and all that you can wish I yield' (1.1.11–12).

Published in 1591, *Fair Em* was bound during the 1630s in a folio labelled 'Shakespeare. Vol. 1' in the collection of Charles I.[25] The play doubtless entered the royal library because it was devised with James' nuptials in mind, as it concerns William's scheme to woo a 'Princess and daughter to the King of Danes' (1.1.52–3), 'in the name of Sir Robert of Windsor' (1.1.77), and leave his deputies in charge while he attempts to 'bring this lady to our Britain' (1.1.71), after he develops a crush on the 'true counterfeit of the lovely Blanch' (1.1.52). To the dismay of English ministers, who had been pushing for a more radical Calvinist match, James had indeed fallen for a painting of the Lutheran Anne. So, perhaps Greene was humouring his government backers, by having William shrink from the marriage with the gynophobia that was his own trademark, when the groom sets eyes on the bride: 'Ill head, worse featured, uncomely, nothing courtly, / Swart, a Collier's sanguine skin. / I never saw a harder favoured slut' (1.3.27–9). This was a risqué twist, given reports that while Anne sat sewing shirts for her fiancé in Copenhagen, 'her affection His Majesty in no way requites'.[26] But then, the entire premise of a play that critics have mistaken for a 'harmless romance' turns on the king's aversion to matrimony, as if quoting James' misogyny back on himself:[27]

> What tellest thou me of ladies?
> I so detest the dealing of their sex,
> As that I count a lover's state to be
> The base and vilest slavery in the world ...
> Let Mistress Nice go saint it where she list,
> And coyly quaint it with dissembling face.
> I hold in scorn the fooleries that they use:
> I being free, will never subject myself
> To any such as she is underneath the sun. (5.1.89–93, 130–4)

In an open letter 'To the Scottish People' James would admit that his 'nature' was indeed such that he 'could have abstained' from marriage, had not 'want of succession bred great [suspicion] of my inability, as if I were of barren stock'.[28] Whoever conceived this 'Danish romance' had picked up, then, on the king's fragile masculinity.[29] But they had doubtless heard, too, about the psychodrama of May 1589, when he 'called his Council into his cabinet' to inform them that, after weeks of prayer, he was abandoning his initial Calvinist choice, Catherine of Navarre, who was 'old and cracked, or worse'; because a similar change of heart is the starting point of *Fair Em*, when the king spurns Blanch for the Swedish princess Mariana, the lover of Marquis Lubeck.[30] Thereafter the plot recycles Greene's hit of the previous year, *Friar Bacon and Friar Bungay*, where Prince Edward and Earl Lacy vie for the fair Margaret, just as Mariana and Lubeck deceive William into eloping with the plain Blanch, 'masked' (5.1.106) in the guise of the Swedish beauty. Anne and James were married on 28 August, in a proxy ceremony at Elsinore that exasperated Elizabeth, who had done everything to prevent this Lutheran alliance.[31] Since *Fair Em* climaxes with a scene of 'Nordic noir', in which 'Britain's mighty conqueror' objects to being ambushed by the 'unconstant Mariana' (5.1.112) and the Danes, it therefore looks as if this Scandinavian stand-off was written from a disbelieving London perspective, during the summer months of uncertainty, prior to Anne's setting sail for Edinburgh:

> Conceit hath wrought such general dislike,
> Through the false dealing of Mariana,
> That utterly I do abhor the sex.
> They are all disloyal, unconstant, all unjust:
> Who tries as I have tried, and finds as I have found,
> Will say there's no such creatures on the ground. (5.1.138–43)

Few suspected that *Fair Em* possessed a Jacobean subtext until, in a revelatory 2012 book on the 'disguised ruler' theme, Kevin Quarmby noticed how its deputising scenario and substitution trick prefigure the shaming of Angelo by a later Mariana, and proposed that a vivid memory of its 'private performance in Lancashire' resurfaced in Shakespeare's reaction to the Stuart king when he wrote *Measure for Measure*, after James came south in 1603. As Quarmby pointed out, when Blanch's father Zweno begs William to forgive her, his ungallant refusal 'betrays bitter distrust' on all sides.[32] In fact, the rejection accords with Greene's *James IV*, possibly acted the following year at Knowsley, before 'The northern lords and ladies hereabouts' it salutes, which depicts the earlier Scottish monarch driven by 'unlawful lust' into plotting with a minion to murder his English queen, who was, in reality, Elizabeth's aunt.[33] The author of this 'un-history play', to apply the term which Lisa Hopkins has invented for *Fair Em*, understood how 'these nations if they join' will prove invincible.[34] Yet overtaken by an 'upstart crow' on the race northwards, Greene the metropolitan writer was persisting in problematising the union with 'anti-Scottish, if not anti-Jacobean sentiment' that would have negative consequences for his own prospects at the court of the earls of Derby, the king-making 'Kings of Lancashire':[35]

> ZWENO: Blanch, thy father loves thee so,
> Thy follies past he knows, but will not know.
> And here, Duke William, take my daughter to thy wife,
> For well I am assured she loves thee well.
> WILLIAM: A proper conjunction! As who should say,
> Lately come out of the fire,
> I should go thrust myself into the flame. (5.1.123–9)

Leeds Barroll has lately demonstrated how alert the king of Scots was to the propaganda value of commercial theatre, not least because the elders of the Kirk liked to warn him how 'certain English comedians' mocked his 'royal person' in 'their plays ... with secret and indirect taunts and checks'.[36] So, if Greene did co-write *Fair Em*, the London dramatist was dangerously Anglocentric in perpetuating suspicion of the son of Mary Queen of Scots as a Frenchified Catholic, prone to sexual 'lust' and 'thralled dumps' (1.1.24, 34), as William admits at the start. Thus, its main 'Saxon' plot is so at odds with James' 'Norman' politics that the play seems not to know which way to turn in response to the impending royal marriage, and everything is set for a battle royal between the Danish and English armies, until at the last moment Lancashire teaches the court a lesson in coexistence and accommodation, when the maid of Manchester steps out of the subplot to show that 'though some deserve no trust, / There's others faithful, loving, loyal, and just' (5.1.144–5). Whoever defused the dramatic confrontation with this tragicomic reversal was thus experimenting with the toleration trope Shakespeare would test to destruction in *The Taming of the Shrew*, itself possibly devised to articulate the conformism of the so-called Church papists in the Knowsley audience, and then elaborate with problem comedies like *All's Well That Ends Well*, of forced marriage as indeed 'a proper conjunction', symbolising political union and religious détente:

WILLIAM: I see that women are not general evils.
Blanch is fair. Methinks I see in her
A modest countenance, a heavenly blush.
Zweno, receive a reconciled foe,
Not as thy friend, but as thy son-in-law.
ZWENO: I joy to see your grace so tractable.
Here, take my daughter Blanch,
And after my decease, the Danish crown. (5.1.221–9)

The Poet from Preston

The union of crowns that concludes *Fair Em*, in place of the expected battle, suggests that its Mancunian matchmaking may have been added to the Danish drama at a late stage, by someone in the Stanley household, '[c]unning in music and the mathematics', and assigned, as the bachelor Petruchio says he hires Hortensio, '[t]o instruct' (2.1.55–7) the groom's future subjects that 'thy sovereign', is 'one that cares for thee, / And for thy maintenance commits his body to painful labour both by sea and land, / To watch the sea in storms' (5.2.151–4), in Kate's compliant words. For if a melodrama about a madcap king's reluctance to marry fits Greene's curriculum vitae as a Queen's Man, its frame story, about the peace-making Lancashire lass, may have been updated by some local insider to meet James' rapidly changing plans. And an indication that this was the case is how this burlesque of the main plot is bookended by extravagant yet supercilious digs at the contemporary sheriff of Lancaster, Sir Edmund Trafford, who routinely descended on Knowsley, as a 'hunter-out and unkenneler of those sly and subtle foxes: Jesuits and seminary Priests'.[37] A kinsman of the queen through Catherine Howard, Trafford had earned notoriety as what Edmund Campion called a 'most bitter enemy of the Catholics' in 1581, when he headed the hue and cry for the priest that led to Hoghton Tower, near Preston: effectively a preparatory school for the English Catholic college at Douai endowed by Thomas Hoghton, after he fled to the Ardennes in 1569, following the Rising of the Northern Earls.[38]

The exiled owner of Hoghton Tower emerged as a choric figure in Ernst Honigmann's 1985 study, *Shakespeare: The 'Lost Years'*, because of his correspondence with his 'conformable' brother Richard Hoghton of Park Hall, Charnock Richard. By the time Thomas expired in 1580, he was hoping to 'come home again', as a 'reconciled foe'.[39] In the event, he was buried in Liège, and when his son did return in 1582, having been ordained at Douai, he was arrested by Trafford, and died in Salford gaol, after the sheriff failed to extract 'any likelihood of conformity'.[40] As a recent discovery in Saint-Omer of a First Folio, read to pieces in the town's English college, has revived interest in Shakespeare's possible contacts with this Catholic diaspora, so has a fact which intrigued Honigmann, E. K. Chambers and others: how five successive Stratford schoolmasters came from Lancashire or had links with Campion.[41] A Jesuit testament of faith, reputedly signed by the poet's father John during Campion's mission, was conveniently 'lost' by Malone. But whether or not, as Honigmann deduced, the dramatist was the William Shakeshafte bequeathed an annuity of £2 in the will that Thomas' brother Alexander Hoghton signed in haste on 2 August 1581 – a day before 'good Sir Edmund Trafford' escorted him to Manchester Castle, where he surely feared he would die in custody – the unnamed yet knowing collaborator on *Fair Em* clearly had cause to remember the sheriff of Lancaster.[42]

Shakespeare's potential Lancashire itinerary has lately been analysed by Michael Winstanley, in the very edition of *Shakespeare Quarterly* where Leeds Barroll opens a new window onto the players' northern world. There the historian sets out to disprove the theory that John Cottom of Tarnacre, near Preston, was the same man as the Stratford schoolmaster of that name from 1579 to 1581, which he believes constitutes 'the crucial link' between the writer and the North.[43] So he asserts that the 'Lancashire connection is predicated' on 'claims that the Hoghton and Cottom families were on intimate terms', and that the teacher 'was a Roman Catholic'.[44] Yet far from having such 'central importance', in the most detailed outline of the Lancashire thesis prior to Honigmann's, *The Annotator* by Alan Keen and Roger Lubbock, Cottom is scarcely mentioned.[45] That is because the longstanding and independent oral traditions that the tyro dramatist worked at Hoghton, Rufford and Knowsley lock into John Aubrey's report that he had been 'a schoolmaster in the country', and the fact that, as Park Honan showed, his 'early plays, and knowledge of his unpublished sonnets, can be linked with people in the circle of Hoghton, Hesketh and Strange'.[46] Thus, no one can deny that his first theatre publication, *Titus Andronicus*, advertises how it was acted by the Earl of Derby's Men, who performed in the earl's palatial mansions in both Lancashire and London; nor refute Honigmann's 'strongly-backed thesis quite independent of other Lancashire connections', that until Shakespeare's playing company became the Lord Chamberlain's Men in 1594, Ferdinando Stanley had been 'the likely patron'.[47]

It was 'Shakespeare's later connections with the Hoghtons' that make it 'irresponsible to ignore' 'William Shakeshafte', Honigmann maintained.[48] These ties include the fact that 'the first writer to address a poem to Shakespeare' was the Prestonian John Weever, who included a sonnet '*Ad Gulielmum Shakespear*' among his 1599 *Epigrammes*, dedicated to Sir Richard Hoghton of Hoghton Tower, in which 'by far the largest group' of poems are addressed to 'Lancastrians, or men closely associated with Lancashire or Cheshire'.[49] Honigmann believed that Weever, a nephew of the powerful Henry Butler of Rawcliffe, was the likeliest of the 'Lancashire connection' to 'lead us to other discoveries'.[50] His Cambridge tutor, William Covell, another Lancastrian, was among the first to praise Shakespeare in print.[51] The inference has to be that the Preston student had seen the sonnets circulating among the 'private friends' of the 'Honey-tong'd Shakespeare' a decade before their publication, such as the manuscript of Sonnet 2 in a collection compiled by the daughter of Sir Richard.[52] The latter became 'a notable hunter of recusants' in the 1590s.[53] Yet, as I remarked in my 2004 *Secret Shakespeare*, the Prestonian Shakespeare was already being celebrated as the post-Reformation seculariser that Milton praised for creating literary 'substitutes for the "hallow'd relics"' of the Old Religion:[54]

> Weever pointedly praises the playwright for 'begetting' a new generation of 'saints', whose votaries 'burn in love', rather than sectarian hate.

Shakespeare's creations are true icons for a post-Reformation society, according to Weever . . . *Ad Gulielmum Shakespear* is confirmation that Shakespeare criticism hinged from the start on . . . vouching the plays' exemption from Catholic influence: 'I swore Apollo got them and none other'.[55]

Since Weever's sonnet was printed among so many that 'celebrate members of the Hoghton family', Honigmann speculated that the epigram might have been written 'to please Sir Richard', who 'may well have been one of Shakespeare's pupils'.[56] And it was followed by a poem to Edward Alleyn, who claimed his mother was a Towneley from Burnley, which would connect the actor to the Heskeths and Hoghtons.[57] Weever's next tributes were to the Lancashire grandee Sir Thomas Gerard, and his brother-in-law, Sir Peter Leigh, the MP for Wigan and a theatre enthusiast.[58] So, *The 'Lost Years'* reiterated that Cottom is 'by no means' the 'only possible link' between Shakespeare and Lancashire, and that Stratford's other Lancastrian educators, Walter Roche, Simon Hunt, who left for Douai, and Alexander Aspinall, of Standen Hall, Clitheroe, further reinforce his 'intricate connections' with the northern county.[59] One would like to know more about Aspinall, who replaced Cottom, and who, among all those in 'the Shakespeare circle', seems to be hiding in plain sight.[60] For this northerner married John Shakespeare's Henley Street neighbour, the widow Anne Shaw, which made him the stepfather of Julius Shaw, a witness to the poet's will.

A supposed model for Holofernes, the Clitheroe schoolteacher is known for a suggestive valentine the Bard is said to have riffed on his behalf, to accompany some kid gloves: 'The gift is small / The will is all / Alexander Aspinall'.[61] But while he served as Stratford's chamberlain, alderman and deputy town clerk, as well as its schoolmaster until his death in 1624, his family maintained its influence in Clitheroe, and nominated the constable there as late as 1618.[62] An Oxford beneficiary of Robert Nowell, of nearby Read Hall, whose trust also funded the university education of Edmund Spenser, it is Aspinall, rather than Cottom, who ought to be considered the firmest of all the possible links between Shakespeare and the Hoghtons, as he was connected to them by the marriage of his kinswoman, or possibly sister, Maud, to another Alexander Hoghton, of the Clitheroe branch of the clan, based at Pendleton Hall. Keen and Lubbock even surmised that between taking his MA in 1578 and settling in Stratford in 1582, Aspinall may himself have worked at Hoghton Tower, as a tutor to its 'singing boys'.[63]

The Warriors of Warrington

The distance from Hoghton to Clitheroe is thirteen miles, and to Tarnacre fourteen. That proximity greatly strengthens the claim that John Cottom of Tarnacre was the Stratford schoolmaster. To recruit successive teachers from the same part of Lancashire looks like carefulness. But Honigmann broadened the grounds for Shakespeare's northern internship by revisiting other points of contact, such as the Globe trustee Thomas Savage, whose mother was a Hesketh; Sir Thomas Hesketh himself, to whom Alexander Hoghton bequeathed his 'play clothes' and musical instruments, if his own brother Thomas chose not to 'maintain players', and whom he then urged 'to be friendly unto Fulke Gillom', a Chester player, and 'William Shakeshafte now dwelling with me', or 'help to some good master'; Ferdinando, who, as patron of Strange's Men, may have been that master, and to whose wife Alice Edmund Spenser dedicated his 1591 *Tears of the Muses*, which praised 'Our pleasant Willy' for his 'joy and jolly merriment'; the Stanleys entombed at Tong in Shropshire beneath epitaphs attributed to the poet by William Dugdale in 1664; and Sir John Salusbury of Llewini in Denbyshire, with his wife, Ferdinando's half-sister Ursula, to whom the collection *Love's Martyr*, containing 'The phoenix and the turtle', was 'consecrated': a publication which proves that 'Shakespeare was in some way connected with the Stanleys'.[64]

Love's Martyr places Shakespeare in the orbit of 'the darling of Wales', the Earl of Essex, for whom Salusbury acted as a Welsh agent, because this overwrought compilation was likely conceived as an homage in the wake of his 1601 revolt.[65] The premature Jacobeans behind the volume were holding a torch for the unionism Shakespeare obliquely hymns in his poem.[1] So, as Kerrigan comments in *Celtic Shakespeare*, since '[i]t is more than likely' that the poet knew Salusbury, it is 'astonishing to find Sir John and Denbighshire missing from the standard biographical studies'. For whether or not he visited Lleweni Hall, 'actors and writers close to Shakespeare will certainly have had contact' with its owner 'and his entourage during the 1590s'.[66] In fact, *The Derby Household Books* record constant gatherings of the Salusbury and Stanley affinity at Knowsley and Lathom, and similar accounts audit how the earls were 'royally entertained' at Llewini.[67] From these, Sally Harper has reconstructed the 1593 Christmas revels there, with songs echoed by Shakespeare, and appearances by Alleyn and the Shropshire-born clown Richard Tarleton.[68] The master of ceremonies was the editor of *Love's Martyr*, and household praise-singer, Robert Chester, and the festivities hailed Ferdinando's elevation to the earldom and petty sovereignty of the Isle of Man. Whether verses to Ursula, embroidered with the Stanley eagle and child, and signed in the name of 'good will', are his thank-you for this extravaganza is disputed; but David George and John Idris Jones have both recently restated the case that they are by Shakespeare:[69]

> From princely blood and royal stock she came
> Of eagle's brood hatched in a lofty nest.
> The Earl of Derby and the King of Man
> Her father was; her brother now possessed.
> Then happy he; but thrice more happy she,
> To match herself with lovely Salusbury ...
> Now must I go, my pen hath run his fill.
> Gold have I not, to girder her withal.
> But yet to show some part of my good will
> The best I have I humbly part with all.
> Accept it then, a portion of my store.
> 'Tis my good will; would God 'twere ten times more.[70]

The 'Denbigh poem' bids farewell to another guest, Ferdinando's daughter Anne, 'last not least', as if the poet was, perhaps, her tutor. So, if this poem was by 'our good Will', as on linguistic evidence David Crystal thinks is 'certainly possible', it would slot beside 'The phoenix and the turtle' in a series of Shakespearean texts possessing what Honigmann termed 'interesting Derby connections': the *Henry VI* plays, with their 'lean towards Lancaster' and nod to the earl's Clifford ancestry; *Richard III*, with its 're-touching' of Stanley fence-sitting at Bosworth; *Love's Labour's Lost*, with its King Ferdinand, and wordplay on the Strange mottos, '*Dieu et ma Foy*' and '*Sans changer ma vérité*'; and *A Midsummer Night's Dream*, with its 'nuptial hour' (1.1.1) apparently synchronised to the shotgun wedding of the sixth Earl William to a granddaughter of Lord Burghley: his brother Ferdinando's possible nemesis.[71] We can add to this sequence *The Taming of the Shrew*, which mitigated its prior version to display the power of weakness; and *Titus Andronicus*, with its recoil from the 'cruel irreligious piety' (1.1.130) exhibited in an opening that was probably drafted by George Peele. Moreover, there is a consistent body of writing which not only supports the supposition that 'Shakespeare worked for a while as one of Strange's Men', but that repeatedly enacts the survival strategy at Knowsley, where, as Honigmann stressed, the young writer would discover that compromise and conformism, rather than resistance or rebellion, were the rules of the house:[72]

> If William served Alexander Hoghton and Sir Thomas Hesketh, two very positively committed Catholics, how can we reconcile this with the anti-Catholic tone of some of his early plays? We may do so by examining the career of his patron ... Ferdinando Stanley ... commended by the Privy Council in 1587 for his diligence against recusants, no doubt felt equally incriminated by his family and his Catholic friends in Lancashire: when he was approached by the Jesuits in 1593 to claim the crown in succession to Queen Elizabeth, he could hardly have been surprised to learn that government spies were closely watching him.[73]

Honigmann's portrait of Ferdinando anticipated that of Manley, who in a 2003 essay saw the earl's 'difficult and problematic' inheritance, as a lineal descendant of Henry VII, mirrored in Shakespeare's dramatic 'balancing of emotion'. The *Henry VI* cycle registers the earl's 'heterodox' confessional identity, according to Manley, as one 'of all three religions', in the aggrieved words of the Jesuit Robert Parsons.[74] Hence, the author of the anti-papal *King John* 'began life as a Catholic' but 'seems to have been a Protestant from the 1580s', *The 'Lost Years'* decides.[75] So, 'like John Donne', Shakespeare 'changed his religion'.[76] And in their survey of Lord Strange's Men, Manley and MacLean analyse the company's 'commitment to ambiguity' precisely in terms of such '*politique* thinking':

> The apparently irenic views of the Stanleys, their local commitments to their northern Catholic domains, and their respect for their Catholic neighbours, on whom it was their unhappy task (at peril of the family's traditional power and standing) to impose the religious policies of the regime, all harmonise with the politically sophisticated repertory of Lord Strange's company.[77]

If the 'little academe' of 'living art' (1.1.1–143) in *Love's Labour's Lost* resembles Ferdinando's 'royal household in the provinces', Honigmann noticed, it is because 'Ferdinand and his friends are caught out repeatedly 'breaking faith'" (1.1.147–55; 5.2.470–1), by pretending 'it is religion to be thus forsworn' (4.3.357). What inspired the setting of the play in Navarre, on this view, was the earl's *politique* equivalence to the little kingdom's chameleon Henri Bourbon, who understood that 'Paris is worth a Mass'. So, far from making Catholicism and Lancashire synonymous, Honigmann insisted that Shakespeare learned to change 'to the opposed ends of our intents' (5.2.746) at Knowsley, where '"in" jokes for a private audience' made religion a game.[78] This chimes with the theories of Manley and MacLean about how the players aligned with the 'Catholic loyalist moderation of the Stanleys' and with the religious 'heterodoxy attributed to the inscrutable Lord Strange'.[79] It also accords with evidence not produced in *The 'Lost Years'*. For as is well known, the first 'review' of *Love's Labour's Lost* occurs in *Alba: The Month's Minde of a Melancholy Lover*, a poem of 1598 where Robert Tofte recalls wasting time on its 'civil war of wits' (2.1.225): 'Which I to hear to my small joy did stay, / Giving attendance on my forward Dame'. Charles Whitney explains that the high-minded poet 'cannot countenance the fun Shakespeare has laughing' at apostasy, which contrasts with his own 'pain' in travelling such a distance to see the show, 'where my fair Angell / doth abide': in the 'Northwest . . . Alongst / Which place, fair Mersey doth glide'.[80] The identity of his cruel mistress is veiled; but Tofte says she resides in a 'Northwest Village far from mine abode', and wages 'WAR IN TOWN' from 'BEAU SE': clues that locate 'Alba' at Bewsey Hall in Warrington.[81]

Editors have always suspected that Shakespeare's comedy was devised as 'a country play' written for a country-house performance; and the 'Melancholy Lover's' recollection that 'I once did see' *Love's Labour's Lost*, 'so called to my pain', implies that this may have been in Lancashire. Recent sleuthing by Matthew Steggle has indeed identified Tofte's 'Alba' in Margaret Aston, wife of Thomas Ireland, who purchased Bewsey Hall from Robert Dudley in 1597.[82] The Astons of Aston, Cheshire, are well known for a portrait of Margaret's nephew at the deathbed of his wife. But if Steggle's identification holds, it opens yet another window onto Shakespearean Lancashire, as Ireland was attorney for William Stanley, sixth Earl of Derby, in the inheritance dispute with the widow, Countess Alice, following the likely poisoning of Ferdinando in 1594. Born at Frodsham on the Mersey, the Gray's Inn lawyer had previously lived in Roby, three miles from Knowsley, where generations of his family were employed by the estate and welcomed at the hall.[83] One of his cousins married Henry Stanley, another son of Earl Henry. So, if 'Alba' was Margaret Ireland, Tofte's disappointment over *Love's Labour's Lost* probably occurred at Knowsley, and says as much about his impatience with the temporising of the real Ferdinand as with the time-wasting of the earl's namesake on stage.

The Miller of Manchester

It is always necessary to return to 'battles long ago' over the 'Northern Shakespeare' Honigmann regretted, because veridical facts are simply ignored by those averse to the theory.[84] The scholar was himself careful 'to distinguish between two groups' of data underwriting the 'Lancastrian Shakespeare': facts about the 'Stanley connection' that make it 'probable' that the dramatist worked for Strange's Men; and the 'Hoghton connection' that remains a tantalising 'possibility', albeit one which the fact that the Cottom and Hoghton families 'must have come into contact' (to use Winstanley's phrase) 'converts . . . into a probability'.[85] What Honigmann did *not* do was make either group substantiate the other, nor claim that 'personal connection' between Cottom and the Hoghtons was a 'crucial link between Stratford and Lancashire'.[86] Above all, he never made the Lancastrian itinerary depend on whether the pupil shared the teacher's 'alleged Catholic sympathies'.[87] It was immaterial to Honigmann whether Cottom was a papist while in Stratford, or remained one after likely being ejected due 'to his relationship to a known Catholic martyr' (his brother had been Campion's chaplain).[88] That was because the concern of this refugee from Nazi Germany was the *collaboration* when 'Queen Elizabeth's government turned the screws' on Lancashire's Catholics, as was witnessed by a squirming petition to the Earl of Leicester to secure the release from prison of Sir Thomas Hesketh himself:[89]

> That whereas he is committed to the custody of Sir Edmond Trafford, Knight, Sheriff of the County of Lancaster . . . in that he hath been over-negligent to see the reformation of some in his family, for which he is right heartily sorry . . . Sir Thomas protesteth before God and your Honour to reform the same offence, in such sort, that those which are under his government and will not henceforth use themselves dutifully and obediently unto Her Majesty and her most godly laws in every respect, shall neither abide in his house nor have any favour at his hands, but all extremity.[90]

Hesketh's professed 'reformation' was belied by a priest hole discovered at Rufford in 1949.[91] After Alexander Hoghton was taken to prison in 1581, this former sheriff was therefore himself 'put under arrest as a "disaffected papist"', and remained in 'the custody of Sir Edmond Trafford' in Manchester Castle at the time of the petition in 1584.[92] Perhaps that was why, if he had been in Lancashire, Shakespeare returned to Stratford, where his children were born in 1583 and 1585. But Keen and Lubbock placed the dramatist back with 'Sir Thomas Hesketh's players' between 1585 and 1587, when they visited Knowsley over Christmas.[93] This is one of many events listed in the *Derby Household Books* that reveal the Stanleys thwarting their other frequent caller, Trafford, by hosting Catholic friends.[94] As the vicar of Prescot complained in 1586, 'they that have the sword in their hands ... to redress abuses among us suffer it to rust'.[95] So, Hesketh was freed from prison. But he died, perhaps as a result of his ordeal, at the time of the Manchester Portrait, on 20 June 1588. If *Fair Em* was staged at Knowsley a year later, the situation of its Lancashire maid and her father, Sir Thomas Goddard, on being compelled to lead double lives, and 'undertake the homely miller's trade' (1.2.4), would therefore resonate with all those in the hall who remained under the eyes of 'Good Sir Edmund'. For clearly, the compliments paid to that 'utterly barbarous man', the 'unrighteous Sheriff', are both loaded and ironic:[96]

Sir Thomas Goddard now old Goddard is,
Goddard the miller of fair Manchester.
Why should not I content me with this state,
As good Sir Edmund Trafford did the flail? (1.2.11–14)

The 'flail' of the 'good' Sheriff was his armorial crest, commemorating a Saxon ancestor, Ranulphus Trafford, who resisted the 'Norman Yoke', disguised as a thresher.[97] *Fair Em* inverts this legend, for now it is Trafford's victims who 'subject / Their gentle necks unto their stubborn yoke of drudging labour and base peasantry', and local Catholics who 'mask to save [their] wretched lives'. Goddard's lamentation on behalf of 'a number of us . . . Threatened by Conquest of this hapless Isle' (1.2.1–10) thereby upstages the king's 'private cares' (1.1.28). Little in the main story supports the accusation of Norman 'tyranny' (1.2.20) against William, who is presented there as the 'temperamental' type of 'Lovesick King' overpowered by strong women, and is even styled the 'Duke of Saxony' (5.1.24).[98] But Em's father's jeremiad also overshadows the story that it is meant to introduce. Instead, the insertion 'of some dozen or sixteen lines' (*Hamlet*, 2.2.517) invests the Miller with a sententiousness that is only explained at the end, when we are told that 'this reverent man' is 'renowned through the world' (5.1.257–9). Sir Thomas will soon forget his rank, when he promises Em to his irreverent servant Trotter. Presumably, there was no call for the maid's father to be 'a knight / And gentleman' in the preliminary draft. But along with the relocation of its denouement to Elizabethan Manchester, Goddard's exhortation 'to shake off pomp' (1.2.1–3) in a menial trade imposes a tragic dimension on the play that can sound virtually Shakespearean:

> And thou, sweet Em, must stoop [from] high estate,
> To join with mine that thus we may protect
> Our harmless lives, which, led in greater port,
> Would be an envious object to our foes,
> That seek to root out all Britain's gentry
> From bearing countenance against their tyranny. (1.2.15–20)

Goddard's homily on 'outward pomp' (1.2.32) will echo through the Forest of Arden, where Duke Senior lectures how 'old custom' is sweeter than 'painted pomp' (*As You Like It*, 2.1.2–12). Yet Greene ridiculed this pulpitry in his 1591 *Farewell to Folly*, where he disowned the additions as the efforts of one who 'cannot write true English without the help of Clerks of parish churches': 'to bring Scripture to prove any thing he says, and kill it dead with the text in a trifling subject of love'. The Protestant playwright particularly scorned the 'blasphemous rhetoric' of the ending, where Em delivers a 'canonical sentence' on her suitor: 'Thy conscience, Manville, is a hundred witnesses' (5.1.157); and Zweno moralises how 'love, that covers multitude of sins, / Makes . . . parents wink at children's faults' (5.1.121–2). The reviser was invoking 1 Peter 4: 8: '[a]nd above all things have fervent charity among yourselves: for charity shall cover the multitude of sins'. Greene's contempt for such sonorous 'abusing of Scripture' has been taken as proof that he had no part in the proceedings.[99] In fact, his comparison of this religiosity to a sermon by a sexton betrays the intensity of his engagement; and Eric Sams infers that he was scandalised by the 'high church' tone of lines that flaunt 'a Catholic background', for there is more than a hint of the parable of the loaves and fishes in the mill scenes of *Fair Em*.[100] What surely irked the Londoner, in any case, was the sanctimoniousness imported into a 'homely miller's trade' (1.2.3), when the flour Goddard doles to Mancunians is intended to '[t]ransfer my soul into a second heaven' (1.2.29), like the Eucharist of the Old Religion:

> Although our outward pomp be thus abased,
> And thralled to drudging, stayless of the world,
> Let us retain those honourable minds
> That lately governed our superior state,
> Wherein true gentry is the only mean
> That makes us differ from base millers born.

Though we expect no knightly delicates,
Nor thirst in soul for former sovereignty,
Yet may our minds as highly scorn to stoop
As if we were in our precedent way. (1.2.32–42)

Greene never forgave the crowing pedagogue for 'killing' his love story with a lesson in civics 'borrowed of Theological poets'. '*The people make no estimation / Of morals teaching education*', he scoffed.[101] Yet for seven years, according to his memoirs, this pedantic 'country author' had reigned supreme as the 'absolute interpreter to the puppets' and 'the King of the Fairies' (presumably, Oberon in *James the Fourth*), even if the voice was 'nothing gracious'. That privileged position had come with 'costly robes' to the value of £200, allowing the 'factotum' to be mistaken for 'a substantial man'. 'So am I, where I dwell', the 'upstart crow' retorts in Greene's 1592 *Groat's-Worth of Wit*, 'able at my proper cost to build a Windmill'.[102] Commentators have automatically assumed that this seeming allusion to a theatre must relate to some contemporary London playhouse, such as the Bankside Rose. But Greene's schoolteacher expressly locates his private 'Windmill' '*where I dwell*'. His boast therefore sounds as if it might well be regarding the Prescot playhouse, which was constructed for Strange's Men, according to George, with a distinctive 'odd-sized' roof.[103] If so, it prompts the question of how funding was raised for this Lancashire theatre, to cover its 'proper cost'.

In *Fair Em*, the 'young men and maids keep such a stir' for corn that Trotter cannot meet demand. Profits from Manchester's flourmills subsidised its grammar school. But the trouble at their mill is that Goddard and Em keep 'weeping and wamenting' their plight, 'as who should say, the Mill will go with wamenting' (1.2.71–6). The city's chief mills were, in fact, owned by the Gerard family, to whom the economic historian, T. S. Willan, thought the name Goddard must refer.[104] For many years Elizabeth's attorney general, Sir Gilbert Gerard had acquired his mills in 1561 from Sir Edmund Trafford.[105] 'A Protestant in London and a papist in Lancashire', it was said of Sir Gilbert that '[t]here is no man that so much shifteth papists from the danger of the law'; and he held properties in trust for Sir Thomas Gerard of Bryn, a recusant, father of a famous Jesuit, and brother-in-law of the exiled Thomas Hoghton, who had been in prison since 1586, after being ensnared in the Babington Plot.[106] The cousins were frequently at Knowsley.[107] So, it looks as if the Manchester mill was dropped into *Fair Em* to honour the marriage of Sir Gilbert's daughter Katherine to Richard Hoghton, which took place forty-eight hours after the actors 'went away'. The bride's brother and brother-in-law, Weever's Thomas Gerard and

Peter Leigh, were surely present. No wonder, in any case, that Greene could smell spilled religion. For whatever the matrimonial occasion, the co-author of *Fair Em* was relaying the family's plea to the queen, that they none of them 'had evil thought against her royal person':[108]

> MILLER: And longer let not *Goddard* live a day
> Than he in honour loves his sovereign.
> WILLIAM: But say, Sir *Thomas*, shall I give thy daughter?
> MILLER: *Goddard*, and all that he hath,
> Doth rest at the pleasure of your majesty. (5.1.265–9)

A Gentleman of Great Habit

'I will go pacify them' (1.2.51): Goddard's words about the bread-starved Lancastrians set the tone for the interpolations in *Fair Em*. Critics believe it 'improbable that a company would entrust to a novice the task of improving' the script in this way.[109] But that reckons without the lift of the 'Windmill' from which the improver preached. George thinks *Fair Em* would indeed 'have been a good choice for a Knowsley performance', which he dates to the autumn of 1593.[110] This must, however, have been before May 1590, when the detested sheriff was buried in Manchester's Collegiate Church, for the play closes with another sardonic tribute, as William, who has sailed from Denmark into Liverpool, swears he is as happy 'to find Sir *Thomas Goddard* / As good Sir *Edmund Trafford* on the plains: / He like a shepherd, and thou our country miller' (5.1.262–4).[111] Those whom the 'good shepherd' harried spoke of 'the furious hate of this inhuman wretch, prepared for any nefarious deed'; but the player king welcomes this 'ferocious man'.[112] The Conqueror has just been inspired to marry Blanch by Em forgiving Manville for betraying her with Eleanor from Chester. For whether or not Shakespeare wrote any of this, the ploys with which the miller's maid has evaded her suitors, playing deaf, dumb and blind, to see, speak and hear no evil, are object lessons in the tactics of toleration that seem hardwired into his creative imagination. Yet if Trafford did shake William's hand, the sheriff must also have been struck by the limits of their imagined 'community of differences', with the heroine's 'visceral recoil' from Manvile's 'limp conciliatory gesture':[113]

> I do forgive thee, with my heart,
> And will forget thee, too, if case I can.
> But never speak to me, nor seem to know me. (5.1.205–7)

In his study of the discursive foundations of the United Kingdom, *Archipelagic English*, Kerrigan shows how the formation of the Stuart state entailed the realignment of 'an entire social order', and how reaction to the 'regal union' was driven as much by local struggle as government policy. The meta-theatre of *Fair Em* thus illustrates how 'in the north of England, magnate power localized' the 'British problem'. It also highlights the complication, that along the borders of the compound state religious differences 'produced a dissonance' that the absolutist doctrine of *cuius regio, eius religio* – 'whose is the realm his is the religion' – could not resolve.[114] So, if he did have a part in it, *Fair Em* signals, decades before *Cymbeline*, how Shakespeare would respond 'to the mélange of myths' that legitimated the union, not with 'easy wish-fulfilment', but with tragicomedy, where 'artifice is of the essence'.[115] And whoever organised its performance had reason to qualify the celebrations in this manner, because just weeks after the actors departed, on 20 November 1589, Thomas Hoghton, whose son Richard married the miller's daughter, was killed by the Catholic Thomas Langton, Baron of Newton, in a feud that tore the community apart along new religious lines. It was from this time of 'Heart-breaking groans and howling misery', in Weever's words, that the young groom became such a 'notable hunter of recusants', and dedicated witch-finder, because, as the Earl of Derby warned Burghley, shortly before the Stanleys were themselves engulfed, the forces pacified in *Fair Em* had the potential to destroy them all:

> If they should be burnt in the hand, I fear it will fall out to be a ceaseless and most dangerous quarrel betwixt the gentlemen that any county of Her Majesty's hath this many years contained.[116]

Fair Em concludes on a Shakespearean note, when Manville concedes that true accord remains tantalisingly out of reach: 'The Fox will eat no grapes ... because they hang too high' (5.1.253–4). So, the bittersweet Lancashire wooing 'doth not end like an old play' (*Love's Labours Lost*, 5.2.851). *All's Well That Ends Well*, *Measure for Measure*, *As You Like It*, *The Merchant of Venice* and *The Two Gentlemen of Verona* are therefore just a few of the dramas prefigured here, which suggests that their author was at least familiar with this problem work. The jest about his lecherous rivalry with Richard Burbage – that 'William the Conqueror came before Richard the Third' – has in fact been heard as evidence that he played the part of its libidinous monarch.[117] We might prefer to believe that the angel-faced young actor disarmed old Trafford in the role of Em, as the pageboy

Bartholomew plays the maid's part for another embarrassing gatecrasher, Christopher Sly, in the later comedy of forced marriage he perhaps composed for Knowsley. We do not know whether he was with the Queen's Men who left so hurriedly for Edinburgh. But it is tempting to imagine that he reprised there the role he had perfected in the Prescot playhouse, and that if *Fair Em* was staged before the king of Scots, while he waited for his bride, it was Shakespeare's alluring presence that impelled James to venture on 'the one romantic episode of his life', and on 22 October 1589 sail 'upon the instant' to fetch his Danish princess, after storms had forced Anne to take shelter in Oslo.[118]

Fair Em can be decoded as a fantasy of the qualified toleration that James would indeed eventually proclaim in 1617 with his *Book of Sports*, when he progressed through Hoghton, Lathom and Bewsey.[119] This might seem to take its Mancunian insertions too seriously. But from the day when Robert Greene refused to credit the impudent 'upstart' in the 'sumptuous silk jacket' as 'a gentleman of great habit', Shakespearean Lancashire has always been underestimated.[120] So, when *Fair Em* was given its first London run for four centuries, all mention of Manchester was cut, even from the title. Moreover, the play staged in 2013 at the Union Theatre in Southwark contained 'little or nothing' by 'Shakespeare', its director confidently stated, because it had 'neither the poetry nor the subtext that we associate with the established canon'.[121] So, this overdue revival was yet another gross undervaluation. For as we discover, the more we study the poetry of its subtext the more 'this fair picture' of the Conquering William, commissioned for a northern house, appears to be 'the true counterfeit' of the artist as a 'beautified' young man: 'Aged 24' in 1588. Of course, we may never discover the identity of the seductive sitter in the Manchester Portrait, nor the name of the author of the attention-seeking Lancastrian additions to *Fair Em*. But for the sake of argument, we might call him William Shakescene.

Notes

1. Tarnya Cooper, *Searching for Shakespeare* (New Haven: Yale University Press, 2006), 62; Catriona Davies, 'Shakespeare portrait a fake', *Daily Telegraph* (28 October 2005).
2. Thomas Kay, *The Story of the 'Grafton' portrait of William Shakespeare, 'Aetatis svae 24, 1588', with an account of the sack and destruction of the manor house of Grafton Regis by the parliamentary forces on Christmas Eve 1643* (London: S.W. Partridge, 1914), 11, 14.

3. Katherine Duncan Jones, *Portraits of Shakespeare* (Oxford: Bodleian Library, 2015), 107, 109.
4. Dowager Lady Hesketh quoted in Ernst Honigmann, *Shakespeare: The 'Lost Years'* (Manchester: Manchester University Press, 1985), 34.
5. Lord Hesketh, quoted in Dowager Lady Hesketh, *Shakespeare*, 33.
6. Alan Keen and Roger Lubbock, *The Annotator: The Pursuit of an Elizabethan Reader of Halle's Chronicle Involving some Surmises About the Early Life of William Shakespeare* (London: Putnam, 1954), 201.
7. Robert Greene, *Groat's-worth of witte, bought with a million of repentance*, in Alexander Grosart (ed.), *The Life and Complete Works in Prose and Verse of Robert Greene* (12 vols, London: Hazell, Watson and Viney, 1883), 12: 144. The authorship of the pamphlet was credited to Chettle by Warren Austin in a 1969 computer analysis that was later partially retracted: Warren Austin 'Groatsworth and Shake-scene', *The Shakespeare Newsletter* (Spring 1992). Richard Westley has since argued persuasively that the work was indeed written by Greene, with Chettle's stylistic fingerprints introduced during the transcription: 'Computing Error: reassessing Austin's Study of Groatsworth of Wit', *Literary and Linguistic Computing*, 21: 3 (2006), 363–78. This attribution has been supported by Steve Mentz, in Kirk Melnikoff and Edward Gieskes (eds), 'Forming Greene: theorizing the early modern author in the Groatsworth of Wit', in *Writing Greene: Essays on England's First Notorious Professional Writer* (Basingstoke: Ashgate, 2008), 115–32.
8. F. R. Raines (ed.), *The Derby Household Books (The Stanley Papers: II)* (Manchester: Chetham Society: 31, 1853), 83.
9. William Axon, 'Did Shakespeare visit Lancashire?', *Lancashire Gleanings* (Manchester: Tubbs, Brook and Crystal, 1883), 127–9; see also K. P. Wentersdorf, 'The Queen's Company in Scotland in 1589', *Theatre Research International*, 6 (1980), 33–6.
10. *Derby Household Books*, 64–5; David George (ed.), *Records of Early English Drama: Lancashire* (Toronto: University of Toronto Press, 1991), 182–3. In his letter of 20 September, Scrope informs Asheby that the Queen's Men 'have made their return hither to Carlisle, where they are, and have stayed for the space of ten days'. Unless the governor was exaggerating his assiduity, this suggests that the players may have first arrived in the border town on 10 September, but then returned to Knowsley for the performance they gave there on 13 September.
11. David George, 'The playhouse at Prescot and 1592–1594 plague', in Richard Dutton, Alison Findlay and Richard Wilson (eds), *Lancastrian Shakespeare: Region, Religion and Patronage* (Manchester: Manchester University Press, 2003), 227–42, 230–1.
12. For an authoritative reprise of the evidence for the existence of the Prescot playhouse, see Elspeth Graham, 'The "longue durée": identity, place, time and performative representations of the Earl of Derby', *Shakespeare Bulletin*, 38: 3 (2020).

13. Lawrence Manley and Sally-Beth MacLean, *Lord Strange's Men and their Plays* (New Haven: Yale University Press, 2014), 262.
14. *Derby Household Books*, 65.
15. See Jane Rickard, *Authorship and Authority in the Writings of James VI and I* (Manchester: Manchester University Press), 53–6.
16. See Edward Phillips, in his *Theatrum Poetarum* of 1675. Richard Simpson proposed that the play was written by Shakespeare as an allegory of the Elizabethan theatre industry, with Em's successful suitor, Valingford, as a self-portrait; see 'On Some Plays Attributed to Shakespeare', *Transactions of the New Shakespeare Society* (1875), 155–80. Other authors credited with the play include Anthony Munday and Robert Wilson; see Terence Logan and Denzell Smith (eds), *The Predecessors of Shakespeare: A Survey and Bibliography of Recent Studies of English Renaissance Drama* (Lincoln: University of Nebraska Press, 1973). Brian Vickers includes *Fair Em* among the plays he attributes in part to Thomas Kyd on stylistic grounds; see Vickers, 'Thomas Kyd, Secret Sharer', *Times Literary Supplement* (18 April 2008), 13–15.
17. Manley and MacLean, *Lord Strange's Men*, 106.
18. Ibid. 104.
19. All quotations from *Fair Em* are from Standish Henning (ed.), *Fair Em: A Critical Edition* (New York: Garland, 1980). See also Charles F. Tucker Brooke (ed.), *The Shakespeare Apocrypha: Being a Collection of Fourteen Plays Which Have Been Ascribed to Shakespeare* (Oxford: Clarendon Press, 1908), 285–306.
20. Caroline Bingham, *James VI of Scotland* (London: Weidenfeld and Nicolson, 1979), 115.
21. Thomas Kyd, quoted in David Riggs, *The World of Christopher Marlowe* (London: Faber and Faber, 2004), 139.
22. John Kerrigan, *Archipelagic English: Literature, History, and Politics, 1603–1707* (Oxford: Oxford University Press, 2008); James VI, *The Trew Law of Free Monarchies*, in C. H. McIlwain (ed.), *The Political Works of James I* (Cambridge, MA: Harvard University Press, 1918), 61–3. For 'william the conkeror', see Manley and MacLean, *Lord Strange's Men*, 106.
23. Christopher Hill, 'The Norman Yoke', in Christopher Hill, *Puritanism and Revolution* (London: Secker and Warburg, 1958), 68–9.
24. Curtis Perry, '"For they are Englishmen": National identities and the early modern drama of medieval conquest', in Curtis Perry and John Watkins (eds), *Shakespeare and the Middle Ages* (Oxford: Oxford University Press, 2009), 172–98, 181; see also Gordon McMullan, 'The colonisation of early Britain on the Jacobean stage', in Gordon McMullan and David Matthews, *Reading the Medieval in Early Modern England* (Cambridge: Cambridge University Press, 2007), 119–40.
25. See Peter Kirwan, 'The First Collected *Shakespeare Apocrypha*', *Shakespeare Quarterly*, 62: 4 (2011), 594–601.
26. Thomas Fowler, letter to William Asheby, English ambassador to Denmark, quoted in David Williams, *James VI and I* (London: Jonathan Cape, 1963), 15.

27. Samuel Schoenbaum, *Internal Evidence and Elizabethan Dramatic Authorship: An Essay in Literary History and Method* (London: Edward Arnold, 1966), 50.
28. 'Discourse of James VI on taking his Voyage' (22 October 1589), in William Boyd and Henry Meikle (eds), *Calendar of State Papers: 10: Scottish, 1589–1593* (Edinburgh: HM General Registry, 1936), 174–5.
29. Lisa Hopkins, 'The Danish Romance Play: *Fair Em, Sir Clyomon and Sir Clamydes*, and *Hoffman*', *Early Modern Literary Studies*, 27 (2017), 1–17, 2.
30. William Melville of Tongland, quoted in Bingham, *James VI*, 115.
31. Bingham, *James VI*, 115.
32. Kevin Quarmby, *The Disguised Ruler in Shakespeare and His Contemporaries* (London: Routledge, 2012), 108–9.
33. J. A. Lavin (ed.), *The Scottish History of King James IV* (London: Ernest Benn, 1967), 1.3.31 and 5.6.180–2.
34. Hopkins, 'Danish Romance Play', 2.
35. Kerrigan, *Archipelagic English*, 15.
36. Leeds Barroll, 'Shakespeare, his fellows, and the New English King', *Shakespeare Quarterly*, 68: 2 (Summer 2017), 115–38, 131–3; James Dibdin, *Annals of the Edinburgh Stage* (Edinburgh: R. Cameron, 1880), 20; Appendix: *Acts and Proceedings of the General Assemblies of the Kirk of Scotland, 1560–1618* (Edinburgh: 1839), 977–1008, para. 191.
37. James Croston, *Lancashire and Cheshire: A Wayfarer's Notes in the Palatine Counties* (Manchester: John Heywood, 1882), 327.
38. Edmund Campion quoted in *The History of Parliament*, 'Sir Edmund Trafford'. Available at: <http://www.historyofparliamentonline.org/volume/1558-1603/member/trafford-edmund-i-1526-90> (last accessed 17 July 2019). The English college at Douai was founded in 1568, and was reliant on donations raised by William Allen.
39. *Acts of the Privy Council*, 13: 149, *British History Online*. Available at: <https://www.british-history.ac.uk> (last accessed 17 July 2019); Thomas Hoghton quoted in Honigmann, *Shakespeare*, 11.
40. Edmund Trafford quoted in George Miller, *Hoghton Tower: The History of the Manor* (Preston: Guardian Press, 1948), 155; Keen and Lubbock, *Annotator*, 97–8.
41. See Jan Graffius, 'A gift from poetry: the First Folio and Jesuit drama in Saint-Omer', *Times Literary Supplement* (6 February 2015), 14–15; E. K. Chambers, 'William Shakeshafte', *Shakespearean Gleanings* (Oxford: Oxford University Press, 1944); and Oliver Baker, *Shakespeare's Warwickshire and the Unknown Years* (London: Simpkin Marshall, 1937), 52–6.
42. John Rylands Library [MSS. 213].
43. Michael Winstanley, 'Shakespeare, Catholicism, and Lancashire: a reappraisal of John Cottom, Stratford schoolmaster', *Shakespeare Quarterly*, 68: 2 (2017), 172–91, 190.
44. Ibid. 173, 181.

45. Ibid. 175; The central claim of *The Annotator* – that a copy of Hall's 1550 *Chronicles* traceable to the Hoghton family is annotated in writing identical to that of the Shakespearean Hand D of *Thomas More* – remains uninvestigated.
46. Oliver Lawson Dick (ed.), *Aubrey's Brief Lives* (London: Secker and Warburg, 1949), 276; Park Honan, *Shakespeare: A Life* (Oxford: Oxford University Press, 1998), 70, 359.
47. Honigmann, *Shakespeare*, 102; Alan Nelson, 'His literary patrons', in Paul Edmonson and Stanley Wells (eds), *The Shakespeare Circle: An Alternative Biography* (Cambridge: Cambridge University Press, 2015), 279.
48. Honigmann, *Shakespeare*, 22.
49. John Weever, *Epigrammes in the oldest cut, and newest fashion* (1599), 4th Week, Epigram 22, 'Ad Guilelmum Shakespear', l. 1: repr. in Ernst Honigmann, *John Weever: A Biography of a Literary Associate of Shakespeare and Jonson* (Manchester: Manchester University Press, 1987), 110; Andrew Hadfield, *The Shakespeare Circle* (Cambridge: Cambridge University Press, 2015), 206.
50. Honigmann, *Shakespeare*, 133.
51. Honigmann, *Weever*, 17–18.
52. John Weever, 'Ad Guilelmum Shakespear'; Honan, 359; Gary Taylor, 'Some Manuscripts of Shakespeare's Sonnets', *Bulletin of the John Rylands Library*, 68 (1986), 222–3.
53. Honigmann, *Shakespeare*, 14.
54. John Milton, 'An epitaph on the admirable dramatic poet, William Shakespeare', prefixed to the Second Folio of the *Works* (London: 1632).
55. Richard Wilson, *Secret Shakespeare: Studies in Theatre, Religion and Resistance* (Manchester: Manchester University Press, 2004), 156–7.
56. Honigmann, *Weever*, 92.
57. John Payne Collyer, *Memoirs of Edward Alleyn* (London: Shakespeare Society, 1841), 3. Peter Farey has made a case for the identification of Edward Alleyn as the co-author of *Fair Em*, in 'The Batillus, The Player, and the Upstart Crow', *Marlowe Society Research Journal*, 6: 2009. But in a 2018 update, Farey has withdrawn this identification, in favour of Anthony Munday.
58. History of Parliament, 'Sir Peter (Piers) Legh, of Lyme, Cheshire, and Bradley Hall, Lancs'. Available at: <http://www.historyofparliamentonline.org/volume/1558-1603/member/legh-peter-1563-1636> (last accessed 17 July 2019); Honigmann, *Shakespeare*, 27.
59. Honigmann, *Shakespeare*, 59–60, 131–2.
60. Alexander Aspinall goes unnoticed by Edmondson and Wells.
61. Samuel Schoenbaum, *Shakespeare: A Documentary Life* (Oxford: Oxford University Press, 1970), 53.
62. Edgar Fripp, *Shakespeare's Stratford* (Oxford: Oxford University Press, 1928), 50–1; William Weeks (ed.), *Clitheroe in the Seventeenth Century* (Clitheroe: Clitheroe Advertiser and Times, 1887), 11, 62.

63. Keen and Lubbock, *Annotator*, 197–8. For Maud Hoghton as the sister of Alexander Aspinall, see <http://landedfamilies.blogspot.co.uk./2016/04/214-aspinall-of-standen-hall.html> (last accessed 17 July 2019).
64. In Honigmann, *Shakespeare*, 3; Edmund Spenser, *The Tears of the Muses*, quoted in Honigmann, *Shakespeare*, 71–2; William Dugdale, *Visitation of Cheshire and Shropshire*, quoted in Honigmann, *Shakespeare*, 78; Robert Chester, 'Dedication', *Love's Martyr*, Honigmann, *Shakespeare*, 91.
65. Arthur Herbert Dodd, *Studies in Stuart Wales* (Cardiff: University of Wales Press, 1971), 81.
66. John Kerrigan, 'Prologue', in Willy Maley and Rory Loughnane (eds), *Celtic Shakespeare: The Bard and the Borderers* (Farnham: Ashgate, 2013), xxxix-xl.
67. Carleton Brown, *Poems of Sir John Salusbury and Robert Chester*, Early English Text Society, Extra Series, 113 (1914); 'Robert Parry's diary', *Archaeologia Cambrensis*, 15 (1915), 121.
68. Sally Harper, 'Shakespearean revels', *New Welsh Review*, 56 (Summer 2002); 'An Elizabethan tune list from Lleweni Hall, North Wales', *Royal Musical Association Research Chronicle*, 38 (2005), 45–98; '"A dittie to the tune of the Welsh Sydannen': a Welsh image of Queen Elizabeth', *Renaissance Studies*, 19: 2 (2005), 201–28; Manley and MacLean, *Lord Strange's Men*, 277. For Edward Alleyn and Richard Tarleton, see Carol Curt Enos, *Shakespeare's Settings* (Tucson, AZ: Wheatmark, 2007), 132, 151, 153, 173–5.
69. Christ Church MSS., 183–4; see David George, 'Young Shakespeare: culture, patrons, and connections', *Selected Papers of the Ohio Valley Shakespeare Conference*, 9: 4 (2018), 45–61, 52–4; and John Idris Jones, *Shakespeare's Missing Years* (Fonthill: Fonthill Media, 2018), 122–33, 127, 133. See also Tom Lloyd Roberts, 'Bard of Lleweni: Shakespeare's Welsh connection', *New Welsh Review*, 23 (1993), 11–18. For a sceptical response, see Jeremy Griffiths, 'Loose sheets and idle scribblings: the case against Shakespeare's Lleweni connection', *New Welsh Review*, 25 (1994), 52–7.
70. Christ Church MSS.
71. David Crystal, quoted in Jones, *Shakespeare's Missing Years*, 133; Honigmann, *Shakespeare*, 62, 64–5, 152–3. See also Ian Wilson, *Shakespeare: The Evidence* (London: Headline, 1993), 176–7.
72. Honigmann, *Shakespeare*, 127.
73. Ibid. 118–19.
74. Lawrence Manley, 'From Strange's Men to Pembroke's Men: *2 Henry VI* and *The First Part of the Contention*', *Shakespeare Quarterly*, 54: 3 (2003), 253–87, 278.
75. Honigmann, *Shakespeare*, 9–10, 65–7, 119; Winstanley, 'Shakespeare, Catholicism, and Lancashire', 172.
76. Winstanley, 'Shakespeare, Catholicism, and Lancashire', 190–1.
77. Manley and MacLean, *Lord Strange's Men*, 6, 246.
78. Honigmann, *Shakespeare*, 65–8.
79. Manley and MacLean, *Lord Strange's Men*, 6.

80. Charles Whitney, *Early Responses to Renaissance Drama* (Cambridge: Cambridge University Press, 2006), 140.
81. Robert Tofte, 'Alba: or the month's mind of a melancholy lover', in Jeffrey Nelson (ed.), *The Poetry of Robert Tofte, 1597–1620: A Critical Old-Spelling Edition* (New York: Garland, 1994), 118.
82. Richard Simpson (ed.), *The School of Shakespeare* (2 vols, London: Chatto and Windus, 1878) 2: 372; Matthew Steggle, 'Two notes on Tofte's *Alba* (1598)', *Notes and Queries*, 54: 3 (1 September 2007), 262–4. See also William Beamont, *Annals of the Lords of Warrington and Bewsey* (2 vols, Manchester and Warrington: Simms and Pearce, 1873), 1: 45–50. Thomas Ireland was knighted by James I when he stayed at Bewsey on his progress in 1617; see John Nichols, *The Progresses, Processions and Magnificent Festivities of King James the First* (4 vols, London: Society of Antiquaries, 1828), 3: 404–5.
83. *History of Parliament*, 'George Ireland (d. 1596), of the Hutt, Halewood, Lancs.' Available at: <http://www.historyofparliamentonline.org/volume/1558-1603/member/ireland-george-1596> (last accessed 17 July 2019).
84. Honigmann, *Shakespeare*, 61.
85. Ibid. 127.
86. Winstanley, 'Shakespeare, Catholicism, and Lancashire', 173–4, 190.
87. Ibid. 183.
88. Ibid. 182.
89. Honigmann, *Shakespeare*, 126.
90. *Calendar of State Papers Domestic*, 175: 2.
91. Honigmann, *Shakespeare*, 38.
92. W. G. Proctor, 'The Manor of Rufford and the Ancient Family of the Heskeths', *Transactions of the Historic Society of Lancashire and Cheshire*, 59 (1908), 93.
93. Keen and Lubbock, *Annotator*, 194; David George (ed.), *Records of Early English Drama: Lancashire* (Toronto: University of Toronto Press, 1992), 180.
94. See Alvin Thaler, '*Faire Em* (and Shakespeare's Company?) in Lancashire', *PMLA*, 46: 3 (1931), 647–58, 652–3; and Barry Coward, *The Stanleys: Lords Stanley and Earls of Derby, 1385–1672* (Manchester: Manchester University Press, 1983), 166–7.
95. Quoted in Christopher Haigh, *Reformation and Resistance in Tudor Lancashire* (Cambridge: Cambridge University Press, 1975), 285.
96. *History of Parliament*: Sir Edmund Trafford; see also William Axon, 'The Traffords of Trafford', *Echoes of Old Lancashire* (London: William Andrews, 1899), 93–4.
97. See Henning, *Fair Em*, 23, n.27.
98. Manley and MacLean, *Lord Strange's Men*, 242.
99. Robert Greene, 'To the gentlemen students of both universities', *Farewell to Folly*, in Greene, *Life and Complete Works*, 9: 233.

100. Eric Sams, *The Real Shakespeare: Retrieving the Early Years, 1564–1594* (New Haven: Yale University Press, 1995), 91, 164.
101. Robert Greene, *Groatsworth*, 144.
102. Ibid. 144.
103. George, *Records of Early English Drama*, 229.
104. Thomas S. Willan, *Elizabethan Manchester* (Manchester: Chetham Society, 1980), 6, 126; Enos, *Shakespeare's Settings*, 4–5, 81–2.
105. John Reilly, *History of Manchester* (London: Judd and Glass, 1865), 117.
106. *History of Parliament*: 'Sir Gilbert Gerard'. Available at: <http://www.historyofparliamentonline.org/volume/1558-1603/member/gerard-sir-gilbert-1593> (last accessed 17 July 2019); *History of Parliament*, 'Sir Richard Houghton'. Available at: <https://www.historyofparliamentonline.org/volume/1604-1629/member/houghton-sir-richard-1569-1630> (last accessed 17 July 2019). See also Pauline Croft, 'The Catholic gentry, the Earl of Salisbury and the Baronets of 1611', in Peter Lake and Michael Questier (eds), *Conformity and Orthodoxy in the English Church, c.1560–1660* (Woodbridge: Boydell, 2000), 262–82, 272. It was from Sir Thomas Gerard of Bryn that the copy of Hall's *Chronicles* discussed in *The Annotator* descended; see Keen and Lubbock, *Annotator*, 93–4.
107. Mary Blackstone, 'Lancashire, Shakespeare and the creation of cultural neighbourhoods in sixteenth-century England', in Dutton, Findlay and Wilson, *Lancastrian Shakespeare*, 186–204, 193.
108. *History of Parliament*, 'Sir Gilbert Gerard'; Honigmann, *Shakespeare*, 12.
109. Schoenbaum, *William Shakespeare*, 116.
110. George, *Records of Early English Drama*, 235.
111. Manley and MacLean propose that additional 'evidence for an early date for the play' includes the title-page reference to its having been acted in the City of London, where Strange's Men performed at the Cross Keys in November 1589; see 105, 43.
112. *History of Parliament*, 'Sir Edmund Trafford'.
113. Richard Dutton and Alison Findlay, 'Introduction', in Dutton, Findlay and Wilson, *Lancastrian Shakespeare*, 1–31, 9; Manley and MacLean, *Lord Strange's Men*, 208.
114. Kerrigan, *Archipelagic English*, 18, 25, 43.
115. Ibid. 133.
116. Weever, Epigrammes, 6th Week, Epigramme 3: 'In tumulum Thomas Houghton Amig', in Honigmann, *Weever*, 115; Henry Stanley, Earl of Derby, to William Cecil, Lord Burghley, quoted in *History of Parliament*, 'Thomas Langton of Walton-le-Dale' <http://www.historyofparliamentonline.org/volume/1558-1603/member/langton-thomas-1561-1605> (last accessed 17 July 2019); Jonathan Lumby, *The Lancashire Witch Craze: Jennet Preston and the Lancashire Witches* (Preston: Carnegie, 1995), 129–33.

117. See Rosalyn Knutson, *The Repertory of Shakespeare's Company, 1594–1613* (Fayetteville: University of Arkansas Press, 1991), 59.
118. James VI, 'Discourse', in Boyd and Meikle *Calendar of State Papers*; David Willson, *King James VI and I* (London: Jonathan Cape, 1963), 85.
119. Nichols, *Progresses*, 396–405.
120. Greene, *Groatsworth*, 131, 144.
121. Phil Willmott, 'Director's note', *Fair Em: Sometime attributed to William Shakespeare* (London: Union Theatre, 2013), xvi.

III

Appropriating Shakespeare in the North

9

'What is Shakespeare to Manchester'? Shakespearean Engagement in the North at the Turn of the Twentieth Century

Monika Smialkowska

Manchester Central Library in St Peter's Square, opened in 1934, is an imposing neoclassical building. Above its main entrance looms a huge stained glass window, which features a portrait of Shakespeare surrounded by fifteen panels depicting characters from his plays. The official website explains that the window was 'given to the library by Mrs Rosa Grindon, in memory of her husband, the famous Manchester botanist, Leo Grindon'.[1] At first glance, this looks like a public display of wifely devotion, with a local luminary's grieving widow deciding to commemorate her departed spouse in a highly visible civic space. But why would Rosa Grindon choose Shakespeare as the theme of her tribute to her late husband? After all, Leopold Hartley Grindon (1818–1904) was renowned as a naturalist, the founder of the Manchester Field Naturalists' and Archaeologists' Society and author of such publications as *The Manchester Flora* (1859), *Manchester Walks and Wild Flowers* (1859) and *The Trees of Old England* (1868).[2] Even the focus of his one Shakespeare-related book, *The Shakspere Flora* (1883), indicates that botany, rather than literature, was his main passion.[3] If his wife wished to commemorate him, why did she not commission a stained glass containing his portrait and images of local plants? Something does not quite add up here. Is there more to the Manchester Central Library's Shakespeare window than meets the eye? By examining previously neglected archival material, this chapter sheds light on this mystery. In doing so, it not only rescues from oblivion a remarkable woman's prolific cultural achievement, but also uncovers a rich history of Shakespearean reception and participation in Manchester in the late nineteenth and early twentieth centuries. This, in turn, adds a new – and northern English – dimension to the current critical understanding of the period as the time which witnessed the consolidation of Shakespeare as Britain's monolithic, national and imperial poet.[4]

What's Hecuba to her or she to Hecuba?

Rosa Elverson Grindon (1848–1923) was a woman of many talents and interests. Born in a Derbyshire village to an agricultural labourer who later became a draper and grocer, she made her own way in life, working in a succession of domestic roles, from an elderly lady's companion to a housekeeper. Always academically minded, she enrolled on what would now be called distance learning courses and obtained an L.L.A. diploma from the University of St Andrews.[5] While working as a housekeeper to John Gilbert, the Mayor of Lichfield, she performed the duties of his Lady Mayoress and, together with Gilbert's daughter Florence, helped transcribe medieval texts at the Lichfield Cathedral Library for the Early English Text Society.[6] Despite her early stated opposition to marriage, in her forties she married Leopold Grindon, thirty years her senior, and moved to Manchester to live with him.[7] By that time Leopold, formerly a cashier, was an established lecturer and author, and the couple seem to have been comfortably off, living in a terraced house and employing two female servants.[8]

Once in Manchester, Rosa Grindon threw herself wholeheartedly into amateur academic, cultural and social work. Sharing her husband's interest in science, particularly botany, she became an active member of the Manchester Naturalists' Society, the first woman to be elected to its council, and was invited to attend the meetings of the Manchester Microscopical Society. She championed causes ranging from encouraging working-class people to establish small gardens by their houses to combatting air pollution and promoting women's suffrage. After participating in meetings of the Manchester Society for Women's Suffrage, in 1913 she was elected one of its vice presidents.[9] The fact that she specified 'Lecturer and Suffragette' as her occupation in the 1911 census indicates that securing votes for women was a particularly important issue to her, but there is no evidence that she approved of violent means of pursuing this goal.[10] As a lecturer, she covered a variety of topics, including literature and natural history, at such institutions as the Manchester Geographical Society, the Chester Society of Natural Science, and the Manchester Working Men's Club

Association.¹¹ A keen supporter of educational and cultural associations, she was the founding member of the Life Study Society, the Ladies' Chess Club, the Manchester Ladies' Literary Club, and other groups.¹²

However, Rosa Grindon's great love was Shakespeare, even if the editor of her collection of lectures was slightly hyperbolic when he claimed that '[i]t was to him she devoted her life'.¹³ By 1901 she was president of the Manchester Ladies' Shakespeare Reading Club, and she steadily built her reputation as a Shakespearean authority in both local and national arenas.¹⁴ She delivered numerous addresses and courses of study on Shakespeare and his plays at various venues in and around Manchester: at her own house, in local libraries, clubs, meeting halls and theatres.¹⁵ Between 1909 and 1913, at the invitation of the Shakespeare Festival Committee, she lectured at the annual Festivals held at the Shakespeare Memorial Theatre in Stratford-upon-Avon.¹⁶ She published some of her lectures in pamphlet format, and a posthumous edited collection appeared in 1930.¹⁷ Moreover, the Manchester Central Library archive reveals that Rosa Grindon associated and corresponded with many of the period's leading Shakespearean actors and scholars, among them Ellen Terry, Henry Irving, Herbert Beerbohm Tree, Violet and Irene Vanbrugh, Frank Benson, Sidney Lee and Edmund Dowden.¹⁸ They not only participated in events at which she spoke or which she organised, but also engaged with her interpretations of Shakespeare's plays and characters. One of the great actor-managers of the time, Henry Irving, found the notes on *Hamlet* which she sent him after he heard her speak at an unspecified meeting 'most interesting'.¹⁹ He did not elaborate on the topic, so perhaps he was simply being polite. However, another established actor, John Martin-Harvey, seems to have been genuinely impressed with Rosa Grindon's reading of Hamlet's speech after the ghost's disappearance: 'I must confess I had not appreciated to so full an extent as you do that extraordinary moment. I shall think of it again from your point of view'.²⁰ By contrast, Johnston Forbes-Robertson, renowned for his rendition of Hamlet's role, disputed her interpretation of the same scene, arguing that 'to treat the passage as you wish would not in my opinion be in harmony with Hamlet's state of mind and body at that awful moment'. Nevertheless, he acknowledged that she 'made a considerable study of "Hamlet"', admitting: 'There is much in what you say'.²¹ Agree with her or not, Rosa Grindon's opinions were heard and valued among the most prominent Shakespeareans of the time.

A detailed investigation of Rosa Grindon's criticism of Shakespeare's plays remains to be undertaken. The brief references to her work in recent publications focus chiefly on her interest in interpreting Shakespeare specifically from a woman's point of view, and locate this interest in the context of the suffragist campaigns and early feminist debates. Thus, Susan Carlson places Rosa Grindon among the 'protofeminist voices' of the time, noting that her insistence on the need to counteract the prevalent masculinist interpretations of *Othello* earned her 'some hostility' from the audience at one of her Stratford lectures.[22] In a later article, Carlson demonstrates that Rosa Grindon 'mock[ed] the predictable tastes of male critics' in her lecture on *Cymbeline*, in which she facetiously suggested that the reason why Imogen was their 'great favourite' lay in 'the fact that she is the only heroine who is spoken of as a good cook'.[23] Similarly, Phyllis Rackin and Evelyn Gajowski comment on Rosa Grindon's challenge to the established, patriarchal approaches to studying Shakespeare, applauding her insight that 'an exclusively masculine perspective may always have been inadequate as an approach to [*The Merry Wives of Windsor*]'.[24] While these observations draw our attention to one important aspect of Rosa Grindon's work, their very scarcity, brevity, and limited focus risk consigning her to a footnote in the history of feminist Shakespearean reception, or pigeonholing her as 'the Victorian apologist for Shakespeare's female characters'.[25] Such a description is historically imprecise, as all of Rosa Grindon's known publications on Shakespeare appeared after Queen Victoria's death. More importantly, it does not do justice to the breadth and originality of her engagement with Shakespeare, which, as we shall see, went well beyond rehabilitating his female characters.

There is certainly a case for conducting a further, more probing analysis of Rosa Grindon's publications. However, for the purposes of this chapter it is more illuminating to examine not what she said and wrote about Shakespeare, but rather what she did to popularise his work in Manchester and beyond. The practical, community-centred activities that she initiated, led and participated in for many years demonstrate her pioneering methods, whilel at the same time shedding light on the lively Shakespearean scene existing outside of the London-Stratford 'Shakespeare metropolis' at the turn of the twentieth century.[26] A good place to start this examination is Rosa Grindon's most ambitious enterprise, the establishment of the Manchester Shakespeare Tercentenary Association in the run-up to the 300th anniversary of the playwright's death in 1916. Her surviving comments on the scope and purpose of this venture give us a unique insight into her approach to Shakespeare as a lived experience and integral part of community life.

The Manchester Shakespeare Tercentenary Association was formed in the autumn of 1912, with the aim of organising in the city a fitting commemoration of the forthcoming anniversary.[27] Three years later, John Cuming Walters, the editor of *The Manchester City News*, credited Rosa Grindon with 'the initiative' to establish it, and with an 'unabated enthusiasm [that] has brought the Association's labours within measurable distance of success'.[28] The ubiquitous presence of Rosa Grindon in newspaper articles, advertisements and promotional materials related to the organisation's activities suggests that she was indeed its primary driving force, serving at different times as its chairman, honorary secretary for Prize Scheme and honorary assistant treasurer, besides organising fundraising events, chairing meetings and delivering lectures and courses of study. Walters emphasised his own role in the enterprise: 'I considered it a great honour as well as a personal gratification to have been invited to cooperate from the first with Mrs Grindon, and practically the Tercentenary Scheme is our joint production'.[29] Nevertheless, although he held the post of treasurer of the Manchester Shakespeare Tercentenary Association, his name does not appear anywhere near as frequently as Rosa Grindon's in the accounts of its undertakings, which indicates that she was more closely involved in the organisation's day-to-day operations. Be that as it may, more important than determining where the credit for the Tercentenary Association's achievements lies are the perceptible differences between Rosa Grindon's and Walters' attitudes to Shakespeare in Manchester. As they seem to embody different views regarding Shakespeare's position in the life of the nation and of local communities, they are worth exploring in some detail.

John Cuming Walters and 'a Shakespearean Temple in Manchester'

Walters has left us an illuminating reflection on one way of approaching the issue, occasioned by his conversation with an unidentified Mancunian regarding the preparations for the Tercentenary celebrations in the city:

> One of our good, strong, commonsense citizens with whom I was discussing our project a few days ago, said 'But why Manchester? What connection has Shakespeare with us?' What indeed! What's Hecuba to him or he to Hecuba? The painful confession has to be made – and we may as well get it over at once – that Shakespeare was not born in Manchester; that he never lived in Manchester; that he never referred to Manchester in his dramas, and that he took no interest in the cotton trade.[30]

This pronouncement reveals some of Walters' tacit assumptions about Manchester's inhabitants. He sees them as parochial and fixated on their immediate surroundings and practical concerns. He thus assumes that they would only care about Shakespeare if he were their neighbour or if he wrote about their city or its chief business, the cotton industry. Needless to say, Walters himself is above such cultural myopia. He refuses to 'extenuate' Shakespeare's lack of Manchester connections 'by emphasising unduly that he gave some attention to the Wars of the Roses and that historic Lancashire men figure conspicuously in his dramas'.[31] Instead, he chooses to minimise the importance of 'localising' Shakespeare in favour of emphasising his universality:

> [I]f Shakespeare is to be localised he is not worth commemorating at all. If he only ranks with Harrison Ainsworth, I want nothing to do with him; if he was only an interesting person connected in some small way with Stratford-on-Avon, let Stratford have him ... The moment we enquire what is Shakespeare to Manchester, and why should Manchester pay him honour, we are reducing him to the level of village mediocrity, and there is no need to discuss the matter further. It is because Shakespeare is universal, because he is permanent, because his genius is all-embracing, because he is the monarch of mind that he belongs as much and as closely and as intimately to Manchester as he does to Blackfriars, and that he is as much our own in Lancashire as he is anyone's in Warwick or Middlesex.[32]

At first glance, Walters seems to be advocating equal access and equal entitlement to Shakespeare, as he states that the playwright is 'all-embracing' and 'belongs' to everybody, regardless of where they happen to live. However, it soon emerges that Walters – consciously or not – privileges certain geographical locations and certain ways of approaching Shakespeare. Notably, his universalism does not preclude an emphasis on Shakespeare's special connection to Englishness. Straight after calling the playwright 'universal', he adds: 'Wherever an English heart beats Shakespeake's [sic] place is in the most sacred chamber', and earlier on he calls Shakespeare's memory 'the most treasured possession of this nation and the proudest legacy of our race'.[33] Writing in 1912, Walters does not seem to notice the potential contradiction inherent in seeing Shakespeare as both universal and a particular 'possession' of one nation or 'race'. Soon, the bitter debates raging between the British and the Germans over the ownership of the playwright during the First World War would, in Clara

Calvo's words, 'expose a fault-line between Shakespeare the national poet and the universal genius'.³⁴

While Walters may not be concerned with the geo-political implications of Shakespeare's 'universality', his statements reveal another facet of 'the paradox of the local and the universal': the tendency to downplay regional differences in pursuit of a homogeneous, national identity and culture.³⁵ Thus, he appears to believe that every 'English heart', whether it beats in Lancashire or in Middlesex, feels – or at least should feel – the same about Shakespeare. But what is this universally English Shakespeare and how should he be approached? First of all, to Walters, he occupies a high position in an implicit cultural hierarchy, as he unquestionably 'ranks' above the popular Manchester-born novelist William Harrison Ainsworth. It is unclear whether Walters denigrates Ainsworth chiefly because the latter's fiction often focused on specific locations, among them Lancashire, because of the genre in which he worked, 'popular historical romances', or because of a combination of these two factors.³⁶ The fact that he proceeds to say that the Manchester Shakespeare Tercentenary Association has an 'elevated purpose' and 'high aim' indicates that the unstated distinction between 'high' and 'low' culture underpins his overt differentiation between the 'universal' and the 'localised'.

Secondly, Walters sees Shakespeare as elevated above the mundane, down-to-earth experiences of everyday life. To him, Shakespeare is 'the monarch of mind' rather than of the body. Consequently, when he outlines Manchester's planned commemorations, he distances them from anything ephemeral, popular or commercial. He explains: 'We are not working up to the ideal of a bazaar' or 'arranging a collection of Shakesperiana [sic] with a view to having a peep-show for a day'.³⁷ By singling out a bazaar and a peep-show, Walters rejects cultural forms associated with the marketplace, crowd participation, profit-making and low-brow entertainment. What he proposes instead is to honour Shakespeare through purely intellectual and spiritual endeavours. He feels that, so far, Manchester has not displayed the right attitude to the playwright: 'I have felt in this city a coldness and a loss in respect of the honour, and particularly to the tributes, to our chief of men'.³⁸ But what exactly does Manchester lack? Walters acknowledges the city's many Shakespearean achievements: 'the valuable relics in the John Rylands Library and the University', 'the excellent labours of the diligent, but far too restricted Shakespeare Society', 'the admirable list of annual lectures arranged on Shakespeare day by the Arts Club', and the presence of 'men and women saturated with Shakespeare lore, and some writers of authority and acknowledged eminence'.³⁹ However, these scattered objects and local initiatives are not enough, as Walters laments: 'we have no Shakespeare library, no Shakespeare museum, no organis[ed] and accessible Shakespeare collection'.⁴⁰ What is missing in Manchester, then, are established, permanent, highbrow institutions devoted to studying and memorialising the playwright.

Walters' juxtaposition between the library/museum on the one hand and the bazaar/peep-show on the other corresponds to Michel Foucault's distinction between 'heterotopias of indefinitely accumulating time' and those heterotopias which are 'linked . . . to time in its most fleeting, transitory, precarious aspect, to time in the mode of the festival'.⁴¹ Foucault sees museums and libraries as peculiarly modern phenomena, dedicated to 'constituting a place of all times that is itself outside of time and inaccessible to its ravages', and contrasts them to fairgrounds, which are 'not oriented toward the eternal' but are instead 'absolutely temporal'.⁴² Tony Bennett develops this insight further, arguing that the modern public museum was conceived as 'representational space' that was 'rational and scientific', associated with progress and order, as opposed to the fair, which was seen as an 'embodiment of the "irrational" and "chaotic" disorder'.⁴³ Applying Foucault's theoretical frameworks, Bennett posits that the museum constructed in these terms became a powerful instrument of social control. This control was conducted through 'plac[ing] the people – conceived as a nationalized citizenry – on the side of power, both its subject and its beneficiary', creating a system in which power was 'made manifest not in its ability to inflict pain but by its ability to organize and co-ordinate an order of things and to produce a place for the people in relation to that order'.⁴⁴ In effect, Bennett sees the modern museum as an educational institution, devoted to inculcating in the population a sense of belonging to a beneficent, well-organised system built on the interrelated notions of tradition and progress: the modern nation state.⁴⁵

Walters' approach to Shakespeare does display an educational purpose, national pride and monumentalising drive towards the 'eternal' at the expense of the fleeting and 'temporal', but it also contains an extra element which Bennett's analysis does not foreground: a set of religious connotations. As we have already seen, Walters uses the phrase 'most sacred' to describe the space in the 'English heart' reserved for Shakespeare, and he calls the Shakespearean mementoes in the John Rylands Library and the University 'valuable relics'. He also says that he is 'connected by friendly ties with many of those Shakespearean scholars and students to whom Stratford is a Mecca, and a shrine'.⁴⁶ These statements chime with the discourse of 'a religion: bardolatry, the worship of Shakespeare'.⁴⁷ Graham Holderness identifies the values which this religion sets out to disseminate as 'truth, authenticity, the assurance and consolation of a vanished golden age, the transcendent illumination of transhistorical genius'. He argues that for many bardolaters these values are embodied in Stratford-upon-Avon's allegedly 'uninterrupted continuum of time and space', symbolising 'an idealised "English" past, picturesque and untroubled'.[48] However, even though Walters claims that 'the midland region', in which Stratford is located, is 'associated with Shakespearean realities', he does not link these unspecified 'realities' to a romanticised, pre-industrial, rural Englishness.[49] Neither does he require a physical connection to Stratford or a ritual transfer of its 'aura' in order to venerate Shakespeare.[50] Instead, he suggests that a site of Shakespeare worship can be established anywhere, and anticipates the creation of 'a Shakespearean Temple in Manchester'. He adds that

> it seems strange, even grotesque, to suggest that this mercantile city should be a place of pilgrimage, yet there is some hope when we, who meet here to-night, are banded together to prepare for the tercentenary celebration, and to show you the nucleus from which may yet swell into a Shakesperian [*sic*] museum.[51]

As he equates a museum with a temple, Walters seems to argue that it is not so much the geographical location as the way of approaching Shakespeare that counts. And the approach he advocates is non-commercial, full of awe and bordering on the metaphysical. While granting that Manchester's Tercentenary movement aims to be 'practical', the proposed activities he outlines are of intellectual or spiritual nature:

> We shall read, we shall have lectures, we shall have illustration, we shall try to get nearer the man, to comprehend the vastness of his message, to plumb the depths of his wisdom, to peer into the chamber of the myriad mind.[52]

Tellingly, the one avenue for engaging with Shakespeare which Walters does not mention is the theatre, the space in which the plays become embodied. In effect, he privileges the mind over the body and intellectual contemplation over enacting Shakespeare in the ephemeral and predominantly commercial space of the playhouse. Overall, Walters' Shakespeare appears to be a national treasure, which should be approached with a reverential, quasi-religious attitude and removed from the sphere of humdrum, mercantile and popular activities. We shall now see how this idea of Shakespeare compares to Rosa Grindon's.

Rosa Grindon's 'practical enthusiasts' and 'Shakespeare aspirations in Manchester'

Rosa Grindon outlined her vision for Manchester's Shakespeare Tercentenary celebrations in a lengthy article, first published in *The Manchester City News* and subsequently reprinted as a stand-alone leaflet. While discussing the same project as Walters – the establishment of the Manchester Shakespeare Tercentenary Association – the article displays quite a different attitude and emphasis. Firstly, Rosa Grindon does not dismiss the local in favour of the national or the universal. She notes that 'London's idea of celebrating the Tercentenary of Shakespeare's death is to erect a National Theatre', and she judges that idea to be '[v]ery good as far as it goes'. Nevertheless, she finds the plan insufficient for Manchester's purposes, as she declares: 'it is quite certain that a new theatre in London, however national it might be, will never fully express Shakespeare aspirations in Manchester'.[53] Thus, she casts doubt on whether a single 'national' culture can adequately represent all parts of the country, especially if the material expression of that culture – the theatre – is to be located exclusively in the capital.

At the same time, Rosa Grindon highlights the distinctiveness of Manchester and its attitude to Shakespeare. The city's key unique trait, in her opinion, is that it is 'very practical'.[54] To Walters, this practical mindset is a flaw, which makes Manchester 'mercantile' and insufficiently reverential towards Shakespeare. By contrast, Rosa Grindon sees it as a strength, and outlines an approach to Shakespeare that plays to and capitalises on this strength. The corollary of this approach, as written into the Manchester Shakespeare Tercentenary Association's Foundation Scheme, is 'the popularising of Shakespeare knowledge, and the understanding of his works'.[55] Elsewhere, Rosa Grindon further explains that the organisation's goal is 'to dispel the notion that Shakspere [*sic*] was for the learned only [and] to make [his] works familiar in every household, high and low'.[56] These statements indicate a desire to take the playwright out of the sphere of high culture and bring him closer to the general population and their everyday concerns. Moreover, the aim of this process seems to be not so much to venerate Shakespeare but rather to offer tangible benefits to the community. To achieve this goal, Rosa Grindon focuses on *doing* (things with) Shakespeare instead of enclosing him in a museum or a shrine; as she explains, 'our wealth consists of Shakespeare knowledge enthusiastically applied'.[57]

But what exactly is the benefit that this 'applied' Shakespeare will bring to Manchester? Rosa Grindon believes that it consists in increasing the population's ethical values and actions:

> It is impossible to over-estimate the effect that would be brought upon the well-being of a community by Shakespeare's ethical standards becoming the living force they ought to be. People there are to whom some of the Bible standards appear out of reach. But Shakespeare brings even the highest within a sweet reasonableness, and makes us realise that after all the highest possesses the most common sense.[58]

While this statement links Shakespeare and religion, it does so in a markedly different way from Walters' pronouncements. Instead of Shakespeare acquiring a metaphysical aura that might lead people to worship him, he takes over some of the practical functions of religion: those related to guiding people's behaviour. However, when Rosa Grindon mentions 'ethical standards', she does not seem to be referring to abstract moral principles regulated by religious taboos, but rather to the down-to-earth rules of everyday social interaction. She anchors these rules in the realm of reason and common sense, within the reach and understanding of normal people. Moreover, she localises them, as she does not refer to large conceptual entities such as the nation or 'the race', but rather a more immediate and potentially more inclusive idea of 'a community'. And she argues that the greatest boon that Shakespeare can bring to the community is to enhance its cohesion by providing it with standards of behaviour that are easy to understand, share and follow:

> Intelligent love of Shakespeare is a stronger bond than even Freemasonry has to offer, and however much the human mind may further develop and enlarge with the ages, Shakespeare will still be the pleasantest path to all right-thinking for this world and the next.[59]

Shakespeare thus becomes an ethical guide and a bonding agent within the community, rather than an object of worship. While Rosa Grindon, like Walters, uses the phrase 'Shakespearean relics', for the most part her vocabulary is not religious but down-to-earth, grounded in everyday, local realities. Accordingly, instead of wishing to enshrine the 'relics' in Walters' 'Shakespearean Temple', she proposes to place them in 'our City Shakespeare Gallery'.[60] In emphasising the municipal and the practical over the national and the abstract, Rosa Grindon is closer to the late nineteenth-century proponents of the 'civic gospel' than to Matthew Arnold's idea of centralised, elevated culture capable of overcoming industrial fragmentation.[61]

If Rosa Grindon's overall attitude to Shakespeare differs from that of Walters, so do the methods which she wishes to apply in approaching and disseminating Shakespearean knowledge. Where Walters tends to privilege high-brow, intellectual and somewhat disembodied activities, Rosa Grindon emphasises active participation, enjoyment and appeal to the senses. Her Shakespeare possesses 'sweet reasonableness' and is 'the pleasantest path' to learning ethical principles. When she advertises 'a reading class' focused on *Romeo and Juliet*, she stresses the 'appeal to the eye as well as the ear': the series of meetings will consist of reading aloud, discussing the play's themes and characters, and 'pictorial illustrations'.[62] The participants will be encouraged to engage with Shakespeare actively, by writing essays about aspects of the play, and Rosa Grindon is not above offering 'small prizes' for the best ones as a tangible incentive. Other activities she proposes are even more fun-orientated and physical in nature, among them 'minuets and other dances of Shakespeare's time done in Shakespeare costume', as well as 'frequent receptions, . . . lectures, dramatic readings, and other Shakespearean entertainments'.[63] The leaflet mentions an event that the members of the newly established Association have already organised, a 'drawing-room entertainment', and the next one planned is an 'Evening with Shakespeare's Songs'.[64] For Rosa Grindon and her associates, 'doing' Shakespeare through the activities of reading, writing, debating, singing, dancing and tasting refreshments at the receptions seems to take precedence over merely contemplating him.

Thus, Rosa Grindon's approach to Shakespeare is active, participatory, social and associated with pleasure and entertainment. Moreover, it is not superciliously divorced from material and monetary concerns. While Walters finds the idea of 'mercantile' Manchester becoming a Shakespearean shrine 'strange and even grotesque', Rosa Grindon unashamedly foregrounds the financial side of the Tercentenary enterprise, admitting that 'our scheme is a costly one' and giving precise details about some of the ways in which money will be raised: '[s]ingle member's ticket covering reading class is 10s. 6d., and being very anxious for the young students we admit them to the reading class at 2s. 6d.'[65] She is also sensitive to the fact that even the highest cultural activities take place within specific economic realities, as she tells the prospective members of the class how much a copy of *Romeo and Juliet* might cost them: 'Heinemain's 6d. edition is recommended'.[66] And she does her best to involve others in the fundraising, as she states that the organisation needs 'some practical enthusiasts' and calls for help and participation in any 'money-making and pleasant functions' to come.[67]

Clearly, 'money' is not a dirty word for Rosa Grindon, and making it can be happily combined with both pleasure and cultural achievement. This attitude echoes that of many women's Shakespeare clubs active in America during that period: as Katherine Scheil demonstrates, their members were involved not only in studying Shakespeare, but also in countless 'civic activities', among them fundraising for local charities and improvement schemes.[68] What makes Rosa Grindon stand out is the fact that her acceptance of the profit-making side of culture extends beyond charitable and high-brow contexts to embrace mainstream, commercial theatre. Thus, she announces that '[t]he course of lectures upon Shakespeare's plays that for the past fifteen of sixteen years I have given in the Queen's Theatre will be continued at the New Theatre in Quay-street during Mr. Flanagan's Shakespeare season'.[69]

This statement is remarkable in several respects. Firstly, Rosa Grindon associates herself here not with a venerable, museum-like institution or with an intellectual, experimental drama movement but with a thoroughly popular type of theatre. Richard Flanagan, in charge of Manchester's Queen's Theatre and later the New Theatre, was 'a commercial manager, with an eye on what some deemed vulgar promotion', steeped in the tradition of 'spectacular "realism"', established by such famous actor-managers as Herbert Beerbohm Tree.[70] By 1916, the type of staging he espoused was being challenged by the avant-garde methods of practitioners like Max Reinhardt, Craig Gordon and William Poel, which many saw as more artistically advanced and intellectually demanding. Indeed, since 1907 Manchester had boasted an establishment catering to such refined tastes, the Gaiety run by Annie Horniman, which Viv Gardner describes as 'Britain's first true repertory theatre' and 'a dramatist's theatre'.[71] As Gardner points out, 'Flanagan has been much derided by critics of Shakespeare and the Gaiety, both in his own day and in subsequent histories', for his allegedly low aesthetic standards, geared towards undiscerning popular audiences.[72] Still, Rosa Grindon chose to run her lecture course at his theatre, demonstrating a preference for popularising Shakespeare over making him artistically cutting-edge, esoteric or intellectually over-sophisticated.[73]

Secondly, in combining the academic activity of lecturing with the embodiment of Shakespeare's plays on stage Rosa Grindon seems to have been ahead of her time. Her lecture programme is rigorously structured, as she assures potential participants that they 'will be supplied with detailed particulars and a copy of the syllabus'.[74] Yet the event is located not in a classroom or a university lecture hall but in a commercial theatre, and it is to include not only academic discussions but also 'a reception of the leading artists during the run of the play, when several members of the cast will discourse upon their parts from their own point of view'.[75] This set-up seems remarkably modern, as it moves the study of Shakespeare from the page, the museum or the shrine to its original but for many years under-appreciated context of the theatre. Moreover, the lecture series is not an isolated event, prepared specially for the 1916 Tercentenary, but a regular occurrence, which has been running for fifteen or sixteen years alongside Flanagan's equally recurrent 'Shakespeare revivals'. The longevity of the project highlights not only Rosa Grindon's ability to attract interested audiences year after year, but also Shakespeare's popularity in Manchester at the turn of the century. An article in *The Manchester Programme of Entertainments and Pleasure* comments on the 'magnitude' of the audience at one of her lectures: '[a]bout four hundred ladies gathered in the bleakest weather in the large theatre'.[76] Similarly, Gardner describes the city's lively Shakespearean scene, with at least seventeen different professional productions between October and April 1907–8.[77]

The sheer number of Shakespearean performances in Manchester seems to contradict Walters' claim that the city displayed 'a coldness and a loss in respect of the honour, and particularly to the tributes, to our chief of men'.[78] However, as we have seen, the theatre did not feature in Walters' pronouncements on how to 'honour' Shakespeare. Rosa Grindon's approach was quite different, as her longstanding collaboration with Flanagan and her friendly exchanges with the leading actors of the day, discussed earlier, demonstrate. Nor was her passion for the theatre limited to the commercial and popular variety. She took a keen interest in the activities of local amateur drama clubs, though there is no evidence of her ever being an actor in one of them. An article in *The Manchester City News* outlines her involvement in a group called The Pastoral Players, who repeatedly performed in a 'transformed waste spot in the rear of Mrs. Grindon's residence, Cecil-street, . . . gradually grown into a pretty open-air theatre'. After one production, the troupe thanked her for 'the time and labour which she has spent in teaching them to "speak the speech trippingly upon the tongue" and in instilling into their hearts a love for the precious gift of Shakespeare'.[79] Rosa Grindon also introduced short performances by 'Shakespeare Amateur Dramatic Societies' at the Town Hall reception to mark the 350th anniversary of Shakespeare's birth in 1914, and she included the best Shakespearean productions by amateur players in the list of prize categories available during the Tercentenary celebrations of 1916.[80] At the same time, she was not averse to avant-garde professional theatre settings and practitioners: the gala performance of selected scenes from Shakespeare's plays during the 1916 Tercentenary took place at the Gaiety, and Annie Horniman chaired at least one of Rosa Grindon's lectures at the Queen's Theatre.[81] It appears that, to Rosa Grindon, all kinds of theatre were valuable and worth supporting.

This pro-theatrical attitude fits well with Rosa Grindon's general preference for active engagement with Shakespeare in the here and now; Shakespeare enacted, embodied and interpreted by generations which came after him. One consequence of this approach was her definition of 'Shakespearean relics' worth collecting and preserving. Her description of the items which she was accumulating for the Manchester Tercentenary exhibition contained no quasi-religious objects which might offer an unmediated access to an 'authentic' Shakespeare, like soil from Stratford or water from the Avon. Instead, she mentions 'play bills, signed programmes of . . . performances', 'signed portraits' of Shakespearean actors, as well as 'portraits and biographies of leading commentators'. She especially valued items of local interest, aiming 'to bring together everything obtainable with regard to the "Irving or Ellen Terry" Shakespeare performances in general, but more particularly of the performances in our own city'.[82] Her Shakespeare is not an exclusive, reified and immutable object, fixed once and for all and memorialised in the museum-like atmosphere of an imaginary English past. Instead, he is an active, evolving, adaptable reality and present as much in contemporary, local performances and interpretations as in the pages of the First Folio or in Shakespeare's tomb in Stratford-upon-Avon.

The Shakespeare Window: The True Story

This brings us back to the puzzling act of memorialisation with which this chapter started: the Shakespeare window on the Manchester Central Library's façade. Monumental, cathedral-like and ornamental rather than utilitarian, it does not look like something with which the practical and ever-active Rosa Grindon would choose to honour her departed husband. There is a very good explanation for this incongruity: in fact, she did not choose it for that purpose. An examination of previously neglected archival documents reveals that she had a rather different plan in mind when she made a bequest to Manchester City Council's Libraries Committee, and only after her death did it morph into what we are left with now.[83]

Rosa Grindon first broached the topic of leaving a legacy to the Libraries Committee in November 1917. She initially approached the committee through an intermediary, none other than John Cuming Walters, who talked informally to its chairman, Alderman Plummer, before sending him an official letter on 30 November. Rosa Grindon's choice of Walters demonstrates that the differences in their approaches to Shakespeare, discussed above, were by no means insurmountable. As we have seen, the pair successfully collaborated in the Tercentenary Association's activities. Moreover, even though Walters did not mention the theatre in his speech about honouring Shakespeare, he was certainly not inherently anti-theatrical. He wrote introductory notes for some of the printed programmes of Flanagan's Shakespearean productions, and he was among the 'dramatic critics' selected to judge the amateur performance competition during the Tercentenary.[84] While his pronouncement in the run-up to the 1916 Tercentenary indicates a predilection for a monumental, national Shakespeare, in practice he participated in many local initiatives dear to Rosa Grindon's heart.

Walters' letter to Plummer outlines Rosa Grindon's proposal to donate £2,000 in order to establish in the planned new library building a hall that would provide a meeting space for Manchester's 'Literary and other Societies', and host her collection of Shakespeareana.[85] The communication mentions neither a stained glass window nor Rosa Grindon desiring to honour the memory of her husband. Instead, it dwells on the learned societies' lack of appropriate 'accommodation' and their need to find 'a suitable and central place of assembly ... to which all could have equal access under the easiest of conditions'. It adds that the Shakespeare Tercentenary Association has accumulated enough materials to establish a Shakespeare Room, where such materials can be held 'for the common object'. These goals are in keeping not only with Rosa Grindon's love for Shakespeare, but also with her characteristic focus on the practical needs of the community.

On 20 December 1917, the Library Committee enthusiastically accepted the offer. In the note to Rosa Grindon, they proposed to name the planned room 'The Grindon Hall', so 'that the name and memory of both your late Husband and of yourself shall be permanently and appropriately associated with the history and development of the public library movement in Manchester'. In response, Rosa Grindon asked for a meeting to discuss the details of the deal, and politely declined the 'Grindon Hall' suggestion, explaining: 'I much prefer the "Shakespeare Hall" as I hope it may give a stimulus to a really good Shakespeare collection, for which I can the more easily work if my name is not connected with it publicly'. This is the only time the bequest documents mention commemorating Mr Grindon, and the suggestion not only does not come from his widow but is rejected by her. A stained glass window is first brought up in Rosa Grindon's letter to Alderman Plummer, dated 15 April 1918. Here, she expresses her belief that '[t]o be truly educative social centres require a beautiful setting', hoping that the Shakespeare Hall might be both 'the Hall Beautiful' and 'the Hall Useful'. Among the room's decorations, she proposes 'as good a stained glass window as we could get, . . . arranged in panels, and containing portraits of our leading Shakespeare dramatic artists and commentators'. In a subsequent letter to the city architect, Henry Price, she specifies that the window should 'face the main entrance to the room and stand over the platform, facing the audience'. She adds that 'it is desired that scenes from Shakespeare's plays shall be given in the Hall', requesting 'small dressing rooms, . . . footlights suitable for stage purposes', as well as 'cloakrooms' that can double as meeting rooms for different committees. These instructions paint a picture of a functional space, devoted to various intellectual, social and theatrical activities. A short note from Price, dated 17 March 1919, confirms that 'The points contained in [Rosa Grindon's] letter are architecturally sound and practical'.

However, the extract from Rosa Grindon's subsequently drafted will, included in the documents, shifts the focus from the Shakespeare Hall and its uses to the stained glass window itself. It states:

> I bequeath . . . the sum of one thousand pounds (£1,000) in trust for a painted glass window containing portraits of Shakespeare Dramatic Artistes and Cormentation [sic] (Medallions) for which special directions are left. The window to be placed in the Shakespeare Hall that the Libraries Committee . . . promised to include in the New Library Buildings.

The will also bequeaths 'all the Shakespeare Material' in Rosa Grindon's possession, but it omits any reference to the key purpose of the proposed hall. It is hard to explain this omission. Perhaps the hall's practical aims were made clear in the 'special directions', now lost. Equally probably, the 'special directions' are the detailed instructions in Rosa Grindon's earlier correspondence, quoted above, and she trusted the Committee's promise to carry them out without repeating them in the will. Finally, the adjustment might have been caused by the unexplained change of the bequeathed sum from £2,000 to £1,000. However, it seems odd that Rosa Grindon would drop the essential part of her plan (providing a space to host the societies and the Shakespearean material) to prioritise the afterthought (including a decorative window).

Whatever the reasons, after Rosa Grindon's death in 1923 things did not go according to her original plan. In 1928, the acting town clerk, H. Dunks, wrote to the chief librarian, L. Stanley Jast, asking whether the Corporation would be able to fulfil the terms of the bequest, as the detailed plans for the new Reference Library were at last being finalised. Jast's response shows how far things had moved away from Rosa Grindon's wishes. He asks 'whether the term "hall" is to be interpreted strictly as a meeting room', explaining that the new building will contain 'a large entrance hall on the first floor', which 'might be the best place architecturally speaking for a stained glass window. If this were called the Shakespeare Hall would this meet the terms of the bequest?' He adds that 'one of the small meeting rooms arranged for on the second floor' could be named the Shakespeare Hall, but they would not provide as good a position for the window. In response, Dunks opines that one of the meeting rooms should become the Shakespeare Hall, referring to the 1917–19 letters and suggesting that the Corporation should 'give sympathetic consideration to the wishes of Mrs. Grindon'. Still, the Library decided to install the Shakespeare window above the building's main entrance. There it presides over an imposing marble hallway, flanked by two staircases and busy with people coming in and out, a space thus entirely inappropriate for holding meetings and theatrical performances or displaying Shakespearean memorabilia.[86] Moreover, the window itself depicts Shakespeare and generic images of his characters rather than the portraits of dramatic artists and commentators that Rosa Grindon specified. In the end, her bequest has been used in the service of the decorative and monumental, not the practical and contemporary. And in the public narrative, its purpose has been changed from serving the living community to honouring the dead husband.

Even though Rosa Grindon's ambitious gift to the people of Manchester failed to materialise in the way she intended, we should still not dismiss her legacy and cultural achievement. Her activities prove that turn-of-the-century Britain had a diverse and exciting Shakespearean scene beyond the London–Stratford 'Shakespeare metropolis'. In local settings, Shakespeare was performed, read, discussed and applied in ways which did not simply reproduce the cultural establishment's attitudes to the 'national bard'. Commercial entertainment, intellectual enquiry and community involvement could and did go hand in hand. Shakespeare could be a practical, down-to-earth and fun reality, rather than a museum exhibit or a relic to be worshipped. There is no space in this chapter to look further afield, but there is archival evidence that locations in the Greater Manchester area such as Oldham, Stockport and Bolton also displayed lively engagement with Shakespeare. It would be profitable to explore such provincial centres in more depth and detail, in order to build a more nuanced image of 'British' – not to say 'Northern' – Shakespeare in the late nineteenth and early twentieth centuries. I hope this chapter offers the first step and encouragement towards such an exploration.

Notes

1. 'History of Central Library'. Available at: <https://secure.manchester.gov.uk/info/500325/central_library_building/4586/history_of_central_library/6> (last accessed 3 January 2019).
2. See L. M. Angus-Butterworth, *Lancashire Literary Worthies* (St Andrews: W. C. Henderson and Son, 1980), 72–3; 'Mr. Leo Grindon', *The Manchester Guardian* (21 November 1904), 12.
3. Leo H. Grindon, *The Shakspere Flora. A Guide to All the Principal Passages in which Mention is Made of Trees, Plants, Flowers, and Vegetable Productions; with Comments and Botanical Particulars* (Manchester: Palmer and Howe; London: Simpkin, Marshall and Co, 1883).
4. See, among others, Graham Holderness, 'Shakespeare-land', in Willy Maley and Margaret Tudeau-Clayton (eds), *This England, That Shakespeare: New Angles on Englishness and the Bard* (Farnham: Ashgate, 2010), 201–19; Richard Foulkes, *Performing Shakespeare in the Age of Empire* (Cambridge: Cambridge University Press, 2002); Jonathan Bate, *The Genius of Shakespeare* (London: Picador, 2008), 187–214.
5. L.L.A. stands for Lady Literate in Arts, an equivalent of an MA, which St Andrews University awarded before women were allowed to obtain regular degrees.
6. Charlie Hulme, 'Rosa Leo Grindon (1923)', *John Cassidy: Manchester Sculptor*. Available at: <http://www.johncassidy.org.uk/grindon.html> (last accessed 5 January 2019).
7. See 'Mrs. Leo. H. Grindon, L.L.A.', *Manchester Faces and Places*, 7: 1 (October 1895), 7–12, 8–9.
8. Hulme, 'Rosa Leo Grindon', n.p.
9. 'Women's suffrage: annual meeting of the Manchester Society', *The Manchester Guardian* (18 January 1913), 12.
10. Hulme, 'Rosa Leo Grindon', n.p.
11. See Bernard Lightman, *Victorian Popularizers of Science: Designing Nature for New Audiences* (Chicago: University of Chicago Press, 2007), 96. I have found no indication of whether or not Rosa Grindon was paid for any of her lectures.
12. 'Mrs. Leo Grindon, L.L.A, F.R.M.S', *The Manchester Programme of Entertainments and Pleasure*, 229 (29 April 1901), 20; 'Mrs. Leo H. Grindon', *The Manchester Guardian* (7 May 1923), 9.

13. G. Vale Owen, 'Foreword', in G. Vale Owen (ed.), Rosa E. Grindon, *Shakespeare and his Plays from a Woman's Point of View* (Manchester: Policy Holding Journal, 1930), n.p.
14. 'Mrs. Leo Grindon', 20.
15. Notices and reports of Rosa Grindon's lectures appeared frequently in *The Manchester City News* and *The Manchester Programme*. In addition, leaflets and other ephemera documenting her Shakespearean activities are scattered in such archives as the Folger Shakespeare Library, Manchester Central Library, Shakespeare Birthplace, and Oldham Local Studies and Archives. Because of the volume of the material, I will provide specific references only to the items which I discuss in some detail.
16. See Roger Savage, *Masques, Mayings, and Music-Dramas: Vaughan Williams and the Twentieth-Century Stage* (Woodbridge: Boydell Press, 2014), 226.
17. Mrs. [Rosa] Leo Grindon, *In Praise of Shakespeare's Merry Wives of Windsor: An Essay in Exposition and Appreciation* (Manchester: Sherratt and Hughes, 1902); *In Praise of Shakespeare's Henry VIII: An Essay in Exposition and Appreciation* (Manchester: Sherratt and Hughes, 1903); *What the Play of Hamlet Says to Us* (Manchester: Marsten and Co, 1906); *The Story and the Poetry of Shakespeare's Play of Cymbeline* (Manchester: Sherratt and Hughes, 1909); *A Woman's Study of Antony and Cleopatra* (Manchester: Sherratt and Hughes, 1909); and G. Vale Owen (ed.), *Shakespeare and his Plays from a Woman's Point of View*.
18. *Autograph Letters, Mrs Leo Grindon Collection*, Manchester Central Library, 7649 H (18535), n.p.
19. Henry Irving's letter to Rosa Grindon (3 November 1900), in *Autograph Letters*, n.p.
20. John Martin-Harvey's letter to Rosa Grindon (23 October 1903), in *Autograph Letters*, n.p.
21. Johnston Forbes-Robertson's letter to Rosa Grindon (20 March 1905), in *Autograph Letters*, n.p. Forbes-Robertson was 'considered the finest Hamlet of his time'; see 'Sir Johnston Forbes-Robertson, British Actor', *Encyclopaedia Britannica* online. Available at: <https://www.britannica.com> (last accessed 12 January 2019).
22. Susan Carlson, 'The suffrage Shrew: the Shakespeare Festival, "A man's play," and new women', in Jonathan Bate, Jill L. Levenson and Dieter Mehl (eds), *Shakespeare and the Twentieth Century: The Selected Proceedings of the International Shakespeare Association World Congress, Los Angeles, 1996* (Newark: University of Delaware Press; London: Associated University Presses, 1998), 85–102, 94–5.
23. Susan Carlson, 'Politicizing Harley Granville Barker: suffragists and Shakespeare', *New Theatre Quarterly*, 22: 2 (May 2006), 122–40, 127, quoting Rosa Grindon's *The Story and the Poetry of Shakespeare's Play of Cymbeline*, 18.
24. Phyllis Rackin and Evelyn Gajowski, 'Introduction: a critical survey', in Evelyn Gajowski and Phyllis Rackin (eds), *The Merry Wives of Windsor:*

New Critical Essays (London and New York: Routledge, 2015), 1–24, 11. The argument here echoes Rackin's earlier comments on Rosa Grindon's approach to *The Merry Wives of Windsor*. See Rackin, 'Our canon, ourselves', in Lena Cowen Orlin (ed.), *Center or Margin: Revisions of the English Renaissance in Honor of Leeds Barroll* (Selinsgrove, PA: Susquehanna University Press, 2006), 91–113; and *Shakespeare and Women* (Oxford: Oxford University Press, 2005), 63–4.

25. Rackin, *Shakespeare and Women*, 134. Apart from the already cited sources, there are passing references to Rosa Grindon in Roger Savage, 'Alice Shortcake, Jenny Pluckpears, and the Stratford-upon-Avon connections of Vaughan Williams's "Sir John in Love"', *Music and Letters*, 89: 1 (Feb. 2008), 18–55, 20–21; L. T. Fitz, 'Egyptian queens and male reviewers: sexist attitudes in *Antony and Cleopatra* Criticism', *Shakespeare Quarterly*, 18 (1977), 297–316, 310; and Philip J. Traci, *The Love Play of Antony and Cleopatra: A Critical Study of Shakespeare's Play* (The Hague: Mouton, 1970), 21. In one recent book, Rosa Grindon is literally relegated to a footnote, as an 'early but obscure' critic of *Antony and Cleopatra*; see Kay Stanton, *Shakespeare's 'Whores': Erotics, Politics, and Poetics* (Houndmills: Palgrave Macmillan, 2014), 163, n.2.

26. For the concept of 'the Shakespeare metropolis', see Martin Orkin, *Local Shakespeares: Proximations and Power* (Abingdon: Routledge, 2005), 1.

27. In a leaflet published in January 1913, Rosa Grindon does not provide a date for the Association's inception, but she describes it as 'recently formed'. Mrs. Leo Grindon, 'A new Shakespeare society. Manchester to celebrate the Tercentenary [reprinted from the *Manchester City News*]'. Undated leaflet [1913], Folger Shakespeare Library, Scrapbook D.8.1 (Shakespeare Celebrations), folder 3 (Manchester Celebrations 1912–1916), n.p. There are also references to the newly established organisation in two newspaper cuttings in the Folger Shakespeare Library archives, which can be tentatively dated to November and December 1912. See 'Manchester Shakespeare Tercentenary Association', cutting from *Manchester Advertiser* (November [1912]), Folger Shakespeare Library, Papers of John Cuming Walters relating to Shakespeare, ca. 1898–1932, Y.d.1417(1462), n.p.; 'Shakespeare Tercentenary Association and the Life Study Association', cutting from an unidentified newspaper, [6 December 1912], Folger Shakespeare Library, Papers of John Cuming Walters relating to Shakespeare, ca. 1898–1932, Y.d.1417(1465), n.p. The date of the latter item is handwritten in the article's margin.

28. J. Cuming Walters, untitled typescript of an address to an unnamed Committee [1915], Folger Shakespeare Library, Papers of John Cuming Walters relating to Shakespeare, ca. 1898–1932, Y.d.1417(1469), 2.

29. Walters, untitled typescript, 2. John Cuming Walters (1863–1933) was a prominent figure in Manchester's cultural life in the late nineteenth and early twentieth centuries. Besides editing *The Manchester City News* for a quarter of a century, he was active in numerous clubs and societies, among

them Manchester Literary Club and Manchester Shakspere [sic] Society, and he published widely on Shakespeare, Dickens, Tennyson, Lancashire topography and other topics. See 'J. Cuming Walters', in Angus-Butterworth, *Lancashire Literary Worthies*, 151–3.
30. 'Manchester Shakespeare Tercentenary Association', n.p.
31. Ibid.
32. Ibid.
33. Ibid.
34. Clara Calvo, 'Fighting over Shakespeare: commemorating the 1916 Tercentenary in wartime', *Critical Survey*, 24: 3 (2012), 48–72, 55.
35. Coppélia Kahn, 'Remembering Shakespeare imperially: The 1916 Tercentenary', *Shakespeare Quarterly*, 52: 4 (2001), 456–78, 461. Similarly to Calvo, Kahn demonstrates how this paradox came to the fore at the critical moment of the 1916 Shakespeare Tercentenary, celebrated at the height of the global conflict.
36. 'William Harrison Ainsworth', *Encyclopaedia Britannica* online. Available at: <https://www.britannica.com> (last accessed 31 January 2019).
37. 'Manchester Shakespeare Tercentenary Association', n.p.
38. Ibid.
39. Ibid.
40. Ibid. The printed article has 'no organisation and accessible Shakespeare collection', but Walters' handwritten correction indicates that he meant 'organised'.
41. Michel Foucault, 'Of other spaces', trans. Jay Miskowiec, *Diacritics*, 16: 1 (Spring 1986), 22–7, 26. Foucault defines heterotopias as 'something like counter-sites, . . . in which the real sites, all the other real sites that can be found within the culture, are simultaneously represented, contested, and inverted' (24).
42. Foucault, 'Of other spaces', 26.
43. Tony Bennett, *The Birth of the Museum: History, Theory, Politics* (London and New York: Routledge, 1995), 1–3.
44. Bennett, *Birth of the Museum*, 67.
45. While Bennett focuses predominantly on the museum, most of his insights apply to the other institutions that Walters mentions: the library and the organised collection.
46. 'Manchester Shakespeare Tercentenary Association', n.p.
47. Graham Holderness, *Cultural Shakespeare: Essays in the Shakespeare Myth* (Hatfield: University of Hertfordshire Press, 2001), 126. The term 'bardolatry' was first coined by George Bernard Shaw in the preface to his *Three Plays for Puritans: The Devil's Disciple, Cæsar and Cleopatra, and Captain Brass-bound's Conversion* (London: Grant Richards, 1901), xxxi.
48. Holderness, *Cultural Shakespeare*, 129–31.
49. 'Manchester Shakespeare Tercentenary Association', n.p.

50. Holderness, *Cultural Shakespeare* (125–6) discusses a notable example of a quasi-religious ritual establishing such a connection, the ceremonial transfer of some soil from Stratford and water from the river Avon to Dallas, Texas, to 'consecrate' a local replica of the Globe Theatre in 1936.
51. 'Manchester Shakespeare Tercentenary Association', n.p.
52. Ibid.
53. Rosa Grindon, 'A new Shakespeare society', n.p.
54. Ibid.
55. Ibid., quoting 'the leading section of our Foundation Scheme'.
56. 'Shakspere Festivals. Scenes at Whitworth Institute', *The Manchester City News* (3 May 1913), 11.
57. Rosa Grindon, 'A new Shakespeare society', n.p.
58. Ibid.
59. Ibid.
60. Ibid.
61. For the ideas of 'civic gospel', focused on the practical improvement of local communities, see Asa Briggs, *Victorian Cities* (Berkeley: University of California Press, 1993), esp. 184–240. Rosa Grindon seems to be espousing these ideas not so much on the level of municipal government, as Birmingham did in the late nineteenth century, but rather on the level of voluntary cultural associations. Matthew Arnold decries 'the evil of the Nonconformists' provincialism', extolling 'the main current of national life', embodied in 'Establishment' institutions; see *Culture and Anarchy: An Essay in Political and Social Criticism* (1869) (London: John Murray, 1949), xiv-xvii. Simultaneously, Arnold criticises the utilitarian focus of contemporary civilisation, which he calls 'mechanical and external', advocating 'a study of perfection', residing in 'an inward condition of the mind and spirit' (*Culture and Anarchy*, 9–10).
62. Rosa Grindon, 'A new Shakespeare society', n.p.
63. Ibid. As the last quotation demonstrates, Rosa Grindon does not shy away from intellectual activities like lectures, but she combines them in a non-hierarchical way with more immediately physical and entertainment-focused ones.
64. Ibid.
65. Ibid.
66. Ibid.
67. Ibid.
68. Katherine West Scheil, *She Hath Been Reading: Women and Shakespeare Clubs in America* (Ithaca and London: Cornell University Press, 2012), xi. While Scheil focuses chiefly on Shakespeare clubs in America, there is no reason to assume that attitudes were substantially different in Shakespeare clubs and other voluntary cultural organisations in Britain. As we have seen, Rosa Grindon was an active member of a number of such organisations.

69. Rosa Grindon, 'A new Shakespeare society', n.p.
70. Viv Gardner, 'No flirting with Philistinism: Shakespearean production at Miss Horniman's Gaiety Theatre', *New Theatre Quarterly*, 14: 55 (1998), 220–33, 222.
71. Gardner, 'No flirting', 220, 230.
72. Gardner, 'No flirting', 222–3.
73. Gardner challenges other critics' disparaging accounts of Flanagan, describing him as 'a popularizer of Shakespeare who provided a necessary complement to the aesthetic experiments at the Gaiety' ('No flirting', 222).
74. Rosa Grindon, 'A new Shakespeare society', n.p. Surviving copies of several programmes of Rosa Grindon's lectures from previous years contain detailed syllabi for each session, covering topics such as 'Effect of Marlowe upon Shakespeare's early tragedy' and 'Sources of the various centres of action'. In one case, the programme includes essay questions to be answered by the participants, with the prize of a guinea for the best answer. Items in the Folger Shakespeare Library, Scrapbook D.8.1 (Shakespeare Celebrations), folder 3 (Manchester Celebrations 1912–1916).
75. Rosa Grindon, 'A new Shakespeare society', n.p.
76. 'Lectures on Shakspere', *The Manchester Programme of Entertainments and Pleasure*, 630 (4 January 1909) 8–9, 8. I have found no evidence that the lectures were aimed exclusively at women, but the article does not mention whether there were any men in attendance.
77. Gardner, 'No flirting', 222.
78. 'Manchester Shakespeare Tercentenary Association', n.p.
79. 'Shakspere Prize Essay Fund. Open-air performances of drama', *The Manchester City News* (28 June 1913), 10.
80. Manchester Shakespeare Tercentenary Association, 'Reception in honour of the 350th anniversary of Shakespeare's birthday, in the Town Hall, on Tuesday evening, April 21st, 1914'. Leaflet in the Folger Shakespeare Library, Scrapbook D.8.1 (Shakespeare Celebrations), folder 3 (Manchester Celebrations 1912–1916), n.p. Rosa L. Grindon, 'Manchester Shakespeare Tercentenary Association: prize scheme for essays, poems and pictures' (1915). Leaflet in the Oldham Local Studies and Archives, MSC 822.33 M/CR. For a comprehensive discussion of Shakespeare on amateur stages, see Michael Dobson, *Shakespeare and Amateur Performance: A Cultural History* (Cambridge: Cambridge University Press, 2011).
81. Manchester Shakespeare Tercentenary Association, 'Completion of the rendering of selected scenes from each of the plays: programme', leaflet in the Folger Shakespeare Library, Scrapbook D.8.1 (Shakespeare Celebrations), folder 3 (Manchester Celebrations 1912–1916); 'Lectures on Shakspere', 9.
82. Rosa Grindon, 'A new Shakespeare society', n.p.
83. All the materials on this topic quoted in this section are located in the Manchester Libraries, Information and Archives, file 143GG, Grindon Bequest, GB127.M740/2/8/2/21.

84. Rosa Grindon, 'Prize scheme for essays', n.p.
85. £1,000 was to be spent on 'the interior fitting and decoration' and the other £1,000 'invested in aid of upkeep in order that the room may be let to Societies at 5/- per meeting'.
86. Rosa Grindon's collection seems to have dispersed after her death. The only item I have been able to locate is the previously mentioned scrapbook of correspondence and theatrical programmes, *Autograph Letters*, at the Manchester Central Library.

10

A Road by Any Other Name: Heaton History Group, a North East Suburb and Shakespeare

Chris Jackson

On 20 June 2016, amateur actors from the People's Theatre, Heaton, Newcastle upon Tyne, appeared in *A Midsummer Night's Dream* in Stratford-upon-Avon alongside professionals from the Royal Shakespeare Company. That performance, a reprise the following night, and five nights at the Northern Stage in Newcastle upon Tyne the previous March, formed part of the national commemoration of the 400th anniversary of William Shakespeare's death. This honour for its local theatre prompted Heaton History Group, of which I am a member, to explore local links with the Bard, not only through theatrical productions but in the fabric and even, it often seems, the soul of the place itself.

Heaton History Group is a community-based history society, which was set up in 2013.[1] The group puts on talks and arranges visits to places of historic interest for its one hundred or so members and others. From the outset, it was keen to carry out original research into the history of its locality. Although most members of the group had no background in history or research, by 2016 it had already published a booklet on the history of some of the area's shops and researched both Heaton's mining heritage and the effects of the First World War on a group of streets known as 'the Avenues' for projects funded by the Heritage Lottery Fund. The group was now looking for another project.

Heaton is a suburb of Newcastle upon Tyne in the North East of England. It is comprised mainly of terraced streets, built in the late nineteenth century and early twentieth century. It is still home to many people who work in the creative industries, including the theatre. This is perhaps because housing costs are relatively low compared to neighbouring Jesmond and Gosforth and might explain why, in Heaton, there seems to be a particular affection towards Shakespeare and his work: there is even a brick memorial to him (Figure 10.1). But is there more

Figure 10.1 Shakespeare mural, South View West, Heaton, Newcastle upon Tyne. Photograph by Chris Jackson.

to it than that? Heaton History Group wanted to find out how long the links went back and why they felt particularly strong. In so doing, we discovered how Shakespeare and one northern location have been intimately connected; in turn, our discoveries offer just one example of how to conceive the ways in which Shakespeare is implicated in making places (far beyond London or Stratford) what they are, and how such places can inform our experience and construction of Shakespeare.

The Naming of the Streets

In the extreme south and west of Heaton, there is a group of terraced streets which appear to be named in honour of Shakespeare and Shakespearean characters: Bolingbroke, Hotspur, Malcolm and Mowbray Streets, and immediately north of them Warwick Street and the Stratfords (Road, Grove, Grove Terrace, Grove West, Villas). This is not unique: Bootle in Merseyside, for example, has a similar cluster of streets which include Macbeth Street, Miranda Road, Rosalind Way, Viola Street, Beatrice Street and Benedict Street.[2] There seems little doubt that these streets were all named after major characters from Shakespeare plays, but could Heaton's literary references be coincidental? Perhaps it was the real life, historical figures who had been immortalised? Why would a housing estate, built around the early 1880s for Newcastle workers and their families, pay homage to Shakespeare and not even his most famous characters at that? Does it indicate that Shakespeare deeply resonated with England's northern working classes at that time? These are questions that have been asked locally many times – indeed this collection's editor, a former resident of Warwick Street, once wrote to the council to see if they could shed any light on the matter – but to no avail.[3] These questions were, therefore, the starting point for Heaton History Group's research before it went on to look at the history of Shakespeare in two local theatres, and, finally, notable Shakespeare-related residents of the streets. This chapter describes what we did, how and why.

Two documents, one in Tyne and Wear Archives and one in Newcastle City Library, provided partial answers. Firstly, in the archives, Heaton History Group's amateur researchers were delighted to find a planning application from Alderman Addison Potter of Heaton Hall and his architect, F. W. Rich.[4] Their plans show Bolingbroke, Hotspur, Malcolm and Mowbray Streets, much as they look now, but bordering them to the south was a Shakespeare Road that certainly is not there now, and which does not appear in any local trade directory.

Not only that, but Siward, Lennox and Umfreville Terraces also appeared on these partly unrealised plans. The Heaton History Group researchers did not purport to be Shakespeare scholars but soon discovered that Siward was the leader of the English army in *Macbeth* and Malcolm's uncle. The real life Siward (d. 1054) was Earl of Northumbria, who became sub-ruler of most of northern England. Lennox is a Scottish nobleman in the same play, who eventually deserts Macbeth in support of Malcolm. Umfreville had a line in the first edition of *Henry IV Part II* and is mentioned by Travers at 1.1.40–2:

My lord, Sir John Umfreville turned me back
With joyful tidings; and, being better horsed,
Out-rode me.[5]

The Umfrevilles were Northumberland landowners, whose family seat was in Redesdale. Robert Umfreville (1363–1437) fought with Henry 'Hotspur' Percy for Richard II, loyally served Henry Bolingbroke (Henry IV) and took part in the Battle of Agincourt with Henry V. He held Prudhoe, Berwick and Warkworth castles at various times. Clearly the inspiration for the street names came from one or more people who knew their literature and their local and national history. But these street plans were rejected by the council for reasons that are unclear, and within a year Addison Potter seems to have sold at least the leasehold of the land to a builder and local councillor called William Temple. Temple submitted new, if broadly similar, proposals. Building work soon started, and many of the streets retained the names in Potter and Rich's proposal. But, by now, Lord Armstrong had gifted Heaton Park to the people of Newcastle and the road to the new public space took its name rather than that of the Bard. It is still called Heaton Park Road today. And nobody lives on Lennox, Siward or Umfreville Terraces either: they became Heaton Park View, Wandsworth Road and Cardigan Terrace.

George Stanley and the Tyne Theatre

But why Shakespeare? Whose idea was it? A newspaper cutting, dated 21 May 1898, in Newcastle City Library provided the next clue. It comprised an interview with former Newcastle upon Tyne councillor, James Birkett:

Mr Birkett himself occupied a cottage on the land which is now known as South View. There was another cottage or two near his, but they had nearly the whole of the district to themselves . . . In front of them was the railway line, and behind was the farmhouse of a Mr Robinson. This house stood on the site now forming the corner of Heaton Park Road and Bolingbroke Street, and one of its occupants was Mr Stanley, who for many years was the lessee of the Tyne Theatre.[6]

This serendipitous find provided the research team with its next lead. Could theatre manager Stanley have somehow been responsible for the choice of names?

Further research showed that George William Stanley, born c.1824 in Marylebone, London, had a deep love not only of drama but of William Shakespeare in particular. By 1851, Stanley described himself as a 'tragedian' and by 1860, he was in the North East.[7] The first mention we have found of him in a local context dates from 28 July of that year, when he is reported to have obtained a licence to open a temporary theatre in East Street, Gateshead.[8] A similar licence in South Shields soon followed. Later, we know that he opened theatres in Tynemouth and Blyth, on the North East coast near Newcastle.

By the 1861 census, he was described as not just (or still) a 'tragedian', but also 'theatre manager'. And in that line he had turned his attention to Newcastle, where his attempts to obtain theatre licences were anything but straightforward. Applying for a six-month licence for theatrical performances in the city, he argued that one theatre (the Theatre Royal) in Newcastle to serve 109,000 people was inadequate; he promised that the type of performances ('operatic and amphitheatre') that he would put on would not directly compete with existing provision; he produced testimonials and support from local rate payers; and he gave guarantees that alcohol would not be served, nor would prostitutes be on the premises.[9] But all to no avail. The Theatre Royal strongly objected, and an editorial in the *Newcastle Guardian and Tyne Mercury* supported the refusal.[10] Appeal after appeal was unsuccessful. Stanley appeared before the licensing committee almost monthly.

In October 1863, George Stanley made yet another impassioned speech, in which he sought to win over the magistrates with his commitment, and high aspirations:

> It is my desire to add to the musical entertainments that I am now able to present to the public, performances of a higher intellectual character. I am, and have been all my life, a member of the theatrical profession, and yet I am prevented from practising my own art in my own premises.

Eventually, he concluded:

> I will not trouble your worships with any further remarks in support of my application, but trust that the year that witnesses the tercentenary of Shakespeare's birth, will also witness the removal of any limitation against the performances of the plays of that greatest of Englishmen in Newcastle.[11]

The Bench retired for thirty-five minutes but finally returned with the same verdict as before.

Despite his latest setback, George Stanley started 1864 determined to mark Shakespeare's big anniversary. In the first week of January, he played Iago opposite Mr T. H. Glenney's Othello in his own Tyne Concert Hall, with the roles being reversed on alternate nights. Reviews praising his efforts made passing reference to Stanley's recent inability to practice his 'own art' in his 'own premises':

> Probably a more excellent representation of these characters has not lately been presented to the Newcastle public. Mr T. H. Glenney sustained the noble Moor with intense energy and power, which contrasted effectively with the subtlety of Iago. Indeed Mr Stanley supported Mr Glenney with undoubted ability, although his want of recent practice in his profession was occasionally evinced in his intonation.[12]

The following week, a preliminary public meeting was held to hear a dramatic oration, 'On the Tercentenary of Shakespeare', by George Linnaeus Banks of London, honorary secretary to the National Shakespeare Committee, and to appoint a local committee to arrange the celebrations in Newcastle. Joseph Cowen, radical political figure (later MP) and owner and editor of the *Newcastle Daily Chronicle* took the chair. Significantly, George Stanley was on the platform and it was he who moved the vote of thanks to Mr Banks for his 'eloquent address'.[13]

Unfortunately, in the end the Tercentenary celebrations were somewhat muted and overshadowed by Garibaldi's visit to England. (He had been expected to visit Cowen on Tyneside that very week, although in the event he left the country just beforehand). There was a half-day holiday in Newcastle on Monday, 25 April 1864 'but the day was raw and cold and the holiday was not so much enjoyed as it might otherwise have been'.[14] A celebration dinner in the Assembly Rooms, 'attended by about 210 gentlemen', was the main event.[15] At the dinner, a toast 'In Memory of

Shakespeare' was proposed, followed by one to 'The Dramatic Profession'. George Stanley gave thanks on behalf of the acting profession.[16]

As befitting someone so clearly enmeshed in thespianism, Stanley continued to pay his own respects to the playwright. He engaged the 'celebrated tragedian, Mr John Pritchard' to perform some celebrated Shakespearean roles. Again, he himself played Othello and Iago on alternate nights.[17] In October 1865, Stanley's wooden concert hall was damaged and narrowly escaped destruction in a huge fire that started in a neighbouring building. This only intensified his determination to open a permanent theatre, and he had found powerful allies. On 19 January 1866, it was announced that an anonymous 'party of capitalists' had purchased land on 'the Westgate' for the erection of a 'theatre on a very large scale'.[18] It emerged that George Stanley would be the new manager. Eventually, Joseph Cowen, with whom Stanley had served on the Shakespeare Tercentenary Committee, was identified as one of the 'capitalists' behind what was to become the Tyne Theatre and Opera House. Stanley's efforts were paying off.

The opening had been set for September 1867, but a licence was still required. On 27 August, Stanley handed in a written application requesting a special sitting of the magistrate's bench. This time the request was countersigned by the mayor.[19] The hearing was held on Friday, 13 September before a panel of magistrates, which included Alderman Addison Potter of Heaton Hall – and this time Stanley and his influential backers were in luck.[20] Just as well, as the new theatre was due to open ten days later. And it did, with an inaugural address by none other than George Stanley himself.[21]

Despite his earlier claims that the Tyne Theatre would not compete with the Theatre Royal, Shakespeare was very much part of the programme in the early years, including productions of *As You Like It*, *The Merchant of Venice* and *King Lear*. It was, however, soon acknowledged that such was the demand that there was room for two theatres in Newcastle. Having worked so hard to secure this theatre, Stanley continued as manager until 1881.

It was in 1878, near the end of his tenure managing the Tyne Theatre, that Stanley moved to Heaton with his family. Their home was Heaton House, which, as noted above, stood on what is now the corner of Heaton Park Road (once planned to be Shakespeare Road) and Bolingbroke Street, but was then in a semi-rural setting. The house was situated only a few hundred yards from Heaton Hall, home of Alderman Addison Potter, one of Stanley's few neighbours, owner of the farmland on which Stanley's house stood and, of course, a member of the panel that finally approved Stanley's theatre in Newcastle.

Potter and Stanley would surely have discussed matters of mutual interest. So, while we might not know exactly how the naming of Heaton's Shakespeare streets came about, we can surely assume that George William Stanley, actor, tragedian, Shakespearean, passionate promoter of theatre, very well known in the city and neighbour of Potter at the time, played a part. It might have taken almost another twenty years and the name 'Shakespeare Road' didn't make the final cut, but Newcastle finally had the long-lasting tribute that George Stanley had wanted for Shakespeare's Tercentenary.

F. R. Benson and the Grand Theatre

The next phase of our research was prompted by an article in the *Newcastle Courant*, dated Saturday, 21 December 1895, announcing that the 'accomplished and popular Shakespearean actor, F. R. Benson', had laid the foundation stone of a new theatre in Heaton the previous Tuesday.[22] The Grand Theatre, Wilfred Street, after struggling for many years to be profitable as either as a theatre or a cinema, finally closed on August 1954. Thus, it is still remembered by some older members of the community as a place where they watched pantomimes as children. We were intrigued by yet another mention of Shakespeare in relation to Heaton. Again, the Heaton History Group researchers had to admit that, at that time, they were unaware of F. R. Benson's importance in the history of the Royal Shakespeare Company.

Francis Robert Benson was born in Tunbridge Wells in 1858. After studying at New College, Oxford, he immediately took to the stage and, soon afterwards, started his own theatrical company. From the outset, he concentrated on Shakespeare and played in Newcastle many times, often in dramatic circumstances. Surprisingly it seems that until 1864 (the year in which, as noted above, George Stanley had served on the Newcastle Shakespeare Tercentenary Committee and put on his own tribute to the Bard), there was little interest in putting on Shakespeare's plays in the town of his birth. Indeed, the suggestion that his plays be performed in Stratford was mocked in *The Times* (1 June 1864):

> We testify our gratitude to Shakespeare by calling for edition after edition of his works, by making household words of his language, and by claiming for him the first place among the poets of all time.

Yet zealous believers have been known to confess that they did not care to see Shakespeare's plays acted, and of those who go from time to time, out of pure love, to see them acted in London, not one in ten thousand would go out of his way to see them acted in Stratford.[23]

What, then, would the London press have made of the tireless struggles of George Stanley to put on Shakespeare's works in even more remote Newcastle? Stratford did, however, put on a successful festival that year, promoted and bankrolled by brewer Edward Flower, mayor at the time. Flower had toured the country to gain support for a school, a monument and a celebration of Shakespeare in Stratford, as opposed to London. He had received enthusiastic support when he met members of the Newcastle Shakespearian Celebration Committee, who empathised with someone prepared to take on the London-based establishment:

> There could be no doubt that Stratford, and not London, was the place where a monument to Shakespeare ought to be erected. London had not been very successful in making monuments, and he [Flower] believed it would be the opinion of many that there would be nothing lost if almost all the figures and statues were swept away from the streets. It was natural that they should have no great confidence in London, or in those who affected to rule London, in that respect . . . if there was to be a national monument to Shakespeare, [in Stratford] it ought to be. The Mayor of Stratford had brought the matter before them in a business-like style . . . The jobs that had been done in London led people to regard London committees with distrust and they had therefore guarded themselves when Mr Banks was there on behalf of the London Committee. They had now moved their interest from the London Committee to Stratford.[24]

The success of the commemoration gave momentum to attempts to raise money to build a theatre in Stratford specifically to put on the plays of its famous son and the Shakespeare Memorial Theatre, Stratford-upon-Avon, opened its doors and launched its first Shakespeare Festival on 23 April 1879, coincidentally the year in which the plans for Heaton's own memorial to Shakespeare, the so called 'Shakespeare Streets', were first submitted.

In 1886, Benson became the director of the Stratford Festival, which was effectively the forerunner of the Royal Shakespeare Company.[25] Nevertheless, he continued with a gruelling touring schedule, so committed was he to promoting Shakespeare far and wide. Indeed, in 1893,

Benson played Richard III at the Theatre Royal in Newcastle with a temperature of 104 degrees Fahrenheit and what turned out to be typhoid. He was seriously ill for several weeks.[26]

The Grand Theatre, where Benson laid the foundation stone, was, despite what the press originally said, actually in nearby Byker, albeit only a couple of hundred yards away from the boundary with Heaton, from where it will have drawn a large part of its audience. It was described as a very fine building, which could seat 2,500 people. The stage was big and could accommodate the largest shows, hence its suitability for Benson's Shakespearean productions. Moreover, it had decent modern amenities which would no doubt also appeal to audiences and actors alike: 'The building is lighted both by electricity and gas and heated with hot water', with 'a commodious suite of dressing rooms on each side fitted with every convenience for the comfort of the artistes'.[27]

Seven months after laying the foundation stone of the Grand, Benson brought his production of *The Taming of the Shrew* to its opening night, which took place on 27 July 1896. Local critics disliked the liberties Benson took with the text but conceded that the comedy had been well received by the audience.[28] The performance was just the first of that week's east Newcastle festival of Shakespeare. Benson's company also put on *The Merchant of Venice, Hamlet* and *As You Like It*, with *Richard III* played al fresco at the nearby Sandyford Park home of a Dr Gibb (later immortalised in the Geordie anthem *Blaydon Races*).[29] Benson was back at the Grand in December 1899. His company had been performing at the Theatre Royal when a disastrous fire destroyed the interior of the theatre and with it most of the company's costumes, props and scenery as well as personal effects. Benson is said to have dashed to London to source replacements and Byker's Grand Theatre was offered as an alternative venue for its outstanding performances of *The Merchant of Venice*.[30] Benson's contribution to the cause of Shakespeare was formally recognised in 1916 during the commemorations for the Tercentenary of Shakespeare's death. He had played Julius Caesar in front of an audience of nearly three thousand people, which included King George V and Queen Mary, when, still wearing the blood-stained robes and ashen make-up of the dead Caesar, he was knighted on stage.[31]

The Royal Shakespeare Company evolved out of the Shakespeare Festival that Benson ran in Stratford between 1888 and 1916. The debt that the company owes to him is acknowledged by a set of stained glass windows in the original Shakespeare Memorial Theatre. But, as someone who understood that Shakespeare's words could and should resonate with the whole country, not just bits of it, Benson is also a part of the story of Shakespeare in the North and specifically of Heaton, Byker and Sandyford's cultural history.

'Thou wall, O wall, O sweet and lovely wall' (*A Midsummer Night's Dream*, 5.1.175)

As Adam Hansen's chapter in this collection shows, Shakespeare has had and continues to have a vibrant, vital presence in Heaton through the productions put on by the People's Theatre. The People's has been a cultural hub of Heaton since it relocated from central Newcastle in 1962. Its links with Heaton, however, go back much further and its history of Shakespeare productions is almost as long. Among the company's founders in 1911 were 32-year-old telephone engineer Norman Kidd Veitch, and his wife, Edith, of 19 Stratford Grove Terrace, and Norman's younger brother Colin Campbell Mackenzie Veitch and his wife, Minnie, who lived just around the corner at 1 Stratford Villas. Fittingly both couples lived in Heaton's 'Shakespeare Streets'.[32]

Beyond the People's, within those streets one of the most obvious and curious physical memorials to Shakespeare locally is a mural on South View West, where a huge copy of Martin Droueshout's contemporary or near contemporary portrait of him has been recreated in brick on the end of a terraced house. Although it is a prominent and comparatively recent addition to Heaton's streetscape, Heaton History Group's researchers have hitherto found it surprisingly difficult to uncover the mural's origins. It had been created in the mid-1980s when the building of a new school (Hotspur Primary School) necessitated the demolition of a number of houses and hence the building of a new gable end. A number of people who lived in Heaton at the time recall it appearing almost overnight but no documentary evidence has yet been found. Eventually the group's quest to uncover the mural's origins was publicised in the local paper, where it was read by the bricklayers assigned to the job. Paul Shucksmith and Bob Spuhler, formerly of Holly Construction, recalled the work taking three to four weeks in mainly inclement weather and described their task as being like painting by numbers with bricks. The paper also interviewed the people currently living in the terraced house, Nicola Rose and Jim Webb, who also said how proud they were of the local landmark.[33] Because questions remain unanswered, the group feels that this part of its research is incomplete. It still wants to know whose idea the portrait was and who designed and commissioned it. But at least the group's members were able to find out a little more about who was responsible for this fitting memorial to Heaton's longstanding connection with the Bard.

Shakespeare in Heaton Schools

Having researched these Shakespearean themes and published several articles on its website, Heaton History Group was ready to move on. But perhaps the most important phase of the project was still to come. The group was at this point approached by Historic England which, like many other organisations in 2016, had chosen Shakespeare as one of its topics for work with schools around the country. Victoria Angel, who coordinated this work in the region, had read the Shakespeare-related articles on the Heaton History Group website and asked whether the group would be prepared to manage a small budget to work with local primary schools based on what we had done so far. Two primary schools, Chillingham Road Primary School and the appropriately named Hotspur Primary School, which is situated on Mowbray Street next to the brick mural, jumped at the chance and the 'Our Shakespeare Streets' project was born. Children from both schools learnt about the origin of the Shakespeare street names, including the part that former resident George Stanley might have played and how, later, resident (and one-time Newcastle United captain) Colin Veitch had not only co-founded the People's Theatre but also starred in its first Shakespeare production. Both schools took part in a joint performance for parents and friends, to which Hotspur's Year 6 (10- and 11-year-old pupils) also brought *Richard III* in a production abridged for them by Chris Heckels of the People's Theatre, who had directed the 'mechanicals' at Stratford a few months earlier.[34] The children had first performed the play to great acclaim in Middlesbrough as part of the Shakespeare Schools Festival. Shakespeare in Heaton is in good hands.

Conclusions

So what conclusions can be drawn from the questions we have asked, answers we have derived, and projects we have undertaken? We found that Heaton's links with Shakespeare's legacy go back over 150 years to the time when Heaton was first becoming a significant suburb and have continued to the present day. Newcastle's, and particularly Heaton and Byker's, excellent relations with Stratford have an equally long history. It may be the case that other places could tell similar stories – about themselves and about what their people have done with Shakespeare in those places.

Although we are not in a position to claim that more people in Heaton feel a deeper affection for England's 'national poet' than elsewhere in the country, anecdotally, Heaton's Shakespearean streets names are often cited as part of the reason for the connection that many local people seem to feel, as well as the fact that Heaton is perhaps home to a disproportionate number of people who work in the arts, the memorable visits of the RSC, and the fact that Shakespeare productions can still be enjoyed at the People's almost annually. But who is to say that Heaton's earlier, albeit not consciously remembered, history has not had some bearing on what the community feels today? And who can doubt that, when the right questions are asked, other communities might find they feel similar things?

We certainly discovered that an understanding and a love of the Bard as well as local history is still being nurtured in our primary schools. That is not unique to Heaton either. But the key thing is that an affection for Shakespeare still exists here and the 400th anniversary of the Bard's death was enthusiastically celebrated in Heaton. Hopefully in 2064 the enthusiastic researchers of Heaton History Group will commemorate half a millennium since Shakespeare's birth and a new generation will find that the emotional, artistic and intellectual ties which bind their community to our national – and local – poet have strengthened further.

Notes

1. See Heaton History Group website, 'About' section. Available at: <https://heatonhistorygroup.org/about> (last accessed 18 July 2019).
2. See the Twitter image publicised by *Shakespeare Magazine* (9 January 2018). Available at: <pic.twitter.com/sE17SszeDF> (last accessed 22 July 2019).
3. Personal communication with the author, 29 February 2016.
4. Tyne and Wear Archives, street plans, Shakespeare Street, V273.
5. William Shakespeare, *The Second Part of Henry the Fourth*, in Jonathan Bate and Eric Rasmussen (eds), *The Complete Works* (Houndmills: Macmillan, 2007).
6. Newcastle City Library Local Studies section, box file labelled 'Heaton'.
7. 1851 Census return, *Ancestry.com* (last accessed 17 July 2019).
8. *Newcastle Journal* (28 July 1860), 8.
9. Ibid. (22 June 1861), 2.
10. *Newcastle Guardian and Tyne Mercury* (14 September 1861), 5.
11. *Newcastle Chronicle and Northern Counties Advertiser* (24 October 1863), 8.
12. Ibid. (5 January 1864), 2.
13. *Newcastle Courant* (15 January 1864), 5.
14. *Newcastle Guardian and Tyne Mercury* (30 April 1864), 6.

15. Ibid.
16. Ibid.
17. *Newcastle Guardian and Tyne Mercury* (30 April 1864), 5.
18. *Newcastle Courant* (19 January 1866), 8.
19. *Newcastle Daily Chronicle* (28 August 1867), 4.
20. *Newcastle Courant* (13 September 1867), 8.
21. *Newcastle Daily Chronicle* (24 September 1867), 3.
22. *Newcastle Courant* (21 December 1895), 4.
23. Sally Beauman, *The Royal Shakespeare Company: A History of Ten Decades* (Oxford: Oxford University Press, 1982), 6.
24. *Newcastle Daily Chronicle and Northern Counties Advertiser* (2 February 1864), 2–3.
25. Beauman, *Royal Shakespeare Company*, 26.
26. Sir Frank Benson, *My Memoirs* (London: Ernest Benn Limited, 1930), 299.
27. *Newcastle Courant* (25 July 1896), 5.
28. *Newcastle Courant* (1 August 1896), 5.
29. Ibid. 5.
30. *Newcastle Courant* (2 December 1899), 5.
31. Benson, *My Memoirs*, 321.
32. See Hansen's chapter in this collection; Chris Goulding, *The Story of the People's* (Newcastle upon Tyne: Newcastle upon Tyne City Libraries and Arts, 1991); and Norman Veitch, *The People's: Being a History of the People's Theatre Newcastle upon Tyne 1911–1939* (Gateshead on Tyne: Northumberland Press Limited, 1950).
33. David Whetstone, 'Brickies recall their Shakespearean triumph 400 years after The Bard's death', *Newcastle Evening Chronicle* (22 April 2016). <https://www.chroniclelive.co.uk/whats-on/arts-culture-news/brickies-recall-shakespearean-triumph-400-11229634> (last accessed 18 July 2019).
34. See <https://heatonhistorygroup.org/2016/12/02/our-shakespeare-streets> (last accessed 18 July 2019).

11

Lancastrian Shakespeares: *Hamlet* and *King Lear* in North West England (2005–2014)

Liz Oakley-Brown

In July 1999, seven years before I travelled from South East to North West England to become a lecturer in Shakespeare and Renaissance Writing in the Department of English Literature and Creative Writing at Lancaster University, a group of that institution's scholars held a conference on 'Lancastrian Shakespeare'.[1] Two of the conference organisers explained how their inspiration for the topic 'was, of course, the possibility that Shakespeare was the "William Shakeshafte" who received forty shillings in Alexander Hoghton's 1581 will'.[2] A member of the gentrified Tudor family from Lea near Preston, the Lancastrian's legacy is often used to link Shakespeare's so-called 'lost years' with the North West,[3] implicitly if not explicitly. To date, there is no proof that Hoghton's beneficiary and the pre-modern author are the same person. Nonetheless, and as witnessed in the two essay collections based on the 1999 conference – *Region, Religion and Patronage* (2003) and *Theatre and Religion* (2003)[4] – the Shakeshaft/Shakespeare quandary facilitates examinations of the relationship between place, identity politics and textual production.[5]

As this current collection shows, others are developing these examinations in new ways. Moreover, this region-specific mode of criticism has inscribed a related texture within a seam of creative writing generated at Lancaster University. If literary scholars consider how Shakespeare's possible proximity to the North West 'opens up wider areas of early modern culture which oblige us to rethink our ideas of Elizabethan England and its theatre',[6] then Lancaster University's creative writers engage with Shakespearean sensibilities as ways of probing local provincial experience. In what follows, I am not especially concerned with tracing direct lines of influence between Shakespeare's texts and these north-western afterlives.

Rather, and in debt to Graham Holderness, my discussion of two texts produced by a former and a current co-worker is concerned with the 'creative collision' of ideas that occurs in a particular place and time. Holderness develops his 'concept of "collision" from the popular understanding of particle physics.' He continues:

> As a term, 'collision' is widely and casually used in Shakespeare criticism, to describe the interaction of characters and forces in a play, especially a tragedy, or to explain the impact of contextual factors on Shakespearean drama. My use of the word is predicated on an analogy with recent discoveries in the behaviour of subatomic particles in experiments such as those conducted in the Large Hadron Collider in Switzerland ... Within this vast machine, subatomic particles are directed towards one another by electromagnetic fields to cause high-energy particle collisions ... when sufficient energy is crammed into a sufficiently small space, particles that were not previously present can sometimes be created out of that energy ... Particle collision between two objects can produce a new object that did not previously exist ... It is my general argument that the concept of 'collision', signifying the impact of a number of forces and objects upon one another, is a useful analogy for describing and accounting for what sometimes happens to produce the phenomenon we know as 'Shakespeare'.[7]

Generated in the particle accelerator-like space of my academic department − a dynamic environment in which critical and creative forces bump against each other to 'produce a new object that did not previously exist' − I suggest that the 2005 film *Frozen* (co-written and directed by Juliet McKoen) and Jenn Ashworth's short story 'Doted' (2014) are striking Lancastrian renditions of *Hamlet* and *King Lear*. Co-scripted by Lancaster University's Jayne Steel (with Juliet McKoen), *Frozen*'s protagonist Kath Swarbrick − a thirty-three-year-old fish filleter − shares some common ground with the playwright's Danish prince. Whereas Shakespeare's privileged man has spectral encounters and roams maritime Helsingør (and beyond) to avenge his father's death,[8] *Frozen*'s working-class woman experiences visions while combing the peninsular town of Fleetwood to find out what happened to Annie, her 'Only relative, an elder half-sister who disappeared without trace two years ago'.[9] Introduced by the line 'Echoes of *King Lear* in modern-day Lancashire', Ashworth's Preston-born narrator self-consciously weaves her recollections of paternal estrangement with the play's tragic plot.[10] Royal courts and monarchical bodies are central to these Shakespearean tragedies, but factories, gender and higher education itself are at the core of what *Frozen* and 'Doted' try to do as they study contemporary culture's economic and emotional terrains.

Frozen: Shakespearean Relocations

Shortly after I arrived in Lancaster in September 2006, I sought out a copy of *Frozen* which had just been released on DVD.[11] I was impressed that one of my new colleagues was involved in this award-winning film and intrigued by the prospect of its Lancastrian setting.[12] To begin with, the film provided my first glimpse of the nearby towns of Preston and Fleetwood; ultimately, *Frozen* has had a lasting impact on my teaching and research of *Hamlet*. In *Demons, Hamlets and Femme Fatales*, her 2007 monograph which explores fictional representations of the Provisional IRA and political discord in Northern Ireland, Jayne Steel writes that *Hamlet* 'is the Ur-text of modern Britain as well as the dilemma of political action'. For Steel, 'within both British and Irish fictions, the high frequency of references to Hamlet reproduces the structure of Shakespeare's play in which a young protagonist agonizes over ethics and the tragic implications of violent political action'.[13] While *Frozen* avoids such direct references, in the 2012-13 teaching handbook for Lancaster University's first-year ENGL100 course, Steel comments that her lecture on the film 'will look at the female protagonist in *Frozen* and consider her status as a universal "Hamletian" figure who evokes grief, loss and haunted memories'.[14] Famously, *Hamlet* begins on 'A guard platform at Elsinore Castle, Denmark'[15] at midnight with 'two sentinels [at several doors]' (1.1.s.d) changing shift. Barnardo asks 'Who's there' (1.1.1), to which Francisco replies, 'Nay, answer me. Stand and unfold yourself' (1.1.1–2). In the words of Jonathan Bate:

> The mood of *Hamlet* is set by its opening exchange . . . The play creates the illusion of asking as many questions of its audience and interpreters as we may ask of it. Shakespeare won't tell us who he is or where he stands. Instead, he makes us – and our culture – reveal ourselves.[16]

Mourning and the mystery surrounding the death of a close familial member are the impetus for both the play's and the film's central figures. Like Shakespeare's prince, *Frozen*'s factory worker is embroiled in an anguished quest which scrutinises identity in comparative ways. Yet, as we shall see, the links between the texts go beyond character analysis.

Shakespearean scholars have comprehensively considered how Hamlet dramatises a fundamental ontological dilemma: 'To be or not to be; that is the question' (3.1.58). Poised on the brink of the Cartesian *cogito*, that dualistic schism between mind and body that later seventeenth-century England would eventually foreground, Shakespeare's tragedy repeatedly stages selfhood's fragile state. In his first soliloquy, the prince proclaims:

> O that this too too solid flesh would melt,
> Thaw, and resolve itself into a dew,
> Or that the Everlasting had not fixed
> His canon reverse 'gainst self-slaughter! O God, O God,
> How weary, stale, flat, and unprofitable
> Seem to me all the uses of this world! (1.2.129–34)

At the turn of the sixteenth century (the supposed period of the play's inception) Hamlet's suicidal meditation on his mechanistic body at the start of this quotation is tempered by his hasty invocation of the Church's edicts ''gainst' such actions. His prolix disquisition is in stark contrast to *Frozen*'s embodiment of grief. In the screenplay, the audience first sees Kath in her place of work, a fish-processing factory in Fleetwood: 'A long, low, white-painted shed open on one side. Rows of women in white coats, hats and scarves stand at marble slabs. They're pin-boning and filleting' (1). At the end of the working day, Kath arranges to meet her fellow fish-filleters for a drink in a local pub and the sterile factory scene gives way to The Crown's divergent location: 'Grubby velvet seats. Flock wallpaper. This pub is spit and sawdust turned swank and then gone to seed' (3). In just three pages of script and approximately four minutes of film, *Frozen*'s juxtaposed settings hint at Fleetwood's economic rise and fall. According to Patrick Maguire's 2018 *New Statesman* article:

> Fleetwood was once the third biggest fishing port in Britain but, as with dozens of northern towns, the particular industry that housed its identity has all but disappeared. Some of Fleetwood's neighbourhoods are among the most deprived in Britain. Where once a third of its population of 250,000 were employed in fishing, no full-time trawlermen remain . . . Irish Sea ferries no longer call at its port, which looms over handsome Victorian terraces.[17]

With a nod to the irony, Maguire notes that now Fleetwood's 'biggest employer [is] Fisherman's Friend – manufacturer of the eye-wateringly strong menthol throat lozenges'.[18] *Frozen*'s fish processing plant is a vivid reminder of Fleetwood's former maritime success. Moreover, with an interior design comprising 'grubby velvet' and 'flock wallpaper' as illustrations of the town's diminished aspirations, a fading opulence only emphasised by their manifestation in a pub named after a symbol of sovereign power, The Crown shows a community under ideological and financial duress.

At first glance, *Hamlet*'s landscape might seem far removed from *Frozen*'s. However, and as Lisa Hopkins makes plain, coastlines are highly relevant to the late sixteenth-century tragedy:

> *Hamlet* is a play in which the relation between sea and land is brought into sharp focus. It is always imaginatively on the shore, echoing the coastal location of the actual Helsingør. It is a play obsessed with water borders, and with their unholy transgression . . . Borders are especially important in this play because geographical borders map so directly onto eschatological ones.[19]

Undoubtedly, and as might be expected in this post-Reformation text, *Hamlet*'s investment in examining the liminal qualities of the four last things (death, judgement, heaven, and hell) is outstanding. Nonetheless, the inhabitants of Shakespeare's Elsinore are under wider material pressures than a narrow focus on the prince's personal sorrow suggests.[20] Margreta De Grazia points out that:

> [A]t his father's death, just at the point when as the only son in a patrilineal system he stands to inherit, Hamlet is dispossessed – and, as far as the court is concerned, legitimately . . . surely the loss of the kingdom affects what Hamlet has within. A prince bereft of his prospective kingdom, like any man deprived of his expected estate, must feel the injury.[21]

Once the view that 'the play is fundamentally about the Prince's political disappointment' is kept in mind,[22] *Hamlet*'s plot turns on a collapsed primogenital system and growing spatial conflict, not least in Denmark's imminent war with Norway.[23] Furthermore, the play's exploration of geographical control is not confined to terra firma. In the wake of Hamlet's accidental murder of Polonius, and under the guise of an 'especial safety' (4.3.39), Claudius acts quickly and sends the prince to England not for wellbeing but for execution by the king. The fact that Claudius can announce that his nephew 'must prepare' himself 'With fiery quickness' (4.3.42) because 'The barque is ready, and the wind at help' (4.3.43) suggests that transportation is nearby. The sea thus has a crucial role in Claudius' swift attempt to rid Denmark of its dead king's son. However, 4.6. begins with a sailor delivering a letter from Hamlet to Horatio which explains how the king's plan to have Hamlet killed in England was thwarted by sea robbers. 'Ere we were two days old at sea,' Horatio reads, 'a pirate of very warlike appointment gave us chase. Finding ourselves too slow of sail, we put on a compelled valour, and in the grapple I boarded them' (4.6.13–16).[24] While this brief epistolary description invites the audience to imagine Hamlet successfully taking control of the pirate's ship, the reported 'grapple' at sea bears traces of topical legal discussions as represented in books such as Hugo Grotius' *Mare Liberum* [The Free Sea] (1609) which examines 'the nature and extent of territorial waters'.[25] *Hamlet*'s plot succeeds because this potentially fatal journey is interrupted by a maritime skirmish impelled by the piratical prospects of financial and spatial gain.[26]

De Grazia's observations about the effects of *Hamlet*'s material politics on the prince's 'injury' are tacitly alert to ways in which sixteenth-century selfhoods are bound up with their surroundings: Hamlet's body is thus sociable rather than solitary. Philip Sidney's often-cited definition of tragedy, for example, shows how sixteenth-century microcosmic corporeality works in tandem with macrocosmic notions of the body politic:

> [H]igh and excellent Tragedy, that openeth the greatest wounds, and showeth forth the Ulcers, that are covered with Tissue; that maketh Kinges feare to be Tyrants, and Tyrants manifest their tyrannical humors; that with sturring the affects of admiration and commiseration teacheth, the uncertainty of this world; and upon howe weake foundations guilden roofes are built.[27]

For Michael Mangan, Sidney's 'fluid definition seems to suggest a conception of tragedy which is both transcendent and topical and whose effect is to be sought both in the abstract world of metaphysics and in the pragmatic world of *realpolitik*'.[28] These points are well made. Yet instead of trying to consider Sidney's observations in binary terms, it is more helpful to think of his 'fluid definitions' in the context of sixteenth-century humoralism, a generally Galenic concept enmeshing the porous somatic vessel with its wider organic surroundings. In its most straightforward form, humoralism (after the French 'humor' and the Latin 'hūmor')[29] is concerned with four kinds of fluids, black bile, phlegm, yellow bile and blood, which flow through the body. Each fluid is allied to a relative temperament – melancholic, phlegmatic, choleric and sanguine – which is tied to a seasonal characteristic: autumn (dry and cold); winter (moist and cold); summer (warm and dry) and spring (moist and warm).[30] Arthur F. Kinney neatly sums up the play's overarching Galenic context when he observes that 'Tudor medicine would describe Hamlet as melancholic . . . caused by superabundance of black bile in his body chemistry that throws health out of balance'.[31] Accordingly, the section entitled 'How melancholie altereth thise actions which rise out of the braine' in Timothy Bright's 1586 regimen *A Treatise of Melancholie* describes melancholics in the following way:

> Such persons are doubtfull, suspitious, and thereby long in deliberation, because those domesticall feares, or that internall obscuritie, causeth an opinion of daunger in outwarde affaires, where there is no cause of doubt: their dreames are fearefull: partly by reason of their fancie waking, is most occupied about feares, and terrours, which retayneth the impression in sleepe, and partly through blacke and darke fumes of melancholie, rising up to the braine, whereof the fantasie forgeth objectes, and disturbeth the sleep of melancholy persons. These persons are also subject to that kinde of suffocation in the night, which is called the mare, wherein, with some horrible vision in dreame they are halfe strangled, and intercepted of speech, though they strive to call. This happeneth through grosse melacholicke vapours in them which cause horrible and fearefull apparitions.[32]

In *Hamlet*'s case, Bright's 'persons' are realised in the guise of 'the melancholic scholar', a specific pre-modern or early modern mode of subjectivity which 'signals a transitional move from a Neoplatonic conception of object-oriented, spiritually inflected sadness . . . to a more Galenically informed model of dispositionally rooted passions'.[33] If we now return to Hamlet's apostrophe 'O, that this too too solid flesh would melt, /Thaw and resolve itself into a dew', his macabre musings align somatic denudation with distillation; human anatomy with the environment. It is impossible to discern if Hamlet's demeanour is caused by humoral imbalance or material loss. Indeed, the audience is ultimately challenged to make sense of 'wild and whirling words' (1.5.137) and the titular figure's self-proclaimed 'antic disposition' (1.5.173) for themselves.

With a title that recalls the play's investment in icy figures, for example Old Hamlet's armour which bespeaks how 'He smote the sledded Polacks on the ice' (1.1.62), or the prince's warning to Ophelia that 'be thou as chaste as ice, as pure as snow, thou shalt not escape calumny' (3.1.136–7),

Frozen inherits *Hamlet*'s preoccupation with systems of tangled signs and the relation of bodies and environments. In a visual equivalent of Barnado's 'Who's there?', the film's narrative starts with a dark flickering screen (accompanied by the low throb of Guy Michelmore's score) which asks its own audience to make sense of the image in front of them. As the camera's focus sharpens, the flicker becomes a flurry of snowflakes. In the background, a man looks out at the falling snow as the voiceover recounts:

> NOYEN (V/O): She told me about her childhood. How she
> imagined that Fleetwood was a special place,
> the only place in the whole world
> Seawater could freeze ...
> She told me about the waves. How she
> Imagined their white spray freezing, mid
> Air, then falling, very gently to pile
> Up along the tideline. When she got older
> She learnt the truth. Sea doesn't freeze.
> And those icy banks are just a thin skim
> Of hoar ice pounded by the sea and washed
> Up with the tide. But the magic of that moment of
> frozen stasis remained with her. (1)

First via sight and then by spoken word, the film calls attention to the environment ('snow', 'seawater', 'air', 'ice') and geographical location ('Fleetwood'). Rather than viewing the genre as an upper-class privilege of melancholic scholars, *Frozen* posits tragedy as an indiscriminate experience. As Kath herself puts it: 'Every second of every day we're just a step away from tragedy. Anything could happen' (14). Hamlet's ghostly father's demand 'Remember me' (1.5.91) functions as his call to action. Kath's spur is her half-sister's last known movements captured on CCTV near Fleetwood's run-down dock. In this way, *Frozen*'s spectrality is brought forth by technology not spiritual belief:

> If the ghost is the revenant ... we live in the midst of ghosts: the voice on the telephone is only ever the reproduction of a voice, an image on television or movie-screen is only ever a reproduction ... we have witnessed the successive ghostly arrivals of the space age, the answer phone, video recorder, camcorder, personal computer, email, the internet, virtual reality ... along with multiple other new forms of interaction via social media.[34]

Whereas Shakespeare's prince uses the conceit of melting flesh to convey the intensity of political/personal grief, Kath's distress – as clearly suggested by the film's title – solidifies the self and immobilises the voice. Instead of the nuanced figures of speech and industrious wordplay which are culturally indicative of Shakespearean drama, and with a trace of Michael Almereyda's cinematically reflexive *Hamlet 2000*,[35] *Frozen* relies on filmic technique to convey ineffable misery. Likewise, Kath's emotional torment is framed by industrial tropes not rhetorical flourish.

For example, when Kath fails to meet her colleagues for the after-work drink in The Crown, her best friend Elsie returns to the factory to look for her:

> EXT. FISH PROCESSING FACTORY – FREEZER ROOM. EVE.
> Elsie peers round the freezer door, squints through the
> dim violet light. Rows of dexion shelves stacked with
> packets of fish.
> ELSIE: Kath?
> Silence. Her breath steams in the cold.
> ELSIE (CONT'D): Kath? You there?
> Again, silence.
> Elsie hesitates. She's about to leave when something
> changes her mind.
> She goes into the freezer, down the aisle, all the while
> Looking left then right.
> When she reaches the final aisle she GASPS.
> On the floor, Kath lies curled in a tight little ball.
> FADE TO BLACK (4)

Albeit for a beat, and as with the earlier frame, the audience is left in darkness. The next scene shows Kath in a counselling session with Noyen, a High Anglican vicar of a local church and, as it turns out, the narrator of the film's voiceover. The 'rest' may not quite be 'silence' (*Hamlet* 5.2.300), but Kath's reticence to speak is a key component of their conversation. The screenplay emphasises 'There is silence' (5) and the ensuing dialogue takes up that trope:

> NOYEN: You seem to be finding it difficult to talk, Kath. Why is that?
> Kath stares down at her hands, doesn't answer. A long pause.
> NOYEN tries again.

NOYEN (CONT'D): Could you tell me what you're feeling?
Kath knots her fingers for a moment then mimics him, angrily.
KATH: What I'm 'feeling' is that I don't bloody wanna be here.
NOYEN: I really do empathise with you. You feel the hospital forced you into coming. But maybe you could try talking a little bit? (5)

In spite of the fact that 'She's not used to talking about herself' (5), Kath begins to recount how her family 'had this hamster once. Dad fetched it when he was in one of his good moods' (5). More information about Kath's familial background is disclosed when Noyen records the meeting in his notebook. His voiceover describes how she was:

> Hospitalised for two days. Told the
> doctors that it 'seemed very simple to
> curl up and drift away into the cold'.
> Alcoholic father left the family home
> when she was eight. Mother died seven
> years later from breast cancer. Only
> relative, an elder half-sister
> disappeared without trace two years ago.
> Obsessive thinking, chronic grieving, the
> feeling of a frozen void within. (8)

The plot overtly follows Kath but her story takes its shape from Noyen's perspective. Kath's grief leads her to locate the CCTV videotape which may (or may not) contain an image of Annie and to apparently experience visions (or hallucinations) of a woman on a distant shoreline. Subsequent counselling sessions include the discussion of these seemingly preternatural events and provide Noyen with the opportunity to talk to Kath about religious and mythological explanations of death and its aftermath. A dialogue between Noyen and his counselling supervisor Donald provides a rich commentary on Kath's case and, markedly, the gender politics of diagnosis:

NOYEN: In the thirteenth century she'd have been exalted as a visionary.
DONALD: (dryly) Or condemned as a witch.
NOYEN: But a figure on the other side of a riverbank? A ferry crossing?
DONALD: Classic Jungian archetypes floating in the zeitgeist.
NOYEN: For a fish filleter with two GCSEs? (36)

Kath may be a 'Hamletian figure', but she is evidently not a university-educated '*Hamlet*ian figure' with a backstory that includes a Wittenberg-like institution of higher education. She is not a 'melancholic scholar'; that role is more aptly Noyen's. Nonetheless, Shakespeare's play and Steel's co-written script 'collide' in noteworthy ways.

In the end, perhaps storytelling is *Frozen*'s most Shakespearean trope of all. Shakespeare's *Hamlet* is an old story – that of Amleth in Saxo Grammaticus' late twelfth-century *Gesta Danorum* – transposed for late sixteenth-century English theatrical reception. In his penultimate speech, Hamlet asks Horatio to 'draw thy breath in pain / To tell my story' (5.2.290–1); *Frozen* upholds that Shakespearean impetus to rewrite a Hamletian figure for its own period and location of production. In so doing, the film asks us to think about the material conditions in which stories are told, recorded and – importantly – where and by whom.

'Doted': Lancastrian Education

Frozen's interests in North West England's declining industry, economy and social mobility are considered far more visibly in Ashworth's short story. Like *Hamlet*, Shakespeare's *King Lear* is derived from a twelfth-century chronicle, on this occasion Geoffrey of Monmouth's *Historia Regum Britanni*. Whereas *Hamlet*'s dramaturgy and *Frozen*'s cinematography exploit the interplay between verbal and non-verbal signs which are obviously absent in the prose source texts, the first-person narrator of 'Doted' revels in the slipperiness of language and close textual analysis. Given its publication in a 2014 UK issue of the literary magazine *Litro* 'devoted to the Bard, as a special gift for his 450th birthday'[36], combined with its direct references to *King Lear*, the short story clearly has a firmer link to Shakespeare than the earlier film. It begins:

> *Doted* is a strange word isn't it? On the one hand it means a fondness or an uncritical affection: the feeling an adult might have for a small child or a pet dog. A couple newly in love might dote on each other too. When our hypothetical couple get to know each other better this doting wears off because the honeymoon stage is just a stage and once it passes there's a tendency for the cold light of day to get into things. The relationship is never the same again; scientists on the internet say you get two years: tops. That first doting is immaturity and foolishness. A kind of infirmity; a lack of sound judgement: caused by love. The word is related to *dotage*; an archaic expression denoting madness, senility, dementia. When Lear

curses Goneril, first with sterility [1.4.240] and then, if she must have a child with an ungrateful one [1.4.243–52] she dismisses his ranting as merely a product of his dotage. Her father's cursing doesn't count because he's too fond and too old. (21)

There is more to be said about the narrator's opening summary of Goneril's rejection of Lear's curses 'as merely a product of his dotage'. Ashworth's titular keyword appears in just two Shakespearean texts: *Henry IV, Part II* (c.1596–7) and *The Rape of Lucrece* (1594). In the history play, the Earl of Westmorland uses the term in the penultimate act to describe how England's 'prayers and love / Were set on Hereford, whom they doted on' (4.1.136). Somewhat differently, the poem invokes the word as an immediate prelude to Tarquin's violent seizure of Lucrece: 'What he beheld, on that he firmly doted, / And in his will his wilful eye he tired' (415–16). Goneril's repetition of the allied (and slightly more common Shakespearean term)[37] 'dotage' in 1.4.256, 1.4.289 and 2.2.362 drives an important dramaturgical dynamic.[38]

'Dotage' is Goneril's word. She is the only character to use it in the play. Tracking its use says something about her increasing agency in the aftermath of her father's abdication and the notorious test he sets his daughters to establish how 'the division of the kingdom' (1.1.3–4) will be shared among them. When France and Cordelia are exiled at the end of 1.1, Goneril considers how Lear's behaviour is age related. Alone with Regan, she implores 'You see how full of changes his age is. *The observation we have made of it hath been little* [my emphasis]. He always loved our sister most, and with what poor judgement he hath now cast her off appears too grossly' (1.1.284–7). With some surprise yet surety at a newly gained perspective, Goneril points out Lear's infirmity to her younger sister. Soon after, she extends this evaluation and observes that as a younger man Lear 'hath been but rash' but his extant impetuosity is now accompanied by 'the unruly waywardness that infirm and choleric years bring with them' (1.2.290–4). In performance, there are many ways in which Goneril might deliver these lines. However, when read in swift succession these two episodes function as the eldest daughter's cool assessment of her father's condition. Lear's desire to divest himself of monarchical responsibilities while retaining symbols of kingly authority (chiefly his Fool, his rowdy entourage of a hundred knights and the expectation that he will retain absolute power) is resistant to Goneril's attempts to address Lear's attack upon her 'gentleman' (1.3.1) and keep order in her household. Lear's misogynistic malediction brings forth her first two uses of 'dotage' as she discusses his outburst with Albany. Goneril's third and final use of the term takes place in Regan's court when Lear rails at the sight of a disguised Kent in the stocks and takes particular issue with his eldest daughter. She responds:

> How have I offended?
> All's not offence that indiscretion finds
> And dotage terms so. (2.2.360–2)

At this point, Goneril's evolving appraisal of her father's behaviour has implicitly established a template for the narrator to review her own experience via inspection, diagnosis and definition.

As Ashworth's narrator insinuates, Goneril's reiterated use of 'dotage' to simultaneously denote immaturity and senility serves as the catalyst for an account of Lancastrian family life. Markedly, though, in the short story, it is the titular word 'Doted' – not 'dotage' – which steers the reader through the subsequent precis of the narrator's difficult relationship with her father, from childhood dialogue, to physical and psychological abuse, to forced and then self-imposed exile. 'It is', the narrator explains, 'the actual word Mum uses to batter back the memories I have' (24). An etymological link is thus forged between Goneril and the narrator's mother. And maternal lines matter for this story. 'When I was little', the narrator recalls at the start of her personal memoir:

> I was close to mum's parents and never met Dad's. It came as a surprise to me that they were dead. When I found out, I asked him when and how his Mum went. I'd never known anyone who had died before. 'It happened some time previously and from a lack of breath,' he said. Then he slapped at his leg and forced out a laugh. It was long and loud: a machine gun rattle. When I was really little, I used to join in the laughing. He had a reputation amongst people who didn't know him, for being a good fun kind of guy. Life and soul. Something like that. When I was a little older, *I noticed something* [my emphasis]. This laugh, be it ever so loud and out of control, was something he performed with his eyes open. He kept his eyes on you because he wanted to make sure, perhaps, that you got the joke. That there would be no more questions. (21)

Like Goneril, the narrator is the eldest daughter (but with a sister and brother rather than two sisters); also like Goneril, she eventually notices her father's behaviour. In this case, it is not aged behaviour which has given the daughter cause for comment. Rather, it is the way in which her father laughs 'with his eyes open' that signals the end of their rapport. By comparison with Cordelia whose own tragedy begins because she 'cannot heave [her] heart into [her] mouth' (1.1.89–90), the narrator's incessant 'demanding infuriated' (23) her father. His response is increasing acts of violence towards the growing child.

In their jointly authored study of *King Lear*, Lesley Koredecki and Karla Koskinen 'argue that the actions of all three daughters, like most of the men in the play, are a result of Lear's erratic and irresponsible behaviour in the first scene'.[39] This is not to say that Lear is held wholly accountable for his actions:

> The character of an increasingly frail man, living through the demise of his body and mind in the story has always elicited great sympathy. The more the all-too-human Lear is pitied, the more his perceived adversaries, first Cordelia, then Goneril and Regan, become guilty.[40]

Indeed, feminist criticism is keen to unpack the social and cultural contexts which allow Lear to act upon his daughters in such damaging ways. 'Feminist thought', Kathleen McCluskie argues, 'need not restrict itself to privileging the woman's part or to special pleading on behalf of female characters'. 'It can', she says, 'be equally well served by making a text reveal the conditions in which a particular ideology of femininity functions and by both revealing and subverting the hold which such an ideology has for readers both female and male.'[41] Lear's line in the penultimate act, 'They told me I was everything' (4.5.102), provides the possibility for an avowedly feminist critic to consider who 'they' are. Writing in the wake of such feminist perspectives, Ashworth's reflective narrator is not immune to the cultural and social impact on her father:

> Despite the laughing Dad never seemed that happy. He worked twelve hour shifts in a factory that turned plain cardboard boxes into waxed cardboard and turned the waxed cardboard into fish finger boxes (I only know this because Grandad worked there too). Dad complained about the long hours and having to come home to an untidy house full of children that were rapidly outgrowing it. (22)

Fleetwood's faltering maritime economy frames *Frozen*'s plot. Likewise, 'Doted' is underpinned by related concerns. Two generations of the narrator's patrilineal ancestors have been employed by the Preston-based 'paper factory' (23) that services the North West fish-processing market by providing packaging for fish fingers. The family home – 'a small terraced house' which 'lay in a warren of terraced houses just like it, between the town centre and one of the arterial roads out of Preston to the south' (22) – is described in terms that mirror Fleetwood's and Preston's proclivity for mass production. The house itself is in a liminal position between the 'nature reserves' on 'the south bank of the Ribble and the dirty footpath alongside the north bank of the river which led along it to the docks' (22). The inhabitants can thus move towards the 'south' and 'nature' or towards 'north' and the 'docks'. There is little sense of a world beyond these immediate binaries and Lear's Lancastrian avatar seems immersed in, and fashioned by, the North West's industrial economy. Crucially, the narrator asks her father about his favourite subject at school. His rejoinder, 'noughts and crosses' (21), encapsulates the local binary sensibility of absence and presence, a configuration of being and not being which seems to underpin the narrator's future plans. She states:

> I go to the best Uni that will take me and study English Literature because he can barely read and it will piss him off. But all reading *King Lear* does is make me want to call Mum. (23)

Studying Shakespeare in an institution of higher education provides the means for this Lancastrian figure to respond to her immediate familial heritage. While close textual analysis does not resolve her personal paternal encounters – notably 'all reading *King Lear* does is make [her] want to call Mum', a figure wholly missing in Shakespeare's work – the play provides the catalyst for recounting the past.

Lancastrian Shakespeares

Produced in Lancaster University's geographical, cultural and intellectual environs, this essay has proposed that *Frozen* and 'Doted' chime with the discourses of Lancastrian Shakespeare and the ideological concerns of North West England. During the decade or so that divides Steel's co-scripted film and Ashworth's short story, the humanities have come under growing pressure to prove their societal worth. As site-specific critical and creative 'collisions', Lancastrian Shakespeares show how the formal study of and writing about literature – canonical, contemporary or otherwise – enables sustained and multiple interrogations of local political and emotional landscapes.

Notes

This essay is dedicated to the memory of our much-missed colleague Dr Jayne Steel (1958–2015). I would like to thank Adam Hansen for his extremely cogent and careful comments on my chapter.

1. The conference took place at Lancaster University and Hoghton Tower, Preston, Lancashire.
2. Alison Findlay and Richard Dutton, 'Introduction', in Richard Dutton, Alison Findlay and Richard Wilson (eds), *Region, Religion and Patronage: Lancastrian Shakespeare* (Cambridge: Cambridge University Press, 2003), 1–31, 1. Richard Dutton and Richard Wilson left Lancaster University in 2003 and 2005 respectively.
3. According to E. A. Honigmann, 'Apart from the records of his baptism (26 April 1564) and licence to marry (27 November 1582), and of the christening of his children, Susanna (26 May 1583) and the twins Hamnet and Judith (2 February 1585), the rest is silence. Then Robert Greene attacked Shakespeare in September 1592, as an upstart crow in the theatrical world'; see E. A. Honigmann, *Shakespeare: The 'Lost Years'*, second edition (Manchester: Manchester University Press, 1998), 1.
4. Richard Dutton, Alison Findlay and Richard Wilson (eds), *Theatre and Religion: Lancastrian Shakespeare* (Cambridge: Cambridge University Press, 2003).
5. See also Richard Wilson, *Secret Shakespeare: Studies in Theatre, Religion and Resistance* (Manchester: Manchester University Press, 2004).
6. Findlay and Dutton, 'Introduction', 1.
7. Graham Holderness, *Tales from Shakespeare: Creative Collisions* (Cambridge: Cambridge University Press, 2014), 16–17.
8. As Pat Reid writes, 'Helsingør is basically a small maritime town, with sailing boats moored in the harbour'; see Pat Reid, 'I Capture the Castle', *Shakespeare Magazine*, 14 (2018). Available at: <https://issuu.com/shakespearemagazine/docs/shakespeare_magazine_14/5> (last accessed 28 July 2018), 56–9, 58.
9. All quotations are from an unpublished draft screenplay that Jayne Steel and I used for our lectures on *Hamlet* and *Frozen* which were given as part of Lancaster University's first-year English Literature course (ENGL100) between 2008 and 2012. The film *Frozen* was produced by Liminal Films, Shoreline Films, Freedonia Films, Freedonia Producciones S. L., RS Productions and Zentropa Entertainments. Distributed by Guerilla Films, *Frozen* had its UK theatrical release in 2005. See further information on IMDb. Available at: <https://www.imdb.com/title/tt0376606/companycredits?ref_=tt_dt_co> (last accessed 6 August 2018).
10. Jenn Ashworth, 'Doted', *Litro*, 133 (2014), 21–7. Subsequent references are given in the text. Ashworth has reflected on her own 'quasi-fictional-autobiographical-reworking' of *King Lear* in her 2019 memoir *Notes Made While Falling* (London: Goldsmiths Press), 137.

11. Distributed by Guerilla Films, *Frozen* was released in the UK on all media in 2006. See further information on IMDb. Available at: <https://www.imdb.com/title/tt0376606/companycredits?ref_=tt_dt_co> (last accessed 6 August 2018).
12. *Frozen* won five awards including the Audience Award at the Commonwealth Film Festival (2005).
13. Jayne Steel, *Demons, Hamlets and Femme Fatales* (Oxford: Peter Lang, 2007), 112, 115.
14. Part One Handbook: Department of English and Creative Writing, Lancaster University (unpublished, 2012), 62.
15. All quotations from the play are from William Shakespeare, 'The Tragedy of Hamlet, Prince of Denmark', Stephen Greenblatt, Walter Cohen, Jean. E. Howard and Katharine Eisaman Maus (eds), *The Norton Shakespeare*, second edition (New York, W.W. Norton, 2008), 1683–1784, 1696, n.1. Subsequent references are given in the text.
16. Jonathan Bate, 'Introduction', in Jonathan Bate and Eric Rasmussen (eds), *The RSC Shakespeare: Hamlet* (Basingstoke: Macmillan, 2008), 1.
17. Patrick Maguire, 'Crumbling Britain: Lancashire's lost world of deep-sea fishing', *New Statesman* (23 May 2018). Available at: <https://www.newstatesman.com/politics/uk/2018/05/crumbling-britain-lancashire-s-lost-world-deep-sea-fishing> (last accessed 1 June 2018), paras 1–2.
18. Ibid. para 1.
19. Lisa Hopkins, *Shakespeare on the Edge: Bordercrossing in the Tragedies and the Henriad* (Aldershot: Ashgate, 2005), 40.
20. Margreta de Grazia remarks that 'Hamlet's disengagement from the land-driven plot is the very precondition of the modernity ascribed to him in 1800'; see *Hamlet without Hamlet* (Cambridge: Cambridge University Press, 2007), 4.
21. Ibid. 1–2.
22. John Curran, 'Margreta de Grazia: *Hamlet without Hamlet*', *Journal of British Studies*, 46: 4 (2007), 930–2, 931.
23. Nearly a decade after de Grazia's observation, Emily C. Bartels' important discussion of 'gender and race in *Hamlet*' comments that 'the political frame is routinely excised from productions as somehow unimportant'; see Emily C. Bartels, 'Identifying the Dane: gender and race in *Hamlet*', in Valerie Traub (ed.), *The Oxford Handbook of Shakespeare and Embodiment* (Oxford: Oxford University Press, 2016), 197–210, 198.
24. Claire Jowitt contextualises this episode in terms of 'Pirates and politics'; see *The Culture of Piracy, 1580–1630: English Literature and Seaborne Crime* (Aldershot: Ashgate, 2010), 130–3.
25. Hopkins, *Shakespeare on the Edge*, 39.
26. In the Introduction to her 2007 edited collection *Pirates? The Politics of Plunder*, Claire Jowitt states that 'In Shakespeare's plays, pirates play small but important roles: in *Measure for Measure, Hamlet, Twelfth Night, Pericles, The*

Merchant of Venice, for example, pirates intervene in the action in ways crucial to each play's plot development'; see Jowitt (ed.), *Pirates? The Politics of Plunder* (Basingstoke: Palgrave, 2007), 3.
27. Philip Sidney, *An Apologie for Poetrie* (1595), F3v-4r.
28. Michael Mangan, *A Preface to Shakespeare's Tragedies* (London: Longman, 1991), 65.
29. humour / humor, n. *OED Online*. Available at: <http://www.oed.com.ezproxy.lancs.ac.uk/view/Entry/89416#eid1142244> (last accessed 30 July 2018).
30. For a detailed discussion of humoralism's significance for Shakespearean thought and *Hamlet* in particular, see Gail Kern Paster, *Humoring the Body: Emotions and the Shakespearean Stage* (Chicago: University of Chicago Press, 2004), 25–76. See also the collection of essays in Valerie Traub (ed.), *The Oxford Handbook of Shakespeare and Embodiment* (Oxford: Oxford University Press, 2016).
31. Arthur F. Kinney, 'Introduction', in Arthur F. Kinney (ed.), *Hamlet: New Critical Essays* (London: Routledge, 2002), 1–70, 13.
32. Timothy Bright, *A Treatise of Melancholie* (1586), 131.
33. Douglas Trevor, *The Poetics of Melancholy in Early Modern England* (Cambridge: Cambridge University Press, 2004), 5.
34. Andrew Bennett and Nicholas Royle, *Introduction to Literature, Criticism and Theory*, fifth edition (London: Longman, 2016), 187–8.
35. New York: Miramax, 2000.
36. Dan Coxon, 'Editorial', *Litro*, 133 (2014), 2–3, 2.
37. *A Midsummer Night's Dream* (c.1594–6) 4.1.44; *Much Ado About Nothing* (c.1598) 2.3.152 and 2.3.92–3; *Othello* (1602–3) 4.1.27; *Timon of Athens* (1605–8) 3.6.98; *Antony and Cleopatra* (1606–7) 1.1.1 and 1.2.106.
38. All quotations from the play are from William Shakespeare, 'The Tragedy of King Lear', in Stephen Greenblatt, Walter Cohen, Jean. E. Howard and Katharine Eisaman Maus (eds), *The Norton Shakespeare*, second edition (New York, W.W. Norton, 2008), 2325–67. Subsequent references are given in the text.
39. Lesley Koredecki and Karla Koskinen, *Re-Visioning Lear's Daughters: Testing Feminist Criticism and Theory* (Manchester: Manchester University Press, 2010), 2.
40. Koredecki and Koskinen, *Re-Visioning*, 17.
41. Kathleen McCluskie, 'The patriarchal Bard: feminist criticism and Shakespeare: *King Lear* and *Measure for Measure*', in Jonathan Dollimore and Alan Sinfield (eds), *Political Shakespeare*, second edition (Manchester: Manchester University Press, 1994), 88–108, 106.

12

Shakespeare's Cheek: *Macbeth*, *Dunsinane* and the Jacobean Condition

James Loxley

What kind of sequel to *Macbeth* can't, or won't, bring itself to mention its predecessor's name? Not once in David Greig's *Dunsinane* is the titular king of Shakespeare's drama mentioned by name. To the English soldiers of the play's early scenes he is merely 'the tyrant', echoing the terms through which Shakespeare delineates his fabled usurper; to his widow, sat beside his corpse, he is first 'a good king', then, repeated, 'my king'.[1] Even in the stage directions the name does not appear: 'Gruach sits with the body of the old king', Greig writes.[2] The occlusion here is total, even if its significance isn't obvious. Is it, perhaps, a metatheatrical echo of the superstition that has those who can't bring themselves to utter the unlucky name reach for the periphrastic alternative, 'the Scottish Play'? Or does it, instead, mark something awkward in this play's relationship to its predecessor, the dramatic forebear which is ever present, unignorable but somehow unnameable?

This chapter is concerned with the nature of this relationship, with the ways in which critics have sought to frame it, and with the kinds of articulation between texts that it prompts us to register. For the play's first reviewers, witnessing it on the stage of the Hampstead Theatre in London in February 2010, it was most readily readable as an allegory of (neo)liberal interventionism in the Balkans, Afghanistan and – most darkly – Iraq. Michael Billington, for example, noted that its 'attack on the danger of military intervention [is] highly topical', while Dominic Cavendish went so far as to suggest that 'Greig overplays the inescapable parallels between the civilising mission then and the stricken project to win hearts and minds in Afghanistan'.[3] Greig himself, in a 2015 interview, put it quite plainly:

It was all about Iraq, and then Afghanistan. I saw a production of *Macbeth* around the time Saddam's statue had been pulled down in 2003, and I thought the interesting thing was not the toppling but what happens afterwards.[4]

In one of the earliest and most acute academic responses to *Dunsinane*, Clare Wallace noted the way in which the play's allegorical framing worked as a strategy of displacement.[5] Considering the play as allegory, its Scottish setting and relationship with Shakespeare are reduced in significance – it is not, in a fundamental sense, 'about' either. It is Scottish solely by coincidence – had the production Greig saw in 2003 been something other than *Macbeth*, he would have had another vehicle for his allegory.

There is plenty in the play to support such a view: as well as the failure or refusal to name Macbeth, or *Macbeth*, it shows a forthright disregard for any kind of continuity with its predecessor. Lady Macbeth is not dead, and she has a living child – both counter-facts that Greig doesn't even attempt to explain. Furthermore, while the Scotland we are shown owes something to common perceptions of the country – most obviously, the supposed inclemency of its weather, as Billington notes – it is at other times rendered in a manner redolent of orientalist visions of the mysterious and dangerous other. For much of the time we see it through the eyes of a verse-speaking choric English soldier, to whom it becomes readily knowable only as unknowable, as a landscape and people that merely invert the certainties of a known world, which is here called England:

> And we began to wonder what sort of country this is
> Where everything that in England was normal –
> Summer, land, beer, a house, a bed – for example –
> In Scotland – that thing would turn out to be made of water –
> This is what you learn here – nothing is solid.[6]

If this is the invader's view, it is also one that the play lets its key Scottish figures articulate. For Malcolm, the Anglicised king called upon to interpret Scotland to his English allies, the nation is not susceptible to being grasped through the 'insistent literalness' shown by the English general, Siward.[7] As he says to him: 'the thinking in this country is so full of traps, you have to walk around in such circular paths, sometimes I forget that another type of thinking even exists'.[8] But Malcolm is not being straight with his ally. Indeed, he manipulates the Englishman's discomfort, disrupting Siward's cognitive and practical grasp of the situation with his performance of a disorientating alterity which appears to have its roots in his clear perception of his own *realpolitikal* interests.

To counterpoint Malcolm's forked tongue the play gives us Gruach, the imprisoned queen and, briefly, Siward's lover. Here, again, orientalist tropes are in play, and again with a degree of self-consciousness on the part of the Scottish character. Gruach's seduction of Siward presents her as a figure of the feminised exotic, a 'witch' whom Siward nonetheless finds 'captivating'.[9] Her difficult alterity is enacted most through her use of Gaelic (left untranslated for a non-Gaelic-speaking audience in the original productions), and the way in which she contrasts this language with English. As she says in one encounter:

> Your English is a woodworker's tool.
> Siward.
> Hello, goodbye, that tree is green,
> Simple matters.
> A soldier's language sent out to capture the world in words.
> Always trying to describe.
> Throw words at the tree and eventually you'll force me to see the tree just as you see it.
> We long since gave up believing in descriptions.
> Our language is the forest.[10]

Here, the valorisation of English and Gaelic not just as different languages but as different kinds of language – the one given over to the instrumental rationality of 'capturing the world', the other by contrast a tongue of symbol, allusion and song – restates the antagonism between the invader and his captive in the epistemological and aesthetic terms of orientalism and its critics. Like Malcolm, Gruach performs Scotland's exoticism, as if for a tourist. Her seduction of Siward is an act of resistance, and imbued with a rationale of its own.

So to some extent *Dunsinane* takes the encounter between England and Scotland and empties it out to work through the past and present of the modern West's colonial and neo-colonial engagement with its Eastern others. This 'Scotland', of course, doesn't exist – indeed, such an allegorical approach actually occludes Scotland's place on the other side of that engagement. As Graham Saunders has noted, any attempt to identify this figurative Scotland with the historical nation quickly runs into problems.[11] But it's also clear that critics understand this staging of the relationship between Scotland and England to be more than allegory – to have some purchase on the sometimes fraught historical relationship between two of Britain's three kingdoms. Ariel Watson, for example, states bluntly that the play is 'about the historical English presence in Scotland', while Saunders argues that it 'is more a play about Scotland's relationship to England' than it is an allegory of Western interventions in the contemporary middle east.[12] Victoria Price has suggested that its meaning and significance changed through spatio-temporal transposition: in London in 2010 the allegorical approach seemed to be the core of things, but revived in Edinburgh in May 2011, in the immediate aftermath of a Scottish National Party landslide which put the prospect of a referendum on Scottish independence firmly on the table, the vehicle intrudes somewhat on the tenor.[13]

It might be thought that in this case the play would enforce upon us an understanding of the Anglo-Scottish relationship as colonial, precisely in the way that Saunders and others have suggested is problematic.[14] But this need not be the case. The mainstream of the movement for Scottish independence that crystallised in the long approach to the referendum of 2014, which Greig supported, did not opt for this kind of framing, and public figures who used the language of coloniality to articulate the case for independence – most notably, Alasdair Gray – found themselves challenged not just by their opponents but also by their own side.[15] Given the extent to which Gruach and Malcolm are in their own distinctive ways both self-consciously playing 'the native' for Siward, acting out the role that the colonial project both expects from, and fears of, its subjects, then a rather more nuanced understanding of the cultural politics of *Dunsinane* becomes possible. Invader and native becomes not the frame for understanding the interactions between the English and the Scots in the play but rather one way in which those cast as 'natives' enact their complicated, indirect, constrained resistance to the power relationship embodied in such casting.

To this extent, then, the play's presentation of Anglo-Scottish relations does not seek to invoke the model of colonialism but instead poses a question about what Scotland is, was, or might be, and who gets to say so. It's interesting, for example, that even though he is alert to the semantic complexity of the play's Scotland, Michael Billington concludes his review with a definitive commonplace: 'Greig also reminds us that Scotland is so contradictory that only one generalisation about it remains permanently true: it's damnably cold'.[16]

But who 'reminds' us of this fact that we, presumably, already knew? Billington is here paraphrasing something said to Siward by Malcolm, as he deploys his disorientating sleight of tongue on his English enabler:

> It's quite ridiculous, isn't it? I'm King of this country and even I don't understand it. Sometimes I think you could be born in this country. Live in it all your life. Study it. Travel the length and breadth of it. And still – if someone asked you – to describe it – all you'd be able to say about it without fear of contradiction is – 'it's cold'.[17]

There is an irony here, though, that Billington's appropriation of Malcolm's sentiment reproduces. The play itself reiterates it, now in the voice of the choric English soldier, at the opening of Scene Two. The English lieutenant Egham repeats it a few lines later.[18] And it lurks in the background of what Malcolm has to say of 'lovely England' in the same scene.[19] As he reminds Siward:

> I was raised in England – in those lovely oak woods where everything is sun-dappled and the forests are full of wild boar and deer and the tables always full of beer and ham – but here we are rock, bog, forest and loch.[20]

Malcolm's Scotland, then, is filtered through his associations with and attachments to England. He is fated to Scotland, but he cannot help but see it at least in part from the outside, with Anglicised eyes. It is this equivocation of perspective that gets lost in Billington's English echo of his insistence on Scotland's coldness. Malcolm is Scottish, but Scottishness nonetheless obtrudes upon him, in blunt, brute terms – just as it does upon the outsiders who come to it. So Malcolm is very much aware of his Scottishness, and its definition through the perceptions of English others even when at home. And for all her difference from her Scottish opponent, Gruach's acutely self-conscious bilingualism confers a similar position on her: there is, of course, a profound asymmetry in a situation in which she can speak Siward's language, but he can't speak hers.

It is in this sense that the play's Scottishness comes most vividly into consideration. To follow on from *Macbeth* is to follow on from the 'Scottish play', to inherit the way in which that work is marked by a Scottishness that comes to it from elsewhere. Greig himself remarked on the strange fact that 'unquestionably the greatest Scottish play was written by the great English playwright'.[21] To this extent, Greig's play is continuous with the kinds of effort to rework the Shakespearean inheritance that we find, for example, in the 1976 translation of a fragment of *Macbeth* into Scots by Edwin Morgan, and the full translations into the same language by Robin Lorimer and David Purves, both of which were published in 1992.[22] Lorimer's translation had to wait twenty years for its first full production by Edinburgh Theatre Arts in May 2012; it was then included in the RSC's Open Stages collaboration with amateur theatre companies that summer, timed to coincide with the London Olympics. These endeavours were matched by the performance in both Glasgow and Edinburgh of Iain MacDhòmhnaill's Gaelic translation of the play, *MacBheatha*, in 2013–14.[23] In his preface to Purves' translation, Paul Scott makes the political resonance of the work clear. This and other translations into Scots of canonical works of Western literature are:

> [P]art of a deliberate and necessary effort to restore Scots and Scottish poetry to the mainstream of European thought and literature and enhance its range and status. This version of *Macbeth* is a notable contribution to this endeavour, even if we have to wait until we have a national theatre before we see it on a stage.[24]

By the second decade of the twenty-first century, that future had arrived, if perhaps not in the form anticipated by Scott or Purves: *Dunsinane* was staged in Edinburgh under the auspices of the National Theatre of Scotland, a cultural development definitive of post-devolutionary institution-building. Within this context, the play's relation to its key intertext can't help but resonate with the ways in which the politics of Scottishness were finding determinate cultural forms.

As I have noted above, that relation is not one of continuity, nor even perhaps contiguity. There is, nonetheless, closeness: *Dunsinane* includes echoes and allusions which mark its deep familiarity with its Shakespearean predecessor. For example, in the opening scene the wounded Egham calls repeatedly for the 'surgeon' (17–18), just as Duncan instructs his attendants to summon 'surgeons' for the bleeding captain who has recounted the victory over Macdonald and his Norwegian allies (Shakespeare, 1.2.44).[25] When Siward hears of his son's death he asks, 'Where's the wound?' just as Shakespeare's Siward enquires 'Had he his hurts before [i.e. on his front]?' when hearing the same news.[26] For both characters, the confirmation that the young man died facing his enemy is enough. Siward himself parallels Macbeth in his tortured journey from warrior to butcher. Malcolm's address to his assembled nobles, stressing as it does the vices of his rule, echoes the encounter between Malcolm and Macduff at the English court in 4.3.[27] When Siward, in the same scene, says 'It's unequivocal' of McAlpin's statement that 'there can be no peace as long as the Queen remains in Dunsinane', the play alludes to the interest in equivocation shown, most notably, by Shakespeare's Porter — though we should note that this is just the most explicit reference to the preoccupation with 'imperfect speakers' which marks *Macbeth* and is a prominent thematic element in Greig's sequel.[28]

Such likenesses, though, coexist with profound narrative discontinuities, which are themselves shaped by the histories of Macbeth and his reign that Shakespeare's apparently authoritative narrative has displaced. As elsewhere in his works, Shakespeare is primarily informed by Holinshed's *Chronicles*, which is itself drawing on Hector Boece for much of its Scottish history. In naming the queen Gruach, and giving her a son named Lulach — as opposed to Holinshed's identification of one 'Lugtake surnamed the foole' as Macbeth's son or cousin, and would-be successor — Greig is instead drawing on Andrew of Wyntoun and John of Fordun's fourteenth- and fifteenth-century chronicles of Scottish history — sources overlooked or ignored by Holinshed.[29] As historians of the medieval and early modern period have argued, the profound incompatibilities between different versions of the chronicles recording English and Scottish histories were always infused with an acutely political charge, since English claims to suzerainty over Scotland were grounded in the mythic history of Brutus most memorably set out by Geoffrey of Monmouth.[30] Scots chroniclers and historians instead promoted a vision of intact Scottish sovereignty traceable to King Fergus, invoking a genealogy and timeline incommensurable with the English narrative.[31] These differences were instantiated in the Edinburgh festivities arranged for the coronation of Charles I in 1633, when portraits by George Jamesone of a long line of 109 Scottish kings, mythic and historical, decorated the processional route, and then again in the decoration of the restored and rebuilt Palace of Holyroodhouse in the 1670s with a similar series of 110 portraits painted by Jacob de Wet, at precisely the point when the veracity of the established chronicle histories was being vigorously queried — it was their value as symbols of sovereignty that mattered more than adequation to new notions of historical fact.[32] They are even echoed in the hugely popular histories of England and Scotland written by Henrietta Marshall in the early twentieth century, which remained influential and in print for decades (her history of England was indeed used, in an abridged version, as a state school textbook between the wars).[33] The genealogies of England and Scotland presented in these two works are entirely incompatible with each other, reflecting the unresolved agonistics at the heart of Britain's mythic history. (It is pertinent, in this context, to note that Marshall herself was a Scot, that her original publisher had offices in both Edinburgh and London, and that when her history of England was twice republished in London in the early twenty-first century its subtitle had been altered to 'a history of *Britain* for boys and girls' (my emphasis), despite the content being unchanged).[34] The Scottish sense that *national* history, in particular, is contested is thus deep-rooted. It is also not necessarily a partisan, nationalist perception: on the thousandth anniversary of Macbeth's birth, it was the Conservative MSP Alex Johnstone who tabled a Holyrood motion 'regret[ting] that Macbeth is misportrayed when he was a successful Scottish king'.[35]

For Robert Crawford, the setting of Shakespeare's play is a prime instance of what he calls 'England's Scotland', a place and nation imagined from an insistently Anglocentric viewpoint. This Scotland is 'linked to perverse inversions, wildness, and disorder'; it is 'a country that is ruinously riven, unnaturally governed, supernaturally disordered, and can be saved only by English orderliness and intervention'.[36] It is, in fact, the same kind of neo-colonial framing of the Anglo-Scottish relationship that we see in *Dunsinane*: as I've noted above, both Malcolm and Gruach work out some space for themselves through their familiarity with the dominant English perceptions of them and their country to which the play readily gives voice. So one of the ways in which the two plays' intertextual relationship operates positions Greig as the subaltern Scot to Shakespeare's English general. In which case, Greig's familiarity with and demurral from Shakespeare's *Macbeth* becomes exactly the kind of intimate entanglement that we see played out consistently in *Dunsinane*, where the antagonism or power play between characters and parties is squeezed into the intimate space of alliance or seduction. Even the extreme hostility of killing, as the actions of the Hen Girl show, happens through a moment of intimacy. The key point, though, is that intimacy does not overcome the kind of fatal or deathly breach in understanding, or narrative, that otherwise subsists between English and Scot. The touch of intimacy is not communion, or a shared perspective. It is, instead, friction.

How, then, to account for it? How to speak of this frictional intimacy which marks not just the kinds of Anglo-Scottish interaction that we see staged in *Dunsinane* but also its own relation to the Shakespearean play from which it takes its bearings? How, too, to make sense of the broader cultural context that generates such national-frictional encounters? In a valuable recent essay, Clare Wallace has described Greig's staging of 'contact zones' in a number of his plays, including *Dunsinane*, through Jacques Rancière's concept of dissensus. As Rancière defines it, dissensus 'is not a conflict of interests, opinions or values; it is a division inserted in "common sense": a dispute over what is given and about the frame within which we see something as given.' Dissensus is 'a conflict about who speaks and who does not speak'.[37] It thus describes the 'fraught contact zone between Scottishness and Englishness' that is evident both in what *Dunsinane* stages and in its complex assumption of its Shakespearean inheritance. It is, as Wallace says, a kind of 'friction'.[38]

There is perhaps another word – 'cheeky' – for this kind of intimate incommensurability, fully alive to its insistence on the *touch* inherent in such friction. It is present in Greig's account of the orientation of Scottish playwrights towards *Macbeth*, which I quoted in part above. 'To some degree for Scottish writers', Greig remarks, 'it's always felt a little bit cheeky that unquestionably the greatest Scottish play was written by the great English playwright'.[39] Interestingly, this is language that Greig repeats elsewhere. As he put it in another interview: 'So the cheeky bit of me thought, "What if the stories of Macbeth being a tyrant turned out to be propaganda, a bit like the weapons of mass destruction?"'.[40] As a play nurtured by both the RSC and the NTS, *Dunsinane* could hardly have had a more institutionally solid origin. *Macbeth* itself could not be more grandly canonical. But it's interesting that Greig should characterise what both he and Shakespeare have done as 'cheeky'. What is cheek? It is impudence, impertinence, a note of resistance within a relation of dominance and subordination, an over-familiarity. There is in that phrasing more than a hint of intimate friction, and one that runs both ways. Shakespeare the English Bard has cheeked Scotland, so Greig, the Scottish playwright, cheeks Shakespeare in return. This is playful, to be sure, but it is also serious. It is where poetics, politics and their histories meet.

Jacobean Dissensus

Greig's generalisation of his own identification of Shakespeare's cheek is significant – it imputes to other and previous Scottish writers the affront he might himself take from this monumental instantiation of 'England's Scotland', and perhaps too the same desire to stage a moment of resistance to it. There is, in other words, a long history of Shakespeare reception in Scotland which might be marked by this dynamic. It is evident, for example, in the framing of Shakespeare in relation to Robert Burns, and vice versa, and in the terms of such a framing. In an earlier essay Robert

Crawford has examined the close but fraught relationship between what we might call the parallel bards of Scottish and English literature, suggesting that it would be 'misguided' to see Shakespeare and Robert Burns as 'jousting competitors', but that 'understandably ... *national* pride may encourage such a view' (my emphasis). He goes on:

> Thomas Campbell in 1819 thought Burns and Shakespeare equal in terms of their education; he says he is making this point 'without intending to make any comparison between the genius of these two bards', but one senses that, like many a speaker at a Burns Supper, he is strongly tempted.[41]

Sometimes, and on precisely such memorial occasions, the temptation has proved too much. In 1864, the 105th anniversary of Burns' birth was marked by a dinner in Edinburgh at which a certain unhomely presence seems to have been felt. Interestingly, though, it is the very work of commemoration that becomes the basis for the comparison, particularly in light of the 1859 celebrations of Burns' centenary. Proposing the toast, the eminent publisher and imminent Lord Provost William Chambers declared:

> I cannot sit down without remonstrating, as every Scotsman ought to do, as to the paltriness and invidiousness of the remarks occasionally made by parties in England concerning Burns. (Hear, hear.) While thousands of Englishmen in their own country and elsewhere join heartily with us in celebrating his birthday in this simple, social manner, others seem to entertain a pleasure in holding such meetings up to ridicule. A few years ago, at the great centenary celebration, the world was petulantly asked by a great organ of public opinion in the South, Will no one give *us* some one to make a centenary about? The answer, I think, has been given with a vengeance. (Hear, hear.) They have lately been trying to get up something of that kind about Shakspeare [sic], and to all appearance are making a great botch of it. (Laughter.) For this, in veneration of Shakspeare, we give our sincere pity; and seeing how things are managed, venture to hint that they had better let that gentleman alone.[42]

There is, of course, the friction of a perceived rivalry here. From a Scots point of view the difficulty of venturing the comparison between Burns and Shakespeare is that it might mean taking the English poet as an original, a pattern, not just in relation to his work but in the way that its continued reception is organised and conducted; to take it as a yardstick would doom the effort at comparison to demonstrate exactly what it sought to shake off. Chambers' rhetoric in 1864 is clearly working to sidestep this trap; Crawford's essay, strikingly, does something very similar. He argues that bardic Shakespeare was in fact modelled on a Scots poetic ideal, and that eighteenth-century English literature press-ganged a celebrated playwright into an Ossianic role it found it needed somebody to play. Not without both awkwardness and a certain inappropriateness, Crawford implies: whereas Burns' mantle fits his popular and radical status, Shakespeare was always 'the King's Man', 'monarch-obsessed', as Crawford says no fewer than three times, representative of an England constitutively incapable of the kind of genuinely popular culture out of and about which Ossian, and later Burns, were able to sing. Thus Shakespeare is indeed a national poet, but not a bard, since the imagined community of England can properly have no such thing:

> Shakespearean ideology has contributed to the myths of England as sceptred isle; the principal intellectual myth of modern Scotland, 'the democratic intellect', finds its bardic correlative in Burns.[43]

Crawford's essay, like Chambers' speech, is an engaging and provocative surrender to the very temptations from which it claims to stand aloof, the creation as much as the analysis of myth. Its disavowal of Shakespeare's centrality is formed as a desire to define him as something like an honoured guest, a representative or ambassador from elsewhere, and thus to give him a stable place. As much is evident in Crawford's phrasing when he describes Shakespeare as 'a *welcome* part of Scottish, as of world, culture' (my emphasis), and dwells, as Chambers does, on the English exclusion of Burns.[44] If this is inclusion, it is exclusion too, in making Shakespeare a stranger: in Scotland, but not of it; a spectre at a Burns supper.

The difficulty with this framing is precisely that it finds a nameable place for Shakespeare in relation to Scottish culture that has to suppress elements in the story. For if Shakespeare was a 'King's Man', then exactly which king was that? We can only think of Shakespeare in Scotland in the tidy terms proposed by Crawford if we ignore the long history of intimate friction which began, perhaps, with his *becoming* a King's Man in the aftermath of James VI's reverse takeover of the English monarchy in 1603, an event without which there would have been no *Macbeth*, and no *Dunsinane*. So we need to appreciate something of the ways in which Shakespeare has played a part in the kinds of contact zone first created at that point – and which, Greig's play and its Scottish political context would suggest, have persisted down to our own time. An understanding of some of the ways in which Shakespeare is a Jacobean writer, and what being Jacobean might mean in this context, can, I think, help to make sense of the contemporary playwright's appeal to cheek and counter-cheek.

There is no evidence that William Shakespeare ever visited Scotland, though that hasn't prevented sometimes wild speculation on the back of a few relevant facts. We do know that James VI patronised English players, and we now also have evidence to suggest that Lawrence Fletcher, 'comediane to his Majestie', who was made an honorary burgess in Aberdeen in 1601, and is listed first, ahead of Shakespeare, among the company of players awarded the patent to perform as the King's Men in 1603, is much more central to the story of that company's establishment than has hitherto been thought.[45] Thus E. K. Chambers, for example, assumed that Fletcher's presence in the remodelled company was marginal – but as Richard Dutton has suggested, his recruitment at the moment of its remodelling would have been of singular value, given his prior involvement with James as one of 'the Kingis Servandis' in Scotland and the inside knowledge of the new royal family's tastes that would have followed from that.[46] Indeed, as Holger Syme has shown, his membership of the King's Men is as well attested as that of Shakespeare and Burbage and his important presence within the world of the London theatres after 1603 is evidenced in a number of recently uncovered sources.[47] Perhaps it is not too far-fetched to imagine Fletcher helping to shape Shakespeare's Scottish history play, which given the sensitivities outlined above could have been a politically risky undertaking. If he was indeed one of the principal players in the company in the first five years of its new existence then we might presume that *Macbeth* was one of the plays in which he acted.

As one of the king's Englishmen, Fletcher reminds us of the meaning and importance of the regnal shift from Elizabethan to Jacobean. James' takeover was not just a change in monarch within a persisting realm, but a major, if ragged and uneven, shift in the relationship between England and Scotland. That the new king was a 'stranger', a foreigner, hardly went unnoticed.[48] We have too often called it a union, and perhaps understood it within the teleological perspective of the coming of a United Kingdom. But in truth it wasn't a union. James, of course, pursued the idea of a full constitutional merger, an idea frustrated in England at least by the constitutional conservatism of lawyers and politicians alarmed by the thought of the state's remodelling. But the fact that full political union on terms that their Scots counterparts could have stomached was blocked did not mean that all the possibilities and implications of a shared monarchy could also be rebuffed. Those in the orbit of the court would certainly have noticed its new and unprecedented bi-nationality, with Scots taking key roles in the English Privy Council and making up the entire company of James' Bedchamber.[49] This was not just the inclusion of a few token northern Britishers in an otherwise English ensemble of courtiers, but a deliberate attempt on the king's part to balance his two kingdoms in the organisation of his personal administration. And there were, too, constitutional consequences despite the lack of movement towards legal union. The most obvious and profound instance of such effects is Calvin's Case, the 1608 judgement which clearly conceded that the English polity, and its ancient constitution, could not remain untouched by James' assumption of his great-great grandfather's throne. Calvin's Case, or the case of the *postnati*, was brought on behalf of a Scots infant, Robert Calvin, and was the occasion for determining conclusively whether those Scots born after James' accession to the English throne could legitimately hold property in England on the same terms and in the same manner as James' English subjects.[50] Settling the case required the invocation and recrafting of politically fundamental questions around sovereignty, allegiance and the rights of the subject or citizen. The successful arguments accepted that the fact that the now king of England was also king of Scots made a *juridical* difference to the former polity as well as a practical one. Calvin's Case marks the constitutional acknowledgment, across different courts, that the Scots were neither properly English nor entirely foreign. They were, as Francis Bacon had put it in Commons debates on the possibility of general naturalisation in 1607, '*alteri nos*', not our others but 'other ourselves', Bacon's English translation making their somewhat *unheimlich* status especially clear.[51]

It is this shift into the political uncanny that needs to be stressed. James' 'Britain' was for the most part a ghostly thing, marked symbolically by new coins, titles and an embryonic union flag, but otherwise only fitfully substantial. And even the imagery of union could not quite establish itself as the ground for a new community of the Britons: like the royal arms, the new union flag had a different arrangement of its elements depending on whether it was in use in England or Scotland – in England, the more familiar design was deployed, but in Scotland, as a few surviving examples from across the period of regnal union show, an alternative arrangement which gave the St Andrews cross the dominant position was used.[52] So the term 'Jacobean' here names a condition in which two previously discrete nations had been opened to each other in unprecedented but profoundly dissensual ways: it was the intimacy which created the conditions for friction.

We can illustrate this further with one illuminating incident which took place during James' return to Scotland in the summer of 1617. A remarkable and insufficiently well-known account of the royal progress was provided by John Crowe, a Scot, in a letter to an English friend, in which he gives a detailed description of a remarkable play performed in the forecourt of Holyroodhouse on the night of the king's birthday, 19 June:

> Then went his Majestie into his pallace and sate in ane window with his nobilles, and beheld a play of fyrwork; their was many thousands beholders of it; I myselff was one. The playe breifflie was thus. It was actet in the nicht. Their was 2 castles erected in the utter court, one castle at the one end off the court and another castle at the uther end, the one called the pallace of Saint Androis, the other the Castle of Envy. It was acted and played by the yong men of Edenborrow. Their was so many fuilles with their belles, so many daunceres, a playmeir [perhaps 'pleymaker', 'a quarreller, a disturber of the peace']⁵³ casting fyr both behind and befor, a maid, so many hagbuttes, so many muscetters, thair ensignes, thair horsmen, thair footmen runing with speires off fyr, the one castle schuiting fyrballes at the other, quheilles [i.e. wheels] runing round about of fyr and so many schotes into it, so many twix the Castles fychting, so many keiping every Castle, sumtymes the one syd winning, then agane retyring bak and flying. Thair was a devys maid, that out off the pallace off Saint Androis cam Sanct Andrew ryding on a hors, with a speire off fyr in his hand, and met the dragon midway, that came out of the Castle of Envy, and out of hir mouth cam fyr spouting, so they foght aspace together; bot Sanct Andrew did overcome the dragon and cam home ryding, and was welcomed home by the men of the pallace. In the mids, betwix the two castles, was a devys set up that schote so many schotes, and a thing going about with horsmen and footmen; then the quheill wald about agane and persew theis men, and at a certaine space so many schottes, and ane man maid of timber in the mids of the quheill, that went ay about as the two troupes of men, did, having an ensigne in his hand, and on it St. Androis cros. Then their was four hieland men, dressed up so of purpos, that came out of the pallace of St. Androis with their boues and arrowes of fyr, that did win the Castle of Envy, quilk castle had for their badge, St George. The castle was throuen down, the men taken prisoners, and the captain sould have bein, as it wer, hanged.⁵⁴

This must have been an astonishing spectacle. Particularly notable, though, from a Jacobean perspective, is Crowe's reading of the national symbolism of the dramatised conflict. There is the emblematic contrast of the two castles, one identified as the palace of St Andrews, the other the Castle of Envy, an implicitly national framing which becomes explicit with Crowe's identification of the latter with St George. There is also the strange mingling of national symbolisms in St Andrew's victory over the dragon, and the deliberate marking out of 'hieland men' as the Scots who eventually sack the Castle of Envy. All of this makes this performance a distinctive staging of the tensions and fusions, the frictional intimacy, of Anglo-Scottish relationships during James' double reign. It's worth noting the multiple layering of contact zones here: the play itself would have been effectively a collaboration between the 'yong men of Edenborrow' and English 'fyrework men', the nobles who watched the play with the king included both Scots and English courtiers, and Crowe the letter writer is describing all this for an English correspondent.[55]

But there is more to consider than that. In the *Accounts of the Master of Works* for 1617 we find the itemised costs of staging the play, including multiple references to the more customary duo of St George and the dragon, rather than to St Andrew. There is also a costing for 'St. George his speire at the fyr warkis', which suggests that the figure Crowe took to be the Scots' patron saint was actually intended to represent the English equivalent.[56] Of course, this utterly changes the symbolic freighting of the play. Where Crowe, and presumably others in the crowd, saw an antagonistic engagement between the forces and emblems of the two nations, the king and his retinue presumably saw something which pitched both nations, in the emblematic figures of St George and then the 'hieland men', against a common enemy. The incommensurable presence of community and conflict within one and the same scene is a paradigmatic instance of the dissensual nature of Jacobean Anglo-Scottish cultural relations.

Wullie Shakespeare

Where does this leave Shakespeare and his relation to Scotland? Insofar as the dramatist and his Scottish play are marked from the beginning by the intimate incommensurabilities of the Jacobean condition, then we cannot simply think of him as a stranger, an English guest or invader like the Siward of *Dunsinane*. He is already *here*, as much as Scottishness was already *there*. The earliest publication of one of his works in Scotland, an edition of *Venus and Adonis*, came only a few years after the publication of the First

Folio; thanks to William Drummond, editions of Shakespeare's plays were on the shelves of 'King James's College', as the University of Edinburgh was then known, around the same time.[57] His plays were in the repertory of Scotland's professional theatres from their beginnings: the Theatre Royal in Dumfries attended by Robert Burns stood then, and still stands, on Shakespeare Street; Edinburgh's Theatre Royal, which opened in 1769 to service the demands of the city's growing population, was established in what was named Shakespeare Square.[58] Purchased by the theatre manager John Jackson, and mentioned in a 1790 list of his outstanding debts, a Coade stone statue of Shakespeare once stood atop the theatre's pediment, flanked by tragedy and comedy.[59]

Of course, such developments occurred long after Jacobean bi-nationality had been overwritten by the English conquest and occupation of Scotland in the 1650s, the multinational upheavals of the later 1680s and the incorporating union of 1707. All of these developments, of course, had radically transformed the cultural and political relationship between Scotland and its southern neighbour. But some remnant of the kind of dissensus here called Jacobean persisted, in often incompatible ideas of what 'union' meant, and very different senses of its importance as a topic of concern – and these are precisely the issues that continue to animate a constitutional debate in Scotland that has no resonance, no place, in English political culture. Indeed, the asymmetrical structure of devolution in the UK, which created levels and institutions of governance that loom large when viewed from outwith England but were designed not to affect the functioning or self-image of the indivisible sovereign centre, created a kind of dissensual constitution. To some extent the fractured polity is, once again, Jacobean.

Jacobean Shakespeare, too, retained something of this currency, even as he was overlaid with other kinds of cultural significance. There was an association between the promotion of or interest in Shakespeare and the kind of Anglicising drive attendant on the cultural domination, with colonial inflections, brought by incorporation – it's notable, for instance, that the 'Grand Shakespearian Amateur Performance' in Edinburgh to mark the Tercentenary of his birth in April 1864 was staged by 'the MEMBERS (LADIES and GENTLEMEN) forming the DRAMATIC CLASS of MR HARCOURT B. BLAND, Professor of Elocution, Glasgow University, &c. &c'.[60] Studying Shakespeare was a way to learn good diction, where 'good' undoubtedly equates to the sounds of southern English speech. But this elevation of Shakespeare went hand in hand with other tendencies: by this time he no longer presided over the Theatre Royal's entrance, having been removed when the building was remodelled after a change in management in 1830, and not just the theatre but Shakespeare Square itself were razed to create a site for the General Post Office by 1861.[61] Along Princes Street, the Scott Monument instead commanded the attention of the city's denizens and visitors. Opened in 1846, this enormous edifice surrounded its statue of Walter Scott with a pantheon of characters from his novels, including James VI and I. Despite the fact that a bust of Shakespeare had had pride of place in Scott's study, and even though he features indirectly in *Kenilworth*, there was no place for him here. The significance of this absence is made clear by the band of writers whose heads do feature on the monument – a canon of sixteen Scottish writers, from James I down to his distant descendant Lord Byron.[62] The inclusion of the latter, more commonly thought of as an English poet, shows how national belonging was here being determined by bloodline. This is an attempt to cluster, around Scott, a Scottish literary heritage defined by ethnicity in which the man long identified as the English national poet would not be at all at home. Jackson's Shakespeare statue was moved out to the grounds of Bonaly Tower, the country residence of the lawyer and writer Henry Cockburn, where its increasingly decrepit and neglected remains still occupy a niche in the perimeter wall.

These contrasting stories testify to Shakespeare's uncertain place in Scottish culture, an ambivalent mixture of high regard, deep familiarity, and a persistent vein of estrangement. This ambivalence is in some ways the persistence of his Jacobean condition, even as it is also the frustrated desire to settle the discomforts of that condition into a clear story about nationality and literature that demarcates more effectively the boundary between belonging and non-belonging, or simplifies the contact zone into the thinness of a border. All of this, perhaps, is implicated in Shakespeare's cheek, and some of its moments seem more than lightly overdetermined. The Shakespeare Tercentenary, for example, was marked in Alloway with a dinner held in his honour at Burns' Cottage, one bard having his birthday party in another's birthplace. The toast was given by Hately Waddell, minister of an independent congregation in Girvan and an 'orator of very exceptional power'.[63] He had a lifelong and passionate interest in Scots and Scottish literature, including editing both Burns and Scott and undertaking work on Macpherson's *Ossian*, and translating into Scots biblical texts including the Psalms of David and the Book of Isaiah. In January 1859 Waddell had presided over a dinner at Burns' birthplace to mark the Bard's centenary; now, five years later, he gave an oration in praise of Shakespeare. It is unsurprisingly marked by its author's vocation, linking Burns and Shakespeare with the distinctive triumvirate of William Wallace, George Washington and Giuseppe Garibaldi as representatives of Christianity's vigour. More interestingly, though, Waddell insists that 'we are assembled for the purpose of doing honour to [Shakespeare's] memory and name on the one spot of all the world, except Stratford-upon-Avon, most appropriate for the purpose'. This region, 'between the Ayr and Doon', and this 'spot of soil' are the most 'befitting for such a rite as this'.[64] There is, in other words, a unique tie that binds Shakespeare to a Scottish locale which draws its singular cultural importance from its native associations with another poet. Shakespeare, somehow, shares in that nativity, even as Waddell has to concede Stratford's higher claim. Later in his toast he expands on the relationship between the two bards, in a series of images that seek both to delineate their different appeal and to explain why Burns might now prove more popular, more celebrated, among Scots:

> Shakespeare was the golden legend, Burns was the golden voice; but a voice or a saying is more available than a legend. Shakespeare was the common universal constitution, Burns was the vital throbbing blood; but we know which of these two will more easily rouse us. Shakespeare was the atmosphere, Burns was the vocal air; and although all men breathe without thinking of it, it is only when men sing that they consciously rejoice together.[65]

What claim might Waddell be making here? It is hard to see Burns and Shakespeare as separable, even – they seem more to be dependent on each other. Nonetheless, Waddell's task is still to give an account of the contact zone between them, to describe or prescribe its shape and its form, in an effort that is at least partly determined, as he admits elsewhere in his piece, by questions of 'nationality'. Such efforts, and their subsumption within the very dissensual condition they are seeking to transcend, are the renewal and perpetuation of an intimate friction. But if cheek is overfamiliarity, or something like it, then the intimacy it acts out is a challenge. And if we check or rebuke someone who cheeks us, it is because we want to insist on a boundary, a distance or estrangement or hierarchy that their cheek has already shown to be inoperative. Because of cheek, it can make sense to claim, as Greig does, that an English playwright wrote the greatest Scottish play. Scotland's Shakespeare, a Jacobean Shakespeare, is a not very proper name for this whole complex of acts and responses. Cheek by jowl; cheek to cheek; never quite not treading on our own, each *other's*, toes.

Notes

1. David Greig, *Dunsinane* (London: Faber and Faber, 2010), 32.
2. Ibid.
3. Michael Billington, 'Dunsinane', *The Guardian* (17 February 2010). Available at: <https://www.theguardian.com/stage/2010/feb/17/dunsinane-review> (last accessed 22 July 2019).
4. Andrew Dickson, 'How playwright David Greig discovered Birnam Wood in Basra', *The Guardian* (24 January 2015). Available at: <https://www.theguardian.com/stage/2015/jan/24/how-david-greig-discovered-birnam-wood-in-basra> (last accessed 17 June 2019).
5. Clare Wallace, 'Unfinished business – allegories of otherness in Dunsinane', in Clare Wallace and Anja Müller (eds), *Cosmotopia: Transnational Identities in David Greig's Theatre* (Prague: Litteraria Pragensia, 2011), 196–213, 198–9.
6. Greig, *Dunsinane*, 39.
7. Ibid. 29.
8. Ibid. 52.
9. Ibid. 69.
10. Ibid. 76.
11. Graham Saunders, *Elizabethan and Jacobean Reappropriation in Contemporary British Drama* (London: Palgrave Macmillan, 2017), 122–5.
12. Ariel Watson, 'Birnam Wood: Scotland, nationalism, and the theatres of war', *Theatre History Studies*, 33 (2014), 226–49, 243; and Saunders, *Elizabethan and Jacobean Reappopriation*, 122.
13. Victoria Price, '"two kingdoms . . . compassed with one Sea": reconstructing kingdoms and reclaiming histories in David Greig's *Dunsinane*', *International Journal of Scottish Theatre and Screen*, 5 (2012), 19–32, 19–22.
14. See, for example, Liam Connell, 'Scottish nationalism and the colonial vision of Scotland', *Interventions*, 6 (2010), 252–63.
15. Dan Rebellato, 'Local hero: the places of David Greig', *Contemporary Theatre Review*, 26 (2016), 9–18, 13.
16. Billington, 'Dunsinane'.
17. Greig, *Dunsinane*, 29.
18. Ibid. 39, 41.
19. Ibid. 49.
20. Ibid. 51.
21. Nigel Wrench, 'Writing Macbeth after Shakespeare', *BBC News* online (10 February 2010). Available at: <http://news.bbc.co.uk/1/hi/entertainment/arts_and_culture/8508803.stm> (last accessed 17 June 2019). Also quoted in Wallace, 'Unfinished business', 200.
22. Edwin Morgan, 'The Hell's-Handsel o Leddy Macbeth', in *Rites of Passage: Translations* (Manchester: Carcanet, 1976); Shakespeare, *Macbeth*, trans.

R. C. Lorimer (Edinburgh: Canongate, 1992); *The Tragedie o Macbeth*, trans. David Purves (Edinburgh: Rob Roy Press, 1992).
23. Sìm Innes, 'Shakespeare's Scottish play in Scottish Gaelic', *Scottish Language*, 33 (2014), 26–50.
24. Purves, *Tragedie o Macbeth*, viii.
25. Greig, *Dunsinane*, 17–18; William Shakespeare, *Macbeth*, Sandra Clark and Pamela Mason (eds) (London: Bloomsbury Arden Shakespeare, 2014), 1.2.44.
26. Greig, *Dunsinane*, 26; Shakespeare, *Macbeth*, 5.7.76.
27. Greig, *Dunsinane*, 80.
28. Shakespeare, *Macbeth*, 1.3.71.
29. Raphael Holinshed, *Chronicles of England, Scotland and Ireland* (London, 1587), Book 5, 176; F. J. Amours (ed.), *The Original Chronicle of Andrew of Wyntoun*, vol. 4 (Edinburgh: Scottish Text Society, 1906), 275; William Skene (ed.), *John of Fordun's Chronicle of the Scottish Nation* (Edinburgh: Edmonston and Douglas, 1872), 193.
30. For an overview of these debates see Roger Mason, 'Scotching the Brut: politics, history, and national myth in sixteenth-century Britain', in Mason (ed.), *Scotland and England, 1286–1815* (Edinburgh: John Donald, 1987), 60–84.
31. Mason, 'Scotching the Brut', 63–6.
32. Duncan Macmillan, *Scottish Art, 1460–1990* (Edinburgh: Mainstream, 1990), 50, 79–81.
33. See Henrietta Marshall, *Our Island Story: A Child's History of England* (Edinburgh: T. C. and E. C. Jack, 1905), and *Scotland's Story: A Child's History of Scotland* (Edinburgh: T. C. and E. C. Jack, 1906).
34. See Rosemary Mitchell, 'Marshall, Henrietta Elizabeth (1867–1941), children's writer', *Oxford Dictionary of National Biography* (2006). Available at: <https://www.oxforddnb.com/view/10.1093/ref:odnb/9780198614128.001.0001/odnb-9780198614128-e-57458> (last accessed 22 July 2019).
35. 'Macbeth gets politicians' backing' *BBC News* online (3 February 2005). Available at: <http://news.bbc.co.uk/1/hi/scotland/4232221.stm> (last accessed 22 July 2019).
36. Robert Crawford, 'England's Scotland', in Gerrard Carruthers and Colin Kidd (eds), *Literature and the Union: Scottish Texts, British Contexts* (Oxford: Oxford University Press, 2018), 331–48, 336–7.
37. Quoted in Clare Wallace, 'Yes and no? Dissensus and David Greig's recent work', *Contemporary Theatre Review*, 26 (2016), 31–8, 33.
38. Wallace, 'Yes and no?', 35.
39. Greig quoted in Wrench, 'Writing Macbeth'.
40. Quoted in Wallace, 'Unfinished business', 203.
41. Robert Crawford, 'The Bard: Ossian, Burns and the shaping of Shakespeare', in Willy Maley and Andrew Murphy (eds), *Shakespeare and Scotland* (Manchester: Manchester University Press, 2004), 137.

42. 'Anniversary of Burns' birthday', *The Scotsman* (26 January 1864), 4.
43. Crawford, 'The Bard: Ossian, Burns and the shaping of Shakespeare', 124–40, 138.
44. Ibid.
45. James Fergusson, *Shakespeare's Scotland* (Edinburgh: Thomas Nelson, 1957), 4.
46. Richard Dutton, *Shakespeare: Court Dramatist* (Oxford: Oxford University Press, 2016), 268; Fergusson, *Shakespeare's Scotland*, 4.
47. Holger Syme, 'The Jacobean King's Men: a reconsideration', *Review of English Studies*, 70 (2019), 231–51, 241–3.
48. Tim Harris, *Rebellion: Britain's First Stuart Kings* (Oxford: Oxford University Press, 2014), 63–4.
49. Neil Cuddy, 'Anglo-Scottish union and the Court of James I, 1603–1625', *Transactions of the Royal Historical Society*, 39 (1989), 107–24.
50. Bruce Galloway, *The Union of England and Scotland, 1603–1608* (Edinburgh: John Donald, 1986), 151–7.
51. Francis Bacon, *Works, Vol. 10: The Letters and the Life 3*, James Spedding et al. (eds) (London: Longmans, 1868), 351.
52. See, for example, the flag depicted flying over the castle in John Slezer's 'North Prospect of the City of Edenburgh', dated around 1690 and included in the 1719 Edinburgh edition of his *Theatrum Scotiae*; or the decorative ceiling boss from Linlithgow Palace, dated to around 1617, in the collections of the National Museums of Scotland; on this see John Keay and Julia Keay (eds), *Collins Encyclopedia of Scotland* (London: HarperCollins, 1994), 623–4.
53. *Dictionary of the Scots Language* (2004). Available at: <https://dsl.ac.uk> (last accessed 22 July 2019).
54. Historical Manuscripts Commission, *The Manuscripts of Lord Kenyon* (London, HMSO, 1894), 22–3.
55. *Manuscripts of Lord Kenyon*, 22; John Imrie and John Dunbar, *Accounts of the Masters of Works for Building and Repairing of Royal Palaces and Castles, vol 2: 1616–1649* (London: HMSO, 1982), 90.
56. Imrie and Dunbar, *Accounts*, 79 and 84.
57. The edition of *Venus and Adonis* was printed and published in Edinburgh by John Wreittoun in 1627. For the catalogue of Drummond's library and his donations to his alma mater, see Robert MacDonald, *The Library of Drummond of Hawthornden* (Edinburgh: Edinburgh University Press, 1971), esp. 2–5 and 46–8.
58. Hugo Arnot, *The History of Edinburgh from the Earliest Accounts, to the Year 1780* (Edinburgh: Thomas Turnbull, 1816), 285.
59. 'Insolvency of John Jackson, manager of the Theatre Royal, Edinburgh', The National Archives, LC 5/181; see James Gowans and Thomas Shepherd, *Edinburgh and its Neighbourhood in the Days of our Grandfathers* (London: John Nimmo, 1886), 91.
60. *The Scotsman* (19 April 1864), 1.

61. See James Dibdin, *The Annals of the Edinburgh Stage* (Edinburgh: Richard Cameron, 1888), 350; Gowans and Shepherd, *Edinburgh and its Neighbourhood*, 91; and Oliphant Smeaton, *The Story of Edinburgh* (London: J. M. Dent, 1905), 372.
62. See N. M. McQ. Holmes and Lyn Stubbs, *The Scott Monument: A History and Architectural Guide* (Edinburgh: City of Edinburgh Museums and Art Galleries, 1989), 17–24.
63. H. Matthew, 'Waddell, Peter Hately (1817–1891), Presbyterian minister and author', *Oxford Dictionary of National Biography* (2004).
64. [Hateley Waddell], 'Hately Waddell on Shakespeare', *The Stirling Observer* (23 April 1864), 6.
65. Ibid.

Postscript: News from the North

Willy Maley

And in a postscript here he says 'alone'. (*Hamlet* 4.4.50)[1]

       Here is yet
a postscript. (*Twelfth Night* 2.5.150–1)

For more uneven and unwelcome news
Came from the North. (*1H4* 1.1.50–1)

The King your father is at Westminster,
And there are twenty weak and wearied posts
Come from the north. (*2H4* 2.4.322–4)

In 2007, I purchased the Minute Book of the British Empire Shakespeare Society (BESS) Glasgow Branch Dramatic Circle for 1929–33, and donated it to the University of Glasgow Library's Scottish Theatre Archive.[2] The Branch met for the first time on Friday, 8 November 1929 at 8pm at Miss Menzies, The Fitzroy Studios, at 7 Fitzroy Place, in Glasgow's West End, near the University. This was an interesting time for a branch of the BESS to be opening in Glasgow. There were moves afoot throughout the 1920s in Shakespeare Studies to bring Scotland to the fore.[3] In 1932 Frederick Harries published *Shakespeare and the Scots* and in his preface pointed out that for 'the last thirteen years of his life' the playwright 'was the subject of a King of Scottish descent'.[4] There were seven 'Ladies' and six 'Gentlemen' present at that first meeting of the BESS in Glasgow, a nice number for a séance, and it was a séance of sorts. A committee was elected, and scenes selected from eight plays, including *Macbeth* (there were no other histories on the list). It was also resolved

> that an advertisement be inserted for new members. The acquisition of a Wardrobe was mentioned. The next meeting was fixed for Saturday 23rd November at 2.30pm at Fitzroy Place. Votes of thanks to Miss Menzies for the use of her studios and to Mrs Davies for presiding were passed.[5]

The British Empire Shakespeare Society was a very active and widespread latticework of reading groups stretching from Dublin to New York – and beyond – that has not had the attention it deserves. The president of the society was Princess Marie Louise, a granddaughter of Queen Victoria. Her memoirs were published in 1956 as *My Memories of Six Reigns*, suggesting that her coverage of monarchical history was on a par with Shakespeare's.[6]

In an essay entitled 'Remembering Shakespeare imperially: the 1916 Tercentenary', Coppélia Kahn has the following note about the organisation:

> The British Empire Shakespeare Society, founded in 1901, aimed 'to diffuse widely among our fellow-countrymen, both in Great Britain and in all parts of the Empire, a knowledge and love of the greatest dramatic poet the world has ever known, whose work incarnates all the noblest and most splendid qualities of the British race' (anon., *The Free Lance*, 1902). Chapters of the BESS sponsored essay and recitation contests and performances of Shakespeare, and published editions of the plays designed for amateur group readings.[7]

It is interesting and ironic that Scotland should have had its own branches of the BESS, first because Scotland never had an Elizabeth I on its throne, and so missed out on that original Bess. There was no Elizabethan Scotland. The first Elizabethan state excluded Scotland. Indeed, from a Scottish perspective, just as there were two James Is – one of Scotland, and later one of England – there can be no Elizabeth II, since there was no Elizabeth I of Scotland. We 'Other' Elizabethans are re-living the reign of Elizabeth I. When England was Elizabethan, Scotland was Jacobean. Jacobean Scotland and Elizabethan England coincided historically. The time is out of joint. Secondly, in Shakespeare's history plays Scotland was presented as a perennial thorn in the side of England's imperial ambitions, and the North as a whole, from the North of England upwards, was variously a source of stress or support for English monarchs and those who would overthrow them, as two of my epigraphs indicate. This anxiety is also present in Shakespeare criticism and this collection, ably edited by Adam Hansen, sets out to investigate the terms of that anxiety from Shakespeare's time to the present.

Just *after* Shakespeare's time, James I visited Carlisle and Westmorland, during August 1617, on his way from his Scottish progress, in what was an event of huge significance in the history of the North because it was the first visit to this region of a reigning monarch for almost three centuries:

> James I's entry into Carlisle was both historic and timely. Not since the early fourteenth century had an English king visited the North-West, and that had been Edward III in 1335 at the head of an army supporting the forlorn hope of Edward Balliol as king of the Scots. James's leisurely journey southwards through the once disorderly Scottish and English marches was symbolic of the new era of peace the region now enjoyed.[8]

Of course, James was more than 'an English King', and where Edward III had come North for war, James came South for peace. Carlisle can no longer be culturally defined as a defensive outpost or a border town in quite the same way with a Scottish monarch on the throne.

If, for early moderns, the location of authorities, borders and peripheries could at times confound encompassing, what is the direction of Shakespeare studies in response? Are such studies, as the Third Citizen suggests in *Coriolanus*, without direction?:

> ... if all our wits were to issue out of one skull, they would
> fly east, west, north, south, and their consent of one direct
> way should be at once to all the points o'th' compass. (2.3.19–21)

Or is it as Lord Hastings reports in *Henry IV Part II*:

> Like youthful steers unyoked, they take their courses
> East, west, north, south; or, like a school broke up,
> Each hurries toward his home and sporting place. (4.1.270–2)

Shakespeare's geography is familiar ground, as is his use of maps; he went so far as to coin a phrase for it: 'They call this bed-work, mapp'ry, closet-war'

(*Troilus* 1.3.204). Here Shakespeare is bolting suffixes onto nouns in order to conceptualise these shifting border-realms in language. It's not just a phrase he coins, but the words used to make up that phrase.

And most of his maps are metaphorical: 'the / map of my microcosm' (*Coriolanus* 2.1.56–7); 'in thy face I see / The map of honor' (*2H6* 3.1.202–3); 'the map of death', 'The face, that map' (*The Rape of Lucrece* 402, 1712); 'Thou map of honour' (*Richard II* 5.1.12); 'I see, as in a map, the end of all' (*Richard III* 2.4.57); 'Thus is his cheek the map of days outworn', 'And him as for a map doth Nature store' (*Sonnet* 68.1, 13); 'Thou map of woe, that thus dost talk in signs!' (*Titus Andronicus* 3.2.12); 'He does smile his face into more lines than is in the new / map with the augmentation of the Indies' (*Twelfth Night* 3.2.68–9). Maps offer pointers: 'if you look in the maps of the world I / warrant you sall find . . . comparisons' (*H5* 4.7.19–20); 'Peering in maps for ports and piers and roads' (*The Merchant of Venice* 1.1.19); 'I am near to th' place where they should meet, if / Pisanio have mapped it truly' (*Cymbeline* 4.1.1–2).[9] But Shakespeare also uses maps as stage props: 'I have forgot / the map! / . . . No, here it is', 'Come, here is the map. Shall we divide our right / According to our threefold order ta'en?' (*1H4* 3.1.4–6; 68–9). This use of 'the map there' (*King Lear* 1.1.35) as an object or piece of stage business is crucial in the staging of the division of the kingdom and in the depiction of the North. 'Hotspur of the North' objects to his designated portion 'north from Burton' being constrained by the River Trent (*1H4* 3.1.94), while Kent considers Lear to have 'affected . . . Albany' (1.1.1–2), that is, favoured Scotland. To see Scotland thus, not merely as a thorn in the side of England but as desirable, prompting the envy of competitors for territory, is a welcome change from the view of the North as arid and economically deprived.

So: what is my North? Who talks of my North? Shakespeare and his appropriators do not always explain what 'the North' actually encompasses. News from the North is a feature of Shakespeare's histories, and the North does not get a good press. Bad news bulletins are common. *Newes from the North* is also the title of a contemporary pamphlet. The narrator of *Newes from the North* (1579), travelling south from Edinburgh to Ripon in Yorkshire, brings bad tidings about 'the Theaters, Courtaines, Heauing houses, Kissing boothes, Bowling alleyes and such places where the time is so shamefully mispent, namely the Sabaoth dayes vnto the great dishonor of God, and the corruption and vtter destruction of youth'.[10] More bad news was to follow with the appearance of *Newes from Scotland* in 1591-2, a witchcraft pamphlet sometimes attributed to James Cunningham and generally considered as one of the sources for *Macbeth*.[11]

The North's distinctiveness as a holdout from southern rule goes back as far as the Norman Conquest.[12] Sometimes the North (of England) is used against the farther North (Scotland). *Henry IV Part I* opens with 'welcome news' of 'Ten thousand bold Scots . . . Balked in their own blood . . . a conquest for a prince to boast of' (1.1.66, 68–9, 76). Hal, a prince who cannot boast such a conquest, later concedes that he is:

> not yet of Percy's mind, the Hotspur of the North, he / that kills me some six or seven dozen of Scots at a break-/ fast, washes his hands, and says to his wife, 'Fie upon this / quiet life! I want work'. (2.4.94–7)

Here Hotspur of the North (of England) acts as a bulwark against the Scots of the (farther) North. More news is broadcast, as later in the same scene Falstaff reports 'villainous news / abroad' concerning 'That same mad fellow of the / North, Percy' (302–5). In *1H6* Mortimer recalls the time of Henry IV:

> During whose reign the Percies of the North,
> Finding his usurpation most unjust,
> Endeavored my advancement to the throne. (2.5.67–9)

In the same play, Joan La Pucelle summons deputies to her aid:

> You speedy helpers that are substitutes
> Under the lordly monarch of the North,
> Appear and aid me in this enterprise. (5.3.5–7)

A note in the Norton edition states: 'The devil and his demons were frequently associated with the North'.[13] There is a much more revealing note in the Arden 3 series edited by Edward Burns, including this reference:

> Nashe, *Piers Penniless*, gives a more detailed account of demonic ecology: 'The second kind of Devils, which he most imploieth, are those northern *Marcij*, called the spirits of revenge, & the authors of massacres, and seedesmen of mischiefe' (Nashe, 1.230.19–21).[14]

In his Introduction, Burns claims Thomas Nashe's text as 'a first-hand description of *1 Henry VI* on stage', and 'the fullest account of a play in the Shakespeare canon by an Elizabethan writer'.[15] Burns finds Nashe's description 'disappointing in its lack of specifics', but if we take Nashe's knowledge of Shakespeare's play as our starting point then we might start to ask some serious questions about the North. With this in mind, Burns' gloss merits further examination, because elsewhere in the same pamphlet Nashe implies that the Devil himself is in the North (as Milton would later in *Paradise Lost* with Satan possessing 'The Quarters of the North', V.689)[16]: 'hee is busie with Mammon and the Prince of the North, howe to build up his kingdome, or sending his spirits abroad to undermine the maligners of his government'.[17] If we revisit the passage cited by Burns we find that Nashe engages in a contrast:

> The second kind of divels, which he most imployeth, are those northern *Marcij*, called the spirites of revenge, and the authors of massacres, and seedsmen of mischief; for they have commisson to incense men to rapines, sacriledge, theft, murther, wrath, furie, and all manner of cruelties; and they command certain of the southern spirits (as slaves) to wayt upon them, as also great Arioch, that is tearmed the spirite of revenge.[18]

Now the North had a bad reputation from Isaiah (14:12, 13) to the fall of Rome, but in the 1590s the North means something very specific. Nashe may be alluding to James VI, the 'Scottish claim' and 'border reiving', that is, the North as ethically lawless; the North as an entity which can consume a more disciplined and 'civilised' part of the realm; the North as a space with inverted territorial ambitions to expand itself to the point where it can no longer even be defined as North (hence Shakespeare's images of the compass points on the map losing their meaning).

Historians have lamented the lack of attention paid to the study of the North in Shakespeare's time.[19] There is no extant work of northern chorography in early modern culture. The North was a deep-rooted problem for the Tudor regime, with the Northern Rising of 1489 a reminder that the dynasty had a tenuous grip on that region.[20] Steve Ellis has shown how the North, and specifically the Anglo-Scottish Border, loomed large for Henry VIII in his efforts to consolidate his power.[21] Elizabeth Bonner demonstrates just how entwined history and drama were when she observes that in 1523 Thomas Cromwell had told the English parliament 'hit be a commen saying that yn Skotland ys nought to wyn but strokes, for that I alledge another commen saying, who that entendyth Fraunce to wyn with Skotland let hym begyn', before going on to note that in *Henry V* Shakespeare puts this latter saying into the mouth of Westmoreland.[22] The crisis of 1536–7 provided evidence that the North was not readily brought to heel.[23] Ten years later, the so-called 'Rough Wooing', or the Anglo-Scottish wars of 1543–50, shook the North once more, as Henry VIII and the Lord Protector, Edward Seymour, 1st Duke of Somerset, sought to persuade the Scots to agree to the marriage of Prince Edward and Mary Stuart, the future Queen of Scots.[24] Links between the 'Far North' and Ireland meant that Ulster became a bone of contention that would not be resolved until the Anglo-Scottish plantation there in 1609 killed two northern birds with one stone. According to William Palmer 'the 1540s . . . had seen a dramatic increase in Scottish migration into Ireland. Rumours quickly appeared that 15,000 Scots had landed in Ireland to support the Irish chieftains'.[25] Ireland had been a Yorkist power base and it became bound up with the problem of the North of England and with Scotland:

> The case of Ireland reveals a curious paradox . . . Ireland, as another rural, highly stratified borderland, should have been, like the English North, one of the last strongholds of a culture of honor and its nobles should have been guarding their reputations zealously. Unfortunately the opposite is true. Irish lords consistently infuriated English authorities by their refusal to behave in accordance with English norms of honorable behavior.[26]

Under Elizabeth the problem of the North persisted and in the Northern Rising of 1569 assumed a more threatening aspect.[27] Henry VII, Henry VIII and Elizabeth I each had a Yorkshire-based rebellion to deal with in their respective reigns as well as a chronic Anglo-Scottish Border problem.

The North is never neutral territory in Shakespeare's histories, or indeed in any of his plays. He may have played there as part of the Queen's Company.[28] In *2H6* Sander Simpcox, the poor man who fraudulently claims to have miraculously regained his sight, hails from 'Berwick in the north' (2.1.81). In *3H6* Richard Duke of York explains how Henry VI escaped his clutches:

> While we pursued the horsemen of the North
> He slyly stole away and left his men. (1.1.2–3)

The gloss in the Oxford edition reads: 'The Lancastrians traditionally drew their strength from the North of England'.[29] But do the Yorkists not also traditionally draw their strength from the North of England? Do we need grounds more relative than this? Perhaps those horses were like the ones the Lord Chamberlain learns from a letter have arrived for Henry VIII: 'young and handsome and of the best / breed in the North' (*H8* 2.2.3–4).

Adam Hansen observes that 'the flexible, inclusive North is often seen as another country', and the North certainly has negative connotations in many of Shakespeare's plays, viewed as a site of rebellion, recusancy and regressive forces. For Richard II, the North means exile and separation, leaving him 'Doubly divorced!', and in a speech that opens portentously with a northern divide and closes with a possible allusion to Mary Queen of Scots, the king declares:

> Part us, Northumberland, I towards the North,
>   Where shivering cold and sickness pines the clime;
> My Queen to France, from whence, set forth in pomp,
> She came adornèd hither like sweet May. (*R2* 5.1.76–9)

Richard III fares no better, advised by a messenger of Lord Stanley's dream and his response:

> Therefore he sends to know your lordship's pleasure,
> If presently you will take horse with him
> And with all speed post into the North
> To shun the danger that his soul divines. (*R3* 3.2.13–16)

When Stanley later tells Richard, 'my friends are in the North',[30] the King says, punning on that region's cooler climes:

> Cold friends to Richard. What do they in the North,
> When they should serve their sovereign in the West? (4.4.397–9)

When the North wind doth blow we shall have geography and politics, so when in *Romeo and Juliet* Mercutio alludes to the 'inconstant . . . wind, who woos . . . the frozen bosom of the North' (1.4.98–9), Benvolio's riposte – 'This wind you talk of blows us from ourselves' (102) – seems freighted with the leaves of history. When Imogen likens her father's entrance to 'the tyrannous breathing of the north' that 'Shakes all our buds from growing' (*Cymbeline* 1.3.36–7), the editorial gloss '*north wind*' seems to underplay the speech. This collection's introduction draws attention to when Emilia declares 'I will speak as liberal as the north' in *Othello* (5.2.214). We might add that this is one of four occurrences of 'liberal' in Shakespeare, and more than any other play, a significance which suggests the Norton gloss – 'As freely as the north wind' – feels limited.[31] Q1 drops the 'north' altogether for 'ayre' (3510), while F capitalises 'North' (3510). What are the implications of this airy elision of location? In *Twelfth Night*, Fabian tells Sir Toby where he stands with Olivia:

> you are now sailed into the north of my lady's opinion,
> where you will hang like an icicle on a Dutchman's beard,
> unless you do redeem it by some laudable attempt either of
> valor or policy. (3.2.22–5)

In *Pericles*, Gower tells how:

> the grizzled North
> Disgorges such a tempest forth
> That, as a duck for life that dives
> So up and down the poor ship drives. (3.0.47–50)

Suzanne Gossett detects in Marina's subsequent statement to Leonine, 'When I was born the wind was north' (4.1.52), 'a geographical anomaly – coming from North Africa Pericles would not be driven by a wind from the north, as Marina reports'.[32] Should we look for contexts closer to home in such geographical anomalies?

If, as the BBC publication cited by Adam Hansen in his introduction suggests, 'the North of England ... is a nation within a nation', then what nation is it within?[33] Discussing 'The function of broadcasting' in *Broadcast Over Britain* (1924), the Stonehaven-born and Glasgow-educated Lord Reith, founder of the British Broadcasting Corporation, did not countenance the neglect of the North, particularly when it came to enjoying the benefits of listening to London and being kept up to date with developments in the British imperial monarchy: 'There is a grumble and a cause of complaining if the crofter in the North of Scotland or the agricultural labourer in the West of England has been unable to hear the King speak on some great national occasion'.[34] Reith believed in spreading the news:

> It seems absurd that Swansea, for instance, should relay from London instead of from Cardiff, or Dundee from London instead of from a Scottish main station. Stations will, I imagine, eventually be grouped

by areas according to the characteristics, national or local, of the people, and a much more satisfactory service be given. Long land lines are treacherous. Any main station programme should be good enough to relay, and on the special London nights the programme is sent to main as well as relays, so the relays would still secure the most important metropolitan events.[35]

This volume addresses the questions of drama, geography, monarchy and nation rehearsed by Shakespeare and still apparent in the reception of his work. The collection's opening gambit sees Paul Frazer explore the ways in which an earlier play with a northern aspect seeped into two later dramas. In 'Shakespeare's Northern Blood: Transfusing *Gorboduc* into *Macbeth* and *Cymbeline*', Frazer develops and extends recent work by Jaecheol Kim, adding Scotland to the northern mix, together with Ireland and Wales, in ways that mark the play as indelibly archipelagic. Next up is Steven Veerapen, who confronts the Border before and after the accession of James I. In '"Here are strangers near at hand": Anglo-Scottish Border Crossings Pre- and Post-Union', Veerapen deals with arguably the most difficult of borders, the border between Tudor and Stuart, made more problematic by the fact that Scotland was Stuart throughout the Tudor period, having had a Stuart – or Stewart – monarch since the succession of Robert II in 1371. Veerapen is alert to the ways in which the plays of the 1590s bear the imprint of the Scottish succession just as those of the next decade testify to the significance of regnal union as an issue. Building on earlier work on Robert Greene and John Ford, he demonstrates that theatrical representations of the Border/Borders often address complexities rather than taking sides in any simple sense, thus making the Anglo-Scottish frontier an ideal stage for dramatic treatment.

Richard Stacey's innovative study of a crucial regional power base in 'Shakespeare, King James, and the Northern Yorkists' offers an ambitious and original reading of Shakespeare's Scottish play as Yorkist. In doing so Stacey extends the reach of the North as examined in this collection in extremely productive ways. This fresh interpretation of a great tragedy situates it firmly within the preoccupations of the medieval history plays of the 1590s and vitally reminds readers of the richness and complexity of the Yorkist impact on Anglo-Scottish politics in the period. This is a new lead on *Macbeth* as a border-crossing drama in terms of genre and geography that others will want to follow.

Lisa Hopkins' work on Shakespeare's regional and national geographies is always engaging, and here she traces the slipperiness of the North in Shakespeare. Picking up where Stacey left off, Hopkins homes in on *Macbeth* as an exemplary engagement with the politics of the North as a site of instability, before moving on to two far less well-known plays by Anthony Brewer and Richard Brome that show the extent to which Shakespeare's successors drew on his work in order to present their own vision of a North that was fractured, fragile and fluid.

Adam Hansen's account of leading North of England company the People's Theatre in 'The People's Shakespeare: Place, Politics, and Performance in a Northern Amateur Theatre' tackles the place of Shakespeare as political theatre in a region where ideas of art and culture differ markedly from those found in London and Stratford. Hansen's account, beginning with J. B. Priestley responding to a rehearsal of *The Trojan Women* in a Newcastle pub in the 1930s by quoting Hamlet on Hecuba, is wonderfully sensitive to questions of language and representation. This chapter is thus about how the North is seen and heard, as well as what Shakespeare is to the North, and the North to Shakespeare. It is also about Shakespeare and socialism, or more precisely about the North and rebellion, a familiar theme from the histories. Hansen's argument utilises archival research into popular culture and in this respect it recalls recent work by Andrew Murphy on an earlier period, building up a detailed picture of Shakespeare for the people and the North.[36]

The essay that comes after Hansen's exploration of the People's Theatre follows like a second act. In 'Only Northerners Need Apply: Northern Broadsides and "No-nonsense" Shakespeare', Caroline Heaton looks at a later development of Northern drama in the shape of Barrie Rutter's company, Northern Broadsides. Rutter, part of the post-war generation of working-class drama students who wanted more than walk-on parts or character roles, pioneered a kind of quickfire Shakespeare performance arguably closer to the original than the RSC, with the focus on substance rather than show. All of Northern Broadsides' shows are in broad Yorkshire dialect regardless of the play or character, so the language does not sound 'authentic' in any historical sense, but Heaton makes a strong case for seeing and hearing Northern (Broadsides') Shakespeare as the real thing, or as real as theatre gets.

Taking a different tack on Shakespearean theatre in the North, Janice Wardle examines how a Stratford production fared on tour, specifically a canonical comedy billed as a popular and inclusive drama. In 'Shakespeare and Blackpool: The RSC's *A Midsummer Night's Dream* (2016): A Play for the Nation?', Wardle is acutely aware of the potential tensions and contradictions around a prestigious national play aiming for local interaction in 'the world's first working-class seaside resort'. Wardle's insights into the production are fascinating, and particularly where the context of the Brexit referendum is flagged with all its negative implications for the arts and for the very diversity that the play stages and which the inclusive notion of nation was meant to convey.

Richard Wilson, in a characteristically robust engagement with Shakespeare's local and global politics, 'William the Conqueror: The Only Shakescene in a Country', grapples with anti-northern prejudice with the bold wit that is his trademark, dismantling discrimination by dint of an unerring eye for detail. His curtain-raiser on the Grafton Shakespeare Portrait in Manchester's John Rylands Library includes the statement that 'English theatre history orthodoxy is violently allergic to a "Northern Shakespeare"'. This awareness is evident in other essays in this collection but Wilson is unwavering and withering in his critique. The best riposte to snobbery – including sniffy scepticism about a northern portrait of the Bard – is an intellectual one. Wilson draws on an anonymous Elizabethan drama variously attributed to Shakespeare and Greene entitled *A Pleasant Comedy of Fair Em the Miller's Daughter of Manchester: With the love of William the Conqueror*. This 'Medieval Conquest' play with a twist of 'Nordic Noir', 'Mancunian matchmaking' and Preston poetry proves fertile territory for Wilson's distinctive brand of playful, probing scholarship. Wilson's conclusion, that we underestimate 'Shakespearean Lancashire' at our peril, is well taken. His contribution to this collection, with its subtle fusion of context and subtext, will have lasting impact on our understanding of Shakespearean reception and depiction in the North.

Monika Smialkowska takes the high road into northern modernity in '"What is Shakespeare to Manchester"? Shakespearean Engagement in the North at the Turn of the Twentieth Century', and takes us back to the world of Wardle, Heaton and Hansen with her incisive study of the ways in which the Manchester Shakespeare Tercentenary Association appropriated the playwright. Her essay is a pioneering piece on Derbyshire-born Rosa Grindon, a distance learning graduate of St Andrews University who became president of the Manchester Ladies' Shakespeare Reading Club. Steeped in the North, Grindon was immersed in Shakespeare, and can be viewed as a key figure in early twentieth-century northern interpretations of his work. This is a door-opening chapter, part of this volume's mission of recovering voices and reclaiming lost territory, and it will no doubt attract future research.

Chris Jackson takes us back to the People's Theatre, to Newcastle and naming Shakespeare in the North, and to that 2016 RSC production of

A Midsummer Night's Dream, when local amateurs rubbed shoulders with professional actors. From this starting point Jackson delves into the rich Shakespearean culture and heritage of the North East of England and the intersection of local history and national theatre, reinforcing the sense that Shakespeare's welcome in the North has been warmer than the North's reception in Shakespeare criticism. It will be interesting to see what the Shakespeare North Playhouse adds to the story.

Liz Oakley-Brown, in 'Lancastrian Shakespeares: *Hamlet* and *King Lear* in North West England (2005–2014)', makes an imaginative and at times ingenious case for seeing Juliet McKoen's *Frozen* (2005) and Jenn Ashworth's 'Doted' (2014) as representing 'striking Lancastrian renditions of *Hamlet* and *King Lear*'. Both film and short story are seen to have structural and thematic links to Shakespeare's two great tragedies, themselves bound up with geography, with sea and land and the elements, and in her exploration of 'site-specific critical and creative "collisions"', Oakley-Brown convincingly argues for the diversity and distinctiveness of Lancastrian Shakespeares.

James Loxley brings us right up to date with 'Shakespeare's Cheek: David Greig's *Dunsinane* and the Jacobean Condition', closing the collection fittingly on a far northerly note and taking us back to the innovative readings of *Macbeth* offered by Paul Frazer and, more particularly, by Richard Stacey. Loxley's analysis of David Greig's sequel to the Scottish play, which makes no mention of the name of its predecessor in keeping with the taboo of theatrical tradition, explores the problem of post-war reconstruction in light of the mass bombing of Iraq and Afghanistan. The question of geography looms large in a play that plays down place in favour of portent, and homes in on climate rather than context. Loxley touches on the cheek of suggesting, 'as Greig does' – tongue-in-cheek? – 'that an English playwright wrote the greatest Scottish play'. But did he? To end this afterword on a personal note, I wrote to David Greig in 2019 telling him that I had been re-reading *The Valiant Scot* (1637) and thought it would make a fine follow-up to *Dunsinane* and a great play to do in the year of the septicentenary of the Declaration of Arbroath.[37] It is certainly a play preoccupied with the North that would resonate with the engaging and informed essays gathered together in this thought-provoking volume. All of the Norths explored in this collection – the North as a kind of projection of southern anxieties; the North as a territory which is never neutral in any of its figurations; the North and its various pejorative associations; the North as a site of theatrical innovation and biographical information; the North as the unruly North of England; the

North of England as a barrier to a barbaric Scotland, later home to a Scottish king who rules from London – are handled in ways that enhance our understanding of Shakespeare's work and work on Shakespeare. From his scholarly stronghold in Northumbria, Adam Hansen has issued an invitation to critics: 'Look North'. We would do well to accept, even if for some of us this might mean looking South.[38]

Notes

1. All references unless otherwise stated are to Stephen Greenblatt et al. (eds), *The Norton Shakespeare*, third edition (New York and London: W.W. Norton & Company, 2016).
2. GB 247 STA Mn 91, Collection, Minute Book of British Empire Shakespeare Society Glasgow Branch, 1929–1933.
3. Lilian Winstanley's *Hamlet and the Scottish Succession: Being an Examination of the Relations of the Play of Hamlet to the Scottish Succession and the Essex Conspiracy*, had appeared in 1921, followed a year later by *Macbeth, King Lear and Contemporary History*, both from Cambridge University Press.
4. Frederick Harries, *Shakespeare and the Scots* (Edinburgh: W. F. Henderson, 1932), 5.
5. Minute Book of British Empire Shakespeare Society Glasgow Branch (1929–1933), 2.
6. Princess Marie Louise, *My Memories of Six Reigns* (London: Evans Bros. Ltd., 1956; London: Dutton, 1957). This work is well worth a visit for gems such as this, when she praises her favourite Shakespeare performers for their diction and adds: 'The Terry sisters had another very striking gift – they could cry real tears without looking ugly; their dear noses did not get red or even pink' (167).
7. Coppélia Kahn, 'Remembering Shakespeare imperially: The 1916 Tercentenary', *Shakespeare Quarterly*, 52: 4 (2001), 456–78, 459, n.13.
8. R. T. Spence, 'A royal progress in the North: James I at Carlisle Castle and the Feast of Brougham, August 1617', *Northern History*, 27: 1 (1991), 41–89, 41. For more on the Stuart solution to the problem of the North see R. T. Spence, 'The pacification of the Cumberland borders, 1593–1628', *Northern History*, 13: 1 (1977), 59–160.
9. All citations here are to the Norton edition except *Titus Andronicus*, ed. Eugene M. Waith (Oxford 1984, 1998).
10. T. F., *Newes from the north. Otherwise called The conference between Simon Certain, and Pierce Plowman, faithfully collected and gathered by T. F. student* (London: John Allde, 1579), sig.F4r. Dedicated to Sir Henry Sidney 'Lord President of Wales, & Marches of the same', with commendatory verses from Anthony Munday and others, this text is part of the Piers Plowman

tradition of petition and complaint. There was of course some good news out of a 'North' that same year in the shape of a new translation of Plutarch's *Lives, The lives of the noble Grecians and Romanes . . . Englished by Thomas North* (London: Thomas Vautroullier and John Wight, 1579).

11. Anon., *Newes from Scotland Declaring the damnable life of Doctor Fian a notable sorcerer, who was burned at Edenbrough in Ianuarie last. 1591* (London: Edward Allde (?) for William Wright, 1592?). Edward Allde was the son of John Allde (the printer of *Newes from the North*, to whom Anthony Munday was apprenticed), so if Edward was indeed the printer of this other work that would be a neat northern news network.
12. See John Le Patourel, 'The Norman conquest of Yorkshire', *Northern History*, 6: 1 (1971), 1–21.
13. *The Norton Shakespeare*, 479, n.3.
14. William Shakespeare, *King Henry VI Part One*, ed. Edward Burns (London: Thomson Learning, 2000), 259, n.27.
15. *King Henry VI Part One*, 1, 2.
16. See Willy Maley and Adam Swann, '"Is this the region . . . that we must change for heav'n?": Milton on the margins', in David Coleman (ed.), *Region, Religion and English Renaissance Literature* (Farnham, Surrey: Ashgate 2013), 139–52, 145–6.
17. Thomas Nashe, *Pierce Penilesse His Supplication to the Divell* (London: Printed by Abell Jeffes, for John Busbie, 1592), 14. This is surely a subtle reference to James VI in the context of the succession and witchcraft debates. On the devilish nature of the monarch of the North, see Waldo F. McNeir, 'Robert Greene and John of Bordeaux', *PMLA*, 64: 4 (1949), 781–801, 784, n.11.
18. Nashe, *Pierce Penilesse*, 85.
19. See for example D. M. Palliser, 'Epidemics in Tudor York', *Northern History*, 8: 1 (1973), 45–63, 45.
20. See Michael J. Bennett, 'Henry VII and the Northern Rising of 1489', *English Historical Review*, 105: 414 (1990), 34–59.
21. Steven G. Ellis, 'A Border baron and the Tudor state: the rise and fall of Lord Dacre of the North', *The Historical Journal*, 35: 2 (1992), 253–77.
22. Elizabeth A. Bonner, 'The genesis of Henry VIII's "Rough Wooing" of the Scots', *Northern History*, 33: 1 (1997), 36–53, 38.
23. M. L. Bush, 'The problem of the far north: a study of the crisis of 1537 and its consequences', *Northern History*, 6: 1 (1971), 40–63. Of course, the notion of the 'Far North' from an English perspective may seem southern from a Scottish standpoint. See Aonghas MacCoinnich, *Plantation and Civility in the Northern Atlantic World: The Case of the Northern Hebrides, 1570–1639* (Leiden and Boston: Brill, 2015). The North as a problem for the Scottish crown went back as far as Shakespeare's histories. See Richard D. Oram, 'David I and the Scottish conquest and colonisation of Moray', *Northern Scotland*, 19: 1 (1999), 1–19.

24. See Bonner, '"Rough Wooing"'.
25. William Palmer, 'High officeholding, foreign policy, and the British dimension in the Tudor far north, 1525–1563', *Albion: A Quarterly Journal Concerned with British Studies*, 29: 4 (1997), 579–95, 590.
26. William Palmer, 'Scenes from provincial life: history, honor, and meaning in the Tudor North', *Renaissance Quarterly*, 53: 2 (2000), 425–48, 442–3. On Ireland and the Yorkist cause, see also Edmund Curtis, 'Richard, Duke of York, as Viceroy of Ireland. 1447–1460; with unpublished materials for his relations with native chiefs', *The Journal of the Royal Society of Antiquaries of Ireland*, 2: 2 (1932), 158–86; Vincent Gorman, 'Richard, Duke of York, and the development of an Irish faction', *Proceedings of the Royal Irish Academy. Section C: Archaeology, Celtic Studies, History, Linguistics, Literature*, 85C (1985), 169–79; and Michael K. Jones, 'Edward IV, the Earl of Warwick and the Yorkist claim to the throne', *Historical Research*, 70: 173 (1997), 342–52. On earlier relations between Scotland and the Yorkists see Andy King, 'The Anglo-Scottish Marches and the perception of "the North" in fifteenth-century England', *Northern History*, 49: 1 (2012), 37–50. On the Yorkist approach to Scotland and how it laid the groundwork for the Tudor strategy see Jonathan Lewis, 'The Yorkist kings and foreign policy', *History Review*, 38 (2000), 3–8.
27. See M. E. James, 'The concept of order and the Northern Rising 1569', *Past & Present*, 60 (1973), 49–83; K. J. Kesselring, '"A Cold Pye for the Papistes": constructing and containing the Northern Rising of 1569', *Journal of British Studies*, 43: 4 (2004), 417–43. For the ways in which this division was depicted in the drama of the period, see Jaecheol Kim, 'The North-South divide in *Gorboduc*: fratricide remembered and forgotten', *Studies in Philology*, 111: 4 (2014), 691–719. For the impact of the Rising on popular culture see Edward Wilson-Lee, 'The Bull and the Moon: Broadside ballads and the public sphere at the time of the Northern Rising (1569-70)', *The Review of English Studies*, New Series, 63: 259 (2012), 225–42.
28. See Karl P. Wentersdorf, 'The Queen's Company in Scotland in 1589', *Theatre Research International*, 6: 1 (1980), 33–6, 35, n.3.
29. William Shakespeare, *Henry VI, Part Three*, ed. Randall Martin (Oxford: Oxford University Press, 2001), 149, n.2.
30. This is a resonant phrase in light of the pioneering TV drama series *Our Friends in the North* (1996), and northern friendship remains topical. See Keith Shaw, '"Our Friends in the North": responses to the independence debate in the North East and Cumbria', *Scottish Affairs*, 23: 3 (2014), 396–406. On the Stanleys and the North see Barry Coward, 'A "crisis of the aristocracy" in the sixteenth and early seventeenth centuries? The case of the Stanleys, earls of Derby, 1504–1642', *Northern History*, 18: 1 (1982), 54–77.
31. *Norton Shakespeare*, 2155, n.7.
32. William Shakespeare, *Pericles*, ed. Suzanne Gossett (London: Thomson Learning, 2004), 129.

33. Hansen is citing Dave Russell, *Looking North: Northern England and the National Imagination* (Manchester and New York: Manchester University Press, 2004), 137.
34. J. C. W. Reith, *Broadcast Over Britain* (London: Hodder and Stoughton Limited, 1924), 15.
35. Reith, *Broadcast Over Britain*, 63.
36. Andrew Murphy, *Shakespeare for the People: Working-class Readers 1800–1900* (Cambridge: Cambridge University Press, 2008).
37. J. W., *The Valiant Scot* (London: Thomas Harper for John Waterson, 1637). See Vimala C. Pasupathi, 'Locating *The Valiant Scot*', in Susan Bennett and Mary Polito (eds) *Performing Environments Site-Specificity in Medieval and Early Modern English Drama* (London: Palgrave Macmillan, 2014), 241–59.
38. The North as a locus of power – and as an alternative power base to London – has a complex and contested history. See Neil Lee, 'Powerhouse of Cards? Understanding the "Northern Powerhouse"', *Regional Studies*, 51: 3 (2017), 478–89. For a more optimistic perspective in keeping with the aims of the present volume see Katy Shaw, 'Writing the Northern Powerhouse: evaluating the Northern Writers' Awards as a potential model of intervention for addressing regional representation in the "London-centric" UK literary industry', *Creative Industries Journal*, 12: 1 (2019), 3–13.

Index

accent, 8, 18, 127, 128, 151–60, 180–1
amateur theatre, 125–6, 132–5, 137, 143–4, 168, 173–81, 232, 244, 281, 291
Anglocentrism, 18, 26, 176, 194, 283
Arts Council England, 161–2, 174
Ashworth, Jenn *see* 'Doted'

Bacon, Francis, 85–6, 94, 288
Bailey, Lucy, 17–18
Barnsley, 4
Benson, Sir Frank, 221, 251–4
Berwick-Upon-Tweed, 60, 66, 105–6, 127, 304
Billington, Michael, 276–7, 279–80
Blackpool, 17–18, 168–84
Blackshaw Head, 1
Bolton, 128, 130, 237
Bootle, 9, 246
borders
 Anglo-Scottish, 13, 15, 16, 19, 20, 45, 60–8, 73–4, 105–6, 109, 112, 207, 303
 border crossing, 45, 61, 69–74
 borderers, 64–5
 as concept, 6, 18–22, 27, 104, 300–1
 and *Macbeth*, 69–73, 88, 89, 92
 see also Britishness; Marches; national identity
Brewer, Anthony *see The Lovesick King*
British Broadcasting Corporation (BBC), 1, 7, 13, 181, 306
British Empire Shakespeare Society, 298–9
British Socialist Party, 128–30
Britishness
 constructed, 20, 42–3, 53, 62, 86, 93
 contested, 19, 24–7, 56, 191
 and inequality, 16–19, 23, 157
 and northernness, 16, 85–6, 104, 207
Brome, Richard *see The Queen's Exchange*
Burnley, 1, 169, 197
Burns, Robert, 284–6, 291–3

Camden, William, 84, 115
Campion, Edmund, 17, 195, 202
Carlisle, 9, 127, 189, 190, 300
Catholicism
 and *Gorboduc*, 42–4
 and the North, 13–18, 43, 82, 84, 195–6, 201
 and Shakespeare, 18, 196–7, 200–4

'Celtic fringe', 19–21, 24, 104
Charles I, 73, 118, 191, 282
Childs, Tony, 140, 144
Clarion Clubs, 128, 130, 131
class, 3–7, 11, 16–18, 25, 130, 152, 154, 157, 161, 181, 246, 259; see also Britishness; Englishness; national identity
Clitheroe, 197–8
colonialism, 21–6, 278–9, 283, 291
Coronation Street, 9
Critical Regionalism, 12, 19, 21, 25
Cromwell, Thomas, 303
Crystal, David, 158, 199

Daniel, Samuel, 61, 86, 88, 104
Dean Clough Mills *see* The Viaduct Theatre
'Deep England', 6–8, 17–18
Doctor Faustus (Christopher Marlowe play), 138
Doctor Who, 103
'Doted' (Jenn Ashworth short story), 259–60, 268–72
Drayton, Michael, 85, 104
Dunbar, 66
Dunsinane (David Greig play), 276–9, 281–6, 290

Eccleston, Christopher, 103, 156
Edinburgh, 80, 104, 193, 208, 279, 281, 282, 285, 291, 301
Edward II (Christopher Marlowe play), 62
Edward IV, 83, 85, 94, 95
Edward VI, 60
Elizabeth I
  and *Gorboduc*, 42–3, 56
  and the North, 13, 15, 16, 105, 299, 304
  and succession, 46–7, 60, 66, 71, 79–82, 91, 104, 108–9, 192, 200

Emerson, Ralph Waldo, 37n
English Touring Theatre, 161–2
Englishness, 2–7, 13, 15, 18–19, 21, 24, 29, 84, 104, 107, 109, 224, 227; *see also* Britishness; 'Celtic fringe'; 'Deep England'; Scottishness
ethnicity
  in Britain, 20–1, 29n, 84, 157, 176
  and James I, 85–8, 94–6
  and *Macbeth*, 93–6
Euripides, 125
Europe, 10, 12, 17, 93, 139, 182, 281

Fair Em the Miller's Daughter of Manchester (anonymous play), 190–6, 203–8
Fleetwood, 174, 259–72
Ford, John *see Perkin Warbeck*
Forman, Simon, 88
Foucault, Michel, 21–2, 226
Frozen (dir. Juliet McKoen), 259, 260–8

Glasgow, 173, 180, 281, 298
Global South, 22–3, 26
Gorboduc (Thomas Norton and Thomas Sackville play)
  and *Cymbeline*, 50, 53–5
  and *Macbeth*, 50–2
  and northernness, 43–50
Greene, Robert
  and *Fair Em the Miller's Daughter*, 190–2, 204–6
  The Scottish History of James the Fourth, 63–8, 193–4
  and Shakespeare, 69, 189–90, 193, 205, 208
Grindon, Rosa (Mancunian Shakespearean), 219–37

INDEX

Halifax, 1, 151, 153
Hamilton, James, earl of Arran, 67
Harrison, Tony, 5, 8–9, 11, 24
Heaton (Newcastle upon Tyne), 9, 145, 244–56
Heckels, Chris (The People's Theatre), 137, 140, 141, 143–4, 145, 255
Henry VII, 46, 53, 81, 82, 87, 106, 200, 304
Henry VIII, 60, 81, 91, 303, 304, 305
Henry, Lenny, 159, 161, 162
Herbert, William, 86, 88
Heywood, Thomas, 89, 93, 95
Hoghton Tower (Lancashire), 13, 195–8
Holderness, Graham, 7, 154, 226–7, 259
Holinshed, Raphael, 50, 53, 62, 91, 117, 282
Honigmann, Ernst, 195–202
Hopkins, Lisa, 45, 50, 61, 65, 73, 262
Hughes, Ted, 1–5, 24
Hull, 11, 151, 162

imperialism, 6, 21, 22, 23, 86–7, 93, 220, 299–300
internal colonialism, 24
Ireland, 19, 20, 84, 90, 93, 140, 304, 307; *see also* 'Celtic fringe'
ITV, 9

James IV, 63, 66
James VI and I, 42, 60–5, 73, 79–83, 104, 189, 286–7, 292, 303
John Rylands Library (Manchester), 187, 225–6
Jonson, Ben, 72

Kassabova, Kapka, 22
Kerrigan, John, 20, 191, 198, 207

Kesselring, K. J., 15
Knowsley (Merseyside), 189–90, 193–6, 198–9, 201, 203, 205, 206, 208

Lancashire, 1, 169, 178
  and Shakespeare, 7, 13, 189–208, 224, 225, 229
Lancaster University, 258–60, 272
Lancastrians, 80–3, 88, 92, 304
Leland, John, 110
Lewkenor, Samuel, 84
The Literary and Philosophical Society (Newcastle upon Tyne), 27
London
  and early modern literary culture, 62–8, 70, 86–7, 193, 205, 287
  and the North, 14–16, 19, 23, 88, 111, 161, 279
  and Shakespeare, 8, 222, 252
  see also Stow, John; Grindon, Rosa
The Lovesick King (Anthony Brewer play), 103, 104, 106–14

McKellen, Sir Ian, 152, 156
McKoen, Juliet *see Frozen*
MacNeice, Louis, 11
Maley, Willy, 19, 24, 93
Manchester Central Library, 219, 233–7
Manchester Ladies' Shakespeare Reading Club, 221
Manchester Shakespeare Tercentenary Association, 228
Marches, 12, 61–5, 74, 103–4, 300; *see also* Borders
Margaret Tudor, 66, 79, 81, 91
Mary I, 43, 60, 62
Mary Queen of Scots, 43, 50, 52, 61, 83, 91, 194, 305
Medea (Seneca), 42, 47, 51–2
Middlesbrough, 127, 130, 255

Miller, Jonathan, 159
Morley, Paul, 9, 11, 178
Murphy, Andrew, 154, 308

Nashe, Thomas, 302–3
National Curriculum, 154
national identity
　conflicted, 2–7, 12–13, 24
　and Shakespeare, 24–6, 56, 62,
　　132, 141, 176, 220, 225,
　　181–3, 220, 225, 227, 236,
　　285–6
　see also accent; borders; 'Celtic
　　fringe'; colonialism; Englishness;
　　ethnicity; imperialism
National Theatre of Scotland, 281
nationalism, 21, 25, 26, 53, 56,
　172, 283
Nelson, Conrad, 162–3
Newcastle upon Tyne, 7, 9, 11,
　105–7, 108–111, 114, 115,
　125–8, 168, 173, 182, 244–56
Niven, Alex, 6, 16, 21
North
　connected to other regions, 14,
　　17–22
　'Deep North', 6–7, 17
　defined, 7, 10–18
　distinct, 14–16
　early modern, 12, 15–16, 20, 22
　incompatible with Shakespeare,
　　7–9
　North-South divide, 3–4, 11, 16,
　　161
　plural, 15, 16, 20, 23, 103
　see also northernness
Northern Broadsides, 9, 151–63,
　181
Northern Ireland, 11, 21, 260, 304
Northern Rebellion, 15, 45, 68,
　303–4
northernness, 7, 16, 45, 127, 180,
　182, 183

Northumberland, 14, 67–8, 88, 89,
　112–13, 118, 127, 247
Northumbria, 45, 109, 112–18, 128
Norton, Thomas *see Gorboduc*

O'Casey, Sean, 132
Ossian, 286, 292

Peake, Maxine, 154, 157
People's Theatre (Newcastle upon
　Tyne), 125–45, 244, 254–5
Percy, Anne, countess of
　Northumberland, 68
Percy, Henry (Hotspur), 5, 14, 15,
　20, 127, 247, 301–2
Percy, Katherine, countess of
　Northumberland, 68
Perkin Warbeck (John Ford play), 73,
　118
postcolonialism, 22–6
Poulton Drama (Lancashire), 173–4,
　178–80
Prescot *see* Knowsley
Preston, 169, 194–6, 258–60, 271–2
Priestley, J. B., 1, 3, 4, 125, 126

The Queen's Exchange (Richard
　Brome play), 104, 115–19
Quick Bright Things (Alison Carr
　play), 143

Rancière, Jacques, 284
Ravenspurgh (Yorkshire), 4–5
Received Pronunciation, 18, 154–8,
　162; *see also* accent
Reivers, 45, 63, 65, 112; *see also*
　borderers
Royal Shakespeare Company (RSC)
　and Blackpool, 168–83
　and 'Deep England', 18
　and Newcastle upon Tyne, 7–8
　and northernness, 17, 284
　and The People's Theatre, 142–4

INDEX

Rutter, Barrie, 9, 151–63 *see also* Nelson, Conrad; Northern Broadsides

Sackville, Thomas *see Gorboduc*
Scotland
  in contemporary drama, 73–4, 276–84
  and *Cymbeline*, 42, 54–6
  and definitions of North, 11, 19, 68, 85, 299–300, 302
  and England, 19, 20, 21, 24
  and *Gorboduc*, 43, 45
  and historians, 62, 84
  and independence, 5, 70–1
  and *Macbeth*, 42, 50–4, 68–73, 88–96, 111–12
  and *The Scottish History of James the Fourth*, 63–8
  and Shakespeare, 190, 284–7, 290–3, 298–9
  and union under James VI and I, 41, 42, 60, 62, 193, 288–90
  and Yorkism, 79–88
  see also accent; borders; Britishness; 'Celtic fringe'; Englishness; ethnicity; imperialism; national identity; North; northernness; Scottishness
Scottish National Party, 279
Scottishness, 62, 64, 84, 280–1, 284, 290
Seneca *see Medea*
Shakespeare
  'Global', 12, 21, 25, 27, 171
  incompatible with the North, 7–9
  Jacobean, 291, 293
  Lancastrian, 13, 29, 188, 191, 202, 208, 258–72
  'local', 12, 24–25
  Scottish, 190, 284–7, 290–3, 298–9

PLAYS AND PRODUCTIONS
All's Well That Ends Well, 194, 207
Antony and Cleopatra, 139, 153
As You Like It, 136, 139, 204, 207, 250, 253
The Comedy of Errors, 139
Coriolanus, 1–4, 139, 300, 301
Cymbeline, 43, 50, 53–6, 136, 207, 222, 301, 305, 307
Hamlet, 104, 113–15, 125, 145, 156–7, 170, 203, 221, 253, 259–68, 298
Henry IV Part 1, 5, 14, 20, 104, 140, 156, 298, 302
Henry IV Part 2, 247, 269, 298, 300
Henry V, 5, 44, 62, 72, 132, 141, 303
Henry VI Part 1, 10, 199–200, 302
Henry VI Part 2, 199–200
Henry VI Part 3, 5, 199–200
Henry VIII, 305
King John, 200
King Lear, 8, 50, 115–19, 134, 137–42, 159, 250, 259, 268–72, 301
Love's Labours Lost, 207
Macbeth, 8, 42, 50–4, 68–73, 88–96, 111–13, 117, 119, 127, 247, 276–7, 280–7, 299, 301
Measure for Measure, 135, 140, 193, 207
The Merchant of Venice, 126, 130, 139, 207, 250, 253, 301
The Merry Wives of Windsor, 134, 155, 158, 222
A Midsummer Night's Dream, 132, 139, 143, 153, 156, 161, 168–83, 190, 199, 244
Much Ado About Nothing, 127, 130, 141
Othello, 10–11, 127, 136, 140, 159, 222, 249–50, 305

Pericles, 306
The Rape of Lucrece, 269, 301
Richard II, 5, 14, 128, 145, 301, 305
Richard III, 89–92, 95, 151–3, 199, 253, 255, 301, 305
Romeo and Juliet, 143, 230, 305
The Sonnets, 301
The Taming of the Shrew, 138, 189, 194, 199, 253
Timon of Athens, 142
Titus Andronicus, 50, 142, 196, 199, 301
Troilus and Cressida, 127, 132, 136, 301
Twelfth Night, 9, 127, 131, 134, 136, 139, 156, 298, 301, 306
The Two Gentlemen of Verona, 138, 207
The Winter's Tale, 9, 17–18, 139, 140, 159
see also national identity
Shakespeare Club (Newcastle upon Tyne), 38n
Shaw, George Bernard, 128, 129, 133–8
Sidney, Sir Philip, 263
Spenser, Edmund, 93, 197, 198
Stanley, Ferdinando, Lord Strange, 189, 196–201
Stanley, George William (North East Theatre impresario), 247–51
Stewart, Elizabeth, countess of Arran, 67

Stewart, James, earl of Arran, 67
Stow, John, 110, 117
Stratford-upon-Avon, 7, 13, 17, 104, 142, 168, 180, 183, 195, 197, 198, 202, 221–2, 224, 226, 227, 233, 244, 251–2, 253, 293

Tamburlaine (Christopher Marlowe play), 108, 115
Tennant, David, 155–6

Union of the Crowns, 42, 53, 60–3, 65, 68–9, 72–3, 81, 85–96, 207, 287–8, 291

Vaughan Williams, Ralph, 26
Veitch, Colin, 128, 141, 254, 255
Veitch, Norman, 129–32, 254
Viaduct Theatre, 153–4

Wales, 12, 14, 20–1, 27, 41–3, 50, 53–4, 84, 86, 103–4, 198; see also 'Celtic fringe'
Walters, John Cuming (Editor of *The Manchester City News*), 223–30, 232, 234
Whyman, Erica (RSC), 143, 172, 174, 176, 178, 180, 181, 182

Yorkism, 79–88
Yorkshire, 1–2, 4, 43, 82, 84, 85, 87, 92, 96, 104, 151, 304
Young, Sandra, 22–4

EU representative:
Easy Access System Europe
Mustamäe tee 50, 10621 Tallinn, Estonia
Gpsr.requests@easproject.com

www.ingramcontent.com/pod-product-compliance
Lightning Source LLC
Chambersburg PA
CBHW051558230426
43668CB00013B/1903